Beyond the Second Sex

Beyond the Second Sex

New Directions in the Anthropology of Gender

Edited by
Peggy Reeves Sanday and
Ruth Gallagher Goodenough

University of Pennsylvania Press
Philadelphia

Copyright © 1990 by the University of Pennsylvania Press
ALL RIGHTS RESERVED
Printed in the United States of America

Library of Congress Cataloging-in-Publication Data

Beyond the second sex: new directions in the anthropology of gender /
Peggy Reeves Sanday and Ruth Gallagher Goodenough, editors.
   p.   cm.
  A selection of edited papers presented at an international
conference held at the University of Pennsylvania in Apr. 1984 and
at a symposium organized for the meetings of the American
Anthropological Association in 1983.
  Includes bibliographical references.
  ISBN 0-8122-8257-4. — ISBN 0-8122-1303-3 (pbk.)
  1. Women—Cross-cultural studies—Congresses. 2. Sex role—Cross-cultural studies—Congresses. I. Sanday, Peggy Reeves.
II. Goodenough, Ruth Gallagher.
GN479.7.B48 1990
305.3—dc20   90-30497
                                                                            CIP

Third paperback printing 1992

Contents

Preface vii

Introduction 1
Peggy Reeves Sanday

1 Gender Meanings: General and Specific 21
  Alice Schlegel

2 Contested Order: Gender and Society in the Southern New Guinea Highlands 43
  Rena Lederman

3 Women's Roles and Existential Identities 75
  Igor Kopytoff

4 Multiple Gender Ideologies and Statuses 99
  Anna Meigs

5 Rethinking Female Pollution: The Beng Case (Côte d'Ivoire) 113
  Alma Gottlieb

6 Androcentric and Matrifocal Gender Representations in Minangkabau Ideology 139
  Peggy Reeves Sanday

7 Gender in an Egalitarian Society: A Case Study from the Coral Sea 169
  Maria Lepowsky

8 Situational Stress and Sexist Behavior Among Young Children 225
  Ruth Gallagher Goodenough

9 Women, Property, and Power 253
  Sandra T. Barnes

10 School Fees and the Marriage Process for Mende Girls
    in Sierra Leone   281
    Caroline Bledsoe

11 The Romance of Resistance: Tracing Transformations of
    Power Through Bedouin Women   311
    Lila Abu-Lughod

Contributors   339

Name Index   343

Subject Index   348

Preface

In April of 1984, the University of Pennsylvania sponsored an international conference "to examine women's status" and "to explore women's scholarship." The conference organizers took as their baseline the work of Simone de Beauvoir and they framed the central issues in terms of the theme *After the Second Sex: New Directions*. When asked to organize a panel of anthropologists, Peggy Sanday decided to focus on ethnographic studies of issues related to Beauvoir's concept of women as the second sex. Not only had her own cross-cultural research shown this notion to have limited validity but at the time of the invitation she had just finished three summers of fieldwork in a society where in certain contexts men, not women, are perceived as the second sex. Discussions with other anthropologists, particularly Anna Meigs, confirmed the impression that labeling women "the second sex" obscured the complexity of gender relations in many ethnographic studies.

In looking for relevant papers Sanday sought studies that fell into one or another of the following criteria: (1) particularistic studies of women actively involved in economic and political negotiation, (2) ethnographic analyses of feminine symbolism as models *of* and *for* behavior, and (3) studies that avoided preconceived theoretical structures in favor of deriving theoretical patterns from women's activities. At the time of the conference, the participants expressed strong sentiment for publishing the papers and for adding authors whose research was relevant for understanding Western sex roles. Subsequently, Ruth Goodenough joined us. Goodenough had studied United States kindergarten classes with the questions we had in mind. Sanday also solicited a paper from Igor Kopytoff, who was interested in writing a cultural critique of Western sex roles from the perspective of his Suku data. Later, papers were also solicited from Sandra Barnes, Caroline Bledsoe, and Lila Abu-Lughod as these authors were writing on topics relevant to one of the themes of the book from the perspective of their fieldwork.

The conference participants agreed to write for a general audience so that the book could be used in Women's Studies courses and general anthropology classes. Ruth Goodenough agreed to edit the papers with this end in mind.

For their help in putting the book together, we wish to thank Anna Meigs, who began it with Peggy Sanday, and the participants in a symposium organized for the meetings of the American Anthropological Association in 1983. We regret that in seeking a united theme it was not possible to include all of the papers presented at this symposium or at the Beauvoir conference. We also want to thank the participants of the conference, especially Judith Shapiro, who served as a trenchant discussant and who, unfortunately, was not able to prepare an Introduction for this volume as we had all hoped.

Peggy Reeves Sanday

Introduction

Anthropological inquiry into male-female relations has evolved and expanded around debates concerning sexual inequality. The authors of this volume enter the debate by posing ethnographic and analytic challenges to assumptions that in the past supported categorical judgments of equality/inequality. Our title, *Beyond the Second Sex,* was chosen to signal a move away from some of the constraining labels and blanket judgments implicit in past formulations in favor of addressing the conflict, variability, and contradictions that we all have encountered in ethnographic field research. Whether describing the actions of women in various social arenas or discussing the cultural construction of gender meanings, representations, or ideologies, our primary emphasis is on context and complicated local process—process that may be, as Lederman (this volume) describes it, "contested rather than shared," more "an argument than a conversation."

This introductory essay proposes to highlight some of the major issues that have informed prior practice and debate and then to provide a brief overview of the contributions of our individual authors, particularly as they move, in the sense defined above, *beyond the second sex*. We start with the work of Margaret Mead and Simone de Beauvoir, who raised the issues that continue to dominate anthropological inquiry into male-female relations. These authors were the first to focus on the question of sexual inequality from a cross-cultural perspective and to offer explanations that accounted for inequality in terms either of cultural or biological universals or of specific, historically constituted social formations.

In *Sex and Temperament* (1963, first published 1935) Mead described the variability in cultural definitions of maleness and femaleness and concluded that "many, if not all, of the personality traits which we have called masculine or feminine are as lightly linked to sex as are the clothing, the manners, and the form of head-dress that a society at a given period assigns to either sex" (1963:280). Her formulation of the relationship between sex and temperament was remarkably similar to our contemporary conventions distinguishing biological sex from gender constructs. Following Ruth Benedict (1934), Mead wrote that each culture weaves a social fabric that shapes the individual born within it to a dominant style of behavior. Every human society has available to it "the point of sex-difference to use as one theme in the plot of social life." By comparing the way in which individual societies "have dramatized sex-difference," she believed it was possible "to gain a greater insight into what elements are social constructs, originally irrelevant to the biological facts of sex-gender" (ibid., ix).

In *Male and Female* (1949), published fourteen years later, Mead focused mainly on sex roles. She also described cultural variability but now argued that this variability was founded on what she defined as "primary sex differences" conditioned by the reproductive functions and anatomical differences between the sexes. She claimed that these primary "precultural" sex differences had consequences for both social roles and temperament.

Women achieve what she called "full sex membership" by realizing their biological ability to have a child, whereas, because paternity remains "to the end inferential," a man's full sex membership is realized through achievement in the domain of culture. Based on this reasoning Mead concluded that male activities would be universally regarded as more important than female activities even where these activities were virtually the same. (See Sanday 1980 for the contradictions in Mead's work.)

The assumption of universal sexual asymmetry also appears in the pioneering work of Simone de Beauvoir. In *The Second Sex* (1952, first published in France in 1949), Beauvoir presented three basic propositions which articulated the view that sociocultural universals are at the heart of universal sexual asymmetry. Her first proposition was that the symbolic structures defining masculine and feminine conform to an essentially static, dialectical pattern of binary oppositions in all societies. The second was that this dialectic follows a universal pattern: the masculine is associated with culture and the feminine is associated with nature. The final proposition was that the nature of the dialectic places males in a position of dominating and exploiting women as culture exploits nature. Hence Beauvoir's title *The Second Sex*. (See Sanday 1988 for further discussion.)

Simone de Beauvoir's universals were based on her acceptance of Lévi-Strauss's and Hegel's views regarding deep structures of the human mind. Beauvoir focused on existential issues having to do with the nature of the individual and social being. She did not conceive of human society as a fellowship sustained by solidarity and friendliness; rather, following Hegel, she saw in each consciousness a fundamental hostility toward every other consciousness. This hostility was necessary in the subject's definition of self:

"The subject can be posed only in being opposed—he sets himself up as the essential as opposed to the other, the inessential, the object" (1952:xix–xx). Men set themselves up as the subject, the essential, by making women the object. The character of female consciousness remained unspecified.

Beauvoir referred to the work of Aristotle and St. Thomas, who defined women in terms of a negation of what the male affirms. It was Aristotle who said: "The female is a female by virtue of a certain *lack* of qualities; we should regard the female nature as afflicted with a natural defectiveness," while St. Thomas called woman an "imperfect man" and "incidental" (Beauvoir 1952:xvii). Beauvoir claimed that in making women the negated self in this way, men everywhere define themselves in superior terms, positioning themselves in the realm of the social and relegating women to the status of the unmarked and the residual other (ibid., xxi).

Thus where Mead introduced the notion of the sociocultural construction of sex roles and temperament and the idea of socially relevant biological differences, Beauvoir saw gender in terms of a semiotic apparatus that followed a universal pattern. Like Mead, Beauvoir had a lasting influence on subsequent developments in the anthropology of male-female relations. Like Mead also, Beauvoir phrased her ideas in terms of universals. In accepting Lévi-Strauss's propositions regarding opposition and duality in the transformation from nature to culture, Beauvoir, like Lévi-Strauss, posited invariant features in the cultural elaboration of sex differences (1952:xx).

The influence of these ideas on the subsequent development of general theory in the anthropology of gender relations was enormous. Anthropologists advanced Mead's early ideas in examining the cultural construction of gender meanings (articles in Ortner and Whitehead 1981) and the sociocultural construction of sex roles and status (Leacock 1978; Sacks 1982; Sanday 1981; Schlegel 1977). The oppositional logic imposed by Beauvoir and Lévi-Strauss on the grammar of male and female was developed by Ortner (1974) in her derivation of the notion of universal sexual asymmetry and by Rosaldo and Lamphere (1974) in their analysis of the relationship of the public/domestic dichotomy to the question of universal asymmetry. Ortner and Whitehead (1981) argued for the cultural construction of gender meanings, while retaining the assumption of universal asymmetry in gender relations. Despite differences on the question of sexual asymmetry, most of these authors employed a common store of analytic categories, like sex status and male dominance, and such dichotomies as public/domestic, nature/culture, and so forth.

Two recent collections of essays have taken steps to move beyond the limitations posed by the foregoing debates and the categories in terms of which the debates were couched. One volume, edited by Strathern (1987), concentrates on Melanesia and presents rich, particularistic analyses of the role of "agency" and "efficacy" in gender relations. The concern in these essays is not with determining "the prevalence of sexual inequality (for instance 'universalist' or not)" or with arguing for the "culturalist" approach; rather it is with anthropological practice, particularly "how we make known to ourselves that inequalities exist" (1987:2). The second collection, edited by Collier and Yanagisako (1987), seeks to revitalize "the study of kinship," situating "the study of gender at the theoretical core of anthropology by calling into question the boundary between these two fields." These editors state at the outset that the coherence of the volume is found in "the commitment to analyzing social wholes" (ibid., 49).

The distinguishing feature of the present volume is the diversity of approaches it offers to the rethinking of major questions in the area of gender relations. Within this diversity run common themes, some inherent in the ethnographic data itself, some in the willingness of the authors to challenge older theoretical conceptions. A number of the papers, for example, present ethnographic challenges to the assumption of universal male dominance (Lepowsky, Schlegel, Sanday, and Goodenough). These essays provide a view of alternatives to female negation and gender inequality by describing accommodating gender arrangements and the ethnographic conditions that support them. Another group of essays (Lederman, Gottlieb, and Meigs) challenges androcentric readings of certain cultural processes that have neglected, distorted, or covered up the significance of female action in many societies. A third major and related focus, found in a number of the essays, is on process and transformation in female political and economic actions in the contemporary world (Barnes, Bledsoe, Abu-Lughod, and Kopytoff). Whether addressing these or other analytic or ethnographic problems, all of the essays share an openness to the complexities and contradiction of local gender practice, as their authors deal with the tensions, conflicts, and paradoxes that they have encountered in the cultures they have studied.

Some Conceptual and Theoretical Issues

It is in the nature of a collection such as this that terminology and its use will vary, depending on the problem or theoretical issue under investigation. It may be helpful to set such differences in context by offering definitions for certain terms and usages the reader will encounter at various points in the text. The work of Schlegel, Lederman, and Kopytoff will figure more prominently in this section because their essays deal explicitly with a number of theoretical distinctions. Of necessity the initial entry in this list is the definition of *gender* itself. A working definition for this key term is taken from Schlegel's opening statement, where she refers to gender as "the way members of the two sexes are perceived, evaluated, and expected to behave."

The next definitions involve a distinction drawn between two terms that are frequently used interchangeably but that present an important difference. These terms are *gender meaning* and *gender representation*. Meaning is the more general term, conveying the idea of what is indicated or implied by how the two sexes are "perceived, evaluated, and expected to behave." Meaning can only be inferred or implied from the symbolic representations of gender we experience, whether from myth, stories, television, ceremonial enactment, or other models *of* or *for* behavior. In our own society for example, one might extract gender meaning from the incessant images of television as well as from the daily input of our peers or elders, both of them affording rich symbolic fields of gender representation.

Schlegel has titled her piece "Gender Meanings, General and Specific." In it she draws a distinction between *general meaning,* "what women and men are in an abstract sense, in that the sexes are ascribed particular characters by virtue of their sex," and *specific meanings,* "the definition of gender according to a particular location in the social structure or within a particular field of action." Schlegel uses this distinction "to simplify and clarify the meaning of gender within cultures," where frequently one encounters contradictory and variable views of maleness and femaleness.

Another related term that the reader will encounter in the text is *gender ideology*. Used sometimes synonymously with gender meaning, gender ideology can be tied more specifically than gender meaning to agency and political process, on the one hand, and to cosmological conceptions of the social order, on the other hand. To understand this definition of gender ideology it is useful first to consider the term ideology.

In some usages of the term, ideology refers both to a system of thought that guides and legitimates social action and to attempts to create a transcendental order by legitimating the power of that order (Bloch 1987: 334–35). Viewed in these terms, gender ideology can be defined as (1) the system of thought that legitimates sex roles and customary behavior of the sexes, and (2) the deployment of gender categories as metaphors in the production of conceptions of an enduring, eternal social order. The difference between these two levels of gender ideology can be seen by contrasting cultural conceptions of appropriate sex-linked behavior with cultural conceptions of the social order based on gender representations. Thus for example, compare the separatist ideology of Hua males, which guides Hua male and female behavior in a number of contexts (see essay by Meigs), with the Minangkabau ethnic ideology based on a "sacralized" matriliny, which is part of the Minangkabau attempt to insure an enduring, ethnic identity (see essay by Sanday).

Since people occupy different positions of relative advantage or disadvantage, they gravitate to those representations and ideologies that they perceive to be strategically appropriate to their concerns. As a result, ideologies are often in competition, and they and the representations on which they rest are under constant negotiation and renegotiation in social interaction (for example, see Lederman, this volume). An extension of Schlegel's distinction between general and specific gender meanings to different levels of ideology is useful here. By examining the deployment of gender representations in a number of contexts, we begin to understand central ideological preoccupations and separate these preoccupations from those of specific contexts. This exercise allows us to make more sophisticated judgments about the meaning of certain behaviors and representations. For example, when approached in this fashion, what appears to mean male dominance in one context in the Hua case may not support such an interpretation when viewed from the more general level. Similarly, what appears to mean female power at the more general level in the Minangkabau case may be contradicted by opposing gender representations in specific contexts.

When representations of gender are used to implement goals in the economic and political marketplace, they may become elaborated into sophisticated technologies. Their use in the marketing of products, the manipulation of opinion, or the mobilization of political support justify De Lauretis's (1987) characterization of them as *gender technologies*. Indeed, in her terms, gender itself "is the product of various social technologies, such as cinema, and of institutionalized discourses, epistemologies, and critical practices, as well as practices of daily life" (ibid., 2). One may speak of institutionalized practices, such as those that surround the concept of female pollution, or of male initiation, as being gender technologies, in that they contribute to the *engendering* of human beings.

Another term of importance in this volume (for example, Kopytoff, Goodenough, Bledsoe) is *social identity* (Linton 1936; W. Goodenough 1963). This term refers to the way people are culturally categorized as socially significant persons in a society. These categorizations are based on such characteristics as age, occupation, family and clan membership, and, of course, gender. Some identities are based on what a person *is*, others are based on what one *does*. In distinguishing between "existential" and role-based identities, Kopytoff (this volume) calls attention to the importance of sorting out in the representations of gender those aspects of female and male identity that are culturally defined as "existential" or "immanent" (in the very nature of being female or male) and those that pertain to the roles people play (such as those of teacher, householder, parent, and so forth).

Kopytoff's essay on the cultural variability in the way people conceptualize "existential" as opposed to "role-based" social identities compares the Suku (Africa) with contemporary North Americans. He points out that for the latter the immanent features of female identity are many, whereas for the Suku they are few. He discusses differences in the cultural conceptualization of the "natural." One society's conceptualization frees women for social negotiation, and the other society's constrains them. His analysis helps us to understand the puzzling fact that in many societies women who appear by Western standards to be socially repressed may move easily into positions of power and authority, whereas in the United States the idea of a woman president is startling, and professional women encounter many obstacles. Thus Kopytoff opens up an analytic approach for resolving apparent paradoxes and contradictions in cross-cultural gender comparison.

Individuals experience themselves as social persons in the identities others perceive them as having, and these perceptions contribute directly to their *self-representations,* that is, how they see themselves. An interesting question is whether women in those societies like Kopytoff's Suku, whose immanent gender attributes are narrowly defined, are less prone to see adverse reflections upon themselves, *as women,* when they are blocked or disadvantaged by social circumstance. Simply because so much of their situation is negotiable they can set about expanding the attributes of their identity by political maneuvering or acquiring new attributes, such as education or status as a property-holder, within the opportunity structures available to them (for example, Lederman, Barnes, Bledsoe, Kopytoff, Abu-Lughod). By contrast, women in modern Western societies, whose gender identities carry a heavy load of immanent features that defy negotiation, are perhaps more often afflicted by feelings of disadvantage or unhappiness at the constraints or derogation they encounter in their existential identity as women.

Lederman's emphasis on social negotiation takes a step in yet another theoretical direction by illustrating how social negotiation intersects Mendi (Highland New Guinea) status concerns, personal identities, and exchange relationships. In her analysis there can be no consistent "general ideology," unless we as analysts choose to accept the Mendi male ideology as the general ideology because males are the predominant actors in the most visible activities. Lederman takes instead a "political approach," one that is "sensitive both to structural contradictions and to diverse local 'voices.'" She shows that while Mendi men are the predominant actors in clan activities, their ostensible status is "neither simply 'true' nor uncontested."

Because of their nature as salient and enduring collectivities, New Guinea clans and the role of men within them have been the usual focus of anthropological analysis for that area. In the case of the Mendi, the organization of clan events may represent a "hegemonic moment," but Lederman demonstrates that "it does not define everyday realities overwhelmingly." The individual involvements of women and men in personal exchange networks represent another arena of activity of considerable significance to the local economy and to women's autonomy and power. The exaggerated value men sometimes accord to maleness in the clan context is an argument in opposition to the gender values enacted in individual network relations. That such an argument is necessary, Lederman suggests, hints at the cultural legitimacy—the political character—of the alternative view, in which gender is not hierarchically organized.

Intracultural Contradictions in Gender Representations

The essays by Meigs, Schlegel, Gottlieb, Lederman, and Sanday are relevant for examining, from a wide ethnographic perspective, the nature and meaning of contradictory gender representations. These essays demonstrate that gender representations are multifaceted and must be understood first in terms of the context in which they appear and second in terms of their fit with other representations in other contexts. Such an approach is a significant change from the usual Western approach to gender as sexual difference that remains invariant across all contexts.

In her essay Meigs points out that three separate and contradictory gender ideologies can be abstracted from the deployment of gender representations by Hua men. The first is "chauvinistic, the second frankly envious of female reproductive power, and the third egalitarian." Meigs associates the chauvinistic ideology with representations separating men from women to prepare them as warriors. Although one might interpret male separatism and its associated ideology simply as male dominance, the evidence suggests that the ideology is a male reaction to the social representation of the reproductive powers of women—a patriarchal social ideology espoused by men in reaction to a matriarchal reproductive ideology held by both sexes.[1] In a sense, one might say that Hua males are engaged in repetitively contesting an order represented by female substances. Meigs's work cautions us against automatically connecting this kind of male ideology with male social dominance.

In tracking gender meanings for Hua men and women through the life cycle, Meigs shows how these meanings change for each sex through time. For Hua females the greatest changes occur in relation to the status of a woman's reproductive capacity, and they center on the positive and negative powers associated with reproductive substances.[2] This argues for the importance not of sexual differences per se but of a *specific* kind or degree of sexual difference. For example, if menstrual blood is the criterion employed for sexual classification, then there are at least three gender classes for Hua adults: menstrual women, postmenopausal women, and initiated men. Other criteria yield yet another classification. Meigs's argument demonstrates also that we cannot think in terms of a single status for women. Status is dependent on context and like the gender ideologies she describes there are multiple, contradictory statuses not only for Hua females but also for Hua males.

The importance of context is a theme repeated in many of the chapters. For example, context is essential for understanding the conflicting gender representations described in essays by Schlegel and Gottlieb. For the Hopi, Schlegel describes representations that disparage and demean women. Yet, as she demonstrates, it would be wrong to infer male social dominance from this fact. She suggests that disparagement is a device by which men assert a common identity within their group in the face of structural tensions that threaten to fragment the communal and patrilineal bonds between them (see also Lederman, this volume). In Hopi thinking there is a balance between women and men in both behavior and symbolism. Schlegel's description of the many contexts in which balance is the rule suggests that the ideology of balance is not only "general" but also hegemonic. She notes that the Hopi brother and sister are complementary—that sibling pairs are thought of as the core of the matrilineage—but that birth and sexual reproduction are not appropriate to the sibling relationship. Thus, incestuous sexuality is what is disparaged in a Hopi sibling rite in which brothers and sisters deprecate one another and hold each other up to ridicule, a practice that is at odds with their usual ceremonial complementarity. Schlegel suggests that the specific ideology of "gross, unbridled sexuality becomes a metaphor for conduct generally, not just incest but any free play of various passions that disrupt harmonious relations and expressions of antisocial feelings that are better suppressed." Disparagement in the Hopi example is best seen as a specific strategy for controlling sexuality, which operates independently of the more general ideology of sexual complementarity.

Perhaps the best known "technology of gender," described by many anthropologists, is the perception that women's bodily substances are polluting. Such systems of belief and practice are often cited as contributing to the subordination of women. Referring to her fieldwork among the Beng of the Ivory Coast, Gottlieb shows how, for this group, the common analogy *male:female::pure:polluting* is not relevant. Like Meigs, who shows that in certain contexts substances associated with women give strength while in others they are polluting, Gottlieb shifts the discussion from female pollution to the *context* in which a substance is said to cause pollution. In doing so she demonstrates how social and symbolic contexts govern the capacity to pollute or to counteract pollution. "Beng women as a category are no more fully defined by pollution than are men as a category. In some contexts women are polluting, in others they prevent or counteract pollution." Gottlieb says that such variability in the symbolic constitution of "female" forms part of a comprehensive and logical system that is reflected in the realm of Beng social structure. She presents two models of sexuality and, through her analysis of sexual pollution in each case, suggests that both provides "different sorts of metaphorical perspectives that the Beng take on their own descent system." Through these concepts she introduces us to the Beng "way of thinking about the entire universe of the basic structural relations that define [their] society" and demonstrates that for these people the supposed negation implied by concepts of pollution have little if anything to do with female subordination.

The centrality of gender constructions to the understanding of social order is a theme we encounter again in Lederman's paper. She speaks of the "thoroughly 'genderized' social discourse" of the Mendi, which makes gender constructions understandable as a "concrete model for the social order." Highlanders use gender constructions in thinking, talking, and arguing about other things, and for action in domains that are not strictly "about" men and women. Genderized language is complex and expresses a range of contradictions that are also seen in the actual activities of the sexes. Lederman points out that genderized "constructions" should not be seen as "reflections" of social reality but rather as "constitutive" of it and "inseparable" from it.

In my own work among the Minangkabau (Indonesia), I found that both men and women used contradictory gender representations to argue for an enduring and uniquely Minangkabau ethnic identity during a historical moment when this identity was at risk. These representations were deployed in two different discourses. One discourse highlighted a symbolic realm associated with women and the other conveyed an androcentric conceptualization of the origins of matriliny. The first representation "mythologized" matriliny by placing the matrifocal bond between mother and child in the realm of the transcendental. The other historicized matriliny by referring to the actions of two semimythic half-brothers who codified the Minangkabau traditional legal system and instituted the principle of matriliny itself. Both representations are deployed as ideologies that legitimate the matrilineal system and its associated kinship bonds. At a time when the demands for national integration tend to undercut all but surface indicators of traditional ethnic life, these ideologies protect the Minangkabau investment in matriliny, whose practices embody Minangkabau ethnic identity. Thus, what appears on the surface to represent simply a "general ideology" can also be seen in its use as a political instrument to preserve ethnic identity.

The Ideology of Balance and Accommodation

Gender ideologies are frequently characterized as hierarchically organized with males occupying symbolically dominant positions over females (see discussion in MacCormack and Strathern 1980). To cite a recent example, Bloch claims that ideology "everywhere" depends on "the creation of a nightmarish image of the world," so that the "irreversible processes of life—birth, conceptions and death—can then be devalued and transcended." In the Merina (Madagascar) case he discusses, Bloch claims that "the construction of ideology depends first on the emphasis on, and then on the expulsion of, the dialectical, biological world represented . . . by femininity" (Bloch 1987:334).

Bloch's position regarding the necessity of creating "a nightmarish image of the world" brings us back to the issues of negation and the universal opposition of the categories male and female discussed by Lévi-Strauss and Beauvoir. The Minangkabau, Vanatinai, and Hopi cases are examples where the transcendental is *not* achieved by negating the feminine, the masculine, or processes associated with birth or death. The absence of such negation in these cases provides the occasion to question its universality and invites us to examine the grammar of gender ideologies that differ from the structure proposed by Lévi-Strauss and Beauvoir.

The oppositional logic of Beauvoir's and Lévi-Strauss's theory of the symbolic association of male/female with culture/nature rests on an either-or conception of the duality of male and female in which men and women exist more in terms of their mutual negation than in terms of their complementarity. Using a both-and logic, we can say that men and women and their different activities could also exist in their mutual relation to one another—not just in spite of but because of one another. Thus the Minangkabau assert that male and female are like the skin and the nail of the finger, and the Hopi stress the complementarity of the brother-sister pair. In both of these societies, male and female are posed in a relationship of synthesis; sexual substances are not cast as representations of gender difference, and the negation of the feminine is not an issue. In their cosmological schema nature is seen not as being transformed by culture but as being in a complementary relationship with culture.

A similar ethic of accommodation motivates the character of social relations on the Island of Vanatinai, a previously unstudied island northeast of mainland New Guinea described by Lepowsky (this volume). Lepowsky examines the range of roles and behavior deemed culturally appropriate for women and men throughout the life cycle of the individual. She finds that women not only figure prominently in traditional exchange activities but participate in the same arena of exchange as men. They exchange with both men and women, and they compete with men to acquire the same ceremonial valuables. In addition to these activities, which comprise one of the Vanatinai's most important prestige arenas, the women also participate in the ritually important mortuary ritual complex.

Lepowsky describes the situational parameters that promote both such egalitarian relations as these and their accompanying ethic of respect for the individual will. This ethic of respect provides a means of handling conflict in potentially divisive situations and guards against the development of social relations of dominance. The emphasis on the resolution of conflict in this matrilineal society can be compared to the way in which the Minangkabau strive to maintain harmony between the sexes.

An interesting light is thrown on the contrast between accommodating societies like the Minangkabau, Hopi, and Vanatinai and other more sexist ones, in Goodenough's essay. She describes situations of egalitarian as opposed to "sexist" relations between male and female kindergarten students in two United States kindergarten classes. Goodenough's research helps us to understand the contexts in which aggressive male representations of American society may become self-representations for kindergarten boys. Her paper also provides us with the insights of a participant observer into the situational factors that lead some young boys to demean and disparage their female playmates.

To gather data for her study Goodenough participated in the year-long daily affairs of the two kindergarten classes. She found that the two groups differed significantly in the character of their cross-sex interaction. In one group the boys developed a sexist ethos. In the second group, the girls and boys interacted as equals. Goodenough's analysis of the situational factors related to the difference between the two groups highlights the role of stress in the development of an "I hate girls" attitude on the part of young boys. At an age when male identity concerns are high, situational stress tends to produce sexist behaviors. In the absence of such stress, boys can express their positive feelings toward girls and do not feel a need to put them down in order to establish their sense of self-worth. Goodenough's paper helps the reader to comprehend, from the point of view of actual behavior in one society, masculine developmental processes that may eventuate in the negation of females. Her material can be compared with that of Meigs, especially as it applies to the developmental needs of young Hua men.

The patterns of accommodation described for the Minangkabau, Hopi, Vanatinai, and the more accommodating kindergarten group have one obvious quality in common: they all involve social groupings in which male and female (in their roles as brother and sister, mother and son, or playmates) cooperate to preserve group harmony. In these kinds of social situations, we also see the cultural elaboration of nurturing as a socially approved style for interaction. This style is particularly evident in the case of the Minangkabau because of the importance attached to the mother-child bond in both ideology and daily behavior.

Social Negotiation by Women in Everyday Life

A comparison of the ethnographic data presented in this volume demonstrates differences between societies marked by the ideological and social prominence of exclusive male groups and those marked by the prominence of sexually integrated ideologies and social groups. An important issue that remains to be considered concerns the social efficacy of women in societies of the former type. The chapters by Barnes, Bledsoe, and Abu-Lughod describe women as active agents and subjects even in their male-dominated societies (see also the chapter by Lederman). In these cases the authors analyze female economic and political activities and examine the multiplicity of social processes and local discourses available to women to achieve their own ends. Each of these chapters demonstrates realms in which women are free to negotiate.

Barnes begins by noting the contradiction between Yoruba women's subservience in some contexts and the "prevalent notion that women are as capable as men in undertaking economic and political endeavors." The key for the urban Lagos women that Barnes studied is acquiring ownership and control of domestic residences. Once they have acquired control of the domestic hierarchy, women are on the same footing as men. The question Barnes articulates "is not whether women have the ability to gain political power and perform effectively in positions of authority, but under what conditions they can transcend the social, economic, and legal obstacles that stand in the way of achieving domestic seniority." Ownership for these women is the crucial bridge to the public realms of economic and political power and authority.

Bledsoe analyzes Mende marriage negotiations. She describes the processual nature of marriage in this African society and illustrates the strategies employed by all the parties to it (a girl's parents, her suitors, and the girl herself). In the "long stretch of marital processing," girls employ strategies that shape their conjugal and career potentials. The processual nature of marriage "creates enormous opportunity for manipulation." Part of the manipulation involves getting a girl's school expenses paid for as a ticket to a highly valued life-style for the student. For the donor, paying school expenses yields a claim on the girl's future "benefits," including influence on her choice of marriage partner. Girls look for donors who might be good marriage prospects. Many girls attempt to manage childbearing and the definitions of their marital statuses "through definitions of school fees." Bledsoe shows how all the parties involved contest one another's rights as they manipulate payment of school fees and the subsequent debts.

Abu-Lughod's analysis of veiling (1986:134–67) has helped to demystify the meaning of the veil and its consequences for the oppression of Middle Eastern women. By veiling themselves, Bedouin women contribute to the perpetuation of a male moral order they undoubtedly helped to create. In her chapter for this volume, Abu-Lughod describes how Bedouin women resist. She uses women's resistance as a way to understand the nature of the changing forms of power in which they are caught up. She demonstrates how, by resisting one form of power, young Bedouin women may be unwittingly caught in other forms of which they are unaware, particularly new forms of power associated with women's incorporation into the capitalist economy. Through this study of practices of women's resistance Abu-Lughod demonstrates how we can learn "about the complex interworkings of historically changing structures of power." It is useful to end with the chapters by Barnes, Bledsoe, and Abu-Lughod because their work provides a powerful reminder of how the world is shrinking and sex roles are changing in response to worldwide economic and social trends.

Conclusion

Taken as a group it is clear that there are differences among the societies described in this book with respect to the cultural phrasing of the relations between males and females and the structure of opportunity open to the sexes. Depending on one's goal, be it a cultural critique of Western sex roles or ethnographic reporting from the native's point of view, issues of power and dominance may be more or less relevant for the writer and the reader.

The essays in this volume were not intended to represent either a single ethnographic area, or a unitary methodological or theoretical point of view. Instead, they were brought together because each of them, on the basis of field research, challenged in some way the prevailing consensus about the nature of gender inequality and the theories that dealt with it. Among the terms and analytic constructs called into question in these chapters are "inequality," "the status of women," "universal male dominance," "the universal negation of the feminine," and the symbolic equation of female:male::nature:culture. Inequality, for example, is an inadequate, or perhaps irrelevant, label for what Barnes and Bledsoe describe. Urban Lagos and Mende women may depend on men for security, but this does not deter them from negotiating to attain the position of property owner or patron. Although the structure of opportunity favors men in these and other cases, women seek and gain positions of power and authority. With the Hopi, the Minangkabau, and the Vanatinai, we encounter three societies whose gender systems are not predicated on male dominance or on the negation of the female. The description of their cultures, in all their variety, provides insight into some of the necessary conditions for more egalitarian gender arrangements.

Through many of the pieces in this book runs a theme of social, economic, and cultural change. Besides providing the opportunities that women are beginning to exploit (see Barnes, Kopytoff, Bledsoe), cultural and social change form the background for several important contributions to our understanding of conflict and accommodation in the area of gender politics. Lederman's view of society as a "contested order" and Abu-Lughod's use of the concept of "resistance" supply ways to understand the maneuvering for advantage that accompanies the erosion of established orders.

Not all of the authors represented here necessarily agree with the approach taken by others. For example, Lederman's approach to culture as a "contested order" takes contradiction as a given, while Schlegel smooths out paradox by introducing the levels of "general and specific" gender meanings. Lepowsky admits that there is "no single relationship between the sexes on Vanatinai," nevertheless she refers to Vanatinai "as an egalitarian society" for reasons spelled out in her text. Since this is a book stressing the importance of context, it is useful to keep context in mind when evaluating such differences. Theory and analysis take shape from the interplay between the problem an author is addressing and the data at hand.

For an example of how context and problem affect theory and analysis we may take the difference between Schlegel's use of "general" and "specific" gender meanings and Kopytoff's distinction between existential and role-based identities. For Kopytoff the problem is one of cross-cultural comparison; this, in combination with his focus on actors in contemporary Suku culture, make his choice of "identity" concepts appropriate. Schlegel, whose focus is on a particular historical moment in the activities of the Hopi people, is motivated to resolve what seems to be a glaring contradiction in that society's gender ideology. The terms she generates to deal with the problem are uniquely adapted to deal with this issue. Schlegel's terms and those proposed by Kopytoff and the other authors will have utility beyond the cases that generated them, but this is not to suggest that these terms will necessarily have universal applicability.

Two issues raised but not adequately addressed are important for future work. The first of these is the relationship between representations and self-representations. The paper by Goodenough describes the gradual erosion of self-esteem that could be observed among kindergarten girls exposed to sexist behavior by their male peers, but we need to understand the process more fully. When and under what conditions does the disparagement of women become subjectively absorbed? When does the gender technology that helps men to define a separate masculine identity for themselves result in internalized oppression such as feminists have described for Western women? Do large areas of autonomy for women, such as exist in many societies otherwise dominated by men, serve to buffer women against self-representations of low value? How does the urban African woman differ from the urban American woman, not only in terms of the gender representations of the two societies, which we can describe, but also in terms of self-representation? These are just some of the questions we raise to foreground women as social actors whose activities, along with those of their male counterparts, shape a social order.

Acknowledgments

This introduction has benefited significantly by the suggestions of Ward and Ruth Goodenough. Rena Lederman also offered useful criticisms, as did Alice Schlegel, Alma Gottlieb, and Sandra Barnes. I am grateful for their comments and insights.

Notes

1. Poole's account (1981) of the Bimin-Kuskusmin paramount ritual female elder also demonstrates the importance of the life cycle in considering contradictory gender representations. The female ritual elder in this case acquires paramount status in a society where agnatic unity is the tie that binds men. She can join the male agnatic group because she is postmenopausal and beyond the restrictive rules related to childbirth and rearing.

2. See essays in Gewertz 1988 for a provocative set of analyses of "myths of matriarchy" touching on similar issues; see also the discussion by Knight (1988).

Bibliography

Abu-Lughod, Lila. 1986. *Veiled Sentiments: Honor and Poetry in a Bedouin Society.* Berkeley and Los Angeles: University of California Press.

Beauvoir, Simone de. 1952. *The Second Sex.* New York: Vintage Books.

Benedict, Ruth. 1934. *Patterns of Culture.* Boston: Houghton Mifflin.

Bloch, Maurice. 1987. "Descent and Sources of Contradiction in Representations of Women and Kinship." In *Gender and Kinship,* Jane F. Collier and Sylvia J. Yanagisako, eds., pp. 324–40. Palo Alto: Stanford University Press.

Collier, Jane F., and Sylvia J. Yanagisako, eds. 1987. *Gender and Kinship.* Palo Alto: Stanford University Press.

De Lauretis, Teresa. 1987. *Technologies of Gender.* Bloomington: Indiana University Press.

Gewertz, Deborah, ed. 1988. *Myths of Matriarchy Reconsidered.* Oceania Monograph 33. Sydney: University of Sydney.

Goodenough, Ward. 1963. *Cooperation in Change: An Anthropological Approach to Community Development.* New York: Russell Sage Foundation.

Knight, Chris. 1988. "Menstrual Synchrony and the Australian Rainbow Snake." In *Blood Magic,* Thomas Buckley and Alma Gottlieb, eds., pp. 55–74. Berkeley: University of California Press.

Leacock, Eleanor. 1978. "Women's Status in Egalitarian Society: Implications for Social Evolution." *Current Anthropology* 19: 247–55.

Linton, Ralph. 1936. *The Study of Man.* New York: Appleton-Century-Crofts.

MacCormack, Carol, and Marilyn Strathern, eds. 1980. *Nature, Culture, and Gender.* Cambridge: Cambridge University Press.

Mead, Margaret. 1949. *Male and Female.* New York: William Morrow.

———. 1963. *Sex and Temperament in Three Primitive Societies.* New York: William Morrow (orig. pub. 1935).

Ortner, Sherry B. 1974. "Is Female to Male as Nature Is to Culture?" In *Woman, Culture, and Society,* Michelle Z. Rosaldo and Louise Lamphere, eds., pp. 67–88. Palo Alto: Stanford University Press.

Ortner, Sherry B., and Harriet Whitehead. 1981. "Introduction." In *Sexual Meanings,* Sherry B. Ortner and Harriet Whitehead, eds., pp. 1–28. Cambridge: Cambridge University Press.

Poole, Fitz John Porter. 1981. "Transforming 'Natural' Woman: Female Ritual Leaders and Gender Ideology Among Bimin-Kuskusmin." In *Sexual Meanings,* Sherry B. Ortner and Harriet Whitehead, eds., pp. 116–35. Cambridge: Cambridge University Press.

Rosaldo, Michelle Z., and Louise Lamphere. 1974. "Introduction." In *Woman, Culture, and Society,* Michelle Z. Rosaldo and Louise Lamphere, eds., pp. 1–16. Palo Alto: Stanford University Press.

Sacks, Karen. 1982. *Sisters and Wives: The Past and Future of Sexual Equality.* Urbana: University of Illinois Press.

Sanday, Peggy Reeves. 1980. "Margaret Mead's View of Sex Roles in Her Own and Other Societies." *American Anthropologist* 82 (2): 340–48.

———. 1981. *Female Power and Male Dominance*. New York: Cambridge University Press.
———. 1988. "The Reproduction of Patriarchy in Feminist Anthropology." In *Feminist Thought and the Structure of Knowledge*, Mary M. Gergen, ed., pp. 49–68. New York: New York University Press.
Schlegel, Alice, ed. 1977. *Sexual Stratification*. New York: Columbia University Press.
Strathern, Marilyn, ed. 1987. *Dealing with Inequality*. Cambridge: Cambridge University Press.
Weiner, Annette. 1976. *Women of Value, Men of Renown*. Austin: University of Texas Press.

Whereas Igor Kopytoff (this volume) develops his terms of existential role identity and role-based identity to explore differences *between* cultures, Alice Schlegel proposes a related but different set of analytical terms to deal with contradictions in the meaning of gender *within* a culture.

Using as her ethnographic example the Hopi of the Southwestern United States, she demonstrates the applicability of an analytic schema that posits two levels of meaning of gender. The first level she characterizes as general: "what women and men are in an abstract sense." The second level is that of the specific: "the definition of gender according to a particular location in the social structure or within a particular field of action." The usefulness of this distinction lies in its ability to clarify situations, not all that uncommon in anthropology, where general and specific meanings of gender are at odds.

By applying this distinction to the Hopi she reconciles a puzzling contradiction: how to account for "the public ritual mocking and teasing between groups classified as brothers and sisters" within a culture where the respect between cross-sex siblings is an overwhelming daily reality. Adopting a situational approach to gender meanings discloses points of structural tension in a society. For the Hopi it uncovers the area of concern (brother-sister incest) that is symbolically rejected by these specific derogatory rituals.

Alice Schlegel

1 Gender Meanings: General and Specific

It is generally agreed that gender, or the way members of the two sexes are perceived, evaluated, and expected to behave, is a cultural construct. As such, gender varies widely from one culture to another, a point that Mead (1935) elaborated in *Sex and Temperament*. The two sexes are the natural basis for two gender categories as a fact of social organization, each defining itself in terms of the other as a contrast set, although the degree to which these categories are differentiated is itself culturally variable.[1]

Every society has to come to terms with the dilemma of a dual-sexed species, finding the common ground of humanity through complementarity of parts. It is not surprising that cross-sexed dyads occur frequently in myth and ritual. Least often, the father-daughter or mother-son pairs, like Zeus and Athena, Mary and Jesus, bridge the gaps of both sex and generation; more commonly, it is the sister-brother and husband-wife pairs that symbolize the melding of divergent categories. (Alternatively, the sexes are combined into an androgynous being that contains the powers of both female and male [compare Poole 1981].) In many societies, particularly those of the middle range between foragers and complex traditional states, gender dichotomy becomes a symbolic grounding for other kinds of dichotomies in the world as perceived: culture and nature, humanity and the supernatural, land and sea, life and death, superior and inferior lineages.[2] One of the finest achievements of symbolic anthropology has been to document the persistence and cultural variability with which this universal dichotomy is expressed.

As more fine-grained analyses of gender ideology are being produced, it becomes increasingly apparent that variability exists within cultures as well as between them, and the researcher has to contend with differing and even conflicting statements that must be taken seriously. There will be contradictory views on femaleness and maleness, hedged with qualifications and contradicted by the "well, but on the other hand" kind of remarks that drive the neophyte field-worker—looking for simple answers to complex questions—to despair.

In this essay, I will lay out an analytical approach to gender as a cultural construct, in an effort to simplify and clarify the meaning of gender within cultures. The gender ideology of the Hopi, a Pueblo Indian society, will be addressed, but the analytic schema I propose may be applicable to other societies as well. I will attempt to demonstrate that, for the Hopi, there are two levels of meaning of gender: the general or what women and men are in an abstract sense, in that the sexes are ascribed particular characters by virtue of their sex; and the specific, the definition of gender according to a particular location in the social structure or within a particular field of action. Thus, it may be that the specific meaning of gender in any particular instance may depart from the general, and that specific meanings may appear to be antithetical to one another. The definition of general and specific meanings is only the first step in gender analysis. The more interesting questions concern the origin of the general meanings (these may not be answerable) and why meanings take on the different, even contradictory, specific forms that they do.

Much of the confusion between general and specific meanings of gender can be eliminated if the context within which the ideology is expressed is considered. General meanings ascribed to women and men as females and males in the abstract must somehow fit with other meanings ascribed to features of the social, natural, and supernatural domains as constructed by a culture. Male and female as symbolic categories do not stand alone or outside the totality of symbolic categories that make up a culture's symbolic system. Rather, they must be coordinated with other categories. There is no need to assume that there is a perfect concordance between a gender as symbolically represented and the behaviors or social roles of that gender in daily life. Symbolic representation is a creative rather than an imitative process: only certain aspects of observed characteristics are likely to be selected, and even these are played with, until the meanings of gender in the general sense are consonant with other meanings in the symbolic system. The context of general ideology of gender is the total ideology of the culture. In contrast, the context of specific ideologies of gender are situations in which relations between the sexes occur; the meaning ascribed to gender has more to do with social reality than with the way these meanings fit with meanings of other symbolic categories.

In many discussions of gender, it is the general meanings that are abstracted from ritual, literature, myth, symbolic objects, and other aspects of expressive culture. Such is the case in the lengthy discussion of the Western tradition that allies females to nature and males to culture. A pair of articles in MacCormack and Strathern (1980), by Bloch and Bloch and by Jordanova, provide an exegetical summary of this pervasive cultural axiom, tracing its expression in medical, educational, and social ideology of the eighteenth and nineteenth centuries.

The nature-culture, or better, the nature-society dichotomy has an old history in European thought.[3] Earlier expressions seem to have been more concerned with bridging the gap than with assigning gender: the wild man (beast-like man) and the bear (man-like beast) seem to have served this function in medieval and early modern European mythology and ritual. In the village rituals of traditional Europe, it was the young woman who "tamed" the wild man or the bear, and thus could be seen as the embodiment of the social, the triumph of culture over nature. (Historical information on the wild man comes from Bernheimer [1952].) The reversal of the female from "culture" to "nature," if such it was, must have had to do with major transformations in gender relations, concomitant with fundamental transformations in other kinds of social relations that followed the restructuring of the economic and political systems under the rise of the modern world system.

Strathern, in the same collection (MacCormack and Strathern 1980), demonstrates that this nature-culture dichotomy does not hold for the Hageners of New Guinea: for them, maleness and femaleness are allied to a series of oppositions such as life and death, birds and pigs, but culture and nature do not fit into the contrast set. This reminds us that the general meaning of gender in one society may not be cross-culturally applicable.

Specific meanings cover a wide ground. In socially heterogeneous societies, for example, status by sex can conflict with status by rank, and the meanings inherent in gender can become confounded by the meanings inherent in social superiority or inferiority. Some societies have devised ways of avoiding anomalous situations: among the Shilluk of Sudan and the Nyoro of Uganda, the power that adheres to men in relation to their wives, and to royalty in relation to their subjects, makes marriage impossible for royal women, who could only marry men of nonroyal clans. In these societies, queens do not become wives (O'Brien 1977:120–21). The specific meanings of femaleness for these women are somewhat different from those for commoner women. But specific meanings can vary even in socially homogeneous societies, as the following case demonstrates.

When particular attitudes toward one sex or the other are expressed, it is instructive to take into account the situation, such as timing or location, of the expression. For example, a situational analysis of gender ideology can help clarify the apparent mismatch between ritual disparagement of women and the domestic felicity of married couples described by Tuzin (1982) for the Ilahita Arapesh. He sensitively portrays the uncertainty and guilt that men feel about this ritual denigration of women, at variance with behavior in everyday life. Although he does not suggest any reasons for this cultural discrepancy in the perception of women, he illustrates in detail the degree to which such disjuncture can go.

Perhaps the answer lies in the nature of the institutional settings of ritual and domesticity. Ilahita Arapesh rituals take place within an all-male setting, which brings into play whatever features of community solidarity, individual competitiveness, and kin-group interactions characterize men's activities within the community. Domesticity is located within the monogamous nuclear family household, a household form that tends to promote partnership and intimacy between spouses wherever it occurs, and which, as a consequence, poses a threat to the bonding of men to one another within the lineage and the community. When any single-sex group is in operation, the opposite sex will be the "other," to use Beauvoir's evocative phrase. Whether or not the "other" is treated within that context in a demeaning manner may have less to do with the way members of that action group actually perceive them to be than with the character of the group itself.

In the instance of the Ilahita Arapesh, ritual denigration of women may be a device by which men assert their identity with other men of the community in the face of structural tensions, of which the nuclear family household may be only one source, which threaten to fragment the communal and patrilineal bonds between them. It is not, therefore, necessary to hunt for some actuality of female inferiority that the ritual is purported to reflect. As Strathern (1981:178) states in another context: "The object of denigration may be less crucially women themselves than what they *stand for*" (emphasis in the original). In the case of the Ilahita Arapesh, women may stand for the various centripetal forces that pull men away from their ties to the patrilineage. In fact, it would not surprise me if some cultural disparagement of women did not exist in *all* patrilineal societies, whatever the actual gender power structure might be. Ilahita Arapesh women may well be subordinate to men, but this cannot be inferred solely on the basis of a ritual ideology that treats them as inferior. Gender as expressed in ritual is not simply a pale reflection of actuality, but rather a construct that is useful for certain purposes. It is one exponent in the total equation of gender relationships.

Like the Ilahita Arapesh, Hopi men ritually denigrate women—but women equally denigrate men in the same manner. This takes the form of public ritual mocking and teasing between groups classified as brothers and sisters. Why such a parody of the most salient cross-sex relationship in this matrilineal society? To resolve this puzzle, and to raise and answer other questions, we look to an analysis of Hopi gender construction, general and specific.

It is a rather simple matter to describe the general meanings attached to gender, for the Hopis themselves philosophize about them and express them so richly in stated cultural axioms, beliefs, and symbolic objects that it takes only a small analytical leap to assemble Hopi gender meanings under terms accessible to European understandings. The specific meanings attached to gender, however, require an awareness of the positions of men vis-à-vis women in the social structure. In this tribal society, the central relationships are those of kinship, both actual and metaphorical, so that we can expect kin positions to be the social facts that are ideologically elaborated and symbolically depicted or dramatized.

Hopi Social Structure and Gender Relations[4]

The social dramas of the Hopi are played out on three stages: the home, the clan, and the community. There is a continuum among them, as clans are composed of member households, and the community, an endogamous village of several hundred to two thousand souls, views itself as a kind of federation of clans. This continuum is conceptualized by the Hopi through the term *kiihu*, or *house*, whose root *ki* is found in terms like *kiva*, used to refer to a ceremonial house. When a child is born, its spiritual "house," consisting of four sets of four lines of corn meal, is drawn on the walls of the room in which it was born. When the ritual clowns enter the village plaza on their ceremonial visits from the underworld, their first act is to draw a similar "house" on the ground, this one of ashes suitable to beings from the land of the dead and the spirits. The village, an independent polity headed by a chief, is metaphorically treated as a house, and the village chief is called *kikmongwi*, or "leader of the houses." The clan, whose members are scattered in individual houses, has its central Clan House, where clan rituals are held and paraphernalia stored. Within the sheltering walls of the physical or metaphysical house—home, clan, or village—the Hopi finds security. In Hopi thinking, the clan supersedes home and community, because it is through the clan that one inherits land, status, political and ceremonial offices, and general obligations to the community.

Hopi clans are matrilineal. This fact gives special character to the relation between cross-sex siblings, for while men reproduce themselves biologically through their wives, they reproduce themselves socially within the matrilineage through their sisters. Thus, men have a double interest in female fertility—in the sexual reproduction of their wives, through which they become fathers, and in the asexual (for them) reproduction of their sisters, through which they become uncles. (The English terms *father* and *uncle* will be used as Hopis today use them. The former denotes any male of the father's clan, while the latter is used for any male of one's own clan in the preceding generation.) Women's primary concern is their own fertility, for as mothers they fulfill their principal role in perpetuating both the household and the clan. While the aunt (father's sister) is tied to her brother's children in an affectionate joking relationship, one that usually gives her much personal satisfaction, this relationship is not central to the kinship system in the way the others are.

The home for the Hopi is the matrilocal extended- or stem-family household. A man's position in this household is problematic until he reaches middle age, at least, for the house and all its furnishings are owned by his wife and she has authority over them. The farm land attached to each house is allocated to it from the wife's clan land holdings. Men do most of the subsistence labor of farming, hunting, and herding, thus paying for house room and domestic comforts; but land, the principal resource, is acquired though women and its produce is turned over to wives to dispose of as they see fit. Since cultivated food is not only the primary subsistence good but also the major item of ceremonial and social exchange and an important item of trade, control over economic resources rests for the most part with women.

This, however, does not put all social power into women's hands. Domestic authority and economic power are balanced by political and ceremonial authority, acted out at the village level of organization. Political activity consists for the most part of settling disputes between clans over land boundaries and control of ceremonial positions. In these matters, the village chief has the final word. The chief and his council are formally in charge of the ceremonial cycle, although each ceremony is produced by the supervising clan or clans and the timing is established by the celestial calendar. The leaders of the four great ceremonies and most of the participants are men, as are the organizers and participants in the ritual kachina dances that enliven village life from January to July. Women have important public or esoteric roles in all ceremonies, but they control only the ceremonies of the three sororities, held between September and November (see below). One of these ceremonies, the Mamraw, is a major ceremony in the cycle.

While households are the setting for most female authority and the village-wide institutions are where male authority is expressed, it is in the clan that male and female authority come together into a cooperative union. The leaders of the clan are a sister and brother pair, Clan Mother and Clan Uncle, who must agree on matters of importance to the clan. The sister is the leader of the clan women and looks after their interests, particularly where land is concerned. She has the final authority over the allocation of clan land among the households of female members. She also organizes female participation in ceremonial activities. It is through her ritual feeding of clan sacred objects that their life is perpetuated and the prosperity of the clan ensured.

The Clan Uncle organizes male participation in clan activities and leads the ceremonies belonging to the clan, except for the women's ceremonies, led by the Clan Mothers of the supervising clans. He is the clan's representative to the outside world and will defend it in case of dispute with other clans. Both Clan Mother and Clan Uncle are looked to as repositories of the wisdom of the clan. The Clan Mother must learn the clan lore and esoteric rituals along with her brother, so as to train his heir if for any reason he is unable to do so or dies before the training is completed. Each depends on the other to perform his or her ritual duties, and each has the power to veto decisions by the other by withholding cooperation. This has been known to happen, although it is very rare and somewhat scandalous.

It was noted earlier that kin relationships were central in Hopi thinking, and no analysis of gender meanings could fail to consider the meanings attached to men and women as embodiments of kin positions. Each of the three major settings discussed above is associated with kin positions in that certain actual or metaphorical kin, that is, persons metaphorically addressed by kin terms, hold authority within them and pattern their actions after the expected behavior of those positions.

The mother is the kin position of highest importance in the house. It is the mother, usually the eldest capable female of the household, who holds at least nominal authority there. While husbands enter and sons leave, and a man's primary economic duty is toward his wife's household, men think of their real homes as their mothers' houses (later their sisters', after the mothers have died). The family house is the abode of women and children; men are somewhat peripheral to it and, in fact, spend little time there beyond eating and sleeping.

The village is a sort of metaphorical house, a bounded place where a person belongs and is safe. In this case it is the father, as the village chief is addressed, who holds final authority in village matters. The role of father is to provide for and to protect his wife and children; as village father, the chief relates to other villagers as his children whose well-being he must assure through meditation and prayer.

The clan comes under the joint stewardship of a "mother" and "uncle." While senior women of the clan are called mothers by junior members, the Clan Mother has the special responsibility to all members of her clan, not just the children of her household. Her brother, the Clan Uncle, is somewhat father-like in that he, too, must provide and protect. As in many matrilineal societies, his role is more instrumental and authoritative than that of the father.

Although men and women participate together in many ceremonial activities, there is a fair degree of sexual separation in public life. Women are not directly involved in either the informal political decision making, which occurs in the kivas when they are in use as men's houses, or the formal decision making, undertaken by the village chief and his council of male leaders.[5] Economic decisions and activities take place within the domestic and clan settings and thereby do not bring women into contact with men who are not kinsmen. Even spectators at ceremonies tend to separate out by sex, the women sitting or standing close to the participants while the men stand to the back or off to one side or on rooftops. The result is that women and men come together most often within the two kin-based settings, the home and the clan. This puts a special emphasis on the cross-sex dyadic relations that are the core of these institutions, husband-wife for the former and sister-brother for the latter.

When anthropologists like Lévi-Strauss (1963, chap. 11) discuss brother-sister and husband-wife as contrasting terms in the structure of cross-sex relationships, they are abstracting and generalizing a contrast that engages the attention of people everywhere. A fundamental distinction in any society is between those who are possible sexual and marital partners and those who are not. Another pervasive distinction is between those to whom you are bound for life through consanguinity and those with whom relationships must be created via affinal or other means, establishing ties of varying degree of fragility.

Two recent works address the issue of sexual status through the analytic framework of these dyads. In *Sisters and Wives,* Sacks (1979) contrasts the symmetrical peer relations of production of siblings with the asymmetrical productive and reproductive character of husband-wife interaction within several African societies, with wives subordinate to husbands. Ortner (1981) compares wives and sisters in Polynesian gender ideology. As sisters, Polynesian women are valued by men because they draw in other men. In societies with cognatic ramages, titles pass through women as well as men, making the sister her brother's peer within the ramage. Wives, however, defer to their husbands, to whom they seem to function primarily as objects of prestige and reproduction, the husband-wife relationship being amicable but rather inconsequential.

The Hopi also have a symmetrical, peer-bond relationship between siblings, grounded in the equality and mutuality of the sister and brother within the clan. The pair-bond of husband and wife, like those discussed by Sacks and Ortner, is asymmetrical; in this case, however, the asymmetry favors the wife, who holds domestic authority. This illustration indicates the pitfalls of looking only to kinship relations, lineage, and household to provide a framework for the analysis of gender relationships within society at large, no matter how prominent these institutions may be. By limiting analysis to these, Hopi society would appear to be a true matriarchy, which it is not.

An important point to keep in mind, and to which we will return later, is that for the Hopi, both the marital and the sibling dyads are reproductive pairs.

General Ideology of Gender: Mothers and Fathers

Out of the primary kin positions in the descent system, the Hopi have selected two for ideological elaboration as the archetypes of gender. These are the mother, the source of life, and the father, the activator of life and the one who protects and cares for his children. As actual or potential mothers, females are accredited by both sexes and on all occasions with higher value than males, since they are the repositories of life. A standard belief about witchcraft is that the heart of a girl, magically stolen by the witch to prolong his own life, will give him twice as much time to live as the heart of a boy.

Girl children are more desired than boys; while sons are welcomed, the birth of a daughter is the occasion for special rejoicing.

Gender is played out on a cosmic stage as well as in the dramas of daily existence. The mundane natures of women and men are reflections, in Hopi thinking, of the principles of feminity and masculinity that characterize the universe and many of its parts. As sacred Earth, identified with the feminine, is the source of all earthly life, so are women the source of human life through their reproductive and nurturant capacities. As the masculine forces of sun, rain, and lightning activate life, so does the human male activate life within the female by providing semen to mix with her blood.

Responsibilities rest heavily on the Hopi man: as a farmer, he protects his young corn plants, Mother Corn, from the hostile elements; as a father, he cares for his wife and children so they will thrive; as a ritual participant, he cooperates with the deities to care for Earth by ensuring that sun and rain will fertilize her and she will yield abundantly. As a mother, the Hopi woman must feed her children and all people the physical and spiritual food from the sacred corn plant. With finely ground corn meal, she sprinkles sacred objects stored within the house, feeding them with spiritual food to keep their sacred power alive. There is general agreement that men should protect and provide for women, who must be cared for if they in turn can care for their children. Even the humblest man can justify his place on earth with the knowledge that by fulfilling his duties, he has aided in the unfolding of the cosmic plan. Even the least significant woman gains satisfaction by providing food and acting as a mother, to her own children and to all those who call her Mother, the children of her clan sisters and others. Far from constraining freedom and thus limiting expression of self, gender difference, as seen by the Hopi, is an element in the cosmic plan, and the fulfillment of these differing responsibilities in the unfolding of the cosmic plan gives meaning and a sense of order to the humble activities of everyday life. It is no small thing to keep the world in balance and the forces of destruction at bay.

The nature of the sexes as construed by the Hopi coordinates with the distinct responsibilities of each sex. As a mother, the Hopi woman has a single, benevolent nature, requiring her to be nurturant only. One might assume that this implies passivity, but such is not the case. The Hopi think of women as quicker to anger and readier to fight, more readily aggressive, than men. By analogy with the animal mother who will only, and then always, fight to protect her young, the human mother will even sacrifice herself to defend her children. She does not, however, take life—she gives it through childbearing and feeding.

In contrast, the duty of Hopi men as fathers requires that they have a dual nature, one that is gentle and nurturant and benevolent, and one that is fierce and deadly. In order to provide for women and children, men must kill animals who are also the children of Earth. There is something awesome about this killing, particularly of large game. Forgiveness is asked of the prey, and it is thanked for sacrificing its life to the hunter. For large game, a kind of funeral rite is conducted.

The killing of humans is more awesome still, but it must be done if men are to protect women and children from enemies. Even though the Hopi believe that death results in a transformation into a new form of life after death, the act of killing is destruction in its purest form. Unlike some North American tribal people, the Hopi do not glorify war. Ritual, not success in battle, is the path to manhood. The warrior absolves his guilt, placates his victim, and snatches life from the grip of death by ritually transforming the scalp of the victim into his child, whom he must then care for ritually with the same devotion as he cares for his living children. The Hopi may not believe in male pregnancy (see Meigs 1976), but they do believe in this form of male childbirth through ritual; and the ritual seclusion of the warrior after battle or homicide is analogous to the seclusion of the woman after physical childbirth. Thus, killing is given a double meaning, for men can reproduce as well as destroy by its means, and this is a form of reproduction that does not require the female.

In all of this, the emphasis is on reproduction as the source of all abundance. Success does not come through raiding or conquest or political maneuvers; rather, it comes through diligence in performing the necessary agricultural and ritual work to ensure the cooperation of the earth and the supernatural beings. Abundance comes about by natural increase, and the means to it is reproduction.

Specific Ideology of Gender: Sisters and Brothers

In light of the high value placed on reproduction, and its even sacred character, it is truly puzzling that Hopi men and women ritually denigrate each other through bawdy songs and gross depictions of the genitals, brandishing comic phalluses made from giant gourds, vulvas constructed out of pieces of watermelon rind, and so forth. Furthermore, this introduces sexuality into an asexual relationship, for the ritual revelers are classed as ritual siblings.

The women and men who engage in this ribaldry are female members of

Mamraw, one of the three sororities, and male members of Wuwutsim and Taatawkyam (often referred to in the literature as Tao, or Singers), two of the four fraternities. Mamraw women are "sisters" to these men.[6] The mockery takes place twice during the ritual cycle, at the Mamraw and Wuwutsim ceremonies. Wuwutsim is the celebration of the Hopi emergence from the underworld, and all four fraternities partake in it even though the ceremony takes its name from only one, the largest. Mamraw is a sort of female counterpart, many of the Wuwutsim elements being employed in the women's ceremony. These are solemn ceremonies, and the ritual denigration is only one event in a series of rites. Particularly within Wuwutsim, which contains awesome and even frightening elements, these little rites serve as comic relief. Titiev (1944:132) describes the scene as follows:

> In the afternoon, the Singers, naked except for breech clouts, and adorned with or carrying realistic phallic representations, revile the women in a bawdy, rowdy exhibition to which the women retaliate by dousing them liberally with water and urine and by smearing them with filth. Some time later, the Wuwutsim men, likewise featuring a variety of phallic signs, emerge from their kiva and try to outdo their predecessors in obscenity, while the women ply them with refuse and even with human ordure.

Not to be outdone, the women respond in kind: in the winter phase of their ceremony, the Mamraw women taunt Wuwutsim and Taatawkyam men with bawdy and obscene songs and receive in turn their dousing with water or urine and smearing with filth. This reciprocal denigration indicates that it is sexuality, or some form of it, that is being disparaged, not one sex or the other.

Wuwutsim, one of the four great ceremonies that involve the total village, opens the ritual cycle. Various mythical events and themes are dramatized in this ritual, most having to do with the Emergence itself. It was at the Emergence that the plan for Hopi life on earth was established, a plan that has unfolded over time. Important moral principles and social arrangements came into being then: Hopis were given stewardship of the land, holding it in trust from the god Masau, and the four fraternities were formed, for example. What place then do bawdy teasing and blatant sexuality hold in such a ceremony?

This ritual disparagement, I believe, is an elliptical statement about incest. The Emergence from the underworld, undergone by the Hopi people in mythical times past, was a kind of birth, the people coming up into the present world through a long hollow reed. The young men, in their late teens and early twenties, who are initiated into the fraternities during this ceremony are treated like newborn infants, another indication of the theme of parturition in the Emergence and its celebration in Wuwutsim. This is reproduction, the birth of a people and the spiritual rebirth through ritual transformation of young males as they move, by means of the ceremony, from adolescent boyhood into manhood. As is frequently, although not universally, found in initiation ceremonies, men give birth to other men by ritually transforming them.

Why, then, bring sisters into it? In Hopi thinking, there is a balance between women and men in the social world and between the male and female principles in the cosmos. Sometimes this is mythically or symbolically expressed as a husband and wife pair. More often, particularly in rituals, the males and females are brother and sister to one another. Kachinas (*Katsinam*), male supernatural beings somewhat below gods and goddesses in importance, have sisters but not wives. If a ceremonial society has supernatural patrons of both sexes, these are a sibling pair.

Thus, it is appropriate to bring sisters into the ceremony, but it must be made clear that birth and sexual reproduction are not appropriate to the sibling relationship.[7] In typical Hopi fashion, the immoral, perverse, or generally unacceptable is turned into a subject for pointed humor, shaming perpetrators or would-be perpetrators with mockery and cautioning spectators about the act or object portrayed in ludicrous fashion. Human sexuality is good in the universal sense, for it is the operator through which life comes into being. A sibling's sexuality, however, is prohibited and thus it is made to seem laughable. Sexual denigration in Wuwutsim and Mamraw rituals cannot be generalized into denigration of sexuality per se. It is not men and women whose sexuality is ridiculous, but brothers and sisters. (For a different but complementary interpretation of this mockery as reflecting emotional ambivalence in the sister-brother relationship, see Schlegel 1979.)

The reproductive but asexual nature of the sibling relationship is an element of another ceremony, whose character is quite contrary to that of the bawdy hilarity of the Wuwutsim and Mamraw activity. This is the Flute Dance.

The Flute Dance begins with a visit to Flute Spring by the Gray Flute and Blue Flute Societies to present prayer feathers to the dead. This is followed by a procession into the central plaza of the village where a small ritual is performed. The principal characters in the drama are the leader of the procession, three children—a boy and two girls—who walk behind him, and the chorus, men dressed in white robes like Kookopölö, Humpbacked Flute Player, a mythological fertility figure, singing or piping on their flutes as they accompany the main players.[8] Its character is peaceful, the association with the dead symbolizing the continuity rather than the destruction of life.

The main activity of the procession is a ritualized form of the ring and dart game that the children play with the leader. As he goes along, he stops and draws three rain and cloud symbols on the ground with cornmeal. One after another, the children toss objects into the designs, the girls throwing small annulets and the boy throwing a dart-like cylinder. Wherever they may land, the leader retrieves them and places one object in the center of each design. The children pick up their objects as the procession continues, and this is repeated until they reach the center of the plaza.

Everything about this ceremony symbolizes fertility. Flutes throughout North America are associated with courtship and life. The annulet crops up in several ceremonies in association with spiritual rebirth. The children are represented as brother and two sisters, the brother-sister pair in its complete form: *naatupkom,* or older sister and younger brother, and *naasiwam,* older brother and younger sister. Sibling pairs are thought of as the core of the matrilineage.

Two major themes emerge from the Flute Dance. One is the continuity of life into the afterworld, through the close association of the dead with the living. Unlike some other kinds of association with the dead, as in some of the rites that comprise Wuwutsim, this is not awesome or fearsome but rather expressive of hope, a celebration of eternity. The other is the continuity over time of life on earth, emphasizing the perpetuation of the clan as represented by sibling pairs. The fertility that assures the continuity of life is represented by the fertility symbols that the ritual siblings employ. However, it is noteworthy that the annulets and dart tossed by the "brother" and "sisters" in the Flute Dance, evocative of vagina and phallus, are never brought into contact with one another. Each is tossed separately into its own cloud design. Sexuality is an element in reproduction, to be sure, but it is not present in the reproduction of siblings.

Reproduction in a matrilineal society is a more complex issue than it is where the sexually and socially reproductive pairs are one and the same. In most matrilineal societies, where the husband resides with the wife and the woman's brother lives elsewhere with his wife, fathers also have some involvement in social reproduction. This is the case for the Hopi, where fathers provide for their children, train and discipline them to some degree, help select their ceremonial fathers, and show them affection and care. The Hopi is recognized as "a child of" and "born for" his or her father's clan, and father's clansmen and clanswomen play important roles in a person's life-crisis ceremonies and throughout his or her existence.[9] But the mother's brother, who depends on his sister's children to perpetuate the clan and to replace him within it, can have no part in the sexual reproduction of his sister. Sexuality, therefore, must be segregated from reproduction, present as an element but not brought into play. This is a central meaning of the brother and sister bond. The asexual nature of the bond is stated in the Flute Dance, within a context that promotes the continuity of life. It is impossible to avoid sexuality in Wuwutsim and its companion Mamraw, for the theme of these ceremonies is birth of various sorts. Since sexuality must be dealt with, it is presented as the Hopi always present inappropriate behavior, through mockery. In the Flute Dance, sexuality can be present but bracketed and set to one side, for the timeless continuity of the clan and of life itself in the ultimate meaning of this ceremony, not the time-bound events of births.

Discussion

A contrast has been drawn between the general meaning of gender, as the Hopi explicate it, and the specific meanings of the sister-brother relationship, as these are interpreted from ritual. The disparagement of sexuality in the Wuwutsim-Mamraw sibling rite is at odds with ideology of femaleness and maleness in the general sense, grounded as it is in cultural elaborations of motherhood and fatherhood, for through sexuality one becomes a father or a mother and is able to realize the highest ideals of human happiness and social duty. Furthermore, the sibling rituals themselves are contradictory in their portrayal of siblingship. On the one hand, sisters and brothers deprecate one another and hold each other up to ridicule; on the other hand, they cooperate in a ceremony that is quiet, solemn, and in spite of its association with the dead, cheerful. How do these fit together?

The total complex of Hopi gender ideology is built around four crucial kinship roles, which are central in the continuity of natural and social life. In spite of the matrilineal descent system, the Hopi define men and women fundamentally as fathers and mothers, the providers of natural and spiritual life. Thus, there is a concordance among the central roles of household (mother) and village (father), the personifications of the cosmos with earth as feminine and celestial phenomena as masculine, and the inherent characters of women and men. Far from a division between nature and culture, each mirrors the other and plays out, on a larger or smaller stage, the principles inherent in both.

The matrilineal clan introduces a new element, replacing the father as leader with uncle (mother's brother). The structure of the clan, also, differs from household or village, in that both of these latter institutions are hierarchical whereas the clan is egalitarian. The female head has domestic authority over all in her household; the village chief and his council, the fathers, have authority over matters of village concern (although not generally over villagers); but the relations among clan members of both sexes is that of peers, the Clan Mother and Clan Uncle being perceived as organizers of activities and representatives to the outside world rather than as figures of authority. Clan Mother and Clan Uncle, as equals and peers who must cooperate, are the models for all clan relationships.

In light of this, the most compelling interpretation of the deprecatory sibling rite of Wuwutsim and Mamraw is not that it is a statement about gender ideology in a general sense but rather a warning against improper clan relationships. Gross, unbridled sexuality becomes a metaphor for unregulated conduct generally, not just incest but any free play of various passions that disrupt harmonious relations and expressions of antisocial feelings that are better suppressed. The Flute Dance, on the other hand, is a model of good clan relations—peaceful and exempt from sexual and other private passions that threaten mutuality and the welfare of the group. Hopis fear and disdain conflict and worry a good deal about maintaining harmony. This concern may well apply particularly to the clan, in which there is no conventional hierarchy to establish order and authority.

Conclusion

Gender ideology has two aspects, the general and the specific. The interpretation of a particular representation of gender must rest on whether it is gender per se that is being represented, in the general sense, or whether some particular aspect of gender relations is on display, in the specific sense. In the case of the latter, women and men may stand for themselves, but they may also stand for other principles, becoming metaphors for social relations on a broader scale. How one interprets any particular representation of gender depends on an understanding of how that representation, be it rite, expression of attitude or belief, mythical figures, or whatever, relates to the complex scheme of social relations in a two-sexed social universe.

The method of analysis proposed here should clarify some of the apparent paradoxes in gender representation, which may exist more in the mind of the ethnographer than in the minds of the natives. By locating representations within the social spaces they occupy, it is possible to determine whether they are general or specific, and if the latter, what messages beyond gender they convey. In doing this, the analyst gives recognition to the fact that gender ideology is not tacked onto other ideologies. Rather, it is an inherent part of a culture's total ideological complex and must be treated within that context.

Acknowledgments

The information on Hopi gender relations and ideology has been collected by me since 1968. I am grateful to Rohn Eloul, James Greenberg, Emory Sekaquaptewa, Judith Shapiro, and Richard A. Thompson for critical readings of the paper and helpful comments.

Notes

1. I am not a proponent of a "three genders" or "multiple genders" position. I see no evidence that societies socialize children for anything but two genders, depending on their sexual identification. Intermediate or anomalous persons such as berdaches or transvestites appear to be trying, to the degree that they are able, to take on the characteristics of the opposite sex, not some intermediate gender.

2. For instances in which gender is or is not the basis of dichotomous categorizations, see papers in MacCormack and Strathern (1980).

3. European thinkers of the Enlightenment and the nineteenth century were talking about society as an integrated whole and not making the distinction between *culture* and *society*, which characterizes twentieth-century analysis.

4. Hopi social structure, described in the paper in the ethnographic present, is that of the mid-nineteenth century and very probably extends back in time. It is reconstructed from the memories of informants and from numerous early accounts of the Hopi. The principle of matrilineality is still strong, although the matrilocal household has given way to the nuclear family household. The villages are no longer independent polities but units within a federally recognized tribe. A subsistence economy has been replaced by a capitalist cash economy, and social relations have

been shifting from clan-based to class-based over the last fifty years. The ceremonies described here are still performed, however, at least in some of the villages.

5. Nevertheless, women's authority in household and clan gives them great influence over the political positions their male kin take. To some degree, women think of men as their representatives in the decision-making process. Thus, women participate, albeit indirectly, in village politics.

6. Another sorority, Lakon, is said to be sister to Al and Kwan, the remaining two fraternities. Whether this association has a long history, or whether it is simply an attempt at symmetry, is difficult to determine. There seems to be no myth establishing siblingship as there is for Mamraw with Wuwutsim and Tao.

7. The Hopi avoid the problem of original incest by not having a first man and first woman (whose children must inevitably marry one another). The origin of mankind is obscure, and references to first people always treat them as multiple rather than an original couple.

8. Children are used to portray a sibling pair in this ritual and also a married pair in the Snake Dance rites, the Snake Dance and the Flute Dance forming a related but contrasting pair of ceremonies. Whether or not there is any special significance in the use of children for these ritual roles is unknown to me.

9. It is the father's clan, not one's own, that has the charge of protecting and promoting a person's sexuality and fertility (compare Schlegel 1989).

Bibliography

Bernheimer, Richard. 1952. *Wild Men in the Middle Ages*. Cambridge: Harvard University Press.
Bloch, Maurice, and Jean H. Bloch. 1980. "Women and the Dialectics of Nature in Eighteenth-Century French Thought." In *Nature, Culture and Gender*, C. MacCormack and M. Strathern, eds., pp. 25–41. Cambridge: Cambridge University Press.
Jordanova, L. J. 1980. "Natural Facts: A Historical Perspective on Science and Sexuality." In *Nature, Culture and Gender*, C. MacCormack and M. Strathern, eds., pp. 42–69. Cambridge: Cambridge University Press.
Lévi-Strauss, Claude. 1963. *Structural Anthropology*. New York: Basic Books, Inc.
MacCormack, C., and H. Strathern, eds. 1980. *Nature, Culture and Gender*. Cambridge: Cambridge University Press.
Mead, Margaret. 1935. *Sex and Temperament in Three Primitive Societies*. New York: W. Morrow.
Meigs, Anna S. 1976. "Male Pregnancy and the Reduction of Sexual Opposition in a New Guinea Highlands Society." *Ethnology* 15: 393–408.
O'Brien, Denise. 1977. "Female Husbands in Southern Bantu Societies." In *Sexual Stratification: A Cross-Cultural View*, A. Schlegel, ed., pp. 109–26. New York: Columbia University Press.
Ortner, Sherry B. 1981. "Gender and Sexuality in Hierarchical Societies: The Case of Polynesia and Some Comparative Implications." In *Sexual Meanings*, S. B.

Ortner and H. Whitehead, eds., pp. 359–409. Cambridge: Cambridge University Press.
Pool, Fitz John Porter. 1981. "Transforming 'Natural' Woman: Female Ritual Leaders and Gender Ideology Among Bimin-Kuskusmin." In *Sexual Meanings,* S. B. Ortner and H. Whitehead, eds., pp. 116–65. Cambridge: Cambridge University Press.
Sacks, Karen. 1979. *Sisters and Wives: The Past and Future of Sexual Equality.* Westport, Conn.: Greenwood Press.
Schlegel, Alice. 1979. "Sexual Antagonism in a Sexually Egalitarian Society." *Ethos* 7: 124–41.
———. 1989. "Fathers, Daughters, and Kachina Dolls." *European Review of Native American Studies* 3: 7–10.
Strathern, Marilyn. 1980. "No Nature, No Culture: The Hagen Case." In *Nature, Culture and Gender,* C. MacCormack and M. Strathern, eds., pp. 174–222. Cambridge: Cambridge University Press.
———. 1981. "Self Interest and the Social Good: Some Implications of Hagen Gender Imagery." In *Sexual Meanings,* S. B. Ortner and H. Whitehead, eds., pp. 166–91. Cambridge: Cambridge University Press.
Titiev, Mischa. 1944. *Old Oraibi: A Study of the Hopi Indians of Third Mesa.* Papers of the Peabody Museum of American Archaeology and Ethnology, Harvard University, vol. 22, no. 1.
Tuzin, Donald F. 1982. "Rituals of Violence Among the Ilahita Arapesh." In *Rituals of Manhood,* G. H. Herdt, ed., pp. 321–56. Berkeley: University of California Press.

The title of Rena Lederman's essay prepares us for a treatment of gender constructs as products of an essentially political process. In concentrating on "the relationship between gender constructions and the behavior of men and women in everyday life" she presents a developing picture of gender relationships among the Mendi (a group from the Southern Highlands of Papua New Guinea) in which the order of things is clearly not only changing but contested.

She contrasts her approach, "political, . . . sensitive to structural contradictions and to diverse local voices," with an earlier, structural analysis of Highland New Guinea sociality: one that viewed clans as central and men as simply dominant over women.

Lederman analyses an exchange relationship among the Mendi in which *both* men and women play active roles. These *twem* relationships are pervasive in Mendi social life; participation in them partly constitutes adult "personhood" for both men and women. Women are excluded only from participation in *clan* transactions, whose purpose is to acquire wealth for display in corporate clan-sponsored ceremonies.

Lederman's analysis replaces a clan-dominated view with one in which *twem* relationships (in which both men and women participate) and clanship (represented as an exclusively "male" relationship) are partially complementary and partially at odds. The ensuing ambiguity defines an arena for argument among social actors concerning the constitution of their social order.

Rena Lederman

2 Contested Order: Gender and Society in the Southern New Guinea Highlands

Introduction

This essay is offered as a contribution to the work of rethinking the ways we have written about inequality in the New Guinea Highlands (for example, A. Strathern, ed. 1982; Josephides 1985; Godelier 1986). Most generally, it is concerned with how "cultures" are to be represented when relations of power are foregrounded. With respect to gender-based inequalities and power, there have long been at least two approaches. Against the common style of ethnography that lets native male statements and actions stand for the whole of social reality, gender-conscious studies of the past fifteen years have either critically dissected these facts as the representations of particular, male interests (and not simply of the "public good") or sought to describe and account for female experience itself. Either way, such feminist-inspired work assists in placing the contradictoriness of sociocultural systems center stage, an orientation fundamental to critical and historicizing movements in anthropology (and other fields).

The case I consider in this chapter is exceptional in certain respects, but I believe that the analytical attitude I have adopted in response—which treats culture as contested rather than shared, and therefore represents social practice more as an argument than as a conversation—is widely applicable. I am concerned here with gender relations in a region that, while technically embedded in a modern state, still retains significant cultural autonomy from state structures (see, for example, Gordon and Meggitt 1985), and in which local relations of power and authority are decentralized and uninstitutionalized relative to political systems found elsewhere with formal councils or ascribed leadership. This paper takes this (non)state of affairs seriously into account in an exploration of gender inequality (see also Lederman 1986b).

The Mendi Valley is located in the Southern Highlands Province of Papua New Guinea (PNG), a region that largely escaped ethnographic scrutiny until the 1970s.[1] By central Highlands standards (see, for example, Brown 1978), the Mendi people are moderately densely settled on their land and have an intensive system of agrarian production based on the sweet potato.[2] Sweet potatoes are the human staple food. They are also fodder for pigs, which, along with pearlshells and PNG national currency, are given as gifts at weddings and mortuary ceremonies, and in the establishment of both personal relationships and political alliances. As in many other Highland societies, exchanges of food and valuables constitute local forms of sociality and agency; that is, sociopolitical distinctions and both individual and group standing are conceptualized as actively produced in gift exchange.

While Australian colonial control in the Highlands was initiated in the 1930s elsewhere, most of the Mendi encountered their first white people only in the 1950s, after district headquarters for the Southern Highlands was set up in the southern end of their valley. Subsequently, political and economic development efforts in the area proceeded quite slowly. Difficulties of access may partially account for the relative lack of attention Southern Highlanders received from ethnographers as well.

In the Highlands anthropological literature—which has, until recently, largely concerned northern Highlanders like the Mae Enga and the Melpa (Meggitt 1965, 1977; A. Strathern 1971, 1972)—social analysis has been dedicated to understanding the organization and political dynamics of what have been called "clans": ideologically agnatic, exogamous landholding collectivities in the names of which people go to war or sponsor public distributions of wealth (like pig festivals and war-death compensation prestations). In the Mendi valley, as in many other parts of the Highlands, intraclan relations appear "corporate," by which I mean only that the Mendi use clan names to talk about transgenerationally enduring communities of social responsibility, and that *as* fellow clan members, persons are held to be equivalent (substitutable for one another) and capable of unitary purpose ("one talk" or "one mind"). However, by and large only men are formally involved in clan affairs.

The pervasive emphasis on clanship among anthropologists working in the northern Highlands may reflect a local cultural weighting; ethnographic accounts that have appeared over the last decade or so concerning the Mendi's Southern Highlands neighbors—for example, the Wola and the Wiru (Sillitoe 1979; A. J. Strathern 1979a, 1984)—suggest that, while clanship is a factor, other forms of relationship are culturally marked there in ways they are not to the north.

The Mendi in particular distinguish two kinds of gift-mediated social relations in which men and women are differentially involved. Exclusively male, "corporate" clan (*sem onda*) relationships are distinguished from ego-centered "network" relationships between exchange partners (*twem ol*). *Twem* relationships are ephemeral insofar as they are created by each person over the course of a lifetime and dissolve upon his or her death. In Mendi, all adults—male and female—establish exchange partnerships and transact with their partners for various reasons. The movement of wealth between exchange partners is premised on a relation of difference and interdependence (culturally, a relation like affinity; pragmatically, a differential need for particular valuables over time). Their *twem* partnerships make for relations of difference (and potential conflict) among clansmen, too, in ways I will outline below.

In what follows, I explore some implications of the exclusion of women from clan affairs, and their joint involvement with men in networks, for an understanding of Mendi society. Relying on definitions of "the political" (and also of value creation and agency) relevant to state societies, we have, for a long time, assumed that clans are dominant institutions in the Highlands, and that the exclusion of women (and nonagnatic men) from clan affairs bespeaks a second-class status (that is, that which is nonpublic or nonpolitical). But while the systematic exclusion of some social categories from dominant institutions may be a good cross-cultural criterion of subordination, I argue here that it is not at all clear that clans are dominant (that the two forms of sociality are hierarchically ordered) in Mendi.[3] Nor then is it clear that exclusion from them is, in itself, evidence of subordination.

In order to assess the significance of female exclusion from clan affairs, we must first situate clanship in a wider frame of reference. For Mendi this means discovering the meaning and relative value with which people invest clan and nonclan (in this case, network) relationships in different contexts. As it happens, nowadays certainly, these cultural matters are also political, because these two types of relationships are evaluated differently by men and women and among men. These discrepant local interpretations pose a challenge to the totalizing conventions of ethnographic description because each version implies not only a different assessment of the statuses and relations of the sexes in Mendi, but also a different account of Mendi society.

Understanding female exclusion from clan affairs is particularly difficult because of how thoroughly "genderized" social discourse is in the Highlands (Herdt 1981). Gender meanings are a concrete model of the social order. Highlanders do not use gender constructions (categorical distinctions made in terms of "male" and "female" qualities) just to refer to the statuses of, or relations between, men and women. They use such constructs also in thinking, talking, and arguing with each other about more elusive matters—about personal agency and ambition, about kinds of social responsibility and the continuity of social identity, and about productivity and value (see, for example, Wagner 1972; Kelly 1976; M. Strathern 1978, 1981, 1985; Herdt 1981; Goldman 1983).

Because genderized terms are used to speak about such a variety of things, and particularly because this language has become important in expressing a range of contradictions implicit in modern social transformations in the Highlands (for example, A. Strathern 1979b; A. Strathern, ed. 1982; M. Strathern 1981), it cannot be analyzed as an abstract and formal system of mutually consistent propositions. Divorced from an account of the contexts and politics of their use, Highlands gender constructions convey ambiguous information about women's social agency and value, and about their relations with men (among other things). Highlands gender constructions involve contradictory idioms and conceptions that may be applied by the same persons in *distinct* social contexts, and by different people in the *same* context. The meaning of a particular idiom is to be found in its partial relations with others—including nongender ideas of greater or lesser explicitness—deployed in practical contexts of social action.

The current state of knowledge about gender and society in Highland New Guinea has encouraged me to agree with those who argue quite generally that cultural constructions (genderized or otherwise) are not "reflections" of social reality but rather are constitutive of it and inseparable from it (for example, Ortner and Whitehead 1981:4–6; M. Strathern 1985). This perspective highlights the internal relations between cultural constructions and social practice (that is, their relations as the terms of a definition), rather than their external relations (as variables in a causal or statistical explanation). In other words, cultural constructions are here understood to define or "create" social reality as it is lived; they order and evaluate events rather than either determining or being determined by them. From within this perspective we can center attention on the strategic or "political" value cultural meanings have for actors in practical contexts, but with different assumptions about "reality" from those implicit in references to "ideology" or "false consciousness."[4]

Women, Men, and Networks in Mendi

I begin by describing what is least familiar: Mendi women's participation in exchange networks. I argue in this section that their activities are not restricted to what we would call a "domestic" domain. Their production and exchange work involves them with people both outside and inside their husband's and their own natal communities. While Mendi women may not be unique among Southern Highlanders (for example, see M. Strathern 1984c on the Southern Highlands Wiru), their involvements do appear to differ from their counterparts in the northern Highlands (for example, the Melpa and the Mae Enga), where women engage in exchange predominantly in support of their husbands and brothers and are not recognized by men as "transactors" (M. Strathern 1972). In contrast, as I show below, Mendi women may participate "in their own names" in exchanges. Both women and men say that women may determine the allocation of sweet potatoes, pigs, and other products of their labor, as well as of objects they have obtained in exchange, and suffer the consequences of their decisions in the event.

In Mendi, each person builds up a network of exchange partners upon whom to depend whenever he or she needs valuables. In contrast to the practice elsewhere in Melanesia, in Mendi people do not inherit partnerships from their parents. The number and type of partners each person accumulates reflect his or her particular level of interest and involvement in transactions and individual strategies of developing exchange relationships. One's *twem* partners may be any kind of relative and (like the Melpa) may also include nonrelatives; for example, someone met on the road while traveling between communities. People sometimes refer to particular members of their own clans with whom they have personal exchange relationships as *twem ol*. Nevertheless, a person's most important *twem* partners are usually related to him or her by marriage, and marriage is a key context for reproducing *twem* relations (compare Feil 1984).[5]

Affinal relations in Mendi commonly involve people from neighboring, allied clans.[6] Similarly, one's exchange partners are likely to live in localities other than one's own. They may belong, for example, to other clans in the tribal alliance with which one's own group affiliates or to groups belonging to other tribal alliances. One may also establish exchange partnerships with (and marry) members of groups with whom one's own is currently or traditionally hostile. Not only may one's partners come from socially distant clans, but they may come from geographically distant ones as well: the

Mendi people I know have partners elsewhere in the Southern Highlands Province (for example, Ialibu) and in other, northern provinces such as Enga (for example, Kandep) and the Western Highlands (for example, Tambul). As far as I can tell from oral accounts, this was true during the generation before a colonial presence was felt in Mendi and contiguous Highland areas. Exchange partnerships typically extend far beyond a person's local community.

So far I have been describing exchange networks as if gender did not matter. And indeed, in many respects, women's networks are similar to men's. Women's exchange partners are both male and female; they may be relatives or nonrelatives, just as is the case for men. Women's transactions are similar to those of men in the sense that they are not domestic or local. They extend not only to the woman's husband's people (with whom she usually lives) and to male and female residents of her own natal community, but also (for example) to her female agnates' affines, to the kin of women and men married into her husband's clan, and to unrelated people in other communities. A number of my female informants reported that in the period just before and after the Australian administration set up headquarters in the Mendi Valley (1950), women used to travel as far as Kandep (a five-day trek northward) in order to get pigs and salt from their maternal relatives.

Although network exchanges are not normatively an exclusive preserve of either men or women, and although men and women transact with one another, men are more active in network exchanges than women are. They have more exchange obligations (gift-"debts" and -"credits"; *saon* in Mendi) and more exchange partners than women do (see Table 2.1 and tables in Lederman 1986b) and may spend more time at these activities than women.

This is, in part, a reflection of the social organization of production. Men are conventionally responsible for clearing forest regrowth in order to make new gardens; but while this work is important and energy-intensive, the need for it is infrequent. Gardens in much of the Mendi Valley are cultivated continuously, sections lapsing into grass fallow occasionally for reasons having less to do with a concern for soil productivity than with location or variations in the household demand for sweet potatoes. The main garden work of Mendi men involves repairing fences and ditches (essential for preventing pigs from damaging gardens as they forage along village paths and in bush areas). While men are also responsible for planting and maintaining special crops (like sugar cane), and may occasionally help

TABLE 2.1. Exchange Networks of 43 Men and Women

Informants	Male partners		Female partners		Average number partners per person
	Average number	%	Average number	%	
Men (n = 23)	54	82	12	18	66
Women (n = 20)	28	67	14	33	42

their wives in the production of sweet potatoes, their work can be done episodically, and need not be an everyday chore.

In contrast, women are responsible for planting, weeding, and harvesting sweet potatoes and greens, a daily cycle of work in a system essentially without harvesting seasons and food storage. Women's garden work provides the staple foods on which both the people and their pigs depend each day. Furthermore, women are expected to do most of the continuous work involved in maintaining the household pig herd (their own pigs, as well as pigs claimed by their husbands, children, and other people). In caring for pigs, women produce one of the most important valuables with which both men and women transact in any context of exchange, a fact of critical importance in the comparative understanding of Highlands political economies and their contemporary transformations (see A. Strathern 1979b; Modjeska 1982; Josephides 1985; Feil 1987; see also Godelier 1986 and Kelly 1988 concerning the limits of this pig-oriented syndrome). Furthermore, unlike men, Mendi women's conventional sense of themselves as social "agents," capable of creating relations and values, is constituted and expressed in their garden work and allocation of garden products.

The quantitative level of involvement of men and women in *twem* exchanges differs also because, to a degree, they transact for different reasons. Women establish new exchange partnerships in order to obtain wealth required to maintain existing ones; that is, they treat the interpersonal relationship as an end in itself. They also transact with their partners in order to contribute in their own names to individually sponsored, public marriage and mortuary prestations. Men establish *twem* partnerships for these same reasons, but they also engage in network transactions so as to acquire wealth for display in clan-sponsored ceremonies (for example, warfare-death compensations), a concern women do not necessarily share and from which, in any case, they are formally excluded.

Although they may demur, even young, unmarried women are not infrequently spoken about as if they are expected to make their own decisions concerning the allocation of wealth. For example, young girls are given pigs by their relatives who say that it would be shameful for them to begin their married lives without valuables of their own. Women do not come to their new husbands' houses empty-handed. As one man commented, arguing privately with his adult son that the latter ought to give his father's brother's daughter a pig in return for a bridewealth pig she had promised him during early marriage negotiations with her prospective husband, "It would not be good for her to be in the middle, without any pigs of her own." Mendi brides distribute their own bridewealth and are held responsible for their decisions by their occasionally disappointed relatives (Lederman 1986b; see also Ryan 1969).

Women routinely have exchange partners who are not part of their husbands' or brothers' networks. A women's exchange obligations vis-à-vis even those partners who are also partners of her husband are not necessarily equivalent to those of her husband; a person may choose to transact separately with a husband and a wife. Women have exchange obligations of their own and do not seek out wealth from their exchange partners merely in response to the requests of their menfolk. Thus, it is not uncommon for men and women to claim that their spouse's transactions are none of their concern, though the degree of husband/wife coordination varies greatly from household to household. Coordination is a widely shared value, but both men and women concede that it is a partnership (sometimes a power struggle) between mutually autonomous persons. Women's autonomy with respect to the exchange interests of their husbands and clansmen is also demonstrated by the fact that network transactions involving female-female links are routine; women are not simply "in between" men—linking or conveying wealth between brothers-in-law—as they are in the northern Highlands (M. Strathern 1972; and compare Feil 1984).[7]

Mendi women's apparent autonomy—in exchange and as persons—may be unusual in the Highlands. But just as we will see that a Mendi man's "autonomy" with respect to his clansmen—his ability (and not infrequent desire) to withdraw from clan projects and pursue his own schemes—is rooted in his unique set of exchange partnerships, a matrix of intensely *social* obligations, a woman's "autonomy" from her husband also presupposes certain social forms. It is underwritten by the typically strong, although personal, support she receives from her agnatic relatives. Mendi women have very close relationships with individual members of their natal clans, with whom they visit frequently and exchange wealth. Even after they have married, many women continue to work regularly in gardens allocated to them by their fathers and brothers.

While many Mendi women today are quite ready to defend themselves in disputes with their husbands or husbands' people, and while they not infrequently take the offensive both verbally and physically, their strongest sanction is their ability to leave their husbands' place either temporarily or permanently. Unlike women in nearby Highland societies (for example, Meggitt 1965), Mendi women are typically welcomed by their brothers or other close clansmen if they return to their natal communities, and may stay indefinitely until a dispute is resolved. While a husband and wife may come to blows, men are restrained by the knowledge that their wives have the power to leave them, and that such a withdrawal of labor and other kinds of cooperation will affect a man's ability to participate in community affairs. Furthermore, a man knows that his wife will be particularly hard to retrieve if she suffers physical injuries at his hand. Male violence is a legitimate basis for divorce; at the least, the woman and her brother can be expected to demand compensation in pigs, pearlshells, or money in such a circumstance.

Mendi women's autonomy in exchange, and the personal support they receive from their agnates, is evident in many everyday attitudes and situations. Whether in domestic or public settings, they are frequently assertive and vocal in their dealings with one another and with men. They are, for example, quick to defend themselves when anyone, male or female, insults them. In local village courts, which are most frequently concerned with disputes between individuals or households (not clans) within or between communities, women play an active public role, contributing both testimony and opinion.[8]

Men and Clans

While women are active and recognized participants in many daily settings in Mendi, they are systematically and conspicuously absent from meetings held to discuss and plan clan-sponsored parades and prestation, and to coordinate preparations by allied clans. Indeed, the exclusion of women is a (perhaps the) distinctive or definitive feature of clan meetings (see Lederman 1980; and, for a description of a comparable, neighboring society in which women are "peripheral sojourners" in clan communities, see Josephides 1985).

Although both men and women have exchange partners with whom they transact for various reasons, only men do so specifically in order to participate in clan ceremonies. Only men are formally involved in clan affairs, determining clan policy and speaking for their clans in discussions with men of other affiliations. Although women may act as an informal audience at meetings held to discuss clan policy, they are explicitly excluded as participants. Such meetings are held either in settings conventionally defined as exclusively male (like men's clubhouses), or in settings that are normally open (like ceremonial grounds where women often congregate) but defined and organized as exclusively "male" for meeting purposes. Not only are in-married wives excluded, but also clanswomen—sisters and daughters who, after all, usually move to the communities of their husbands upon marriage. More surprisingly, married agnatic women resident in the community are excluded, and *even* when they are more active in network exchanges and more articulate than their husbands (who, although they be in-married men, and therefore not formal members of the collectivity in question, *do* take an active part in clan meetings). This, despite the respect and strong sense of *personal* identification and responsibility that Mendi men often express and demonstrate toward their clanswomen.

As such, Mendi society is similar to others in the New Guinea Highlands, which together have an anthropological reputation for male dominance. In these societies, men are the predominant actors in ritual and in public political meetings and exchange ceremonies. Highland men have, for this reason, been more accessible than women to Western outsiders (male and female anthropologists included). But their accessibility may also be due to our own presuppositions about their activity (for example, concerning the relevance and relative value of categorical distinctions like "public"/"domestic"). Either way, our understanding of the symbolism and socio-political uses of gender constructions has been based predominantly on statements made by Highland men in the context of discussions about or performances of male fertility or initiation cults, and public, clan-sponsored wealth exchanges. Highlands ethnographers have long recognized, but have not always emphasized, that the idioms of agnation or brotherhood that Highlands men use for talking generally about the "maleness" of collective social identities and of transgenerational social continuity (if not specifically about group membership) might in fact articulate an interested perspective—an "ideology" of male dominance over women (for example, A. Strathern 1969; Langness 1974; see also Lederman 1986b, chap. 2).

Nevertheless—despite both a widespread discomfort with the application of "Africanist" segmentary lineage models in the description of Highlands sociality and an awareness of other kinds of relationships since virtually the beginning of research in the area (see, for example, Barnes 1962)—central Highlands ethnography has foregrounded clans, clan-sponsored ceremonial exchange, and the role of leaders ("big-men") in organizing them. For the most part, we have been left with the impression that clans are the integrative and taken-for-granted framework of social life. From this vantage, the part is taken for the whole: clans *are* the "social structure," and clan prestations and warfare drive Highlands political economies.

Our attention to collective male action, and lack of attention to the cultural value central Highlanders also accord to exchange partnerships, households, and other kinds of noncollective social relations—not to mention alternative local "models" of sociality—have had the effect of implying that the latter are simply strategic means to the end of spectacular public prestations made in the names of clans, at which prominent men officiate.

Exchange partnerships and the like have not, until recently, been a focus of research in the central Highlands. But this has not been the case elsewhere. While there have been hints about the significance of other sorts of relations in this region all along (for example, in Meggitt 1967; A. Strathern 1971; Glasse 1968), more recently—and especially because of research in societies on the southern Highland "fringe"—attention has shifted from descent to exchange, siblingship, and other relational principles and logics (see, for example, Wagner 1967, 1974; Schieffelin 1976; Kelly 1977; see also Schwimmer 1973). Although some of this work (notably that of Sillitoe 1979; see also Feil 1984) threatens to replace a clan-centered understanding of Highlands social action with an equally one-dimensional, individual-centered analysis by denying the cultural reality of collectivities altogether, all of it has contributed to a rethinking of the ways in which we represent both collective and personal relationships, and has opened up for productive debate whether or not a clan-centered interpretation accurately reports even Highland men's perspectives on the social order.

In any case, an analytical focus on clanship has, by the by, also constrained our understanding of male/female relations; the power of its particular presuppositions concerning "political" identities and contexts derives from a tangential convergence between Highland male categories and Western ones. For the Mendi case, this interpretation would force us to conclude that ("personal") network exchanges (not to mention "domestic" production) merely facilitate the ("public") staging of ("political") clan prestations, and have no distinct rationale of their own. Given women's exclusive involvement in network transactions, and their formal absence from clan ceremonies, this interpretation implies not only that women are political nonpersons but also that even their claims to personal agency—based on the control of their own labor and transactions—are a delusion.

That is, in this interpretation, Mendi women's control over the pacing of their garden work and over the allocation of garden crops they have planted, and their assertions about transacting "in their own names," are illusory or superficial despite male concurrence, because men control the timing, planning, and import of clan-sponsored wealth distributions. If we treat male collective relations as the overarching context and "end" of all work and all network exchanges, we would have to conclude that, regardless of how indirectly their power is expressed and regardless of their intentions or interpretations, men ultimately control both the function and the meaning of women's creative energies. In the local idiom, women would not even control their own "names"—which they claim to make through the skillful execution of garden work and through hospitality and gift-giving—if their ("personal") reputations were in the final analysis subsumed or encompassed by ("political") clan meanings that only men make (see Lederman 1980; and also Josephides 1985 in which a related argument is forcefully made for the Kewa, southeastern neighbors of the Mendi, who differ from the latter in certain respects).

But if clan-centered social structural analyses constrain our understanding of male/female relations, analyses centered on gender constructions and relations contribute to the general reinterpretation of Highlands sociopolitical structure now underway by attending to the signs of a dialectic of cultural perspectives and practices.

Networks, Groups, and the Structuring of Exchange

A clan-centered interpretation of Mendi social structure is partial in both senses of the word. In fact, as I will argue below, two contradictory but equally real perspectives on how *twem* and clan relations articulate are operative in Mendi (although they are not any more reducible to a "women's" and a "men's" model than are the secular and ritual models in the Avatip [lowland New Guinea] case described in Harrison 1985; compare Feil 1978:276). It makes as much sense to argue that *twem* partnerships constitute an alternative principle of relationship to clanship—that the two parallel and oppose one another as cultural possibilities, or stand reciprocally to one another as both source and product (Lederman n.d.)—as it does to argue that they simply facilitate clan prestations and are in that sense subsumed by male collectivity.[9] If we privilege one or the other of these perspectives analytically, in the interest of consistency, perhaps, we produce one of two different conclusions concerning women's and men's socioeconomic relationship. My point is that while such consistency may be rhetorically satisfying to us, and may even accord with particular Mendi actors' arguments and interpretations in specific circumstances, it obscures the "objective" ambiguities of the social-historical process.

In order to demonstrate this, my presentation of the cultural contrast and structural relation between networks and clans must be sharpened. As I have already noted, clan (*sem onda*) relations can be described as "corporate" in the limited sense that clan names are used to define collectivities that are represented to endure beyond the lifetimes of individuals (and are manifested tangibly in conventions concerning transgenerational access to garden land and bush resources). A man's clan affiliation defines his collective social identity and community of responsibility. All of this helps to create a sense (at the very least for the observer) that clan relations are historically "given" facts of cultural structure. But the sociopolitical reality of any particular clan must also be actively demonstrated in exchanges, violent or amicable, aimed at reestablishing or redefining the clan's relationships with other clans. The specific political significance of such events is mooted at public meetings, during which men seek to establish a persuasive interpretation of events. In order to organize clan prestations, a collectivity of what are represented as "brothers" (*aeme*; a metaphor widely applied—even to members of intermarrying allied groups—to invoke unitary purpose, also conveyed in the idiom "one talk") must agree to coordinate their activities and in particular, they must hold onto their wealth in preparation for the event. Women are formally excluded from clan policy-making; indeed, the "agnatic" biasing of clan genealogies conveys the sense that clan unity and transgenerational continuity are "male."

Twem networks are unnamed, ego-centered, and unique; each exists only relative to some particular person. The members of one's own network are not necessarily members of one another's networks. Networks are unbounded and inclusive, in the sense that the network of any person articulates with the networks of each of his or her exchange partners, linking that person indirectly with thousands of others. *Twem* networks are as ephemeral as particular persons; at the same time the specific, cultural sense of personal agency and "autonomy" (a man's with respect, specifically, to fellow clan members; a woman's with respect to her household) is, in large measure, actualized through network exchanges of wealth (pigs, pearl-shells, and money, the same items exchanged in clan ceremonies). Moreover, these relations are the main way in which a person extends himself or herself beyond the social circle of childhood, a status culturally associated with antisocial consumption.

In contrast to the years-long pacing of a clan's exchanges, the events of active exchange partnerships have a weekly or monthly rhythm. The relationship of clanmembers involves diffuse, generalized reciprocity, whereas *twem* partners actively request wealth from one another and keep accounts of their gift-debts, often specifying when and how they ought to be repaid (see note 7). In contrast to the mutual identification and substitutability of clansmen, the *twem* relationship is premised on difference: *twem* partners have a differential need for wealth, and stand to one another alternately (and simultaneously) as givers and receivers of gifts. A premium is placed on the rapid circulation of wealth between *twem* partners: one reproduces partnerships and expands one's network by quickly distributing the wealth one has on hand. Finally, as I have noted, both men and women may engage in network transactions, although men are significantly more active in them than women are.

It is especially important to understand that the exchange rationales of *twem* partnerships and of clanship are potentially in conflict. Clan and network exchanges demand a different and sometimes mutually incompatible allocation of wealth. That is, while clan ceremonies require the periodic *accumulation* of wealth, the etiquette of exchange partnerships demands the rapid *circulation* of wealth. Exchange partners have what is, in effect, joint or equivalent claims on the wealth any one of them currently holds. Therefore, when a partner arrives requesting something that one has on hand, one is under some moral pressure to relinquish it. At the same time, men know they ought to coordinate with their fellow clansmen in holding on to wealth in preparation for group-sponsored prestations.

Network and clan obligations are in an important sense necessary to one another, and *may* be fulfilled simultaneously (as when a man manages to orchestrate his network obligations so that he can call in his "credits" and pay off his "debts" in the very act of participating in a clan event). Moreover, certain exchange conventions may be used to conjoin group and network obligations. For example, the expectation that a man will repay with an incremental value any gifts given to him by his wives' and mother's kin, *if* they wait for the repayment until his clan festival, encourages those relatives to be patient (see Lederman 1986b, n.d.). But men do not always take full advantage of these rules.

However, without such a premeditated effort of orchestration, the mutual expectations of exchange partners only partially and fortuitously feed into the coordinated projects of a community of clansmen, and may well conflict. In such an event, a man may find himself forced to delay meeting his *twem* partners' requests for wealth and to make heavy demands on his network for gifts or repayments in order to have sufficient wealth available in time for his clan's ceremony. Conversely, a man's diverse commitments to his respective *twem* partners may limit his participation in a clan event. Indeed, whether as a deliberate strategy in interclan politics or for want of collective purpose, clan events are often delayed and sometimes canceled in the name of *twem* responsibilities.

For women this conflict is not the same problem that it is for men. Women are excluded from participation in clan affairs and have no voice in discussions concerning the collective significance of this or that action or event. This implies that in precolonial times of interclan warfare, women sometimes suffered the violent and dislocating effects of men's decisions without the hope of the compensatory increments to their personal standing that helped to make warfare more meaningful to their menfolk. These costs have not been levied recently in Mendi, and nowadays decisions made by men concerning the staging of clan prestations have more benign implications for women. Unlike men, they need take no initiative in the reordering of network obligations preparatory to those events. Married sisters may choose to give valuables to their brothers in support of those men's participation in their clan's prestations; wives expect that they and their kin will receive incremental repayments for any gifts or labor they provide their husbands when the latter sponsor such an event.

But despite the apparent asymmetry in the means available to men and women for shaping the conditions of their own and other's actions, and despite the memory and possibility of warfare, these days women do not seem to care very much about their exclusion from clan meetings. While enjoying aspects of the festivities organized in the names of clans, they admit little envy concerning male control over public wealth distributions. On the contrary, they often express indifference or bemusement—and sometimes scorn—about time better spent in other pursuits. That is, women do not accord special value to male clan involvements; their acquiescence to exclusion does not itself demonstrate that they share the values in terms of which they are excluded.

How exactly can female complacency about exclusion from clan affairs be understood to make sense? By asking this question, I do not mean to suggest that, in place of privileging a male voice, we substitute Mendi women's interpretations as a better truth. They are also partial and reflective of perceived interests. The point is that in making anthropological analysis more sensitive to "history," we need to understand how the contradictions among significant, local perspectives are reproduced. If it is true in class societies that one needs to consider how and to what extent the social order is accorded legitimacy by both its advantaged and its disadvantaged members, and how a sense of legitimacy is itself the precipitate of incomplete or only apparent compromises over the value of persons and the meaning of events, then it is surely true in places like Mendi, where relations of power are structurally ambiguous. Such considerations are essential for an open-ended understanding of political relations insofar as they outline the potential, *internal* to a social order and inherent in cultural process, for a realignment of powers and values.

Mendi women explain their husbands' clan prestations as a means of fulfilling obligations to themselves and their own agnates (with whom, as I noted earlier, women have mainly dyadic, network-type relationships), and men offer this interpretation on occasion as well (see Lederman 1986b:174). After all, prestations sponsored in the names of clans are most often received by members of allied clans, the natal groups of in-married wives. What is more, the wealth accumulated for clan distributions is not held out of networks for long. Major clan events like the Mendi *sai le* (pig kill, the last event in a decade-long series making up the *mok ink* or Pig Festival) are organized as a large number of simultaneous, public distributions, first of pearlshells and money and then of pork, by individual clansmen directly to their respective *twem* partners. It is the public discussion beforehand, and the general coordination of personal obligations, that gives these separate prestations their collective effect. Even those prestations formally represented as passing from one clan as a corporate entity to other clans (for example, components of warfare compensations or the parades leading up to the pig kill) are shared out on the spot to individuals, who are subsequently free to reinvest the wealth in their personal networks in an uncoordinated fashion.

Nor is a network focus exclusive to women. Men agree that *twem* relationships are not simply the sources of wealth to be displayed during clan events. For men no less than for women, *twem* relationships also produce other *twem* relationships. Moreover, clanship may be considered one of the sources of wealth needed to create *twem* partnerships insofar as clansmen are expected to contribute to one another's marriage prestations, and to establish personal exchange relationships with one another's affines.

Of course, some men rarely attend clan meetings and do not make any special effort to accumulate wealth in preparation for clan events. While extreme male inactivity is usually derided by both men and women, even most well-respected, ordinary men do not play an active role in defining the political contexts and setting the dates for clan prestations. When these terms are established, the success of collective events becomes a matter of each prospective participant separately reorganizing his own *twem* obligations so that they will coordinate with those of his clansmen. Each man attempts to meet the demands of both his exchange partners and his clansmen simultaneously, preferably with the same valuables. For example, he may attempt to convince particular exchange partners to redefine what were initially simple gift-debts (*saon*) as "initiatory" gifts (*ol topowe*), that is, gifts that solicit group prestations and are repaid with an increment. To the women who have looked after the pigs he plans to kill, he arranges to give "pig rope" gifts (*mok ya ri*). That is, with some effort of reorganization aimed at engaging *twem* (and also specifically female) interests, the two kinds of obligations need not necessarily conflict (see Lederman 1986b for a detailed consideration of this process of articulation; see also A. Strathern 1979a).

But this is a risky process, and men often face an explicit, politicized choice between two different kinds of relationships with potentially incompatible material implications. They cannot hope to coordinate all of their network obligations with their group responsibilities and must occasionally decide between allocating wealth to exchange partners or withholding it so as to be able to participate with their fellow clansmen in a group prestation. This necessity is experienced—either positively or negatively depending on individual temperament—as a major challenge by most men; it is also what much of the discussion at clan meetings is about. For, if clan events are to take place as such, men *have* to accord them special value some of the time, and give priority to those *twem* obligations that are compatible with their participation.

Although women must make choices, too, theirs are not a focus of explicit, public discussion the way men's alternatives are. A woman may choose to give a pig at the request of one or another of her exchange partners outside of any collective project, or she may give the animal to her husband or brother specifically to support his participation in a clan event. The amount and timing of repayment will be different in each case. But she is likely to talk about these alternatives as equivalent, personal relationships. While women who tirelessly support their husband's clan projects are praised (especially by men, but more likely by reference to proper *domestic* relations and not in terms of clanship either), women with other sorts of exchange involvements are also respected.

In probable contrast to some northern Highland societies, ordinary Mendi men's attitudes are often similar to those of women. They express a preference for uncoordinated network involvements over the coordination of clan events. While they may support particular clan projects, they are more actively concerned with their own *twem* partnerships and preparations for small-scale, individually sponsored marriage and mortuary prestations. But, unlike women, their preference for network relationships has a negative aspect because they cannot affect extreme indifference to clan festivals without risking a loss of personal standing. Consequently, they regard the arrangements they must make to sychronize their exchange network obligations with a clan ceremonial timetable with at least mild distress.

However, big-men do not share with ordinary men this ambivalence of structural commitment. While they are also concerned with developing their network relationships and amplifying their renown by sponsoring small-scale prestations in their own names, big-men consistently initiate and organize collective events. It is this active association with the collective identity that makes a man "big." As in some northern Highlands societies, the Mendi are quite explicit that one cannot build a regional reputation as a big-man without organizing and performing well in clan-sponsored events; that is, without playing a creative role in the reproduction or reordering of clan names and interclan relationships.

It might be noted that from a comparative perspective, the ambivalence of ordinary Mendi men's engagement with the clan ethic is not entirely anomalous. In some other Southern Highlands societies (for example, the Wola and the Huli: see Glasse 1968; Sillitoe 1979; Frankel 1986), even big-men do not so clearly attain their special status by arguing for and participating in collective events. In exchange and even in warfare, Huli and Wola men appear to act simply in their own names. Big-men are recognized as such simply by being particularly active in network exchange relations in these societies.

In Mendi, however, the difference between big-men and ordinary men that I have been describing is explicit. More generally, particular *twem* obligations differentiate *each and every* clansman, regardless of status, from his fellows—and not simply with respect to the allocation of wealth but also in terms of the evaluation of particular clan projects and interclan relationships. But these various differences must be negated if clan events are to take place (Josephides 1985; see also A. Strathern 1979b). Prominent among the means by which the advocates of clan projects create a conviction of common male interest is the strategic use of gender constructs in public speech-making during meetings. Emphasizing conventional differences between maleness and femaleness and ranking their respective value, but alluding to sentiments of support and reciprocity about which there is general agreement, a rhetoric of gender idioms deflects attention from and obviates differences between men while simultaneously effecting a hierarchical ordering—a ranking—of their common, clan concerns over their differentiating, network ones. The marked and remarked upon differences of social involvement between men and women in clans and networks are in these contexts made to stand for (now tacit) differences among men.

At meetings in which clan events are discussed and planned, and in which men address members of their own and allied communities, big-men and other proponents of particular clan actions argue for the importance of elevating the collective project over the divergent commitments of clansmen to their respective exchange partners. Successful persuasions define the collective and interclan significance of specific past or future actions taken by individuals. That is, they have a substantive (though necessarily never conclusive) effect on how the actions of individual persons are interpreted both by those who take part in the meeting and by the larger social universe (for example, by interested members of neighboring communities).

In order to create a consensus for clan action, orators contest the value of a concern with *twem* relationships by arguing that to put network obligations first is to be "like women": concerned with personal affairs rather than with the collective interest. Because of their differentiating effect, which works against a unity of purpose ("one talk [or voice]," as the Mendi say), networks have a "female" value, even though men are in fact more active in them than women are (refer back to Table 2.1). Outside of this rhetorical context, network involvements are not any more simply "female" than they are simply "male": they are what all adults do. Furthermore, normally neither personal, network involvements nor women are denigrated (see also M. Strathern 1981, 1984b).

Analytically, the problem is that the particular ordering of relations argued for during clan meetings happens to converge with the ordering of personal (domestic, female) concerns as against political (public, male) ones familiar in the West. No wonder they appear definitive. But in Mendi, while the clan view is surely compelling, it is neither simply "true" nor is it uncontested. The evaluative rhetoric of clan meetings is itself a sign of the problematic character of what it advocates. The successful organization of clan events—that is to say, the persuasive representation of certain actions as collective—is, in fact, a political *achievement*. While one may wish to consider this achievement a hegemonic moment for one version of "male" interests, it is not canonical. Collective "clan" identities and concerns are not taken-for-granted or ritualized inevitabilities in Mendi—they need to be argued for. They do not take precedence over "personal" identities and involvements as they appear to do in some northern Highland societies (see Meggitt 1977 on the Mae Enga; but see Meggitt 1974, and Feil 1984 on the contrastive Tombema Enga, concerning the significance of differentiating exchange relations to the north).

The de-emphasis of clanship in Mendi becomes more significant when viewed as part of a broader, regional pattern. Elsewhere in the Southern Highlands (for example, among the Huli, Wola, or Wiru), collective styles of male agency are muted still further with respect to their alternatives. In the Mendi case, the value and priority sometimes accorded to male collectivity are not objective facts but rather relative weighting. It cannot be understood without a simultaneous appreciation of what it is an argument against. That such an argument is necessary hints at the conventional value of the alternative construction, in which gender difference is not hierarchically organized.

The Cultural Is Political

In short, the cultural values of both personal and collective identities are contested in Mendi. Because these values are constituted in gendered terms, and because women's and men's orderings of them differ, the relative social position and agency of men and women become analytically ambiguous as well. Gender constructions have a bearing on how Highlanders think about men and women as such; but the male/female distinction also contrasts kinds of men (or women), gives meaning and value to relations among men, and defines kinds of social responsibility and other qualities of *persons* generally, regardless of their sex. In the Highlands, gender constructions have also been among the most potent local media for remaking social value and relationships in dramatically changing times, and for redefining the very contexts (and therefore the meaning) of both men's and women's action.

For all the revisions we have made recently in our understanding of Highlanders, wider ethnographic conventions still encourage us to represent their cultural systems as unitary or shared. Summed up—with internal arguments adjudicated as they appeared at the "moment" of observation, and the necessary ambiguities of practice clarified for a final analysis—social relations appear static or, if in motion, mostly reactive to external challenges.

Stressing ambiguity—viewing Mendi culture politically as a contested ordering of relations—may reduce the usefulness of the case for comparative analysis, just as raising doubts about the analytical utility of identifying dominant institutions may undermine our usual frame of reference for understanding relations of power comparatively.

But to the extent that we are interested in understanding Highlands societies historically, we need to retain something of the perspectives of social actors—that is, of those with an interest in where they are going. If those perspectives have no contractual center, our challenge will be to invent ways to convey that fact (see Price 1983; compare Bourdieu 1977). Sensitivity both to particular, local "voices" and to the structural implications of their diversity (to the intentional and unintentional ways in which particular arguments and purposes mutually constrain, define, and agitate one another) is necessary if we seek to account for the indigenous means available for both making and responding to new social circumstances.

Along with nearly everything else, both male and female roles and the very ways in which gender is used rhetorically are changing throughout the Highlands. These changes are not simply the product of external forces. Highland peoples have also been making a difference, and their actions have been informed by historically constituted interpretations of their circumstances. In Mendi and elsewhere, people argue about exactly how the cultural reworking of new situations ought to be accomplished. In contemporary struggles for cultural control over a changing social world, women are actively engaged in limiting the development of new forms of male power and expanding their own, just as leaders and ordinary men are, each in their own ways, attempting to regain some of the power they lost during a generation of state and mission challenges to local clan autonomy.

In the Eastern Highlands Province, Sexton (1982, 1984) has observed the emergence of women's groups and a women's movement created as innovative extensions of existing social relations and values. Organized as a series of financial savings and credit associations, these collective female responses to new kinds of male economic appropriation (involving cards and beer) are paralleled by related male innovations in the western Highlands. For example, A. Strathern (1979b; A. Strathern, ed. 1982) has analyzed Hagen men's responses to their womenfolk's access to money, this access itself being a creative application of existing conventions concerning women's control over vegetable products.

Rural Hagen men's present-day preoccupation with conserving the precolonial ordering of gender relations may even supersede their commitment to the *moka* system of ceremonial exchange. M. Strathern's comments concerning young Hagen wage labor migrants (for example, 1984b:28–30) outline an equally threatening play on the system of values aligning "maleness"/"femaleness" with "prestige"/"rubbishness" and the distinctions between collective ceremony, interdependent domesticity, and socially irresponsible "personal" interests. But the terms in which the threat to male collectivity is couched are not entirely alien, nor do they signal the total dissolution of an indigenous sociality. The reordering of values bears some resemblance to that which holds in the south.

On the other hand, in Mendi, Wiru, and perhaps some other Southern Highland societies, a gender hierarchy may never have been as important to men as it is today in Mt. Hagen, though it is likely to have played more of a role in the past than it has in the present generation.[10] Nevertheless, here as elsewhere, the changes taking place specifically in male-female relations reverberate with other transformations, and gender is, here no less than in the north, an idiom for talking about the alien social orientations and inequalities associated with state politics and an expanding market economy.

As I have been concerned with the political uses of cultural constructions, one small story will serve as an appropriate coda to suggest how anthropological representations are implicated in the relations they seek simply to describe. It involves an argument about the accessibility of one new sort of "place" and its discourse. It is not at all as idiosyncratic as it might seem; the principles articulated in this exchange were also expressed in arguments taking place in other more common, contemporary situations (for example, local village courts) in Mendi today.

> One day, very early in our stay in Wepra, my husband and I sat in our house talking with a prominent tribal leader, Walipa, about details of the commu-

nity's history, with the aid of two or three male acquaintances who acted as interpreters. I had begun by asking him about the community's involvement in pig festivals, but one thing led to another, and he wound up giving us an account of precolonial warfare practices, with special attention to the particular battles in which he had been involved. While we were listening to an especially vivid description of how he had acquired two scars, Walo (one of Walipa's wives) and Nande (a woman on whose husband's land our house was built, but whom we did not know very well at the time) came by and called out to us. One of the men in the house opened the door at my request. "Why are you letting them in?" Walipa asked, as the women entered the house. "Women aren't allowed in here!" he asserted (ignoring the sex of the anthropologist).

Walo and Nande seated themselves just inside the door, smiling all the while, and Walo asked her husband, "What is it you want to say now, that we cannot hear? Something about sorcery, perhaps?"

Against her husband's view of the matter, Walo suggested that, however it might have appeared, the anthropologist's house was not a "men's house" (*ensa*), where a prohibition against women entering would have been appropriate, nor was the content and form of our discussion the sort from which women are conventionally excluded. Walo made this point indirectly but without much subtlety (and not *entirely* for the anthropologist's benefit), by alluding to sorcery: the only sort of activity that is conventionally secret (though it is so for men and women equally; see Lederman 1981). She was making fun of Walipa's attempt to apply rules concerning the exclusion of women to what she judged as an inappropriate context; choosing to ignore the legitimacy of women's exclusion from some gatherings, she asserted that this one was open. By alluding to what is very widely agreed, in Mendi culture, to be a negative kind of "exclusive" activity (sorcery, which is contrasted with normal social interaction), she attempted to undercut the legitimacy of Walipa's interpretation of the situation: that the activity was exclusive in the positive (that is, male) sense. In the abstract, both distinctions are culturally recognized, but their application to particular contexts is subject to debate. Walo and Walipa each used the distinction that suited his or her respective meaning, construing the context in which they were involved in contrastive ways.

I agreed with Walo—my house was not a men's house. But the reason was not just because I was a woman. As an anthropologist, I had to attend to diverse voices and to create a space in which I might hear them. For this and other reasons, I was an outsider and unlike either Walo or Walipa, or most other members of their community. However, we are all alike in bearing responsibility for the stories we choose to tell. For how people represent themselves and how they are represented by others (both within and outside of their communities) have serious implications for their worldly behavior by giving it particular meanings and values. From this point of view, a central question in understanding relations of power concerns how notions of difference and value are themselves innovated or transformed (for example, Munn 1986) and, particularly, how different categories of person come to create the means by which they may effectively make their case. And the challenge in writing about those relations, ethnographically or otherwise, is to find ways of weaving into the critical dissection of things as they are an evocation of the openness of experience.

Acknowledgments

Reproduced by permission of the American Anthropological Association from *American Ethnologist* 16:2, 1989. Not for further reproduction.

This paper began as a talk given during a symposium on "Sexual Antagonism in Melanesia" organized by Fitz Poole and Gilbert Herdt at the 1983 American Anthropological Association meeting; versions were also presented during 1984–85 at a symposium organized by Peggy Sanday for the Simone de Beauvoir conference held at the University of Pennsylvania, and in Anthropology Department seminars at the University of Michigan and Princeton University. Herewith much delayed thanks to the participants and sponsors of those events. Finally, with this paper I repay (however inadequately) a long-outstanding debt to Robert Murphy.

Notes

1. Exceptions include Ryan 1961, Franklin 1965, and Glasse 1968. Others (for example, A. Strathern, E. Schieffelin) began research in the Southern Highlands Province in the 1960s, but their relevant published work dates primarily since 1970. The fieldwork on which the present chapter is based was conducted during 1977–79 supported by the National Institutes of Mental Health and National Science Foundation, and in 1983 with grants from the American Philosophical Society and Princeton University. I thank all of these institutions for their aid.

2. By "central Highlands" or "New Guinea Highlands" I mean the cultural/geographical zone of relatively high population density and intensive cultivation in mountain valleys over about 5,000 feet above sea level running east to west across the New Guinea island (which comprises two political subdivisions: independent

Papua New Guinea in the east, and Irian Jaya, an Indonesian possession, in the west). In this chapter, I occasionally highlight a distinction between two central Highlands regions in Papua New Guinea: the southern Highlands (Southern Highlands Province), and the northern Highlands (for example, Enga and Western Highlands Provinces).

3. The argument may apply to other Southern Highlands societies (as well as to some of their northern neighbors), but I will not develop it here. Conservatively, there is reason to argue that, among at least some non-Westernized Highlanders, hierarchically organized, "taxonomic" modes of representation—conceptualizations of mutually consistent "levels" of inclusion and subsumption—are not conventional. Instead, they favor "making twos"—a relativistic mode of classification based on "pairing," which applies principles of complementarity and opposition—as a means of ordering the natural and social worlds (see Lancy and Strathern 1981). I believe that Lancy and Strathern's argument is compatible with a more inclusive and radical analysis Wagner (1981) has made of "differentiating" symbolization characteristic of nonstate societies, and that it ought to be taken account of in our interpretations of local notions of value and power (see also Wagner 1974; M. Strathern 1984a).

4. See, for example, in different ways, Wagner (1972, 1981), Sahlins (1976, 1981), Bourdieu (1979), and Munn (1986). Although Bourdieu's notion of symbolic power is close to my sense here, his emphasis is on the legitimation of domination in state societies (see also Bourdieu 1977). While keeping this process in view, I am especially interested in understanding the critical or subversive potential of any symbolic construction, for example, by paying special attention to how received meanings and values are reworked by disadvantaged persons. Following Wagner (for example, 1978), I take this as a special case of the most general cultural processes.

5. This is an accurate but also a somewhat male-centered view of *twem*. More generally put, "network" relationships are differentiating and dyadic, and involve explicit obligations to reciprocate specific gifts; "clan" relationships are collective and involve more diffuse obligations of mutual aid. Generally, women tend to conduct their relationships—including agnatic ones—within a *twem* idiom and ethic. In contrast, from time to time men convert even their male affines into "brothers" (for example, those affines belonging to allied clans within their tribe or an allied tribe) and expect to stand together during pig kills and major warfare compensation payments (and formerly, in warfare). These practical ambiguities are a background condition for the matters discussed in the following two sections of this chapter.

6. The named social units I am calling "clans" (*sem onda*) are exogamous. However, as implied in note 5, marriages can take place within the "tribe" (also *sem onda;* a named alliance of clans that acts as a unit in the largest ceremonies and in warfare). Marriages also take place between members of enemy clans; unlike among the Melpa, in Mendi an individual's personal relationships are not necessarily consistent with intergroup political relationships.

7. In network exchanges, objectively everyone is "in-between." Men not uncommonly receive an item from a woman in order to give to another woman; women frequently do the same for men, and for other women, as men do for other

men. The point is that women are widely expected to be responsible for their own gift-debts. Nevertheless, "in-betweenness" implies that the source of and responsibility for any gift are ambiguous and must be actively attributed; indeed, *twem* partners expect one another to be explicit concerning the conditions for the repayment of gifts.

8. During the time of my fieldwork there were no formal women's groups in upper Mendi (compare Sexton 1982, 1984). However, such forms are clearly not unthinkable. Occasionally women informally demonstrated a mutual identification that ignored clan affiliation and personal relationship, and appeared specifically female. This was most evident in court cases involving male sexual assault, but was also true in some mundane social contexts as well.

9. As I suggested in note 3, it is not at all clear that the Mendi think hierarchically about their social relations most of the time. While it is clear that clanship is given priority by some of the people some of the time, this does not necessarily demonstrate the existence of a *generalized* hierarchy of forms of sociality.

10. In precolonial times, the ideological association of maleness with the social reproduction of something like "society as a whole" might have been stronger than it is today (bearing in mind the cautions implied in notes 3 and 10; but compare Godelier 1986). Up until the 1960s, men controlled a number of cults concerned with the fertility of people and the land (compare A. Strathern 1970). Female participation in these cults, even as spectators, was quite limited. In contrast, male participation was organized in such a way as to obviate the usual distinctions between political allies and enemies. Members of major enemy clans found themselves on both sides of the moiety division created during cult performances, raising the gender division to the level of society as a whole in the interests of the general welfare. Even boys participated in the cults; only females as a class were excluded.

Nothing remotely like this exists today. However, ways of writing historically about noncollective, cross-sex relations must be found in order for the significance of exclusively male forms to be understood. A more general comparison between Southern Highlands societies and societies in the better known northern Highlands may prove particularly enlightening because the two regions contrast in their relative commitment to clanship and its alternatives.

Bibliography

Barnes, J. 1962. "African Models in the New Guinea Highlands." *Man* 62: 5–9.
Bourdieu, P. 1977. *Outline of a Theory of Practice*. New York: Cambridge University Press.
———. 1979. "Symbolic Power." *Critique of Anthropology* 13/14: 77–85.
Brown, P. 1978. *Highland Peoples of New Guinea*. New York: Cambridge University Press.
Feil, D. 1978. "Enga Women in the Tee Exchange." In *Trade and Exchange in Oceania and Australia*, J. Specht and J. P. White, eds. (*Mankind,* special issue, 11: 220–30).
———. 1984. *Ways of Exchange*. St. Lucia: University of Queensland Press.

———. 1987. *The Evolution of Highland Papua New Guinea Societies.* Cambridge: Cambridge University Press.
Frankel, S. 1986. *The Huli Response to Illness.* Cambridge: Cambridge University Press.
Franklin, K. 1965. "Kewa Social Organization." *Ethnology* 4: 408–20.
Glasse, R. 1968. *The Huli of Papua.* The Hague: Mouton.
Godelier, M. 1982. "Social Hierarchies among the Baruya." In *Inequality in New Guinea Highlands Societies.* A. J. Strathern, ed. Cambridge: Cambridge University Press.
———. 1986[1982]. *The Making of Great Men.* Cambridge: Cambridge University Press.
Goldman, L. 1983. *Talk Never Dies.* London: Tavistock.
Gordon, R., and M. Meggitt. 1985. *Law and Order in the New Guinea Highlands.* Hanover, N.H.: University Presses of New England.
Harrison, S. 1985. "Ritual Hierarchy and Secular Equality." *American Ethnologist* 12 (3): 413–26.
Herdt, G. 1981. *Guardians of the Flutes.* New York: McGraw-Hill.
Josephides, L. 1985. *The Production of Inequality.* London: Tavistock.
Kelly, R. 1976. "Witchcraft and Sexual Relations." In *Man and Woman in the New Guinea Highlands,* P. Brown and G. Buchbinder, eds., pp. 36–53. Washington, D.C.: American Anthropological Association Special Publication No. 8.
———. 1977. *Etoro Social Structure.* Ann Arbor: University of Michigan Press.
———. 1988. "Etoro Suidology: A Reassessment of the Pig's Role in the Prehistory and Comparative Ethnology of New Guinea." In *Mountain Papuans,* J. Weiner, ed., pp. 111–186. Ann Arbor: University of Michigan Press.
Lancy, D., and A. Strathern. 1981. "'Making Twos': Pairing as an Alternative to the Taxonomic Mode of Representation." *American Anthropologist* 83 (4): 773–95.
Langness, L. 1974. "Ritual, Power and Male Dominance in the New Guinea Highlands." *Ethos* 2: 189–212.
Lederman, R. 1980. "Who Speaks Here? Formality and the Politics of Gender in Mendi." *Journal of the Polynesian Society* 89: 479–98.
———. 1981. "Sorcery and Social Change in Mendi." *Social Analysis* 8: 15–27.
———. 1986a. "Changing Times in Mendi." *Ethnohistory* 33 (1): 1–30.
———. 1986b. *What Gifts Engender.* New York: Cambridge University Press.
———. n.d. "'Interests' in Exchange: Increment, Equivalence, and the Limits of Big-manship." In *Big Men and Great Men: The Development of a Comparison in Melanesia,* M. Godelier and M. Strathern, eds. Cambridge: Cambridge University Press, forthcoming.
LeRoy, J. 1985. *Fabricated World: An Interpretation of Kewa Tales.* Vancouver: University of British Columbia Press.
Meggitt, M. 1964. "Male-Female Relationships in the Highlands of Australian New Guinea." In *New Guinea: The Central Highlands,* J. Watson, ed. (*American Anthropologist* 66 [4, pt. 2]: 204–24).
———. 1965. *The Lineage System of the Mae-Enga of New Guinea.* New York: Barnes and Noble.

———. 1967. "The Pattern of Leadership among the Mae-Enga of New Guinea." *Anthropological Forum* 2 (1): 20–35.
———. 1974. "'Pigs Are Our Hearts!': The Tee Exchange Cycle among the Mae Enga of New Guinea." *Oceania* 44 (3): 165–203.
———. 1977. *Blood Is Their Argument*. Palo Alto: Mayfield.
Modjeska, C. N. 1982. "Production and Inequality: Perspectives from Central New Guinea." In *Inequality in New Guinea Highland Societies*, A. J. Strathern, ed., pp. 50–108. New York: Cambridge University Press.
Munn, N. 1986. *The Fame of Gawa*. Cambridge: Cambridge University Press.
Ortner, S., and H. Whitehead, eds. 1981. *Sexual Meanings*. New York: Cambridge University Press.
Price, R. 1983. *First-Time*. Baltimore: Johns Hopkins University Press.
Ryan, D'A. 1961. "Gift Exchange in the Mendi Valley." Ph.D. diss., The University of Sydney.
———. 1969. "Marriage in Mendi." In *Pigs, Pearlshells and Women*, R. Glasse and M. Meggitt, eds., pp. 159–75. Englewood Cliffs, N.J.: Prentice-Hall.
Sahlins, M. 1976. *Culture and Practical Reason*. Chicago: University of Chicago Press.
———. 1981. *Historical Metaphors and Mythical Realities*. Ann Arbor: University of Michigan Press.
Schieffelin, E. 1976. *The Sorrow of the Lonely and the Burning of the Dancers*. New York: St. Martin's.
Schwimmer, E. 1973. *Exchange in the Social Structure of the Orokaiva*. London: Hurst.
Sexton, L. 1982. "*Wok Meri:* A Woman's Savings and Exchange System in Highland Papua New Guinea." *Oceania* 52 (3): 167–98.
———. 1984. "Pigs, Pearlshells and 'Women's Work': Collective Response to Change in Highland Papua New Guinea." In *Rethinking Women's Roles*, D. O'Brien and S. W. Tiffany, eds., pp. 120–52. Berkeley: University of California Press.
Sillitoe, P. 1979. *Give and Take*. New York: St. Martin's.
Strathern, A. 1969. "Descent and Alliance in the New Guinea Highlands." Proceedings of the Royal Anthropological Institute for 1968: 37–52.
———. 1970. "The Female and Male Spirit Cults in Mount Hagen." *Man* (n.s.) 5: 571–85.
———. 1971. *The Rope of Moka*. New York: Cambridge University Press.
———. 1972. *One Father, One Blood*. London: Tavistock.
———. 1979a. "It's His Affair: A Note on the Individual and the Group in New Guinea Highlands Societies." *Canberra Anthropology* 2: 98–113.
———. 1979b. "Gender, Ideology and Money in Mt. Hagen." *Man* 14: 530–48.
———. 1984. *A Line of Power*. London: Tavistock.
Strathern, A., ed. 1982. *Inequality in New Guinea Highland Societies*. New York: Cambridge University Press.
Strathern, M. 1972. *Women in Between*. New York: Seminar Press.
———. 1978. "The Achievement of Sex: Paradoxes in Hagen Gender Thinking." In *Yearbook of Symbolic Anthropology*, E. Schwimmer, ed. London: Hurst.

———. 1981. "Self-Interest and the Social Good." In *Sexual Meanings*, S. Ortner and H. Whitehead, eds., pp. 166–91. New York: Cambridge University Press.
———. 1984a. "Discovering 'Social Control.'" Paper prepared for Conflict and Control in the New Guinea Highlands, William Wormsley, ed.
———. 1984b. "Domesticity and the Denigration of Women." In *Rethinking Women's Roles*, D. O'Brien and S. W. Tiffany, eds., pp. 13–31. Berkeley: University of California Press.
———. 1984c. "Subject or Object? Women and the Circulation of Valuables in Highland New Guinea." In *Women and Property, Women as Property*, R. Hirschon, ed., pp. 158–75. London: Croom Helm.
———. 1985. "Kinship and Economy: Constitutive Orders of a Provisional Kind." *American Ethnologist* 12 (2): 191–209.
Wagner, R. 1967. *The Curse of Souw*. Chicago: University of Chicago Press.
———. 1972. *Habu: The Innovation of Meaning in Daribi Religion*. Chicago: University of Chicago Press.
———. 1974. "Are There Groups in the New Guinea Highlands?" In *Explorations in Cultural Anthropology*, M. Leaf, ed., pp. 95–122. New York: Von Nostrand.
———. 1978. *Lethal Speech*. Ithaca: Cornell University Press.
———. 1981[1975]. *The Invention of Culture*. Chicago: University of Chicago Press.

Kopytoff opens his essay with a puzzle: Where is the American equivalent of Indira Gandhi, or Margaret Thatcher, or Benazir Bhutto? Given America's "long-standing egalitarian ideology and progressivist tradition," he asks, why "does the election of a woman president remain elusive" for the United States? To explore the ramifications of this question, Kopytoff looks to the differences in constraint built into cultural definitions of women's identities in different societies.

His analysis starts with a refinement of the terms used to describe social identity. He draws a distinction between what he refers to as *existential* identity, defined as a state of being, and *role-based* social identity, based on roles individuals perform or occupations they engage in. As Kopytoff develops the argument, the critical element determining the relative ease of entry into positions of power by women resides in the nature of their existential identity as defined by their society. In this view, if a broad spectrum of traits and behaviors is thought to be intrinsic to women's existential identity in a particular society, it will prove to be more constraining than a correspondingly narrower band of immanent features in another.

He describes the Suku, of southwestern Zaire, as a group whose existential identity for women has fewer non-negotiable features and therefore allows for greater freedom. He contrasts the situation of the African "free women" with that of career women in the United States, making the point that our heavily loaded expectations of "what women are in their being" burdens and handicaps American women in their move out from the domestic world—and certainly limits their access to positions of power. In his words, "The sheer weight of the American woman's immanent role-load . . . [makes] the taking on of other identities and roles a daunting prospect."

Igor Kopytoff

3 Women's Roles and Existential Identities

A commonplace yet puzzling phenomenon has given rise to this exploration. Why is it that in many changing "traditional" societies, where the burdens of inequality so obviously rest on women, we see women claiming and assuming positions of political power with relative ease? One thinks of Indira Gandhi in India, Sirimavo Bandaranaike in Sri Lanka, Corazon Aquino in the Philippines, Benazir Bhutto in Pakistan, Khalida Zia Rahman and Skeikh Hasina Wazed in Bangladesh, Shirley Kuo in Taiwan . . . the list is a long one. By contrast, in the United States, with its longstanding egalitarian ideology and progressivist tradition, the election of a woman president remains elusive and the reality of women cabinet members rare. Moreover, what occurs at the top of the political pyramid in these "traditional" societies also happens at lower political levels and in bureaucracies and the professions. One encounters innumerable cases of women smoothly pursuing independent careers that put at their beck and call unresentful male subordinates.

Nor does the conventional liberal wisdom that conflates "traditionalism" and "conservatism" with "sexism" always hold in the West. After all, the first British woman prime minister turned out to be a Tory rather than a Liberal or a Laborite, and in the American Congress, more women members have been Republican than Democrat.

This does not mean that the assumption of new careers by women in all these instances has necessarily been easy. But it does mean that the conventional view of these matters is somehow out of tune with the facts. The problem clearly calls for a new perspective on the dynamics of gender roles. I shall begin the task here by examining these roles among the Suku of Zaire—a society in which I have done ethnographic fieldwork and whose cultural subtleties are consequently more accessible to me than those of the larger Third World societies I have mentioned.

The Suku, numbering about 100,000, live in hamlets and small villages scattered across the rolling savannas of southwestern Zaire (for a brief general sketch of Suku society, see Kopytoff 1965). Traditionally—that is, before the colonial period and into the 1950s—they were organized into small matrilineages averaging some thirty-five members. The division of labor followed gender very closely. Subsistence agriculture was entirely in the hands of women, who also kept chickens, did a little fishing in the swamps, and trapped small rodents. The women kept house, cooked, gathered firewood, and carried water. Their one craft was pottery, and a few engaged in herbalism.

Men did no subsistence agriculture. But they did keep miniscule gardens of herbs, tobacco, bananas; occasionally and more recently, some imported "European" vegetables and tended small groves of raffia palm from which they extracted fiber and "wine." They hunted and trapped wild animals and kept the larger domestic animals—goats, pigs, and hunting dogs. Most of Suku craftwork was done by men: they built houses; they made baskets and wove raffia cloth, mats, fishing weirs, and nets; they manufactured all the household utensils; and they did the woodcarving. The outstanding male craft specialist was the blacksmith, who produced hoes, knives, arrowpoints, and axes. In addition, the men controlled the professions, involving medical practice, divination, dispute settlement, and the organization of rituals such as circumcision. The men also held the formal political positions, such as the headmanship of lineages, various chieftainships, and the kingship.

A Terminological Excursion

Now, to move directly toward the central issue of this discussion, let me point at once to an omission from my lists of occupations of men and women. I did not include among men's occupations the impregnation of women and their provision of semen in the production of children. Nor did I point out that it is the women and not the men who bore children. Had I mentioned these occupations in the same breath as woodcarving and household chores, the average reader would have been startled. But why? The question raises some serious cognitive and cultural issues.

I am, of course, writing as an anthropologist, within the anthropological tradition of listing certain things when describing the division of labor by gender. In this tradition, one explains who weaves baskets and who makes pots but not who gives birth to children. The latter piece of data is "obvious" and it is redundant and pedantic to mention it. Childbearing by women is "natural" and shows no cross-cultural variation—unlike basket weaving and pottery, which are variable, "cultural," and worth mentioning.

This way of approaching the division of labor by gender is indeed more anthropological than Western. After all, in many Western groups, people would draw the line differently between what is obviously natural and what is arbitrarily cultural. They might, for example, insist that women are no less "naturally" meant to do household chores, rear children, and support their husbands' egos than they are meant to bear children. That is, which roles in a society are seen to belong naturally to certain persons and which are seen as being in some sense artificial is itself a cultural artifact. Granted that bearing children is part of what we assume to be a core (physiological, psychological, sociological) of objectively natural functions that go with femaleness, no society restricts itself to that core in its definition of what is "natural." And even the core's boundaries are by no means objectively obvious, as the various shifts in anthropological ideas on the subject over the past century have shown.

In the folk anthropology of a society, the distinction between what is natural and what is artificial (or to the anthropologist, "cultural") is reflected in its treatment of social identities and the roles associated with them. This statement requires a brief terminological excursion.

I owe my use here of the term "social identity" to Goodenough (1965), who incisively clarified Linton's (1936) original conceptualization of role and status. Beginning with role (an easily observable piece of behavior), Linton carried his theoretical discussion toward the more abstract status—that is, in the direction of social structure. By contrast, Goodenough began the discussion with the individual in a given concrete ethnographic setting, and moved in the direction of cognition, identity, social psychology, and culture. Briefly defined, social identity (recognized by a native term) is an aspect of the social (as opposed to personal and idiosyncratic) self. In this perspective, a social structure may be said to consist of actors who are expected to behave in terms of their various social identities (such as in the English terms father, policeman, teacher, doctor, prime minister, and so forth, in our society).

I would like to suggest here that in examining social roles in a society, it is useful to make a further distinction within Goodenough's notion of social identity. The distinction is between what people in a society regard as *existential* social identities and those they regard as *role-based*. Some social identities are culturally defined as having to do with what people "are" in a fundamental sense, indicating a state of being (for example, in the West, father, woman, or priest). This is in contrast to social identities that are culturally perceived as being derived from what people "do" that is, identities based on their roles (for example, physician, teacher, or policeman).

Some features of an existential identity and the roles attached to it (what they visibly do) are culturally defined as immanent in the state of being: people do X because of what they are. Thus, in the West, certain nurturing roles are immanent in the existential identity of father. By contrast, in role-based identities, the causal relationship is reversed: people are X because of what they do. The identity here is circumstantial, derived from the role that has been taken on, and the identity lapses when the role is shed. To say that X has a policeman's identity is a shorthand way of saying that X performs a certain kind of role. The identity is a label for a role and it does not exist in and of itself, the way an existential identity—qua state of being—does.

Roles and features that are culturally defined as immanent in an existential identity are, of course, relatively immutable and subject only with great difficulty to social renegotiation. People do not welcome the subtraction from existential identities of their established immanent features, and they resist the addition to them of new immanent features, especially when these threaten to contradict established ones. On the other hand, there are other features of existential identities that, even if prevalent, are not regarded as immanent. Such features are far more open to debate and negotiation. To take a rather trivial example, even fifty years ago the wearing of skirts by women in America, though a prevalent feature of the female identity, was not an immanent one, as the wearing of pants by men was and still is. As a result, the expansion in the wearing of pants among women in the 1960s did not entail any serious debate.

Let me now apply these distinctions to male and female roles among the Suku.

Gender Identities and Roles Among the Suku

Traditionally, a Suku was a human being (*mutu*, pl. *batu*) not immediately upon birth but rather after a "coming-out" and naming ritual—the first rite of passage in the life cycle—that took place several weeks after birth. At this time, formal recognition was given to the child's sex as well as to the socially crucial existential identities of membership of one's matrilineage and that of one's patrikindred (for a sketch of the organization of these groups, see

Kopytoff 1964). Circumcision, traditionally at the age of sixteen or older, took the male into social adulthood—he became a *yakala* (pl. *bakala*), a "man" as in the narrower English term for a postboyhood male. Although no ritual marked the onset of menarche (or of menopause) in the female, she became a "woman" in the narrower sense of adult woman (*muketu,* pl. *baketu*) with the onset of menstruation. I shall focus my discussion here on such mature men and women.

Looking back, I realize that in my conversations with the Suku there emerged a kind of operational definition for existential identities and the immanence of their features. The definition rested on the form taken by explanations of a role's raison d'être. To begin with the simplest case, the reason given for the fact that women bore children was simply that "they are women." The role of childbearer was seen as flowing directly out of the woman's identity—out of her state of being a woman. The appeal to this existential identity constituted a terminal explanation for her role of childbearer; the statement was sufficient and nothing more needed to be added to it. That, in the case of childbearing, this explanation should be terminal seems obvious to us—because we happen to share it. (And we are tempted to think that we share it because the relationship between woman and childbearer is biologically given. True, but the terms of the relationship may be reversed. It is conceivable that, in some societies, the term we might gloss as woman may in reality be seen as an immanent feature of the existential identity of childbearer.)

The Suku proffered similar terminal explanations for roles that were not so obvious to the foreigner. Thus, a woman could not be initiated as a lineage head and she could play one but not another ritual role because, again and without further explanatory ado, "she is a woman." This mode of explanation obviously leaves very little room for logical probing or social negotiation.

What is significant for the argument of this essay is that, among the Suku, few immanent roles were specifically linked to the man or the woman qua existential identities. This is not to say that these roles were not important, but importance focused on the symbolic rather than the pragmatic aspects of life. Among these immanent roles, the ones that loomed largest for a woman were, precisely, childbearing (with its great weight as a realization of the female identity) and the profoundly immanent role, in this matrilineal society, of reproducer of offspring on whom she conferred their crucial existential identity of members of their corporate kin group. Certain rituals involving "medicines" required participation by a woman, others by a man, and still others by both. The "contamination" by dangerous "medicines" through the sexual act followed different rules with women and men. The ritual initiation into chiefly positions was restricted to men, and so were hunting, warfare, and ironworking (all three ritually encrusted occupations), as well as house building and toolmaking. Men were said to do these things simply "because they are men."

A complex system of reciprocal existential identities, with associated immanent features, was found in the sphere of kinship relations (father-son, mother's brother–sister's son, older brother–younger brother, and so forth), of what we like to call ritual kinship (as in blood brotherhood and the adoption of acquired persons—"slaves"—into the kin group), and of certain entirely ritual spheres (such as the identity of Kita, see Kopytoff 1980). All of these identities and relations, it should be noted, were heavily ritualized.

One set of identities deserves special comment—that of husband and wife. The immanent roles associated with them were clearly defined but they were few in number. They focused primarily on the various dangers of ritually unsanctioned sexual unions. But most features of the husband-wife relationship (though they could have mystical significance) involved the contractual side of marriage. Here, bridewealth transactions established (and renegotiations could change) the precise rights of the mates in one another and in the children. These rights were not immanent in the husband-wife relationship as such. They included such matters as the wife's role as grower and maker of food and as provider of sex to the husband; and the husband's role of provider of meat, cloth, and utensils to the wife. In brief, the numerous roles that Westerners consider to be immanent in the identities of husband and wife derived, among the Suku, from specific and discrete contractual, circumstantial, and negotiable arrangements. The boundary between the immanent and the circumstantial was reflected in two sets of terms. When the immanent features of the marriage were involved, this was better conveyed by using the terms *mununi* (husband) and *mukasi* (wife). On the other hand, the contractual and circumstantial features were better conveyed by the terms *yakala* (literally man, male) and *muketu* (literally woman, female). The distinction is reminiscent of the two terms used for wife in French: *épouse*, with its implications of legalism and formality, and *femme*, conveying sociability and informality. The more formal Suku set of terms was, in fact, rarely used, simply because the contexts in which they were relevant were rare. The statement by Vellenga (1983:145) about Akan marriage—that "generally it could be said that marriage was considered more of a *process* that a state of being"—conveys very well the flavor of the non-existential side of Suku marriage arrangements.

When pressed further for explanations, my Suku informants attributed the immanence of certain roles in certain existential identities to the nature of human existential identity itself, as in the case of injunction against sex between siblings. The immanence of other roles they attributed to the "injunctions of Suku elders/ancestors" (*misiku mya bambuta*). Here, the Suku posited a Suku existential identity separate from their neighbors'. More recently, however, with the growing awareness of startling variations in customs, such explanations have become less satisfying. When I once mentioned to a group of Suku that in some parts of Africa women are "circumcised," the information was greeted with disbelief and hilarity. One person, who had literally fallen on the ground with laughter, asked in jest whether women in those places also impregnated women. In Suku folk anthropology, to be circumcised was as immanent a feature of being a man as the begetting of children. Circumcision was not a variant practice but an invariant, "natural" attribute of masculinity—of human masculinity before the appearance of uncircumcised Europeans and, since then, of African masculinity (though my story about female circumcision among some distant Africans suddenly threw uncertainty over that). Circumcision was also, above all, a "natural" nonattribute of femininity—the sort of thing that a Suku anthropologist might think it pedantic to mention in a report on gender attributes in a foreign society, in the same way that Western anthropologists think it pedantic to mention childbearing as an attribute of femininity.

But when it came to the fact that Suku women did agriculture, the reason given was not that "it is because they are women," or that there was an ancestral injunction that women should do agriculture. The Suku recognized that there is a kind of custom that is different from one naturally or ancestrally imposed. This is the *mutindu* or *mpila*, or, in the Kikongo-based lingua franca of the area, *faso* (from the French *façon*). The distinction between the two kinds of customs is, of course, reminiscent of Sumner's (1906) classic distinction in sociological theory between the coercive "mores" and the merely habitual "folkways," that is, "social practices." What I refer to as immanent features of existential identities carry the kind of coercive force that Sumner's mores do; in contrast, like practices, the circumstantial features of existential identities do not.

The Suku recognized that they shared some of their practices with their neighbors, and they could point to specific instances of the diffusion of practices in the region. Practices were seen as changeable and some were known to have changed within Suku society. There was nothing startling, then, in the idea that some Suku practices may be reversed among other peoples—that, in another society, for example, men might do subsistence agriculture and women might weave baskets.

Agricultural work by women was not a matter of ancestral injunction but rather a practice. As I have mentioned, Suku men did traditionally do some planting inside the village and in the form of little gardens of herbs, tobacco, and imported vegetables. In the late 1940s, men had begun to plant coffee trees in the very few places in Sukuland where the soil allowed it. My suggestion that men might plant manioc, the staple food, if there were a market for it, was acceptable. However, the idea of planting it for one's own consumption was rejected on pragmatic grounds. They could do it, but it would make no sense since the women already planted all the food they needed. I do not wish to convey the impression that these pragmatic discussions lacked all emotional overtones. Suku men did not like to engage in agriculture and they did feel somewhat demeaned when they did, even if, as in the case of coffee, the profits seduced them into it. But the point is that they were seducible for pragmatic reasons. Not doing agriculture was a circumstantial feature of male identity and a socially negotiable one.

The overwhelming majority of the tasks that I have mentioned as being on the women's side in the division of labor were of this circumstantial rather than immanent kind—matters of negotiable practice. Unlike mores and "injunctions from the elders/ancestors," which are self-justifying and beyond rational discussion and rational defense, circumstantial features of women's identities could be discussed and defended, even if the defense was circular. For example, when I raised the issue of men planting subsistence crops, one of the reasons advanced for their not doing so was that since women cooked, they might as well know what they are cooking. Later, when I broached the idea of cooking by men, I was told that since women grew the food, they knew it and might as well cook it. And when I reminded them of the earlier argument, the response was not embarrassment at having been caught at a fallacy but rather a triumphant reassertion of it all along the lines of "that's exactly right, you see, these things go together." The point is that the strands in this circular functionalist web are pragmatic, and the very possibility of engaging in such a defense implies the negotiability of these particular gender roles.

To the extent that the new occupations introduced in the colonial period had no established place in the Suku folk anthropology of gender, all of them lacked immanence and represented circumstantial roles. Their relationship to gender should thus have been negotiable—in principle. In fact, a certain amount of cultural pre-sortment occurred. Some of this was achieved by obvious equations—a policeman's or soldier's role easily joined that of warrior and hunter as an attribute of male social identity. But whether these new roles were unquestionably immanent in the male existential identity remained unclear (it is significant, I think, that in many parts of Africa where women had never been warriors, they nevertheless have become soldiers without any sense of profound anomaly). Many other new roles, such as schoolteachers, clerks, or nurses, had no obvious traditional counterparts. Pragmatically, however, their allocation was conditioned by the fact that the women had little time to spare beyond their routine work while the men were definitely, in the economist's language, underemployed.

It was largely in these terms that the embryonic modernization of the Suku area began to take shape after the Second World War. For example, in the matter of cooking—traditionally, a circumstantial but almost universally female role among the Suku—the issue was sorted out very early on. Suku males took work as cooks for resident European and African officials; the job, with its regular pay, gave them some status. Similarly, young men took on jobs caring for expatriate children—an occupation that traditionally fell on the women. The women's heavy responsibilities would not allow them to become engaged as nannies or indeed as anything else. One might be tempted to say that men took on these jobs *because* it gave them money and status. This explanation would be too easy. The far greater status and rewards of being a Christian schoolteacher, for example, would not have been sufficient to make men even remotely consider the possibility of abandoning circumcision. The Christian missionaries from the beginning did not press the attack on what they recognized as a pagan but non-negotiable feature of men's existential identity.

Although growing vegetables for sale to the small local stranger community was rather more frequently done by men, some women did it too in the midst of their busy schedules. The little trading that was available in this economically depressed region was again done mostly by men, though a little by women. Clerking was all done by men at the beginning, but then literacy was until the 1950s almost monopolized by them. As more women became literate, a few of them began to move into clerkish positions.

In brief, the definition of many old roles and most of the new roles meant that these roles remained open to both genders—in principle. Their statistical distribution was, however, skewed, and that for pragmatic reasons.

But even pragmatically Suku women did not invariably give preference to old established roles. This is shown by the emergence among the Suku of that contemporary pan-African figure: the free woman. Unlike other groups closer to the centers of modernity, the Suku had very few such free women—in the late 1950s, a few score at most. But this makes their emergence no less significant as a systemic cultural phenomenon.

The colonial authorities of what was then the Belgian Congo recognized a formal status of *femme libre*. In the official view, a free woman was one who had detached herself from the obligations and constraints of African custom. She could claim to be subject not to the customary tribunal but to that held directly by colonial administrators enforcing the written legal code of the colony. This creation of a legal status was a case of law following African sociological reality. Legalities aside, de facto free women had been a feature of most colonial African societies.

Among the Suku and neighboring peoples, free women engaged in such varied occupations as traders, small businesswomen (such as keepers of the rudimentary shops, hotels, bars, and restaurants in African townships), prostitutes, temporary concubines of expatriate European and African functionaries, and common-law wives of the relatively de-tribalized and mobile males involved in the modern sector (mechanics, drivers, male nurses, businessmen, clerks, and the like). Free women often moved between these various roles. When they had children, these either joined the burgeoning urban population or were brought up by their mothers' relatives back in the village. The children had no problem of social placement among these matrilineal populations, being automatically members of their mothers' kin groups.

What was the social position of these free women from the Suku point of view? They were simply women who had not married, for whom nobody had paid bridewealth, and who exercised scarcely any of the main traditional female occupations, that is, cultivation and minor crafts. But their existential identity as women remained intact. They bore children and, like other women, thereby asserted their womanhood. They conferred on these children what was in women's power to confer—that essential quality of "blood" that made these children members of their matrilineage. In principle, they could fulfill any of the women's ritual roles.

If they were not, in fact, called upon by their kin groups to take up female ritual roles, the reason was practical, for these roles imposed considerable constraints on sexual activities. If many of them did not bring up their own children, this conformed with certain traditional understandings.

As in most of Africa (where fosterage of children is very widespread), rearing children (as opposed to bearing them) was not a role immanent in a Suku woman's existential identity. The task was easily delegated to other relatives, sometimes for the convenience of parents, sometimes at the request of relatives. A childless woman might ask her sister to let her have a "spare" daughter to bring up and help out around the house (as elsewhere in Africa, children represented an important part of domestic labor resources).

The negotiability, in Africa, of various aspects of the marital and parental role is striking from the Western perspective, where so many immanent features are embedded in the identities of husband/father and wife/mother. For example we are now aware of the very wide distribution throughout Africa of what Herskovits (1938:i:319–22) first called "woman-marriage" in Dahomey (for examples, see Strobel 1982:120–21). In this kind of marriage, it is possible for a woman, by paying bridewealth for another woman, to acquire the legal role of "husband" to that woman and the legal role of "father" to her children (the children being sired by a designated male who does not thereby acquire legal paternal rights in them). The very possibility of a woman being a "husband" and "father" puts very vividly to the test the Western cultural assumptions about which features are naturally immanent in the woman's social identity. But "woman-marriage" is only one expression of a more general tendency in African cultures to have a great variety of different kinds of heterosexual unions, all surrounding the woman's existential identity with negotiated arrangements whose formal recognition makes them all akin to what Westerners feel compelled to see as some kind of "marriage." Thus, Herskovits lists thirteen kinds of such unions for Dahomey, and Vellenga (1983:145) refers to twenty-three for the Akan (for an example of the bewildering number of strategies such systems permit, see Bledsoe 1980). In this perspective, the Suku free woman represented a radically stripped down version of essential Suku womanhood—stripped, that is, of most of its traditional panoply of circumstantial features, with the remaining existential core being endowed with a set of new circumstantial features and roles.

It is not surprising, then, that at no time had I heard anyone disparage Suku free women as "loose" or suggest that they were doing anything they should not or not doing something they should. The flavor of the attitude is conveyed by the fact that some informants compared free women to nuns, African and European, whom the Suku saw as having taken on special circumstantial roles rather than, as in the Christian view, having adopted a profoundly new existential identity. The difference, amid the similarities, between the free woman and the nun was that the nun had also chosen to agree not to bear children. When people expressed moral judgments about free women, they talked not about the category as such but about the conduct of some individuals within the category. A promiscuous trader woman, whose promiscuity led to unseemly public behavior, would be condemned in the same way that a married woman would. The same held for a full-time prostitute whose behavior (but not her role) might or might not be shameful.

The absence of evaluative comments on such role transformations is related to another aspect of the Suku definition of woman's existential identity. The Suku did not focus on *what* in some essentialist sense that existential identity—what we would call womanhood—was. The identity of woman existed as a concept, but it was not described in terms of some general internal content. In effect, there was no general pattern of "femininity," no generic "feminine role" as such, describable in terms of some characterological qualities.

Linton (1945:130) coined the term status-personality to indicate the linkage, in a given society, between a particular status and the personality configuration required by that status. For example, we generally recognize that to be a successful psychologist or university administrator calls for a personality different from what it takes to be a successful army sergeant. We may transfer Linton's idea to Goodenough's concept of social identity and talk of an identity-personality.

In discussing chieftaincy—an existential identity established by a ritual—the Suku very willingly described the identity-personality desirable in rulers. The chief should be dignified in bearing, reserved, slow to anger, judicious, generous, nurturing, stern with transgressions but understanding and forgiving. Similarly, one could easily elicit broadly sketched identity-personalities (in such reciprocal existential relationships as that of father-son or mother's brother–sister's child) and narrowly sketched ones for diviners, judges, or guardians of ritual medicines. I could never, however, elicit an identity-personality for either woman or man as such. Characterologically, that is, males and females were not differentiated, the character of a particular person being regarded as a matter of individual variation that cross-cut gender. One sometimes heard it said that women in their childbearing years had a greater tendency to be talkative and impulsive and to lack discretion. But this was not said of women in general. And the traits were also said to be present in some individual men. It is significant that I have not heard anyone say about an indiscreet man that he was "like a woman"—a very common formulation in Western, Middle Eastern, and, I am sure, other societies.

The Suku do not say that "women should not be forward." What they will say is that a woman should be quiet on such and such an occasion, as should also a man on certain occasions. The Suku do not say that "women should be obedient." They will say that a wife should obey her husband in certain contexts, as a son should obey his father in certain contexts. Even when disapproving of breaches of roles immanent in the identity of the postpubertal woman, the Suku would not phrase the issue characterologically, as is done in so many societies, by saying: "Do not walk naked in the street because women should be modest." What they will say is: "Do not walk naked in the street because it is shameful for big women to walk naked in the street." The avoidance of characterological judgments is related to the general pattern of what might be called "externality" in African cultures—the unwillingness to probe into the inaccessible interior of persons (precisely what modern Westerners so excel at). The African preference is for dealing with behavior in terms of external and visible features, without conflating them into a global statement about the interior person.

In any analysis of women's roles in a given society, it is important to discover whether the society conceptualizes a singular identity of "woman" (as the West does), and whether that identity is kept quite distinct in certain contexts from such identities as wife, or adolescent, mature, or postmenopausal females. Thus, among the Suku, while there was no answer to the question of what women are or of how they should behave in general, such a description was available for the identity of a wife. But the description—in any case clearly contextual—was bare: above all, a Suku wife should be respectful of her husband and her in-laws, as he should be of her and his in-laws. Beyond that, being a wife entailed circumstantial features and roles, defining not what one was but what one did, such as providing food and sex, cooking, and keeping house. These task-oriented roles were derived from the contractual side of Suku marriage, which involved negotiated payments by the husband. Legally, a wife was to fulfill these roles without also playing a personality-role. If she failed in her obligations, the failure was legal, and narrowly so. For example, if one's mate misused one's property, one could take him or her to court, but this act did not threaten the marriage itself.

An analogy will perhaps clarify the point: in some contemporary American marriages, the wealth of the respective mates is kept legally separate.

How each chooses to use it is a matter lying outside the obligations immanent in the marriage relationship. A spendthrift with his or her money is immune from accusations of being a spendthrift in the context of the marriage partnership. Since marriage in America is an overwhelmingly existential relationship, such variations in marriage are regarded in mainstream American culture as having been deliberately put outside of the marriage relationship. In Africa, on the other hand, such negotiated variations *constitute* the marriage in one of its several possible guises.

In this perspective, the African free woman is at the extreme of a continuum of acceptable women's roles, including her relationship with men. To a Westerner, one end of the continuum is clearly recognizable as "marriage" while the other end appears as a most ephemeral relationship with one or more men. The significance of the free woman lies in showing the ease with which an apparently radical transformation of women's roles can occur by what is in fact a slight variation in role shedding and role acquisition. Many other African women, Suku and others, have gone some but not all the way on this road. And more recently, they have taken these transformations in new directions—into the professions, the bureaucracy, and politics. They perform these new roles with little evidence of being victims of the kind of wrenching role conflicts that so often accompany the careers of their Western, and especially American, sisters. These transformations have taken place without any notable public debate in most African societies (some Islamic African societies being apparent exceptions that demand, however, close analysis).

The free African women were usually seen as a new phenomenon, attributable to the destabilization of old customs by modern forces. But the phenomenon clearly has deeper cultural roots. Together with the principles that underlie it, it is widely distributed in Africa, and the dynamics of identity I have described have worked as smoothly and thoroughly in the big cities as in backwaters such as Sukuland. All this militates against the idea that the free African woman has arisen only since colonial times or solely in response to modern conditions. A considerable literature has developed (for one review, see Strobel 1982) that indicates this. We are now also aware of the large number of African women who rose as large-scale entrepreneurs and political and even military leaders in the past (see, for example, Sweetman 1984). The literature also points to the wide specific variation in the social condition of African women in different places and historical periods. What I would stress here is that these concrete variations become understandable precisely because they deal with the circumstantial elements (that are highly responsive to external changes) that cluster around a very narrow existential core.

Women's Identities in the West

The crucial question I have been posing is this: granted that most and perhaps all societies posit that being a woman is an existential identity with a set of features immanent in it, how many such immanent features are there and what are they? Or, to put it most simply, the problem of women's roles is not whether a society recognizes women as being different from men (they invariably do) but how it organizes other things around the difference.

I am not competent to extend this perspective from the Suku and Africa to other areas of the Third World. Let me try, however, to bring the perspective to the very different situation found in the West and more particularly in the United States. What is there, then, in the modern Western conceptualization of women's identities and roles that makes the Western configuration so different?

Two things come immediately to attention: (1) the astonishingly greater number of immanent features associated with the Western woman's existential identity, and (2) the elaborate interior characterization of the Western female existential identity itself—what Betty Friedan (1963) so aptly called the feminine mystique.

The modern American conception of womanhood—by which I mean the most recent and still culturally dominant synthesis in mid-twentieth-century "mainstream" American culture—had been in the making over the preceding century and a half of Anglo-American history. Its emergence was part of a larger transformation that included the spreading cultural hegemony of an expanding middle class that became the carrier of a progressivist ethos of antitraditionalism, individualism, egalitarianism, and democracy. Before that, both in northwestern Europe (see, for example, Howell 1987) and in America (Jensen 1987), role definitions were rather differently and more loosely organized.

In the modern synthesis, the range of the immanent features of womanhood is very wide indeed and it is familiar enough to need hardly any extensive discussion. In addition to the role of childbearer, the woman's identity has come to include numerous immanent features embodying a vast array of responsibilities. There is the rearing, socialization, and education of one's own children, in a society where "correct" socialization is believed to determine the child's future success in life. There is the role of providing a physically and psychologically encouraging ambience at home for the husband. There is the management of the social life and social calendar of the family unit. There is housekeeping, which merges into the more elusive homemaking. There is the responsibility to present to the world attractive and physically cared-for house, children, husband, and, not least, one's own self as a significant indicator of the state and status of the family. And, perhaps hardest of all, there is the requirement of presenting to the world a characterologically, rather than merely behaviorally, defined femininity: charm, docility, good sense, seductiveness, controlled sexuality, a certain impracticality in business matters combined with a no-nonsense managerial efficiency in home matters, and so on.

These features began to be built up gradually, beginning early in the nineteenth century, with the development of what Matthews (1987) refers to as the cult of domesticity. Increasingly, the identity of wife-mother came to be seen as immanent in the very identity of being a woman. This was not always so. In the nineteenth century, the spinster—like the bachelor, widow, and widower—was culturally well-recognized as an alternative identity (see, for example, Chambers-Schiller 1984). The identity had its own cluster of integral roles (including such roles as schoolteacher, nurse, nanny, or companion) and was not unlike the alternative gender identities of nun and priest. But by the mid-twentieth century, spinsterhood and bachelorhood ceased to be seen as equal and mature identities in and of themselves. They became increasingly defined as incomplete identities, representing an unachieved journey toward the mature identity of married person. The redefinition was further exacerbated by the invasion of American popular culture by psychology and especially a vulgarized Freudianism; spinsterhood changed from an alternative identity into a flawed one, into a public statement of sexual, and therefore existential, incompleteness. The very terms spinster, bachelor, widow, and widower became somewhat embarrassing and began to drop out of common usage, to be replaced by the vague "single." Not surprisingly, this trend coincided with the questioning of the existential legitimacy of the identities of nun and priest.

By the mid-twentieth century, American society seemed to have arrived at the point where most small-scale societies like the Suku have been all along—where all "normal" men and women are somehow incomplete unless they are married and have progeny. But there is a difference with African societies that lies in the circumstance that each of the American gender identities is encrusted with numerous immanent features. Many unmarried African women could repair their incompleteness and have mates and children by resorting to one of a dozen or more available recognized unions. The modern American woman can achieve this "normal" identity only by way of marriage, with its burdensome and cumbersome package of immanent roles. Once existentially complete, she can then turn to other occupations. But everyone is realistic enough to know that few can manage that with any ease, and if a woman does, the achievement is publicly recognized by the obligatory and congratulatory aside about how it had all been done without her ceasing to be a woman-wife-mother. To give such high praise is to reiterate the rarity of success in reconciling the role contradictions. And if success is rare, then it is too risky to entrust to women such crucial positions as, say, the presidency of a company, let alone of a country.

The sheer weight of the American woman's immanent role-load continues to make the taking on of other identities and roles a daunting prospect. It is true that the workload of Suku women's roles was heavier and more time-consuming, but the roles themselves were overwhelmingly circumstantial and negotiable. In America the existential identity is enveloped in a huge mantle of non-negotiable roles. If an American woman wishes to take on a new circumstantial role (say, that of professional), she cannot easily trade it for an old one (say, that of her family's hostess).

Moreover, if an American woman wishes to chip away at the immanent roles, the dominant liberal social ethos often makes this course of action ideologically and pragmatically difficult. An ethos of personal achievement discourages the delegation to others of tasks considered to be properly one's own. An egalitarian ethos frowns upon the hiring of the less advantaged as servants to do onerous tasks, and it also makes the social handling of the inherently unequal relationship with servants difficult (in a way that a class society does not). An individualistic ethos prizes individual privacy; this makes the presence of servants and their involvement in the intimate details of everyday life uncomfortable (in a way that aristocratic societies do not, with their exclusion of the lower orders from the community of manners and their notorious lack of personal shame before servants). And just when the use of servants becomes increasingly unacceptable, the use of relatives as surrogates for the fulfillment of one's roles becomes increasingly difficult, for the ethos of antitraditionalism questions the sincerity and the obligatory nature of culturally mandated relationships, including those of kinship, and extols instead voluntary relationships.

While there is some room for rearranging housekeeping roles, many of the other roles immanent in womanhood are by their nature utterly non-negotiable. A woman can scarcely delegate to someone else the psychological caretaking of her husband. Nor can she, while pursuing her education or profession, delegate entirely to others the rearing of her children, steeped as the task is in innumerable psychological subtleties; to do so would make her an "unnatural mother" in her own eyes no less than in others'. Moreover, the greater the sheer number of immanent roles, the greater the chances of substantive conflict with new circumstantial roles that one might be contemplating—for example, conflicts between schedules demanded by a job and by the socialization of one's children.

But the greatest source of difficulties may be traced to the development of a characterological model of existential womanhood itself. The existence of this model in the West is itself part of the rise of individualism and the idea that a knowledge of their "internal" core yields a superior understanding of people. This internal perspective leads, in turn, to especially subtle characterological formulations of existential social identities, be they of gender, race, or ethnicity. Once an internal personality-like characterization of womanhood exists, the problem arises of its congruence with the identity-personality (Linton's status-personality) of various occupations. For example, can one who is "naturally" docile, impractical, and seductive take on occupations demanding aggressiveness, hardheadedness, and professionalism? For the American woman, the conflict between different pursuits is very often existential—a personality conflict that also involves values, responsibilities, and ethics. This is in contrast to the Suku, for whom, in the absence of a characterological model of womanhood, the conflict is pragmatic.

The issue is further complicated by the different views of the relationship between the natural and the cultural. In the Hobbesian and Durkheimian views, society is an artificial—hence, cultural—construction that transcends and often contradicts nature. On the other hand, American folk anthropology (and, frequently, American social science) is Lockean, seeing society as a natural phenomenon beholden to natural laws. Hence, to Americans, social change must conform to the demands of Nature. And it is Nature (as revealed by Science) that, in the absence of an active deity, becomes the validator or invalidator of proposed social changes.

This poses special problems in dealing with gender roles. If what is natural is right, then whatever one believes or wishes to be right must be proven natural; and whatever one wishes to be wrong must be shown to be unnatural. This injects American debates over social policy with an extraordinary amount of theory, measurement, and scientific pretensions. In so eminently cultural an issue as civil or educational rights, the opposing sides both argue over the latest word on I.Q. tests and the latest ruminations of social scientists. For the same reason, in the first flush of feminist agitation, one saw the drive to demonstrate scientifically the biological equivalence between the sexes, while antifeminist rhetoric seized on the latest experiment to claim biological nonequivalence. The legitimacy of civic arrangements is made to depend on the latest reports from the laboratories.

In the popular expression of this system, when a role hitherto played by men (as, for example, the role of secretary and typist at the turn of the century) is taken up by women, the new reality is eventually justified on natural grounds. This can be accomplished relatively quickly, given the shallowness of modern historical awareness (itself a part of its antitraditionalism). Once an occupation threatens to become the preserve of one gender, there occurs a flight from it by the other—not unlike the flights that make for ethnic successions in American neighborhoods.

What I wish to stress here is that the development in the modern West of what we generally think of as the basic progressivist package of values has been a double-edged weapon when it came to the transformation of women's roles. Egalitarianism, individualism, personal independence, refusal to exploit others for one's personal comfort, and the need for an objective and scientific rather than a traditional (and therefore "arbitrary") basis for social action—even as these values called for redefining gender roles in an egalitarian direction, they also rigidified these roles and made venturing into new roles and occupations for either sex more difficult. It is an obvious paradox that the liberation of the servant girl necessarily imposed, in practice, more domestic chores on her mistress. Other such paradoxes are more than practical. The humanitarianism that specifically banished women from work in the mines, for example, necessarily gave moral sanction to the idea that women are existentially unfit to do certain kinds of men's work.

Conclusion

We find ourselves back where we began—with the puzzle of "traditional" rather than "progressive" societies producing women prime ministers and assertive professionals that take on with startling ease positions hitherto reserved to men. My analysis depended primarily on a paradigmatic contrast between Africa and the United States. It left untouched the question of what specifically this says about gender conceptualizations in the West outside of the United States and in the rest of the Third World (a label without much content in any case). I can only hope that at least the mode of my analysis and the terms I have coined for it can be usefully applied elsewhere in the elucidation of similar problems.

A final point—in my discussions with colleagues, I have sometimes encountered a reaction worth noting. They point out that, after all, the Indira Gandhis and the Corazon Aquinos get where they are "not on their own" but "because" of their relationship to their fathers and husbands. And if Third World professional women often find it easy to pursue their careers and to administer men, it is "because" they live in a class society in which servants make their independence of action possible and in which lower-class men are used to accepting orders from superiors, whatever their gender. These objections do not always apply to Africa, with its mostly classless traditional societies, but they deserve an answer with respect to places such as India.

The objections are really expressions of disapproval of the social conditions that allow Third World women of the higher classes to be free of certain burdens. At the very least, the critics refuse to be impressed with women's progress when the costs of success are so culturally unacceptable. This argument, then, is essentially about price. It also reflects the contradictions within the modern progressivist ethos that I have discussed, an ethos whose many different values are not all reconcilable. Western progressivist ideology is notoriously cultureless, while the structure of identities and roles cannot exist, even in the abstract, in a sociocultural vacuum. To say that it is Indira Gandhi's kinship position that has given her power is precisely to say that in many societies certain factors (unpalatable though they are to the Western progressivist ethos) do override gender distinctions in a way that they cannot be overridden in America. In India, the kinship-dynastic factor overrode them twice: first it transmitted the political charisma of a man, Pandit Nehru, to a woman, his daughter Indira Gandhi, and then from her to a man, her son Rajiv. The factor of gender, that is, worked in both directions. What the critics would have liked was for Indira Gandhi to have achieved it entirely on her own. But how, speaking concretely? Like Margaret Thatcher, perhaps? But ideology intrudes. . . .

That a hierarchical or class structure may give some women authority over some men merely reminds us that societies will always rely on many different kinds of criteria when they confer or transfer authority: family connections, class, caste, religion, education, race, majority or minority status—the list is endless. Each of them has at one time or another, in one place or another, been considered objectionable. It has been left to our age to consider all of them objectionable. In societies where existential social distinctions—based on what we usually call "ascribed statuses"—have been drastically reduced (as they have been in most Western societies), those that do remain, gender included, will be all the more visible and irritating to progressivist sensibilities. All of these different systems of gender identities and roles carry their particular social costs—costs in terms of their own values and costs in terms of the values of observers from other societies. How such costs are to be compared and weighed is a question that belongs in a forum other than this one.

Bibliography

Bledsoe, Caroline. 1980. *Women and Marriage in Kpelle Society.* Stanford: Stanford University Press.
Chambers-Schiller, Lee Virginia. 1984. *Liberty, A Better Husband—Single Women in America: The Generations of 1780–1840.* New Haven: Yale University Press.
Friedan, Betty. 1963. *The Feminine Mystique.* New York: Norton.
Goodenough, Ward H. 1965. "Rethinking 'Status' and 'Role': Toward a General Model of Cultural Organization of Social Relationships." In *The Relevance of Models for Social Anthropology,* M. Banton, ed. London: Tavistock.
Herskovits, Melville J. 1937. "A Note on 'Woman Marriage' in Dahomey." *Africa* 10: 335–41.
———. 1938. *Dahomey: An Ancient West African Kingdom.* 2 vols. New York: J. J. Augustin.
Howell, Martha C. 1987. *Women, Production, and Patriarchy in Late Medieval Cities.* Chicago: University of Chicago Press.
Jensen, Joan M. 1987. *Loosening the Bonds: Mid-Atlantic Farm Women, 1750–1850.* New Haven: Yale University Press.
Kopytoff, Igor. 1964. "Family and Lineage among the Suku of the Congo." In *The Family Estate in Africa,* Robert F. Gray and P. H. Gulliver, eds., pp. 83–116. Boston: Boston University Press.
———. 1965. "The Suku of Southwestern Congo." In *Peoples of Africa,* James L. Gibbs, Jr., ed., pp. 441–78. New York: Holt, Rinehart, and Winston.
———. 1980. "Revitalization and the Genesis of Cults in Pragmatic Religion: The Kita Rite of Passage among the Suku." In *Explorations in African Systems of Thought,* Ivan Karp and Charles S. Bird, eds., pp. 183–212. Bloomington: Indiana University Press.
Linton, Ralph. 1936. *The Study of Man.* New York: Appleton-Century.
———. 1945. *The Cultural Background of Personality.* New York: Appleton-Century.

Matthews, Glenna. 1987. *"Just a Housewife": The Rise and Fall of Domesticity*. New York: Oxford University Press.
Strobel, Margaret. 1982. "African Women." *Signs: A Journal of Women in Culture and Society* 8: 108–31.
Sumner, William Graham. 1906. *Folkways: A Study of the Sociological Importance of Usage, Manners, Customs, Mores and Morals* (1959 ed.). Boston: Ginn.
Sweetman, David. 1984. *Women Leaders in African History*. London: Heinemann.
Vellenga, Dorothy Dee. 1983. "Who Is a Wife? Legal Expressions of Heterosexual Conflicts in Ghana." In *Female and Male in West Africa*, Christine Oppong, ed., pp. 144–55. London: Allen and Unwin.

On the basis of behavioral and institutional evidence of the denigration of women, ethnographers have long attributed an ideology of male dominance to societies of the Eastern Highlands of Papua New Guinea. Anna Meigs has studied one of these groups, the Hua, and finds that indeed males of the society have such an ideology, in terms of which they view females as "disgusting, dirty, and dangerous." But this is not the end of the story, for Meigs's data reveal two other ideologies of at least equal importance in defining the Hua view of gender relations.

Along with the "brutally chauvinistic" ideology, which is most apparent in the ritual beliefs and practices that surround the initiation of young males, are two entirely contradictory ones. The first of these is one of envy of women for their power, endurance, and longevity, based on the view that the female body is superior to that of the male. The second is an ideology of complementary interdependence of males and females, an egalitarian view "enshrined in the interaction of everyday life in which males depend on females and females depend on males."

Meigs points out that within the culture of the Hua these different ideologies are necessary to meet the "combined needs of reproduction and defense." Her essay details the elaborate system of compartmentalization and turn-taking that allows the Hua to minimize the ideological conflict among these contradictory positions. Time provides one dimension for this ideological sorting, and to illustrate it Meigs gives us a rich picture of the life cycle of both males and females in terms of the three prevailing gender ideologies. Another dimension is spatial, "across scenes and local contexts," which permits the Hua to compartmentalize their opposing ideologies in defined situational contexts.

Anna Meigs

4 Multiple Gender Ideologies and Statuses

Anthropological discussions of sex-gender systems have been shaped by three closely linked assumptions. They are

(1) that a society has a gender ideology, a single monolithic outlook on male and female;
(2) that female status is similarly singular and monolithic; in other words, that one can describe "female status" in a society in a unitary and composite way; and
(3) that there are two simple and monolithic categories: male and female.

In this chapter I argue that gender ideology, female status, and gender categorization are all highly complex and multifaceted cultural constructions and, as such, are characterized by a high degree of multiplicity of conception in any single society. No society, in other words, has a definitive gender ideology, a simple "female status," or a single way of categorizing male and female. I will illustrate these points with examples drawn from the Hua, a population of 3,100 horticulturists in the Eastern Highlands of Papua New Guinea.

Gender Ideology: Single or Multiple?

Ethnographers and students of the New Guinea Highlands, in particular the Eastern Highlands, have focused ever since the inception of ethnographic work on a set of ideas, behaviors, and institutions that is widespread in the area and that has come to be described as a manifestation of an ideology of "male dominance." This ideology certainly exists among the

Hua as well. Several months of fieldwork, however, led me to the realization that, at least in the Hua case, this ideology was only one among several to which Hua males subscribe. Hua males, in fact, have three separate and contradictory gender ideologies. One is brutally chauvinistic, the second frankly envious of female reproductive power, and the third egalitarian (for a more detailed discussion of these options, see Meigs 1984).

According to the chauvinist ideology, females are disgusting, dirty, and dangerous. All feminine body substances, but particularly menstrual blood, have the power to destroy not only male growth and strength but also any male endeavor. The inside of a woman's body is alleged to be dark and putrid like that of scavenging animals. Males by contrast are like the birds: clean and pure and associated with the arboreal heights. Female degradation in this ideology is not only physical but also moral and social. Woman are stupid and lack information, perspective, and insight. Their loyalty and honor are suspect. Their ability to cooperate and subordinate personal to group interest is denigrated (see M. Strathern 1972 for discussion of this point among the Hageners). This ideology is enshrined in many ritual and institutional devices, among them the men's house, the cult of the flutes, the early stages of initiation, but particularly in the food rules enjoined upon a young male initiate. These rules equate most items of the extensive Hua food inventory with some aspect of the female's reproductive anatomy or physiology, which food is then labeled as disgusting and dangerous and tabooed to the male initiate for a varying period of time. In the process males are taught an ideology of male contempt for, disgust at, and fear of female reproduction.

Males *also* believe, however, that the female body is superior to the male. The original Hua people were females who through being impregnated by immigrant males created the Hua people. The original rulers of society, producers and owners of the cult flutes, were women (this according to a secret male myth). Males feel intense insecurity about the more rapid growth exhibited by females (the sanction on numerous male food taboos is stunting of growth) and females' allegedly greater endurance and longevity. Hua males imitate menstruation and believe they can become pregnant. In secret ceremonies they eat food directly associated with the soft, juicy, fast-growing quality of the female body that they supposedly abhor. They ingest these substances, they say, to compensate for the lack of vitality inherent in the male body. This gender ideology in which females are granted natural superiority is enshrined in myth, traditional belief (for example, that males can become pregnant), and ritual practice (bloodletting in imitation of menstruation and consumption of foods associated with feminine qualities).

The third gender ideology or idea complex is neither chauvinistic nor envious but egalitarian. Male bodies are dryer, harder, less rapid in growth, less long-lived, less capable of endurance but stronger for action than female bodies. These facts do not mean, in the terms of this third ideology, that male bodies (and males) are better or worse than female. Only that they are different. Males would like their bodies to have, like the females', a greater proportion of fluid but recognize that in the interest of defense they must be dry and hard. Similarly, both males and females would like the female body to be less wet. Not only would this make her more pleasing aesthetically but would better suit her to a life of action. Both sexes, though, recognize that the feminine excess of fluid is necessary for reproduction. The male body is too hard and dry; the female body is too soft and wet. Both represent extremes of the same continuum, extremes recognized as unfortunate but necessary, given the combined needs of reproduction and defense. This essentially egalitarian ideology is enshrined in the interaction of everyday life in which males depend on females as females depend on males. There is a recognition of this complementary dependency and a cross-sex respect deriving from it.

Clearly it is not possible to state that the Hua have a single gender ideology. Probably there is no such thing as a single gender ideology in any society. On a topic like the relationship of males and females, each society undoubtedly has many ways of thinking—complex, subtle, and even contradictory ideological options.

There are a variety of different ways in which ideological complexity can operate. Ideological multiplicity and, much more, ideological contradiction, create cognitive dissonance. The Hua attempt to quiet some of this dissonance through a turn-taking system. The multiple ideologies are sorted to separate contextual niches in order to keep up the appearance and the feel (at least temporarily) of singularity and simplicity. Ideologies are sorted both vertically through time (connecting with the life-cycle stages of individuals) and horizontally across space (connecting with the various scenes and local contexts of the culture). I examine briefly here first a vertical and then a horizontal example drawn from my Hua data.

The first example illustrates how individuals are cycled through different, even contradictory, ideological positions in the course of growing up. Young Hua males initiated at adolescence are taught the chauvinistic doctrine on females in its pure and unadulterated form. They must not look at women, they may not eat foods from women's gardens, foods that women have prepared, or foods that resemble any aspect of the female reproductive system or its products—to name only a few of the hundreds of rules enjoined on young male initiates. For them the appropriate message is the dangerous and repugnant inferiority of the female body and of females in general. But this complex of ideas, taught in the early grades of initiation, slowly weakens. Prohibition after prohibition on substances that look like something female or on various kinds of interaction with females are relaxed through a scheduled sequence of ritual releases worked on the age mate group as a part of, and then as a sequel to, their initiation process. The initial list of several hundred rules shrinks, until by middle age the male need hardly observe more rules than the female. As the rules drop away, the ideology of chauvinism and sexual avoidance is replaced by one of relative egalitarianism and cooperation. Middle-aged males may sleep, eat, have sex, and work with their wives. Far from seeking distance from femaleness (represented in Hua thinking as that which is *korogo*: wet, juicy, fast-growing, cool, and fertile) males now seek access to it. Ritual retreats focus on consumption of soups made of *korogo* substances that are eaten by males to improve their vitality and virility. Femaleness is represented in this stage as equal in value to maleness (represented as that which is *hakeri'a*: dry, hard, slow-growing, hot, and strong). An ideological transformation has occurred. Males see females no longer as repugnant inferiors but as desirable, although different, equals. This is a transformation that all males go through as they switch from being *kakora* (young male initiates) to being *ropa ve'de* (middle-aged men).

 This ideological transformation is orchestrated by Hua society in order to achieve the satisfaction of competing needs for defense and reproduction. The Hua were traditionally a warring society competing with their neighbors for increasingly scarce land. Like any warring society, the Hua had to create a solidary male fighting force. In a small society (total Hua population is under 3,500) occupying very limited amounts of land, it is difficult to create the isolation and social segregation of, say, Fort Bragg. The Hua drive the wedge between the military and the civilian population with only very minimum quantities of space (all they have available) but make up for their deficiencies in space with an abundance of rules, in other words, with an ideology. Ultimately, however, the society needs these men for more than defense. They need them for reproduction. The chauvinistic message must be weakened, the males must be brought closer to the females to allow heterosexual intercourse (not allowed in early stages of initiation).

A new gender ideology is gradually introduced to allow for male-female cooperation in the raising of a family.

In addition to cycling diverse ideologies to different ages (vertical cycling through time), Hua culture assigns different gender ideologies to different relationships (horizontal allotment over space). Consider, for example, the bride newly married into a Hua village. Hua males of approximately her age will treat her as highly polluting, her body and its substances as contaminating. She will be avoided and isolated in accordance with the above-mentioned chauvinistic ideology. Older Hua males will view her body similarly although to a lesser degree. There is, however, a whole class of Hua males who will not relate to her as polluting in the slightest. These are men who, through their mothers or mother's mothers, are consanguineously related to the new bride. This group of men, often quite sizable given the Hua practice of concentrating their marriages, relates to the new bride as a classificatory sister or daughter. The chauvinistic ideology, which they would normally apply to a new bride, has no relevance here. Instead males relate to her through the ideology of egalitarianism and cooperation. Thus men of the same age in the same village adhere to different and contradictory gender ideologies in relation to the same woman.

I have not mentioned an age grade, a context, or a relationship in which the second gender ideology, that of female superiority, predominates. I will do so briefly here. The idea that the female, far from being inferior to the male, is actually his superior, is a secret inner lining of initiation taught when the young males are well into the initiatory process. This teaching revolves around rules regulating the eating of possum and human blood and around the practices imitating female menstruation (for detailed discussion see Meigs 1984). At the earlier stages of initiation, the young males are taught that they can under no circumstances eat possum or human blood (otherwise considered edible). Possum is prohibited because it is, according to the direct statements of male informants, the counterpart of women. Blood is prohibited because all blood in Hua thinking is female. What the initiands soon learn, however, is that the doctrine of male chauvinism and avoidance of female substances has a complex and secret wrinkle in it. When males are sick, their growth stunted, or their virility or vitality impaired, those substances that can best effect a cure are substances associated with women. A secret suppressed ideology is revealed: that the female body is the ultimate source of power and vitality. This knowledge is restricted to secret contexts of the men's house society. No male is supposed to reveal this ideology to any noninitiated person. No woman or child is supposed to know it. But this ideology exists within the men's house society and the culture of initiation as an alternative to and contradiction of the males' oft-proclaimed public posture of ideological chauvinism.

Problems in the Concept of "Female Status" Among the Hua

Statements such as "Female status is high in society X" or "Female status is low in society Y" are not infrequent in the literature. I myself expected to be able to make some such assessment of Hua female status, yet I found I was unable to. In some respects female status seemed low, in others high. As evidence of low female status, I could cite such facts as patrilineality and patrilocality, residential segregation of the sexes (male residence in "sacred" men's house for all of initiation and intermittently in later years), strict division of labor (males build fences, hunt, and fight; females garden and raise pigs and children), strict division of behavior styles (males and females sit, sleep, eat, dress, carry loads in radically different fashions legislated by local custom), a warrior code of bravery and toughness, proud tales of gang rape, exclusion of females from ritual knowledge, a cult of the flutes in which males claimed the right to kill women who discovered the secret, denigration of the female body, and so on.[1] All these facts support the idea of male dominance and high male status with a corresponding low status for females. But one can produce a second set of facts that create an image of relatively high female status and thus contradict the image created by the facts listed above.

For example, within the last twenty years males and females have begun to live together more continuously (residential integration) and to cooperate in garden labor and child care (weak division of labor). I have seen males carrying babies on their shoulders to work in their gardens.

There are now and probably always have been informal techniques by which women have some significant control of marriage placements. Women, for example, claim that they would never agree to be married into an area into which numerous kinswomen had not already married. Further, women maintain that their husbands' kin's marriage choices are determined by their own recruiting efforts. Women recruit their own kinswomen as brides for their husband's patrikin in an effort to build up their own kinship network in their community of marriage.

Some women now have and perhaps have always had the liberty to go looking for husbands. It was not uncommon for a young woman to arrive for an extended visit with relatives in a Hua village for the express purpose of finding herself a husband.

There was, during the period in which I was living with the Hua, one elected village head who was female.

Females have now and always have had the ability to undermine male exchange and prestige schemes (negotiated with foods raised by women) through noncooperation (not producing garden surpluses or providing adequate care for pigs).

Similarly, according to men, Hua women now have and always have had the power to destroy male growth and strength (perhaps the most highly valued of all male qualities) through manipulation of the potentially polluting substances of their bodies. Women are suspected of introducing bits of dried menstrual blood into the food of males they dislike. The effect, according to males, is severe debilitation of their bodies.

Females participate alongside males in local fights over land.

The male appreciates female fertility as the most awesome of all powers.

Female status among the Hua clearly presents a confusing picture. One can only say that in some respects their status is high, in other respects low. A composite statement seems impossible. There is no formula by which to reduce all the complexity of variables into a single status "score."

If the Hua complexity on the twin issues of gender ideology and female status is not somehow exceptional, then such statements as "Female status among X is high [or low]" must represent some kind of simplification. Furthermore, this is a kind of simplification and distortion that is not perpetrated upon the male category. One never, to my knowledge, reads sentences like "Male status among the X is high." The status of men in any community is recognized to be heterogeneous depending on the political maneuvers of ambitious individuals and groups. It is only females who are alleged to have a homogeneous status. They are in this a kind of residual category. After the political and economic structures in which men manipulate and maneuver for power have been discussed in detail, one comes to the women, whose status is there, simple and composite, as a leftover of the real system. The variegated, tangled, and blurred nature of the indirect if relatively high female status (such as was listed earlier) leads toward awareness of the crucial issue: female status in any ethnographic context, like male status, is constructed out of a complex variety of components.

Females, like males, operate within complex systems (whether sexually integrated or segregated) and make difficult choices as political actors. Even where the female world is separate from the male, which is by no means always the case, that female world is a world of power and politics (see Lederman this volume; for an earlier formulation of the neglect of females as political actors see Collier 1974). Viewed as political actors within structures of power, women have and achieve statuses as individuals or as members of groups. Clearly not all individuals or all groups within a society have equal access to power or equal skill at using it. Differentials in status will arise due to variable access to the structure of opportunity (see Barnes this volume) or variable definitions of negotiable attributes of sex-roles (see Kopytoff this volume). But these differences do not necessarily define women as a group separate from men as a group. Women and men of certain classes or groups may experience distinctly different opportunities and sex-role possibilities from women and men in other classes or groups.

Gender and Multiplicity

The tendency to see gender ideology and female status as single and unitary, homogeneous and simple, perhaps derives from the biological determinism with which anthropologists originally viewed females. The status of women was given by nature—subordinate. It was a simple and universal biological fact. Female status was not constructed by culture (in which case it would be variable, complex, and highly differentiated both within and across cultures) but given by nature.

In the context of a pervasive biological determinism, gender ideology like female status seemed simple and relatively uninteresting. The ideology of male and female tagged along behind the universal biological facts. Although anthropologists have long since ceased viewing female status and gender ideology through the lens of biological determinism, we have perhaps failed to realize the incredible complexity and multiplicity that cultural determination allows in the construction of both female status and gender ideologies within even a single society.

In regard to the categorization of male and female, it has generally been assumed that these are natural categories discriminated by genital differences. Where the genitals are female, the sex is female, and where the genitals are male, so is the sex. The Hua, like presumably all other cultures, do differentiate individuals by genital characteristics. *Vi* are those individuals who possess the male genital organs and *a'* those with the female. Theoretically, though, sexual classification could be based on a number of different criteria. Consider for example behavior. Certain behaviors are markedly female and others male, so that a person who is genitally female can in certain contexts be classified as male, and vice versa. (Wikan 1977 describes a system among the Omani in which the sexual act rather than the organs defines the gender.) Another mode of classification would be through the substances associated with sexuality, namely menstrual blood, vaginal secretions, parturitional fluids, and semen. As these substances are transferable between the two genital classes, the classification permits crossovers: a genitally male person may be classified as female and a genitally female as male.

Such a mode of classification exists among the Hua as an alternative to the genital one. The relevant substances are female. Those people regardless of genital identity whose bodies have been in contact with and thus contain varying amounts of menstrual blood, parturitional fluids, and vaginal secretions are called *figapa* "uninitiated person" and are said to be "like women" (in the genital sense). They need observe relatively few food proscriptions, can publicly eat possum (the most tabooed of all foods), need observe relatively few avoidance rules, and do not participate in men's house activities. Included in the class *figapa* are children of both sexes, premenopausal women, postmenopausal women who have borne two or less children, and old men. The bodies of all of these people contain female substances and, as a consequence, all may be classified as *figapa* "like a woman." (Children contain female substances because of the continual exchanges of body substance that occur as a natural part of everyday interaction between mother and child.) The mature woman is the origin of all substances relevant to the *kakora-figapa* distinction. Her body at menarche becomes the possessor of a large but finite amount of menstrual blood. This blood plus the closely linked parturitional fluids and vaginal secretions are steadily spent through the reproductive activities of the premenopausal years. Each act of sex involves the release of a small quantum of these fluids (some of which is transferred to her partner), each menstrual period a larger release, and each childbirth a massive one. By menopause the women who have given birth to three or more children (have been massively cleaned out three or more times) are understood to have been defeminized. They are now, as the Hua say, "like men," are called *kakora,* take up residence in the men's house and become privy to male secret knowledge. Some of those substances released by females are taken in by males in the act of eating foods prepared by reproductively active women (which food is contaminated in Hua male thinking with traces of female reproductive fluids transmitted from the vagina through the hand to the food), in the act of sex, and in the process of everyday casual contact.

These intakes of female substances gradually feminize the male so that by old age he is reclassified as *figapa* and said to be "like a female."

Little boys classified as *figapa* become *kakora* through the forced removal of female substances from their bodies (vomiting, nose bleeding, and sweating), their isolation from any further contact with female substances, and then in this context of purity (in regard to female substances) the ingestion of male substances (older males feed initiates blood let from their veins, their hair sprinkled on food, and their semen in acts of oral sex [compare Herdt 1981], and rub the initiates' bodies with sweat and oils removed from their own). It is through this massive reorganization of male and female substances that the genitally male but "like a female" *figapa* becomes a *kakora* and thus takes up residence in men's house. This state, though, is not permanent. As noted earlier, the male's separation from the substances of female sexuality is limited to the period after the boy leaves his mother to take up the life of an initiate and before he takes up a sexual, eating, and residential relationship with his wife. Once his relationship with his wife begins, so also begins the refeminization that culminates in his reclassification in old age as *figapa*.

Among the Hua, then, male-female is not a singular and simple opposition. Multiplicity and complexity pervade this cultural construction as they do those of female status and gender ideology. In addition to the male-female opposition based on genital differences (*vi-a'* in Hua), there is an alternative opposition (*kakora-figapa*) based on the substances of female sexuality.

In regard to the *kakora-figapa* mode of classification, it is important to note the categorization is not crisp and simple. In genital classification (*vi-a'*), in almost all cases ordering is simple, obvious, and immutable: an individual does or does not have male or female genitals. Classification by substances is more subtle and allows for degrees of maleness and femaleness. The young male initiate whose body has been "purified" of all the substances of his mother and other female consanguines and has not yet come into contact with the substances of his real and classificatory wives (wives of agemates) is the quintessential *kakora*. He is pure male because he is pure of all female substances. Marriage gradually will destroy and vitiate his maleness. The female from menarche to the birth of her first child is femaleness at its strongest. Her body is imagined by males to be awash in reproductive fluids. As these are gradually released through the reproductive activities of her adult years, she becomes steadily dryer and harder; she becomes masculinized.

The *kakora-figapa* classification, being based on substances that seep and flow, admits of degrees of maleness and femaleness and as such approximates the notion of prototype. Psychologists and linguists, frustrated with the overly simple, crisp, black-and-white nature of the traditional notion of category (in which an item either is or is not a member depending on whether it does or does not fit certain criteria), have suggested the notion of a prototype that allows semantic categories blurry edges and degrees of membership (Rosch 1975; Coleman and Kay 1981).

The Hua provide us with two alternative constructions of male and female. There is *vi* and *a'* that conform to our notion of a class as a homogeneous and definitively bounded set. A person is a *vi* if and only if he possesses what we call male genitalia; a person is an *a'* if and only if she possesses the female genitalia. Only in very exceptional circumstances is there room for confusion and ambiguity in this mode of classification.

Kakora and *figapa*, on the other hand, sorts people less crisply. *Figapa* are those individuals who possess greater amounts of female substance and *kakora* those who possess lesser. These substances are always in motion and each individual's quotient varies with age and (genital) sex class. Being a *kakora* is a matter of degree of absence of female substance and being a *figapa* a matter of degree of presence. There is a quintessential or prototypical *kakora*: the young initiated male whose body has been purged of the substances of his real and classificatory mothers and who has not yet been contaminated with the substances of his real and classificatory wives. He is *kakora* par excellence. All other *kakora* are *kakora* to a lesser degree than he. Similarly, there is a prototypical *figapa*: the postmenarcheal young married woman whose body contains a nearly full quotient of reproductive fluids. All other *figapa* are *figapa* to a lesser degree than she. As one moves outward from the prototypical *figapa* and the prototypical *kakora* one gets to a blurry area of ambiguity. It is difficult to determine the exact moment at which a *figapa* (whether adolescent male or postmenopausal female) has been drained of sufficient female substance to qualify as a *kakora*. Similarly, it is difficult to determine when a *kakora* has been sufficiently pervaded with female substance to qualify as a *figapa*.

Conclusion

It was the original assumption of anthropological scholarship that female status was simple and unitary. This chapter raises the question of whether our assumption that there is such a thing as female status, a singular gender ideology, and a single mode of differentiation of male and female is not, in fact, a legacy of biological determinism. Recognition of multiplicity, complexity, and the role of context is essential to seeing women, the female role, femaleness, and femininity as cultural constructions rather than as natural facts.

Notes

1. I should note that neither residential segregation/integration nor a strong/weak division of labor in and of itself connotes sexual asymmetry of any kind, a point made to me by an anonymous reviewer of this manuscript.

Bibliography

Coleman, Linda, and Paul Kay. 1981. "Prototype Semantics." *Language* 57: 26–44.
Collier, J. F. 1974. "Women in Politics." In *Woman, Culture and Society*, M. Rosaldo and L. Lamphere, eds., pp. 89–96. Stanford: Stanford University Press.
Herdt, Gilbert. 1981. *Guardians of the Flutes*. New York: McGraw-Hill.
Meigs, Anna. 1984. *Food, Sex, and Pollution: A New Guinea Religion*. New Brunswick, N.J.: Rutgers University Press.
Rosch, Eleanor. 1975. "Human Categorization." In *Advances in Cross-Cultural Psychology*, Neil Warren, ed., pp. 1–72. London: Academic Press.
Strathern, M. 1972. *Women In Between*. London: Seminar Press.
Weiner, Annette. 1976. *Women of Value, Men of Renown: New Perspectives in Trobriand Exchange*. Austin: University of Texas Press.
Wikan, U. 1977. "Man Becomes Noman: Trans-Sexualism in Oman as a Key to Gender Roles." *Man* (n.s.) 12:304–19.

Alma Gottlieb starts her essay with a statement of what she sees as the prevailing view among anthropologists who deal with the comparative symbolism of gender. It is the familiar one that holds that "all women, everywhere, have been viewed by their societies in varying degrees as . . . a source of mystical contamination, and that this symbolic system in turn reflects the sociopolitical subordination of women to men."

Without wholly rejecting this model of "the second sex" Gottlieb questions its universality. To substantiate her position she presents the case of the Beng of the Ivory Coast, where the usual analogy "male:female::pure:polluting" is clearly not relevant.

She examines the religion and the gender ideology of the Beng and finds them woven together in such a way that the dimensions of male-female relations form "part of a comprehensive and logical symbolic system that comprises much of Beng religion." This system in turn she links to the structure of the matriclan, a dominant feature of Beng society.

In her conclusion Gottlieb suggests that societies with patrilineal descent groups, where newly wed couples move in with the groom's family, would be more likely to exhibit an ideology of female pollution "as a metaphor for the marginality of women." Societies like the Beng, however, "may prefer alternative ideologies that permit far more symbolic flexibility in gender conceptions than much of the recent literature has pointed to."

Alma Gottlieb

5 Rethinking Female Pollution: The Beng Case (Côte d'Ivoire)

Introduction

Over the past decade, anthropologists interested in gender roles have begun turning to several dynamic approaches to social life now glossed as "practice anthropology" (Ortner 1984; and see Collier and Yanagisako 1987; Strathern 1987). Those anthropologists who are especially interested in gender symbolism have started to ask new questions of their data: How do women see the wider cultural system of values, and their role in producing it? When reliably documented, do indigenous notions of female pollution always signify a local denigration of women in general? Are such ideas complemented by less visible notions of male pollution? Might pollution ideologies go beyond notions of gender as such and relate to wider social features?

The researchers who are now investigating these issues offer a refreshing departure from the more rigid dualist models that long dominated anthropological discussions of gender symbolism—models that inevitably culminated in paired columns listing male and female traits and associations that not only appeared unchangeable but were discomfortingly degrading to women (strong/weak, active/passive, auspicious/inauspicious, stable/wild, and of course pure/polluting) (see Needham, ed. 1973 for many classic examples of this mode of analysis; for a recent example, see Parkes 1987). In its purest form rather procrustean, this model of gender relations de facto assigned females to the role of eternal Other, thereby denying women any active place in social life. But dualist models themselves may conceal deep pockets of negotiation. As Beidelman has recently written:

> Dualism is a deceptive term in that, misunderstood, it might wrongly lead some to believe that this refers to a system that is ever present in one form and always activated in its entirety. . . . Yet different situations, demands, aims,

and roles are so varied and contradictory that only some segments of this cosmology are meaningful or usefully activated at any one time. (1986:26–27)

Current successors to the dualist model of gender relations include an exciting group of works that present a variety of approaches, all of which share the aim of restoring to women the role of subject.[1] Beginning with an early article of Faithorn (1975), which discussed the polluting qualities of semen among the Kafe of Papua New Guinea as an alternative to the classic focus on women's menstrual and vaginal pollution of men (for a critique of the literature on the former, see Buckley and Gottlieb 1988), those writing today have moved on to more balanced accounts that now embed interpretations of male and female in multilayered systems of thought—systems whose meanings can alter significantly in different social contexts, affording both women and men an active role in making meaning in society (e.g., Herzfeld 1984).

For instance, on the basis of data from Mount Hagen (Papua New Guinea), Strathern offers an important refinement of a common earlier assumption that all women invariably constitute the "second sex." Strathern argues that Hageners do use gender as an abstract basis for classifying the world, but that the gender categories do not necessarily exhaust the range of possibilities for individual men and women: "Women can totally dissociate themselves from the handicap of being female, as males have to prove they can utilize the potential of being male, because these gender markers do not totally encompass the person" (1981b:178; and see Strathern 1981a, 1986). Such a statement is a significant modification of the earlier view that implied that individual women (and men) were wholly bound in their behavior to a single ideological model offered them by their society (compare Kessler and McKenna 1985:142–69).

A recent work on Southern Bantu-speaking groups of southern Africa by Kuper similarly shows how not all items in a symbolically meaningful repertoire can be made to fit into a dualist scheme linked with the gender opposition, though such items are not necessarily "liminal." Kuper (1982: 18ff.) lists three fundamental categories, "hot" and "cool"—which are linked, respectively, with female and male—and a third category of "neither hot nor cool," into which the many Southern Bantu-speaking peoples classify the world around them. Such a model leaves room for a typology of objects and concepts that are not associated with gender at all, which demonstrates a significant refinement of the structuralist emphasis on binary classification schemes. Both Kuper's and Strathern's work, like the others to be mentioned here, develop logically from the general premise, now well accepted in anthropology, that, as LaFontaine has put it clearly, "the 'facts' of biology are culturally determined" (1981:337) and more specifically that "the physiology of each sex and the process of human reproduction are . . . subject to social construction" (ibid., 336).

If such "facts" are culturally constructed, those very constructions may be unstable. Substances that are seen as symbolically polluting in some contexts may be symbolically neutral, or even purifying, in others. Meigs (1984) has shown this to be the case for food and sex taboos among the Hua of Papua New Guinea. In West Africa, Bledsoe (1984:465) has written of men's and women's initiation societies (Poro and Sande) in a similar vein. Where these interethnic associations exist, both masculine and feminine elements are seen as pure or polluting, depending on context:

> An important key to the symbolism in the Poro and Sande . . . is the interstitial region between the safely bounded categories of "pure" male and "pure" female. This region contains messily combined elements of both sexes; it is the realm of supernatural resources from which categorically ambiguous initiates are removed and shaped into categorically pure men and women. Because the messy, intermediate area is necessarily composed part of male elements, they too are regarded as potentially contaminated and polluting. . . . In the external, categorically pure domain women are as ordered as men; but in the interstitial domain, male elements are as messy as female ones. (Bledsoe 1984:465)[2]

This chapter aims to contribute to this emerging body of literature. As the historian of religion Jonathan Smith has written: "There is nothing that is inherently sacred or profane. These are not substantive categories, but rather situational or relational categories, mobile boundaries which shift according to the map being employed" (1981:115; and see Smith 1978: 291). The data that I present here illustrate Smith's statement with striking clarity. I explore gender notions among the Beng of Côte d'Ivoire, among whom the specific classic analogy male:female::pure:polluting is simply not the dominant model. In keeping with the emerging theoretical shift in focus from the substance to the cultural context of pollution, I investigate how crucial is the latter for an understanding of Beng religion. In some contexts Beng women are indeed polluting, while in others they can prevent or even counteract pollution. In still other situations, men and women are equally, and mutually, polluting. In short, Beng women as a category are no more fully defined by pollution than are men as a category. The varying contexts of pollution reveal a good deal more about the constitution of male and female than does the mere fact of pollution.

Following from this, I also aim to show how a given society may contain a more multilayered understanding of gender relations than a single model would allow. In the Beng case, I will argue that two models of symbolically defined sexual pollution exist as distinct statements concerning gender relations. One model emphasizes female responsibility but in both creative and destructive guises, while the other focuses on male-female complementarity. I will suggest that these two models of gender-based pollution are parallel to two models of social organization that are present in Beng society. In the concluding section, I continue along this line of analysis and explore briefly a type of society that often contains an all-encompassing ideology of female pollution, and contrast this with the Beng, who prefer alternative ideologies that permit far more complex possibilities in gender conceptions.

"Female Dirt" and "Female Pollution" Among the Beng

The Beng are a minority ethnic group of some 10,000 living in east-central Côte d'Ivoire. Their social structure is based on double descent, with corporate matriclans and patriclans. Until recently they practiced their own traditional religion, which focused on worship of earth spirits. Some recent converts to Islam and Catholicism have begun to substitute a monotheistic god, but for the most part the traditional modes of worship still remain viable. All Muslims and Catholics still participate in the symbolic system of gender images and rituals that I explore in this article.

GBRE: THE "DIRTY" DISEASE

There is one indication that Beng females are indeed symbolically "polluting" in the sense normally understood by anthropologists. Children are said to be vulnerable to a disease called *gbre* (literally, "dirt"), which is seen as contagious by the medium of the vagina. Specifically, it may be carried by women who defied the norm and were not virgins before they were engaged to be married—a violation that is fairly rare. During the period of engagement, a girl nowadays almost always takes a lover—whom she must renounce upon marriage—but I was told that this too was rare precolonially, though never the cause for much concern. However, it is still quite unusual for a girl to take a lover before she is engaged, and it is the violation

Rethinking Female Pollution   119

of this rule that causes her to carry the disease, *gbre*.³ This is a potentially fatal illness for the afflicted infant, and some mothers may endeavor to guard against it by attaching strands of certain beads around the baby's waist, which are held to be magically efficacious (Gottlieb 1981).

Tempting though it may be to interpret this disease as evidence of a general view of females as polluting, this interpretation would conceal more than it would reveal. The stated carrier of the disease is specifically that group of women who were not virgins before their engagement. By no means is all female sexuality being posed as polluting; rather, it is a question of pollution by a certain small proportion of women, those who have engaged in premature sexuality. Why, then, should premature sexuality be symbolically problematic?

Among premenopausal women, sex is associated with fertility, and fertility, in turn, should normatively be associated with marriage. For this reason, any child born of a pre-engagement union was traditionally killed: drowned in a bucket of soapy water (though the mother was not punished per se in any other way). Hence the traditional rule that girls remain virgins before their engagement is a way of confining fertility to marriage. This in turn reflects the strong emphasis on an alliance system based on arranged marriage, which was, and to a great extent still is, an extensive and complex system that is central to the wider social structure (Gottlieb 1986b). A baby should be the product of a relationship that is an element in this alliance system, and the infant is considered vulnerable (potentially fatally) when exposed to the opposite of this norm: sex before a woman's engagement.⁴ It is true, of course, that women and not men are the carriers of this pollution, and this does point to a "female bias" to the situation. I will have occasion below to discuss further the nature and extent of this female bias.

Now, one of the symptoms of the infant disease *gbre* is a cough, in which case it is called *gbre drɔ*, or "dirt cough." A mother may prevent her baby from catching *gbre drɔ* by using a certain medicine regularly.⁵ Significantly, this preventive medicine makes indirect use of the female genitals, revealing that female sexuality—even, in this case, inappropriate female sexuality—may have positive uses. To protect her baby, a mother must find a woman who is a potential carrier of *gbre* (that is, a woman who was not a virgin at the time she became engaged) who also happens to be pregnant. The night before the pregnant woman gathers the cure's ingredients, she must have sex with her husband. The next morning, she gathers some ash from her cooking fire; because it is being gathered by a "dirty" woman (who might potentially transmit *gbre*), the ash is called *gbre yepe*, or "dirt ash." The pregnant woman gives the ash to the mother of the child who is to be protected, and the baby's mother mixes the *gbre yepe* with some leaves. The mother gives the baby a small amount of the mixture to swallow very early in the morning. When repeated regularly, this acts as a prophylaxis against *gbre*.

The symbolism involved in this preventive medicine is complex. First, to guard against a baby catching the disease, the ingredients to the preventive medicine must be procured by precisely that category of woman who can transmit the disease. But why must this woman be pregnant, and why must she have had sex with her husband the night before procuring the cure's ingredients? In a sense, her earlier act of inappropriate sexuality is being (temporarily) nullified by her present act of sexuality, which is now appropriate: fertile sex with her legitimate sexual partner, her husband. By now having contact, via the medicine, with a *gbre*-carrying women who has "reformed"—gotten married and had legitimate sex with her husband, producing a legitimate fetus—the baby can have the potential effects of a future *gbre*-carrier countered.[6] In addition, the baby to be protected against *gbre* has a symbolic tie to the fetus inside the pregnant woman. For this fetus, as the product of a now legitimate sexual relationship, will (unlike its predecessor) be permitted to live, and so too will the protected baby.

The major ingredient to the *gbre* medicine is also symbolically resonant. The primary item gathered by the *gbre* woman for the cure is ash. Ash, of course, constitutes the leftover and cool remains of a fire and as such has important symbolic implications. Interestingly, these associations are rooted in a scheme that is quite binary in its logic.

Specifically, cold is associated with fertility and heat with infertility. To cite but one example: if a woman has not menstruated for several months but she is not pregnant (amenorrhea), the Beng recognize that she is infertile, for they explicitly acknowledge the connection between regular menstruation and fertility (Gottlieb 1988b). They view amenorrhea, and thus the infertility it represents, as the result of what they term *nɔ̄ batú*, or "hot womb/stomach"; the main remedy involves bathing with an infusion of certain leaves that are mixed with fresh water that must never have been heated (*yi yɔ*, "raw water"). (This is in stark contrast to the vast majority of herbal remedies for other diseases, which almost always require that the leaves be *boiled* in water before being used as a wash.) In this cure, cold, in the form of "raw" water, is associated directly with attempts to attain fertility.[7]

These symbolic associations of heat and cold give meaning to the use of ash in preventing *gbre* in a baby. As a cooled-down version of a fire, ash is a highly apt symbol for counteracting the possibility of contracting *gbre:* the latter is caused by "hot," inappropriate sexuality, and is thus treated by ash, which represents the *cooling down* of heat. Furthermore, ash is a female symbol par excellence, as fire is said to be owned by women. It is women who chop firewood in the forest, carry it back to the village where they store it in piles outside their kitchens, then burn it in their hearths to cook food and heat bath water. The metonymic associations of ash with women's work further reinforce its appropriateness in the context of its medicinal use in preventing a disease that is itself transmitted by women.

In sum, the case of *gbre* shows how the common notion of intrinsic female pollution is at best only partially relevant to the Beng. First, symbolic principles relating to fertility and heat are at work and have only an indirect relationship to gender. Even more interesting, *gbre* reveals that the female genitals may both cause *and prevent* a disease of infancy that the Beng view as mystically engendered. Here femininity is associated with inauspiciousness *and* auspiciousness, pollution *and* purity. Such ambivalence concerning women's sexuality is an important modification of the binary meanings of hot and cold that we have traced out in our analysis. It reveals that the presence of binary oppositions at one level of a system of thought is not necessarily an indication of a thoroughgoing system of absolute polarities.

Indeed, ambivalence concerning the female genitals is present in a related malady, one that again concerns young children.

LATE WALKERS

If children of about the age of one-and-a-half years are still crawling and have not shown any inclination to begin walking or to perfect the skill (described by the phrase, ŋo wɔ diŋ ŋo sɛ̃—"their wrists hurt them"), the parents begin to worry. Various herbal and other remedies are available, but they may or may not work. For our purposes, the cure that is the most interesting is not herbal but again deals directly with symbols of female sexuality.

The mother of such a baby rises before dawn and removes her cache-sexe (a small piece of cloth that every woman wears as an undergarment). She puts the cloth over a kerosene lamp to heat it and then pulls the baby's wrists with the warm cloth. This action is said to enable the baby to begin walking. In this cure we see a vaginal symbol—something that was physically connected to the vagina—used in a curative rather than polluting way. The heated piece of cloth serves as a double symbol of infertility. First, as we have seen, its warmth is associated with sterility. Second, due to a postpartum sex taboo in force until the baby can walk competently, the wearer of the cache-sexe herself should be celibate, hence infertile. Perhaps the cloth is being applied to convince the baby that its parents have not yet resumed sexuality (and fertility), and hence there is no reason for the baby to delay starting to walk.[8]

Alternatively, it may be that the cache-sexe of a woman whose child is a late walker represents, by metonymic connection, her vagina that *has* been illegitimately active sexually: in other words, her inappropriate and premature resumption of sexuality before her child began walking. On this interpretation, the mother would be using her cache-sexe to cure in her child a disease that her vagina, in effect, caused.[9] In this case, the cure might be seen as an example of the principle that "two negatives equal a positive," a principle that is operative in other spheres of Beng thought, including other examples of Beng medicine (Gottlieb 1981).

In either case, we are far from viewing the vagina merely as a symbol of pollution. In the phenomenon of late walkers as culturally defined by the Beng, the vagina is a symbolic means for curative powers; moreover, on one interpretation, it may also generate the same disease that it cures.

THE AMBIGUOUS VAGINA

The discussions of *gbre* and late walkers have revealed a direct focus on female sexuality. What is striking is that the female genitals are viewed by the Beng as symbolically powerful in both constructive and destructive senses. I want to suggest that this ambivalent view of the vagina is consistent with the structure of Beng matriclans that form part of the system of double descent (see Gottlieb 1988a). Beng matriclans are the focus of intense emotional commitment on the part of their members, but that emotional commitment has both positive and negative implications (see Beidelman 1971 for a similar case among the matrilineal Kaguru of Tanzania). Among other things, matrikin see each other as a source of emotional comfort, economic aid, and potential means of access to political office. The soul is inherited through the matriline. Matriclan endogamy, though not practiced exclusively, is nonetheless perceived as an ideal form of marriage (Gottlieb 1986b). I view all these traits as combining to form what I term a common fund of identity that unites all members of a given matriclan (Gottlieb 1988a). Despite this—or perhaps because of it—the matriclan also defines the scope of all witchcraft. First, witchcraft is aimed only at matrikin (for the political side to this, see Gottlieb 1988b). Second, the ability to conduct witchcraft is inherited matrilineally (it can also be bought). Thus the matriclan is itself a highly ambivalent grouping, based as it is on a paradox: the people on whom one should most rely are also those whom one should most distrust.

In stark contrast, patriclans, which are exogamous, have a more moderate feel to them. Patriclans focus on what I term difference: it is the differences *between* patriclans that are highlighted in Beng thought, rather than any deep notion of substance or identity that would be said to be shared by members of a given patriclan. Beng say that matrikin are in effect too close to be friends, but the same is not said of patrikin; indeed, it is overwhelmingly among patrikin that one finds one's friends. Patrikin relations are in general much less highly charged in either direction than are matrikin relations.

I take the matriclan, then, with its ambivalent structure, as consistent with the kind of symbolism I have found concerning the female genitals: also ambivalent, with both positive and negative associations. And this should not be too surprising, since matriclan membership is of course determined through women. In short, rather than viewing the vagina, which on occasion is seen as responsible for causing pollution and sickness, as representing the inherent pollution of women, I am suggesting that the Beng view of the female genitals and of their own matriclan structure act as metaphors for one another, each reflecting back to the other domain. Both are ambivalent entities, powerful, and capable of promoting good as well as harm.

Sexual Pollution

Until now, I have presented a case for the ambivalent view of the female genitals. But this ambivalent view emerges through various symptoms and cures for only two diseases, *gbre* and delayed walking, and I cannot state that it is a dominant motif in Beng thought (see Gottlieb 1988b for Beng views of menstruation, which in some ways fit in with this pattern). Indeed, it is only one of two views expressed in Beng symbolism about the genders. In contrast to this analysis of *gbre* and late walking, another level of Beng religion presents a much more gender-balanced view of sexuality as compared to many other societies that often reveal a single-minded preoccupation with female sexuality. I now want to explore another group of ideas about sexuality in the Beng symbolic repertoire that do not focus on female sexuality at all but, rather, the sex act performed by male and female.

"FOREST SEX"

The sex act is not only a mutually involving experience; it is seen by the Beng in some ways to be symbolically dangerous and, as in other societies, there are many rules concerning where, when, and how it may occur. Unlike some other societies, however, both partners share equal responsibility for many acts of sexual impropriety.

According to informants' direct statements, the most important of all Beng rules *of any category* in fact relates to sex: humans may not copulate in the forest. The taboo is said to be dictated by the Earth, which is worshiped by the Beng (see below and Gottlieb n.d.). Should a couple violate this taboo, the Earth will announce its anger in one of two ways: the guilty woman will have a difficult childbirth, and/or the rains will not come—both resulting in aborted fertility in, respectively, the village (human) and the farm (crop) spheres.

The guilty parties generally confess forthwith. Significantly, both partners are punished equally, protected equally, and held equally responsible, though one may have seduced or even forced the other to participate. (In fact, some of these cases of "forest sex" are cases of rape, which is, in turn, generally interpreted as having been caused by bewitching.) As punishment, the couple is led to the spot in the forest where they committed their act. They are accompanied by old and middle-aged men of their own and some surrounding villages. A Master of the Earth (a ritual leader who offers sacrifices to the Earth) oversees the ritual punishment: the couple is made to repeat the sex act while jeered on by the angry crowd, who beat and burn them with switches and firebrands. To prevent the guilty couple from being excessively injured or even killed, each of the two is protected by a same-sex elder who tries to deflect the blows and burns of the switches and firebrands. The punishment over, a cow is sacrificed to the Earth by way of apology for its having been polluted. The couple's clothes are taken away permanently, and they are given new clothes to wear.

Both the man and woman who have sex in the forest/fields are considered permanently "dirty" (*gbre*) as well as "polluted" (*zozoa*). This manifests itself in patterns of language and luck. It is said that any such "dirty/polluted" man or woman brings "bad luck" (*yɔŋ tri,* literally, "black face") all day to someone who speaks to him or her early in the morning, before the "dirty" person has rinsed out his or her mouth or has eaten. To prevent against being so afflicted, one may eat a tiny bit of any food (especially chili pepper or yam), which is said to nullify the bad luck caused by speaking with such a person.

Because of this unfortunate effect on people, if such a polluted person happens to be single, or is later divorced or widow(er)ed, he or she will have a difficult time finding a (new) spouse, since anyone would be reluctant to marry a "dirty" person who continually brought them bad luck from conversing in the early morning. The prospect of acquiring a co-wife who is *gbre* is generally considered a legitimate reason for a married woman either to refuse the co-wife or to threaten divorce. One middle-aged woman I knew virtually forbade her husband to take as a second wife a woman who was *gbre* in this manner. Most likely, then, someone who is *gbre* will either remain single or will marry someone else who is "dirty."

BATHING AND SEXUALITY

A related rule concerns another aspect of sexuality. On moving into a Beng village, the visitor cannot help noticing how seriously the Beng observe their rules of hygiene, even in periods of drought. All Beng invariably wash twice a day: once in the morning, before setting out for the fields (which are located in the forest), and once in the evening, after returning to the village from the fields. The evening bath is taken to wash off the soil from working in the fields. However, the underlying motive for the morning bath is not hygiene, strictly speaking, but rather relates to certain ideas emerging from Beng religion, as focused on worship of the Earth. Here I summarize briefly what I see as the fundamental Beng view of the Earth as it relates to bathing practices (see Gottlieb 1986a, 1988b).

The Earth, which is associated with certain shrines outside the village, is seen as a separate realm from the village, and there are many rules necessitating the symbolic separation between the two areas. In particular, the rules pertain to the separation of the two kinds of fertility produced by these two realms: crops (Earth) and babies (village). One such rule concerns washing.

All adult Beng are required to bathe in the morning. The stated purpose is to "wash off sex" from the preceding night, before coming into contact with the named Earth in the forest later that day when out in the fields. If an adult—male or female—does not wash in the morning after having had sex the night before and then goes to the fields, it is said that he or she will get bitten by a snake in the forest.[10] Moreover, if an adult—again, male or female—does not wash after having had sex and then he or she touches a nursing baby who is not yet walking, the baby will develop a bad cough. These rules demonstrate that sex is viewed as a mutually involving act for which both partners are held equally responsible.

A related bath rule is that people must use only the right hand when washing the genitals. The explanation relates to the Beng reason for bathing (especially in the morning): symbolic cleansing of sexual pollution. Purifying the body should appropriately be done, then, with the "good" hand. Again, there is no distinction made here between male and female practice.

This egalitarian treatment of men and women's sexuality is echoed in another set of practices. During the sex act, it is required for both partners to use only the left hand, never the right. I was told that this is so because the genitals are said to be "bad" (à gèŋέ), and the left hand is also considered "bad" and is thus appropriate here (aside from sex, the left hand is used for wiping feces and little else). This rule is in dramatic contrast to some systems reported elsewhere in Africa. For example, Beidelman (1963:329) has written that among the Kaguru of Tanzania, during sex, men lie on their right sides and use the left hand for sex play, while women lie on their left sides and use their right hands. Being more polluting in and of itself, the left hand is thus appropriately used by men while touching the bodies of women, which are also seen as symbolically polluting to men. The same set of practices is reported for the Swazi of Swaziland (Beidelman 1973:393), the Nyoro of Uganda (Beattie 1976), and the Lele of Zaire (Douglas 1975:13). This view of women's intrinsic pollution (especially in comparison with men) could not contrast more starkly with the Beng system, in which there is a decided emphasis on *mutual* and/or equal symbolic pollution by men and women. To put it simply, in the Beng understanding of sex, the woman does not emerge as the polluter of the pure man.[11]

In view of the "badness" of the genitals, a final rule concerning hand-genital contact might seem perplexing. When putting on or removing underwear, both males and females should use the right hand, which is said to be "good" (ò gέŋ). Considering that the genitals are themselves "bad," why should the good hand be used? It may be that the potential "badness" of the genitals is in a sense activated only when they come in contact, explicitly or implicitly, with the genitals of the opposite sex. Without this contact, the "badness" of one's own genitals may not come into play and the right hand is acceptable. In any case, once again the rule on dressing focuses on both male and female sexuality treated alike, with no hint of greater pollution by women of men. Rather, what is potentially polluting in all three rules discussed in this section is the sex act itself (for a similar case among the Kayapo Indians of Brazil, compare Basso 1985:307).

AN INTERPRETATION OF BENG SEXUAL POLLUTION

Why should the sexual union of male and female be construed by the Beng as so symbolically dangerous and potentially polluting? As with the problem of vaginal pollution, I suggest that this is best understood in relation to the sociological correlates of what male and female mean in Beng society. Here my case fits Mary Douglas's predicted correlation (1966:113): "Pollution is a type of danger which is not likely to occur except where the lines of structure, cosmic, or social, are clearly defined." In the Beng case, those clearly drawn lines are those of descent.

Matriclans and patriclans are viewed by the Beng as fundamentally different sorts of descent groupings (Gottlieb 1988a). While I cannot supply a causal explanation for this general pattern, I do think it clear that the Beng system of descent seems to "aim" as much as possible to keep the arenas of each of these clan types as distinct as possible in a way not always found in other descent systems (for example, Chauveau and Richard 1975: 11–12). I suggest that the Beng view of the sex act and the specific nature of the Beng system of double descent may be seen as metaphors for one another. By uniting in the sex act, one ipso facto crosses two boundaries: physically, one's body, and conceptually, one's gender. Thus it is that the act of sex is potentially the ultimate liminal act, defined as it is by the crossing of boundaries. The sex act is a symbolic means of "straddling a fence," separating two discrete realms. To straddle this fence metaphorically through sex is to combine metaphorically the two types of clans, which should not be combined; hence the sex act, as metaphor, must be strictly regulated in order to control and contain the meaning for which the liminal act stands. One partner of the act is not given more responsibility than the other, for in a basic way, male and female are not seen as comparable, but jointly and complementarily responsible (for similar cases, compare Buckley n.d.; Rogers 1978; Schlegel this volume; Weiner 1977)—just as the matriclans and patriclans are not ranked in relation to one another, but are viewed as complementary social groupings and jointly responsible for the wider social structure. In short, I propose that the Beng symbolic elaborations of the human sex act make a sociological sense relevant to Beng society.

Conclusions

I have proposed an understanding of Beng gender symbolism that relates to sociological considerations. In so doing, I resist the temptation to link isolated cases of feminine pollution to notions of essential impurity defining all women. At the same time, I borrow from a venerable tradition in anthropology that seeks to understand systems of symbolism in relation to social features. As Marcel Mauss suggested earlier in this century (1979 [1935]) and as Douglas (for example, 1970) has continued to demonstrate, ideas about the body must be tied intimately to ideas about society, and notions of gender pollution should be no exception.

Indeed, in scanning the now voluminous literature on female pollution, one cannot help but notice that many, though not all, of the societies described have a system of patrilineal descent, and a newly wed couple moves in permanently with the groom's family. It is possible to hypothesize that it is precisely in this type of society in which one would expect to find notions of feminine pollution, as a metaphor for the sociological marginality of women. Strathern (1972) showed this to be the case for the Mount Hageners of Papua New Guinea. Others have since remarked on this connection between the sociological liminality of women in patrilineal systems, and the corresponding presence of conceptions of female pollution (for example, Bennett 1976; Ngubane 1977:90ff.). But this simple correlation of social marginality with symbolic dirt, while seductive, should not be taken as all-encompassing.

In the Beng case, I have suggested another correlation. While the Beng system at first glance might appear binary, in fact we have seen how it contains far more complex systems of thought operating at several levels. For when it comes to female sexuality, I found sources not only of pollution but of healing as well. I have suggested that this ambivalence concerning women's genitals is parallel to an ambivalence that one finds at a sociological level—at the heart of the matriclan. Yet another aspect of sexuality shifts the focus to relations between men and women and sees shared sexuality (in both legitimate and illegitimate phases) as potentially polluting, and here I look to the entire system of dual descent for a parallel social form. The important point is that in both cases—in patrilineal and bilineal settings—feminine sources of pollution derive not from intrinsic notions of female culpability, but are correlated with sociological factors existing outside the purview of women themselves.

The Durkheimian overtones to this discussion must be apparent. Yet I resist the temptation to make the ultimate Durkheimian argument of causality by insisting that it is the descent form that provides the initial direction to society, with the symbolic system limping along placidly in its footsteps. Instead, I point out more simply that the two levels of society—which we can gloss crudely as social structural and symbolic—seem to "work" in tandem. The theoretical advances of the 1960s and 1970s concerning the symbolic dimensions of society have surely gone a long way toward documenting the extraordinary powers of symbolic formulations. Given this, a feedback loop between symbol and society seems reasonable (for an analogous argument in relation to myth and society, compare Gottlieb 1986c).

At this stage, however, even a noncausal connection between descent systems and ideologies of gender pollution can only be a hypothesis, to be tested more systematically on a comparative basis. We should continue to remain open to explanations that offer other kinds of connections not relevant to descent structures, for not all the societies already reported to have female pollution complexes do fit into this categorization of their descent and residential systems. For example, Okely (1975) proposes that notions of female pollution among the cognatic British Gypsies are related to a prevailing concern about maintaining *ethnic* boundaries between the Gypsies and the settled peoples who surround them. While strict unilineal descent is lacking here, there is nevertheless a more general and striking correlation between a concern with symbolic boundaries and a concern with sociological boundaries. Further ethnographic and comparative studies are clearly needed to explore systematically the many possible relationships that might exist between social formations and ideologies of sexual pollution.

In the meanwhile, the present article is offered as a case study of one situation that diverges from what we have come to expect. Unlike, apparently, so many other systems, Beng symbolism cannot be classified as having a binary model of gender relations that sees women as no more than symbolic threats to men. Instead, one finds *two* very distinct models of gender symbolism: one that stresses female sexuality alone but in both negative and positive guises and that emphasizes female responsibility; another that stresses mutual male-female sexuality and blames the sex act itself as polluting. I have argued that when taken together, the two kinds of symbolic models of gender provide a way of thinking about the complete universe of basic structural relations that define Beng society: matriclans alone, and the entire system of double descent. In short, the Beng case challenges us to consider the possibility of multiple models existing within a single society (compare Gottlieb 1986c, 1989a), as well as to look at varying social contexts that define and redefine what could only be glossed crudely as female pollution.

While Simone de Beauvoir's classic model of women as the second sex is probably relevant to a good many societies, there is less and less reason to suppose that it is applicable everywhere (for example, Appell 1988; Etienne and Leacock, eds. 1980; Harris 1978; LaFontaine 1978; Sacks 1979; Tiffany 1982; Weiner 1976). Recent work, including other chapters in this collection, points to many cases that reveal significant departures from the model of simple universal female subordination. The current chapter offers one specific case in which the predicted symbolic correlate to supposedly universal female subordination—an all-encompassing notion of women sexually polluting men—must be replaced by a more complex pair of models that includes women's power both to pollute and to purify, as well as men's power to pollute.

The sort of approach to traditional systems of thought I have used here, one that seeks to transcend the limitations of the classic binary schemes so prevalent in anthropology for many years, is now finding reinforcement in other allied fields: in the history of religion (Smith 1978, 1981) as well as in social and cognitive psychology. Eleanor Rosch and her associates, for example, have been researching human thought processes as rooted in a Wittgensteinian notion of "family resemblances" (for example, Rosch and Mervis 1975; for an earlier anthropological use of this important concept, see Needham 1975). Although we do construct "prototypes" of objects and concepts that revolve around polar oppositions (compare Semin and Rosch 1981), we create such binary oppositions via a series of cognitive family resemblances, which are predicated on relative rather than absolute differences involving finely graded distinctions based on context rather than substance (for a discussion of the complementarity of these two different modes of thinking, see Rosch 1983). According to Rosch and Mervis (1975), this mode of thinking is characteristic of adults as well as children and is presumably universal—though this point remains to be thoroughly tested before it can be assumed (for a useful summary and critique of Rosch's work, see Scholnick 1983:46–52). In any case, this emerging body of experimental work is a powerful though tentative reinforcement at the psychological level of the sort of approach I have taken here, which, at the philosophical level, has emphasized context over substance, and ambiguity and even ambivalence over strict binarism.

Acknowledgments

The initial fieldwork on which this chapter is based was funded by a Social Science Research Council Predoctoral Grant in 1979–1980, which I acknowledge with gratitude. I also thank that body, the American Association of University Women, and the Woodrow Wilson Foundation (Program in Women's Studies) for dissertation write-up support. I am grateful to the University of Illinois at Urbana-Champaign for support of a summer trip to the Beng in 1985, via the following programs: United States Information Agency Linkage Agreement between the University of Illinois at Urbana-Champaign and the National University of Côte d'Ivoire; International Programs and Studies (for a Flora and William Hewlett Award); the Center for African Studies; and the Research Board. I am also indebted to Liesl Gambold and Bill Wood for invaluable library help on this article.

This chapter appeared in *Dialectical Anthropology* (special issue: A Tribute to Irving Goldman) 14 (2) in a slightly different form and appears here with permission of the journal editor. Earlier versions of this chapter were presented as talks given to the Department of Anthropology at New York University and to the School of Social Sciences at the University of Illinois at Urbana-Champaign. I am grateful for the invitations and for the audiences' comments. The following have also read various drafts of this work: Lynne Brydon, Robert Carlson, Mona Etienne, Eric Gable, Philip Graham, Janet Keller, Charles Piot, Peggy Sanday, J. David Sapir, and James R. Wilkerson. I hope I have done all their comments justice.

Notes

1. This is particularly the case in Melanesian studies, which have long been concerned with issues relating to gender (for a summary of recent work, see Strathern 1986).
2. A recent article by C. Thompson (1985) on Hindu perceptions of gender symbolism offers a compatible perspective: here what is emphasized is women's own perceptions of their capacity to pollute as well as to exert more productive powers (also see Shore 1981). For West Africa, a body of writing by contemporary art historians focuses on positively valued images of women and/or femininity in cultures such as the Yoruba of Nigeria (Adams 1984; Drewal and Drewal 1983) and the Senufo of Côte d'Ivoire (Glaze 1981). This emerging body of work is now beginning to be noticed by anthropologists (see Ottenberg 1987).
3. Girls are traditionally engaged at about the age of 15 to 17 years and usually marry about a year after engagement.

4. Children born from adulterous unions involving a married (or divorced or widowed) woman were not killed. They were perceived as illegitimate in a general sense and were mocked by other children, but were not disadvantaged legally: they belonged to their fathers' patriclans and mothers' matriclans, and could inherit from their maternal uncles or older brothers. I explain this difference in treatment of children born illegitimately to pre-engaged girls, on the one hand, and to mature women, on the other, as a sign of the crucial importance of the (arranged) marriage system in assigning a social identity to young people. Before being incorporated into this system via engagement (which usually but not always results in an arranged marriage), girls are considered children and their wombs are not a fair option for exercise.

5. The Beng medical system is quite extensive (see Gottlieb 1981 for one type of medical treatment). Both healers and diviners have knowledge of only portions of the Beng pharmacopoeia: no single individual knows all the Beng remedies practiced. Though no Beng consultant put it this way, it is clear to me that there are two radically different kinds of remedies for diseases. One kind of remedy is essentially herbal (or uses other natural substances) and its action seems to be purely chemical (though the chemical effects of pharmacological plants used by Beng healers have yet to be tested by Western science). The other kind of remedy may utilize herbal ingredients but is also characterized by ingredients and/or modes of gathering and treating those ingredients that we would have to call symbolically constituted, including sacrifices, prayers, color symbolism, and so on. In these cases, it seems clear that the action of such cures is deemed symbolic rather than chemical. It is with this latter class of diseases and remedies that we are concerned in this article.

During field research, my husband and I adopted by popular demand the role of Western medicine supplier. Most Beng were enthusiastic about Western medicines, but for diseases seen as caused by sociosymbolic rather than purely biological complications, patients made clear that the Western remedies would remove the disease's symptoms, but that other symbolic actions were necessary to deal with their cause if the cure was to last.

6. Beng recognize that a single act of sex is all that is required to effect conception. Once pregnant, it is neither forbidden nor required for a woman to continue sexual relations with her husband: this is left to her own preference. However, it would seem that sex with her husband while a woman is pregnant underscores the fertile relationship that the two legitimately share. An alternative explanation would be that pregnant sex, being unnecessary for the fetus' formation, is a redundant act and, as such, makes a mockery of sexuality, whose ultimate purpose is fertilization. On this interpretation, a *gbre*-carrying woman having pregnant sex would be mocking the serious goals of sex at two stages in her life: before her engagement, and while married. In this case, using such a woman to prevent against a baby catching *gbre* would be in line with the Beng principle that "two negatives equal a positive," a principle that appears frequently in Beng curing (see below). Determining which of the above two interpretations is seen as relevant by Beng themselves must await further field research.

7. The symbolic association of cold with fertility (or general auspiciousness) and heat with sterility (or general inauspiciousness) is found widely in Africa: for

example in Ghana among the Avatime (Lynne Brydon, personal communication), the Akuropon (Gilbert 1987:318, 324 n. 3), and the Aowin (Ebin 1982:149); among the Ndembu of Zambia (Turner 1969:77ff.); among the Kaguru of Tanzania (Beidelman 1986:123); and among many Southern Bantu-speaking groups of southern Africa (Kuper 1982:18–20), including the Lovedu and Thonga (de Heusch 1986:90) and the Barolong boo Ratshidi (Comaroff 1985). R. Thompson (1973) has termed a wider version of this as "aesthetic of the cool" that pervades the world view not only of much of Africa but of many New World African-derived societies as well. (For related ideas concerning hot/cold symbolism in Afro-Caribbean and African-American groups, see Laguerre 1987:64–72.) However, the association is not completely universal even in Africa: for another configuration, see Fernandez (1982:112) on the Fang of Gabon.

8. That the mother is seen as more responsible than the father is shown in the "double standard" that the Beng have concerning the postpartum sex taboo. A nursing mother may not have sexual relations with any man, including her husband. Her husband, however, may have sexual relations with any of his other wives (or with other unmarried women, or with prostitutes). The reason for this asymmetrical rule relates in the Beng view to the breast milk: the semen of any man, it is said, will spoil the milk of a nursing mother. (This is a fairly common line of reasoning throughout sub-Saharan Africa.) One informant speculated that if a woman were to bottle-feed her infant exclusively, she might resume an active sexual life with her husband soon after the birth. In any case, the rule puts more symbolic weight on the mother's role than the father's in abstaining from sex while their infant nurses, hence my extrapolation that in effect, it is the vagina of the woman who transgresses this rule that is responsible for the baby's resultant affliction.

9. In Beng thought, although cold is associated with appropriate fertility, it is also seen by the Beng as dangerous to what we might call newly realized fertility: the baby. In particular, dew and drizzle, both cool substances in the Beng view, are said to afflict babies with disease, and some mothers put certain necklaces, kneelets, or anklets (as "amulets") on their babies for several months as preventive medicine against the diseases "Dew" and "Drizzle" (Gottlieb 1981). Once the baby has reached the walking stage—joining humanity on one level, by gaining a certain measure of independence—the child is no longer seen as vulnerable to cold.

Also of note is that for the Beng, cold is associated symbolically not only with human fertility but with crop fertility as well. It is said that if there is a good cold spell during the months before planting crops, the seeds will grow well and there will be a good harvest. Hail is welcomed during the initial growing season for the same reason: it is cold rain, and is said to fertilize the soil well.

A further association of cold with general auspiciousness is found in Beng greetings. After greeting someone, one may ask how things are. Assuming there is no bad news, the required response is: *no nyilɛ*, literally, "Here it is cold." Brydon (personal communication) reports the same for the Avatime of Ghana. This sensibility has traveled to black populations in the New World; Afro-American speech has now penetrated "standard" English with the phrase "that's cool," among many others (see R. Thompson 1973).

As for heat, not only barrenness but also inappropriate sexuality/fertility is associated with it, as is noted in the discussion of babies who are late walkers. Heat is also associated with death (the ultimate barrenness). At a funeral, those women who attend a cadaver before the burial should pat a certain mixture (which must be uncooked) on their bodies to chase the ghost (*wru*) of the deceased. If they fail to take this precaution, the ghost will linger, and the bodies of such women will always be hot: specifically, whenever the ghost touches them, they will run a fever.

10. Snakes make a frequent appearance in Beng thought; I hope to analyze the system of snake symbolism in a future article.

11. There is another custom practiced by all Beng that again reveals how intimate and mutual the sex act is viewed. To clean their teeth, Beng use small twigs of various trees and shrubs: they peel the bark and use the twigs, in much the same way that Westerners use toothpicks. All Beng, including young children, know that one may only use these "toothpicks" in the morning and very early afternoon; after about 3 P.M., it is forbidden to use them. The explanation concerns sexuality. It is said that if one were to violate this rule, the person with whom one first had sexual relations would soon die. (Obviously the motivation behind this rule would not be relevant for children. However, children are still taught to observe the rule as a means, I was told, for training them to observe it when it will "count," later in their married lives.) Here, I am not concerned with the possible Freudian symbolic associations between teeth and sexuality. Instead, what interests me is the connection revealed between male and female sex partners: a connection that is permanent as well as mutual, and once again entails mutual responsibility on the part of man and woman. (Compare Gray 1960:41, for a somewhat analogous case among the Sonjo of Tanzania: a husband and wife married for the first time have enduring ties, and the two unite in the afterlife.)

Bibliography

Adams, Monni. 1984. "The Aesthetics of Power: Gelede Festival of the Western Yoruba." Mary Ingraham Bunting Institute of Radcliffe College. Unpublished manuscript.

Appell, Laura. 1988. "Menstruation Among the Rungus of Borneo: An Unmarked Category." In *Blood Magic: The Anthropology of Menstruation,* Thomas Buckley and Alma Gottlieb, eds., pp. 94–112. Berkeley and Los Angeles: University of California Press.

Basso, Ellen. 1985. *A Musical View of the Universe.* Philadelphia: University of Pennsylvania Press.

Beattie, John. 1976. "Right, Left and the Banyoro." *Africa* 46 (3): 217–35.

Beidelman, T. O. 1963. "The Blood Covenant and the Concept of Blood in Ukaguru." *Africa* 33: 321–42.

———. 1971. *The Kaguru.* New York: Holt, Rinehart and Winston.

———. 1973[1966]. "Swazi Royal Ritual." In *Africa and Change,* Colin Turnbull, ed., pp. 382–421. New York: Knopf.

———. 1986. *Moral Imagination in Kaguru Modes of Thought.* Bloomington: Indiana University Press.

Bennett, Lynn. 1976. "The Wives of the Rishis—An Analysis of the Tij-Rishi Panchami Women's Festival." *Kailash (A Journal of Himalayan Studies)* 4 (2): 185–207.

Bledsoe, Caroline. 1984. "The Political Use of Sande Ideology and Symbolism." *American Ethnologist* 11 (3): 455–72.

Buckley, Thomas. n.d. "The Articulation of Gender Symmetry in Yuchi Culture." To appear in *Semiotica*. In press.

Buckley, Thomas, and Alma Gottlieb. 1988. "A Critical Appraisal of Theories of Menstrual Symbolism." In *Blood Magic: The Anthropology of Menstruation*, Thomas Buckley and Alma Gottlieb, eds., pp. 1–50. Berkeley and Los Angeles: University of California Press.

Chauveau, Jean-Pierre, and Jacques Richard. 1975. *Organisation socio-économique Gban et économie de plantation*. Abidjan: O.R.S.T.O.M., Sciences Humaines VIII, no. 2. Centre de Petit Bassam.

Collier, Jane F., and Sylvia J. Yanagisako. 1987. "Theory in Anthropology Since Feminist Practice." Paper presented at the 86th Annual Meeting of the American Anthropological Association (Chicago), November.

Comaroff, Jean. 1985. *Body of Power, Spirits of Resistance*. Chicago: University of Chicago Press.

Douglas, Mary. 1966. *Purity and Danger*. New York: Praeger.

———. 1970. *Natural Symbols*. New York: Random House.

———. 1975[1955]. "Social and Religious Symbolism of the Lele." In her *Implicit Meanings*, pp. 9–26. London: Routledge and Kegan Paul.

Drewal, Henry John, and Margaret Thompson Drewal. 1983. *Gelede: Art and Female Power Among the Yoruba*. Bloomington: Indiana University Press.

Ebin, V. 1982. "Interpretations of Infertility: The Aowin People of South-West Ghana." In *Ethnography of Fertility and Birth*, Carol P. MacCormack, ed., pp. 141–59. London: Academic Press.

Etienne, Mona, and Eleanor Leacock, eds. 1980. *Women and Colonization*. New York: Praeger.

Faithorn, Elizabeth. 1975. "The Concept of Pollution Among the Kafe of the Papua New Guinea Highlands." In *Toward an Anthropology of Women*, Rayna Reiter, ed., pp. 127–40. New York: Monthly Review Press.

Fernandez, James. 1982. *Bwiti: An Ethnography of the Religious Imagination in Africa*. Princeton: Princeton University Press.

Gilbert, Michelle. 1987. "The Person of the King." In *Rituals of Royalty*, S. R. F. Price and David Cannadine, eds. New York: Cambridge University Press.

Glaze, Anita. 1981. "Art and the Women's Sphere." In her *Art and Death in a Senufo Village*, pp. 46–88. Bloomington: Indiana University Press.

Gottlieb, Alma. 1981. "Beng Baby Decoration: The Efficacy of Symbols and the Power of Women." Paper presented at the 24th Annual Meeting of the African Studies Association, Bloomington, Ind., October.

———. 1986a. "Changing the Calendar: Economics and Religious Innovation Among the Beng of Côte d'Ivoire." Paper presented at the 29th Annual Meeting of the African Studies Association, Madison, Wis., November.

———. 1986b. "Cousin Marriage, Birth Order and Gender: Alliance Models Among the Beng of Ivory Coast." *Man* 21 (4): 697–722.

———. 1986c. "Dog: Ally or Traitor? Mythology, Cosmology and Society Among the Beng of Ivory Coast." *American Ethnologist* 13 (3): 477–88.

———. 1988a. "The Ideology of Double Descent Among the Beng of Côte d'Ivoire." Paper presented at the 87th Annual Meeting of the American Anthropological Association, Phoenix, November.

———. 1988b. "Menstrual Cosmology Among the Beng of Ivory Coast." In *Blood Magic: The Anthropology of Menstruation*, Thomas Buckley and Alma Gottlieb, eds., pp. 55–74. Berkeley and Los Angeles: University of California Press.

———. 1989a. "Hyenas and Heteroglossia: Myth and Ritual Among the Beng of Côte d'Ivoire." *American Ethnologist* 16 (3): 487–501.

———. 1989b. "Witches, Kings, and Identity: or, the Power of Paradox and the Paradox of Power Among the Beng of Ivory Coast." In *Creativity of Power: Cosmology and Action in African Societies*, William Arens and Ivan Karp, eds., pp. 245–72. Washington, D.C.: Smithsonian Institution Press.

———. n.d. *Under the Kapok Tree: Identity and Difference in Beng Thought*. Bloomington: Indiana University Press. In press.

Gray, Robert. 1960. "Sonjo Bride-Price and the Question of African 'Wife-Purchase.'" *American Anthropologist* 62: 34–57.

Harris, Olivia. 1978. "Complementarity and Conflict: An Andean View of Women and Men." In *Sex and Age as Principles of Differentiation*, J. S. LaFontaine, ed., pp. 21–40. London: Academic Press.

Herzfeld, Michael. 1984. "The Horns of the Mediterraneist Dilemma." *American Ethnologist* 11 (3): 439–54.

Heusch, Luc de. 1986. *Sacrifice in Africa: A Structuralist Approach*. Alice Morton, tr. Bloomington: Indiana University Press.

Kessler, Suzanne J., and Wendy McKenna. 1985[1978]. *Gender: An Ethnomethodological Approach*. Chicago: University of Chicago Press.

Kuper, Adam. 1982. *Wives for Cattle: Bridewealth and Marriage in Southern Africa*. London: Routledge and Kegan Paul.

LaFontaine, J. S. 1978. "Introduction." In *Sex and Age as Principles of Differentiation*, Jean LaFontaine, ed., pp. 1–20. London: Academic Press.

———. 1981. "The Domestication of the Savage Male." *Man* 16 (3): 333–40.

Laguerre, Michel. 1987. *Afro-Caribbean Folk Medicine*. South Hadley, Mass.: Bergin & Garvey.

Mauss, Marcel. 1979[1935]. "Body Techniques." In his *Sociology and Psychology: Essays*, pp. 95–123. Ben Brewster, tr. London: Routledge and Kegan Paul.

Meigs, Anna. 1984. *Food, Sex, and Pollution: A New Guinean Religion*. New Brunswick, N.J.: Rutgers University Press.

Needham, Rodney. 1975. "Polythetic Classification: Convergence and Consequences." *Man* 10 (3): 349–69.

———, ed. 1973. *Right and Left: Essays in Dual Symbolic Classification*. Chicago: University of Chicago Press.

Ngubane, Harriet. 1977. *Body and Mind in Zulu Medicine: An Ethnography of Health and Disease in Nyuswa-Zulu Thought and Practice*. London: Academic Press.

Okely, Judith. 1975. "Gypsy Women: Models in Conflict." In *Perceiving Women,* Shirley Ardener, ed., pp. 55–86. New York: John Wiley.
Ortner, Sherry. 1984. "Theory in Anthropology Since the Sixties." *Comparative Studies in Society and History* 26 (1): 126–66.
Ottenberg, Simon. 1987. "The Anthropologist as Art Historian: The Art Historian as Anthropologist." *Reviews in Anthropology* 14 (1): 53–60.
Parkes, Peter. 1987. "Livestock Symbolism and Pastoral Ideology among the Kafirs of the Hindu Kush." *Man* 22 (4): 637–60.
Rogers, Susan Carol. 1978. "Woman's Place: A Critical Review of Anthropological Theory." *Comparative Studies in Society and History* 20: 123–62.
Rosch, Eleanor. 1983. "Prototype Classification and Logical Classification: The Two Systems." In *New Trends in Conceptual Representation: Challenges to Piaget's Theory?* Ellin Kofsky Scholnick, ed., pp. 73–86. Hillsdale, N.J.: Lawrence Erlbaum Associates, Publishers.
Rosch, Eleanor, and Carolyn B. Mervis. 1975. "Family Resemblances: Studies in the Internal Structure of Categories." *Cognitive Psychology* 7: 573–605.
Sacks, Karen. 1979. *Sisters and Wives: The Past and Future of Sexual Equality.* Westport, Conn.: Greenwood Press.
Scholnick, Ellin Kofsky. 1983. "Why Are New Trends in Conceptual Representation a Challenge to Piaget's Theory?" In *New Trends in Conceptual Representation: Challenges to Piaget's Theory?* Ellin Kofsky Scholnick, ed., pp. 41–70. Hillsdale, N.J.: Lawrence Erlbaum Associates, Publishers.
Semin, Gun R., and Ekkehard Rosch. 1981. "Activation of Bipolar Prototypes in Attribute Inferences." *Journal of Experimental Social Psychology* 17: 472–84.
Shore, Bradd. 1981. "Sexuality and Gender in Samoa: Conceptions and Missed Conceptions." In *Sexual Meanings,* Sherry Ortner and Harriet Whitehead, eds., pp. 192–215. New York: Cambridge University Press.
Smith, Jonathan Z. 1978. "Map Is Not Territory." In his *Map Is Not Territory: Studies in the History of Religions,* pp. 289–310. Leiden: E. J. Brill.
———. 1981. "The Bare Facts of Ritual." *History of Religions* 20 (1–2): 112–27.
Strathern, Marilyn. 1972. *Women in Between: Female Roles in a Male World.* London: Seminar Press.
———. 1981a. "Culture in a Net Bag." *Man* 16 (4): 665–88.
———. 1981b. "Self-Interest and the Social Good: Some Implications of Hagen Gender Imagery." In *Sexual Meanings,* Sherry Ortner and Harriet Whitehead, eds., pp. 166–91. New York: Cambridge University Press.
———. 1986. "Dual Models and Multiple Persons: Gender in Melanesia." Paper presented at the 85th Annual Meeting of the American Anthropological Association, Philadelphia, November.
———. 1987. "An Awkward Relationship: The Case of Feminism and Anthropology." *Signs* 12 (2): 276–92.
Thompson, Catherine. 1985. "The Power to Pollute and the Power to Preserve: Perceptions of Female Power in a Hindu Village." *Social Science and Medicine* 21 (6): 701–11.
Thompson, Robert Farris. 1973. "Aesthetic of the Cool." *African Arts* VII (1): 41–43, 64–67, 89–92.

Tiffany, Sharon. 1982. *Women, Work and Motherhood*. Englewood Cliffs, N.J.: Prentice-Hall.
Turner, Victor. 1969. *The Ritual Process: Structure and Anti-Structure*. Chicago: Aldine.
Weiner, Annette B. 1976. *Women of Value, Men of Renown: New Perspectives in Trobriand Exchange*. Austin: University of Texas Press.
———. 1977. "Trobriand Descent: Female/Male Domains." *Ethos* 5 (1): 54–70.

The Minangkabau of West Sumatra, as one of the most populous matrilineal and matrifocal societies in the modern world, provides an interesting case study of the continuity of a female-centered ideology despite modernization. With a prevailing ethic of accommodation, one that looks to nature for models for living, the Minangkabau have fashioned a society that has ridden out the storms of successive occupations by powerful historical groups without surrendering their central matrilineal heritage.

The record of history shows at least four major cultural assaults upon the Minangkabau, including the well-documented ones of Islam, the colonial Dutch, and the modern nation-state of Indonesia, all of which have supported contrary patriarchal institutions. Priding themselves on their ability to reconcile differences, the Minangkabau have adopted elements of the occupying ideologies while maintaining their own matrilineal identity and their ethic of nurturance and accommodation.

As Sanday describes the modern Minangkabau, we see them living out many of the contradictions of this complicated heritage. Buried in folk tales and ceremonial performances are two dominant and contradictory strains, or as Sanday terms them, "templates" for constructing social reality. The one, presumed to be primordial, is matricentric; the other, interpreted as the result of historical contact, is androcentric. In the reconciliation of these two potentially antithetical strains, the Minangkabau resort to rich imagery and the wisdom of their philosophers and poets to rationalize the contradictions in a way that preserves the matrilineal core of their society.

Peggy Reeves Sanday

6 Androcentric and Matrifocal Gender Representations in Minangkabau Ideology

I was first attracted to studying the matrilineal Minangkabau of Indonesia by Nancy Tanner's (1974) description of Minangkabau matrifocality, a term she defines as the cultural and structural centrality of women. Tanner describes Minangkabau women's economic power and their extensive participation in decision making. Tanner also notes that the structurally central position of the Minangkabau mother is evident in a wide range of cultural beliefs, at the center of which is the figure of Bundo Kanduang, a mythical (some say real) queen, whose name is used as a contemporary label of respect for senior women of the matrilineage. More recently, Tanner and others have described the association between Minangkabau matriliny and significant female power and authority (see especially Prindiville 1985; Tanner and Thomas 1985; F. and K. von Benda-Beckmann 1985; F. von Benda-Beckmann 1979).

My research goal when I arrived in West Sumatra in 1981 was to study the relationship between the practices of matrifocality and worldview, particularly Minangkabau concepts of nature, of self, and of society.[1] Almost immediately this project ran into difficulties, because where I expected to find a single, consistent worldview I found paradox and contradiction.

The contradiction first emerged in the following form. In the mountain villages and cities, the homeland of Minangkabau tradition, I observed men and women engaging in activities and rhetoric that I interpreted as reproducing matrifocality both as an ideology and as a lived reality. In the coastal capital, on the other hand, I encountered male rhetoric that articulated a "matriarchal" ideology for a national and international audience. From a Western perspective this rhetoric was interesting because it contrasted so sharply with analogous Western ideology. Whereas the strong male is the dominant gender metaphor in the West, the authoritative mother is the dominant gender metaphor of Minangkabau ethnic ideology articulated not only in the coastal capital but in the villages. Yet exclusion of women from intellectual and governmental activities in the capital was reminiscent of Western practices. When I raised this point in a seminar to an all-male group of intellectuals, they defended their exclusion of women on the ground that the traditional system of roles includes one defined as "intellectual" that is assigned exclusively to men.

The matriarchal rhetoric voiced by city men is empty—all skin and no core as the Minangkabau would say—because it was articulated in an environment (that is, the city) where people are living apart from clan property, the matrifocal household, and the important traditional ceremonies. This rhetoric is meaningful only as long as men and women in the villages continue the ceremonial activities and traditional exchange relations that perpetuate the core of the matrifocal system.

Contrary to the state of affairs in the capital, women hold positions of prominence in the system of village authority as well as in the general ideology. This prominence, however, occurs in some but not all contexts. In this chapter I examine the meaning of the deployment of contradictory gender representations in Minangkabau ideology.[2]

This discussion is primarily focused on Minangkabau ideology called *adat Minangkabau*. When examining this ideology it is obvious that there are androcentric and matrifocal gender representations deployed in different contexts. I suggest that the deployment of such contradictory gender representations is part of a larger sociocultural process related to developing and protecting a historical and enduring ethnic identity.

The Minangkabau claim that they live according to two interconnected ideological systems: one is constituted by religious codes and the other by the code of traditional custom (*adat*). The matrilineal social system is defined by the code of traditional custom. *Adat* intellectuals use several terms to define matriliny: "blood line from one stomach" (Manggis 1982:106); "matriarchaat" (meaning "system of descent from the mother," Nasroen 1957[1971:34]); and "matrilinial" [*sic*] (descent through the line of the mother, Hakimy 1984:77). Generally, these terms refer to identifying with the clan (*suku*) of the mother, having rights in property through the clan of the mother, living in the home of the wife, and maintaining a lifelong allegiance to one's mother and siblings. In the following discussion, the term matriliny will be retained for issues regarding descent; the term matrifocal will be employed to refer to residence with the wife and allegiance to the mother and siblings. For sake of clarity the phrase matrilineal social system will refer to matriliny and matrifocality.

Minangkabau intellectuals speak of their matrilineal social system with pride, saying that it has survived a history of external patrilineal influences. As informants describe this history, primordial time was interrupted by the early semicentralization of the Minangkabau kingdom and the influence of a Javanese-Minangkabau king who was associated with patrilineality. Next there was the acceptance of patrilineal Islam, which was rationalized by Minangkabau social theoreticians as supporting, not destroying, the matrilineal system. From Europe there was Dutch colonialism, a period of time when men, not women, were identified by the colonial government as representing lineage affairs. Finally, and most recently, there are pressures to develop national integration and a "national culture" in the postcolonial era. Despite these pressures, Minangkabau matriliny has survived. Indeed, as Abdullah, a Minangkabau social scientist, stresses, "whatever economic changes that have taken place so far, there has always been an inclination among Minangkabau to safeguard their matrilineal social system. It is a sacred system; it has been religiously legitimated" (1985:155).

Today, matrifocal and androcentric gender representations are a common feature of the Minangkabau ethnographic landscape. The Minangkabau recognize that contradictory gender representations exist, at least in the minds of outside observers, and they take great pride in explaining them away. As Abdullah says about the widely discussed contradiction between matriliny and the patrilineal bias of Islamic law, it incites the Minangkabau "ethnic pride on 'the genius of Minangkabau' to synthesize contradictions harmoniously" (1985:141).

In what follows, examples of matrifocal and androcentric representations are described in more detail. The Minangkabau argument for the harmony between their matrilineal system and patrilineal Islam is then presented to demonstrate their interest in resolving contradictions. Finally, the plot of the Minangkabau "state myth" is presented to illustrate the tensions and conflicts that create contradictory gender representations and the ideological solution that resolves the contradiction. I conclude that, more often than not, gender representations of women dominate at the mythical—or timeless and eternal—level, while representations extolling male actors emerge in specific historical, political, and religious contexts. This foray into Minangkabau ethnography leads me beyond an earlier concern with female status to consider the production of ideology as a means to protect ethnic identity and provide continuity in a rapidly changing world.

Matrilineal and Matrifocal Gender Representations

Minangkabau informants, particularly educated men, like to refer to their society as a "matriarchate." By this they mean that women inherit all ancestral property and husbands must go to live with their wives. In their roles as husbands, men frequently complain that theirs is a poor lot in life. If they are divorced or widowed they must leave the home of their wives and find a home either with their matrilineal relatives or in a local prayer house. While men may complain about their lot as husbands, they view as barbaric the Javanese custom that forces women out of their husbands' homes if a marriage ends through death or divorce.

Indeed, Minangkabau men feel morally superior to men in more patriarchal societies because of the power Minangkabau women have, which, as a matter of masculine pride, they feel they must protect. Traditionally, men were expected to leave their homes and villages as young men in order to prove their worth and leave their sisters and mothers securely in charge of the matrilineal property. Thus, men derive a certain sense of moral superiority from their efforts to promote matrifocal control of family property. In the words of a well-known male leader, Idrus Hakimy Dt. Rajo Penghulu, whom I interviewed in the capital,

> Women and men are the same, but women are more respected and given more privileges. All ancestral property goes to women. The house goes to women. Women keep the key to the rice house because women are more economical. Young boys sleep in other houses (usually mosques) to show their sisters that they do not own the houses. Men feel proud because they don't take anything from their mother's house. Men who take from others' houses are accused of being weak or robbers. Women are given more privileges because people think that women determine the continuation of the generations. Whether the next generation is bad or good depends on women. Women's role will determine future generations, because children stay most of the time with their mother and mothers are primarily responsible for teaching children. In the home *adat* is taught by the oldest sister who is called *Bundo Kanduang* (real mother).

A comparable sense of moral responsibility is voiced by women, who claim that they must remain in the village with their kinswomen to manage ancestral property and uphold traditional custom. Women live either in matrilineal longhouses, occupied through the generations by kinswomen, or in houses built for them by their husbands, which they own and will pass on to their daughters. Senior women are likened to the supporting pole of the Minangkabau longhouse, a major symbol of matrilineal custom throughout Indonesia. As one senior woman said: "Women cannot leave their home to go somewhere like men do. A woman stays in the place where she was born and upholds Minangkabau tradition [*adat*]. The way a woman behaves is part of custom; she keeps *adat* going through her behavior."

Although there is consensus about the moral authority of women, informants in the villages are divided in their opinion regarding the relative social position of the sexes. It is interesting to examine what informants say about the relative social status of males and females, because from this we learn that each sex has its own realm of social responsibility and leadership. Women are responsible for economic matters related to the use of ancestral property as well as for matters having to do with the visual and alimentary representation of the lineage in ceremonial affairs. Men, on the other hand, in their roles as senior lineage males (*mamak*) and titled male leaders (*penghulu*), are responsible for formal political matters as well as for matters having to do with verbal expositions in ceremonial affairs.[3]

Generally speaking, informants agreed that women hold more power with respect to the disbursement and use of ancestral property, while men hold more power in "government." In the village and council house, informants said, male leaders are the highest; in the home women are the highest. This statement will mislead the Western reader who assumes that the domestic realm is unimportant or peripheral to the center of power. In fact the domestic realm is conceptualized as the center of power because all decisions are made first in discussions with women in the domestic realm before moving to the council house. In many villages, male leaders must discuss matters with matrilineal relatives, male and female, before moving into a meeting where each member acts as a representative in a decision-making process that operates by consensus. In most villages these meetings are held in the village council house and are attended by men alone. These differential rights and duties of Minangkabau men and women are codified by the ideology represented in Minangkabau *adat*. According to this ideology males and females may have different rights, but since both are necessary to perpetuate *adat* the two are at the same level (*sama tinggi*).[4]

Adat *and the Matrilineal Ideology*

The Minangkabau are guided by a hegemonic ideology called *adat*, which legitimizes and structures traditional political and ceremonial life in the villages. The dictates of *adat* must be distinguished from the political and ceremonial forms dictated by the national government and by the practices of Islam. Today *adat* forms exist in complex interrelationship with these national social and religious forms.

According to F. von Benda-Beckmann (1979:113), "*adat* is the symbolic universe by which the peoples of the Indonesian archipelago have constructed their world." For each ethnic group, *adat* has specific meanings spun from a group's early history and, in some cases, centuries of interaction with various external influences. Many people believe that *adat* is a word of Arabic origin. However, the Minangkabau believe that their *adat* existed long before Islam came to West Sumatra. One *adat* scholar points out that the word is actually derived from the Sanskrit words *a* and *dato*, and refers to worldview (Manggis 1982:145). All agree that *adat* pervades Minangkabau thinking and philosophy. Abdullah defines *adat* as "the whole structural system of society"; it forms "the entire value system, the basis of all ethical and legal judgment, as well as the source of social expectations" (1966:1).

A male leader describes *adat* as "central to our life, it determines the way we act, and gives us rules for living. Without *adat* people would be like wild animals in the jungle: the strong would conquer the weak, the tallest would defeat the shortest, and the strongest would hold down the smallest." A female *adat* leader, discussing the etymology of the word, said: "*A* means not; *dat* means stress or tension. So, *adat* means without stress or tension. *Adat* is a system which does not put stress on the people because it is flexible, practical, democratic, rational, and systematic."

A folk saying makes *adat* part of natural law, the principle that existed before all else:

> When nothing was existent, the universe did not exist
> Neither earth nor sky existed
> *Adat* had already existed.

The Minangkabau refer to this saying in distinguishing between "*adat* that is truly *adat*" and "*adat* that is made *adat*." The first kind of *adat* refers to those aspects that are enduring and cannot be changed, such as the matrilineal principles of clan exogamy and matrilineal inheritance. These principles, they say, have not changed over the centuries despite numerous external influences such as patrilineally oriented Islam and modernization. The other type refers to *adat* rules that are the result of local, historical circumstances decided by the consensus of village household leaders. The principle of flexibility means that different *adat* rules develop in each village because of the process of forming consensus regarding expected behavior in new circumstances. This process is reflected in the following proverb:

In different grass there are different grasshoppers
In different ponds are different fish
In different villages there is different *adat*.

Discussions about *adat* quickly become discussions about rules for behavior and the underlying philosophy that forms these rules. *Adat* precepts are expressed in proverbs, epigrams, and house carving, and are enacted in ceremonies and curing practices as well as encoded by the motifs of traditional textiles. Folk exegesis of sung narrative drama, the motifs of textiles, and the organization of traditional clothes and ceremonies are phrased in terms of the grammar of *adat Minangkabau*. *Adat* is expressed through all the senses: speaking, eating, seeing, touching, and hearing—and is rendered in mundane, abstract, performative, and even magical forms.

Adat ceremonies are rife with meaning. Food prepared and served by women, ceremonial words spoken by men, ritual interaction in same-sex groups and between men and women, and the way in which traditional dress is worn are glossed in terms of *adat*. Informants say that traditional ceremonies and dress are "the skin of *adat*." They also say that matriliny is the "skin of *adat*," which indicates the close interconnection between ceremonial life, matriliny, and *adat*.

Adat ceremonies mark major episodes in the life cycle (birth, circumcision, marriage, and death) and other major events, such as building a traditional house and the ascension to hereditary titles by men. In all of these ceremonies actors play their roles according to their matrilineal or affinal relationship to the family sponsoring the ceremony. The traditional clothes and headdress worn by men and women on these occasions are woven with motifs which can be translated by an expert into a series of proverbs and epigrams. The linguistic and visual signs mediated by proverbs and textiles often signify expected behavior of the senior woman as the center-pole of the house and senior men in their roles as mother's brother or father. Even the way the clothes are worn and the form into which the headdress is shaped tell a story about rules for living according to matrilineal ties.[5] In these ceremonies matrilineal *adat* becomes a living form; the message and the medium are merged with the performance.

Adat ideology expressed in proverbs provides the legitimating principles for Minangkabau matriliny and matrifocality. One proverb, in particular, is widely discussed and understood. This proverb is of particular interest because of its conceptualization of nature as a model for culture. The Minangkabau do not conceive of nature as wild, but as providing models for culture. Indeed appropriate behavior entails the studied imitation of growth in nature. The reconciliation of nature with culture in this manner also demonstrates the importance attached to harmonizing differences.

> Take the small knife used for carving
> Make a staff from the *lintabuang* tree
> The cover of *pinang* flowers becomes a winnow
> A drop of water becomes the sea
> A clump of earth becomes a mountain
> Growth in nature becomes a teacher.

The first three lines of the proverb refer to human dependence on nature for tools (knife, staff, and winnow); the last three lines demonstrate that humans should look to natural growth and development as a model for the emotions and social life. For example, people say that "as there are hills and valleys in nature, there will be ups and downs in life." Or, in a more philosophical vein, "no matter how small something may be it can grow into something big. A gift may be small but, like the growth of a child or a seed, its intention can grow in the heart and yield many fruits."

According to many informants, the matrilineal system of the Minangkabau in which all ancestral property is owned, regulated, and inherited by women is the most important social consequence of looking to nature for models of and for living. As Idrus Hakimy Dt. Rajo Penghulu said in an interview:

> As we all know, Minangkabau *adat* comes from nature according to the proverb *Alam takambang jadi guru* [the unfurling, blooming, expansion of nature is our teacher]. In nature all that is born into the world is born from the female, not from the father. *Adat* knows that the mother is the closest to her children and is therefore more dominant than the father in establishing the character of the generations. Thus, we must protect women and their

offspring because they are also weaker than men. Just as the weak becomes the strong in nature, we must make the weaker the stronger in human life.

On a more practical note, informants also noted that while we do not always know who a child's father is, we always know the child's mother. If the father is not known, a child cannot get food from him. The mother is always known and can always provide security in a matrilineal system. This respect and care for the weak is a key element in the Minangkabau general ideology and is consistent with the importance attached to looking to "the unfurling of growth in nature" as a teacher.

There is no dialectical struggle between nature and culture, male and female, weak and strong. The potential opposition between these polarities is reconciled by making one the actualization of the other. Thus, culture is the actualization of the messages of nature just as the child is the actualization of birth and adulthood the actualization of childhood. As matriliny is associated with divine nature so is the senior woman, Bundo Kanduang, whose son actualizes the messages she teaches (see below). In this complementary sense women are associated with nature and men with culture.

Thus, the Minangkabau make a distinction between female/weak and male/strong, but the logic of the Minangkabau ideology does not permit the strong to obliterate or subordinate the weak (see Jordanova 1980 for a discussion of these dichotomies in Western thought). Informants say: "Here we elevate the weak instead of the strong. Women *must* be given rights *because* they are weak. Young men *must* be sent away from the village to prove their manhood so that there will be no competition between them and their sisters." Sending males away also ensures the durability of matriliny by providing an outlet for the pressures created by *adat* in the modern world. Individuals may give conceptual allegiance to Minangkabau thought and ideology and retain their lineage identity and village residence even though their primary residence is outside the Minangkabau heartland where they follow a more modern way of life. Living outside of West Sumatra (*rantau*), as Abdullah notes (1985:155), "provides whatever outlets are needed to release the pressure caused by the system in the period of economic changes," a point also made by F. von Benda-Beckmann (1979: 378).[6] Here again we see the Minangkabau acting to preserve a primordial, enduring matrilineal identity.

Thus, according to *adat* ideology, matriliny, nature, and mothering represent the seeds for a Minangkabau reflective philosophy privileging women as mothers and as the perpetuators, along with their brothers, of lineage identity. Today, matrilineal identity for the Minangkabau is more than a basic principle connecting individuals with their lineage ancestors and contemporaries, it is the ground for their social being. The Minangkabau are proud that they are among the few matrilineal peoples left in the world. Ancestral property passed on matrilineally is treated with reverence and respect because it associates each person with the all-important lineage identity. Ancestral property includes lineage titles, ancestral lands, and heirlooms. Alienation of this property from the clan would provide "a real breakdown of both the *adat* ideological system and the behavior relating to it" (F. and K. von Benda-Beckmann 1985:278). Lineage identity is a source of power, authority, and prestige for both sexes. More important, without affiliation with a matrilineage, individual males and females cannot achieve Minangkabau personhood.

The model of the feminine as the source of life, the potentiality from which the human generations are derived, is found in other contexts not directly related to *adat*. For example, in several villages I heard stories about the original ancestress who founded a given clan. Interestingly, this mythical woman, associated with the wild, was described as making her home in an egg, a symbol for the eternal seed and all first things. In one story, this woman was brought to society by a male to become a clan ancestress. Today her grave is visited by pilgrims seeking magical power and her help in problems of life. In other villages, I heard stories about the eternal woman of the jungle, who as the mother of wild pigs forces humans to show reverence for the things of the jungle by following certain rules that show respect for her jungle domain. These stories about the eternal woman are conceptually similar to ideas about eternal *adat* and the eternal queen mother, Bundo Kanduang.

The Androcentric Template and Adat *Ideology*

In the specifics of male and female role definition, *adat* ideology is decidedly androcentric, particularly as this ideology is interpreted in contemporary rhetoric. A male leader I interviewed in the highlands listed what he called "five potencies for developing and improving the country and villages in Minangkabau." What Kopytoff (this volume) discriminates as immanent and negotiable traits of gender roles, this man refers to as "potencies" and "vitalities." A description of these terms identifies the major features of an idealized system of roles. A paraphrase of the interview follows:

First there are the *ninik mamak,* the men who have the authority to decide in accordance with *adat* law. *Mamak* is the word for mother's brother. *Ninik* is the word for leader. Senior women of a clan choose the *ninik mamak* in conjunction with male clan members. The *ninik mamak* have authority over their nephews and nieces. They are the heads of the *suku* (clan) in the villages. *Penghulus* (titled male leaders) are chosen from the ranks of the *ninik mamak.* As the senior woman is like the center pole of the household, the *ninik mamak* is like a big tree in the middle of a wide (flat) field. He gives advice and is informed about the actions of individuals.

The second "potency" is the *alim ulama* (religious leader). In every village religious leaders advise the people about religious law. They give "light in the night" by instructing people in religious truths and defining acceptable and unacceptable behavior. Today many people say that *adat* is based on religious law. While *ninik mamak* have authority over their nephews and nieces, *alim ulama* have authority over their followers. In every village there is a place for the *ninik mamak* to meet called the *balai adat.* The unity of *adat* and religion, of *ninik mamak* and *alim ulama* provides the foundation for behavior. *Adat* and religious law are like the bamboo trees that grow on the side of the canyon walls; they lean against each other for mutual support.

The third potency is the intellectuals. Intelligent people are supposed to "tell good things." They plan for the future. They are brilliant, healthy, and strong. They put forth effort, they are full of "vitality," and they have many ideas for developing the village.

The fourth potency is the senior women, Bundo Kanduang, who have vitality to support the other groups. Women are superior to men in their feeling, inspiration, and dedication. Women also have more ability in the areas of morality, art, friendliness, and religious matters.

The fifth potency is the young people who will manage the world. Young people are supposed to be diligent and fast without making mistakes. Young people fill up the village and give it its vitality. Whether the village becomes good or bad depends on the young people.

The male bias of the above conceptualization is repeated in the following well-known *adat* proverb.

Nephews and nieces are subject to uncles
Uncles are subject to *penghulu*
Penghulu are subject to *mufakat* [consensus]
Mufakat is subject to the truth
The truth is according to human feelings and what is appropriate.
(Tr. from H. I. Hakimy Dt. Rajo Penghulu 1984:91)

According to this proverb, men or women in their roles as nephews or nieces (*kamanakan*) are governed by uncles (*mamak*) and titled male leaders (*penghulu*). However, even in this system *adat* is perceived as having final authority, and democratic consensus is the means by which *adat* precepts are interpreted. What is appropriate and true is decided by reference to *adat*. In some villages, however, decision making is exclusively in the hands of the *penghulu* and there is a titled leader, *penghulu pucuk,* who may be thought of as the highest authority. In a few cases informants claimed that the *penghulu pucuk* was superior to men and women in the village, while in the domestic realm a *penghulu* was superior to his matrilineal relatives. This interpretation, however, was not as common as the notion that senior women and men, in the context of *adat,* form a single unit that cannot be split.

Such differences in local rhetoric regarding the position of men and women, or the superior position of the leading titled male leader, reflect the considerable variation that exists among villages in the structure of traditional political forms (as opposed to those forms imposed by the national government from the provincial capital). Interviews in a variety of villages disclosed that some villages follow a democratic structural form where equality is emphasized while others stress hierarchy. Generally speaking, the differences can be tied to a village's perceived historical relationship to the Minangkabau kingdom, which some say was instituted by an immigrant king from India. Those villages that connect their history to this kingdom tend to be more hierarchically structured, while the more democratically oriented villages tie their history to a different, more egalitarian historical model. This contradiction between democracy and hierarchy is believed to be the result of the work of two legendary half-brothers who accommodated the influences of an immigrant royalty to a local democratic tradition. According to folk history these two brothers codified a legal system that included contradictory local forms of government and a descent system that was matrilineal.

In the body of folk history, called *tambo* (stories of old times), the origin of *adat* law is traced to the work of two half-brothers. These men, Datuk Katumanggungan and Datuk Perpatih nan Sebatang (Datuk is an honorific title given all *penghulu*), are said to have created *penghulu* titles and engaged in activities leading to the federation of Minangkabau villages under a common *adat*.

Regarding the origin of matrilineal inheritance, Kato (1982:150–51) summarizes one of the versions presented in the *tambo*. Originally property passed from father to children. Dt. (Datuk) Perpatih and Dt. Katumanggungan decided that they wanted to sail to North Sumatra. On the way their ship ran aground. The two men gathered their children, nieces, and nephews to ask for help. Only the nieces and nephews would help them, saying, "If that is the wish of our elders, let us tow the ship. It does not matter even if we might be run over by the ship and killed in the process, for it is the ship of our elders that ran aground." They pulled the ship off the sand and, assisted by spirits, the ship floated again. Later, "the two Datuk decreed that from that time on all the property be given to the (sororal) nieces and nephews as a reward of their services, instead of to the children."

Many informants associate this story with the advent of a powerful Javanese-Minangkabau ruler in West Sumatra in the fourteenth century, Adityawarman, who threatened the democratic basis (*mufakat*) for Minangkabau decision making by imposing more autocratic forms. It is impossible to determine the accuracy either of this association or even of the historical reality of the two half-brothers. For our purposes here, what is important is that informants refer to this story when explaining the political basis for the codification of a social ideology and the federation of villages under a common umbrella, called *alam Minangkabau* (the Minangkabau world).

In their codification of *adat* precepts, Dt. Perpatih and Dt. Katumanggungan incorporated elements of royalty, indeed Dt. Katumanggungan, the son of an immigrant king, embodies royalty in his personage and the *adat* associated with him is more hierarchical than the *adat* associated with Dt. Perpatih. Dt. Perpatih was the son of a commoner, said to have been the advisor to this king. Dt. Perpatih embodies the ethos of harmony and decision by consensus and the *adat* associated with him is democratic. The two half-brothers symbolize contradictory but real historical forces known to have been present in the Minangkabau heartland. In the lengthy historical tale detailing their codification of *adat*, these forces are accommodated and synthesized. In contemporary village life the legacy of these differences is still discernible in the structure of traditional political roles and the degree to which democracy or hierarchy is emphasized.

Harmonizing Contradictions: Adat *and Islam*

The Minangkabau see no contradiction between matrifocality and the tale of the origin of matriliny as codified by the two half-brothers. Likewise they see no contradiction between their matrilineal *adat* and patrilineal Islam. Although these two principles of social organization clashed in the nineteenth century, resulting in a lengthy and violent civil war, today Islam and *adat* exist in mutual reinforcement.[7] Today Islam is considered to be part of the *adat that is truly adat*. Although Islamic doctrine was not intended to replace local practices, it was put in the highest *adat* category from the outset. The Quran and Hadith together with the natural law were viewed as the eternal principles that guide human spiritual and secular activities and from which actual practices and "lesser values" emanate. Later when the Dutch government introduced Western criminal law, this was included in the other category of *adat (adat that can be changed)*.

According to Idrus Hakimy Dt. Rajo Penghulu, there is no contradiction between matrilineal *adat* and Islam. In an interview he emphasized, as do many informants, the close association between *adat* and Islam.

> The practices of *adat* go together with practices of Islam. Many are overlapping and the same. The reason that *adat* is quite strong in our villages is because they are supported by religion. In *adat* the possessions go to women. In Islam possessions go to men and women. But actually the two things are not contradictory. In *adat* there are two kinds of possessions—clan and individual. Clan possessions go to women, from one woman to another. Individual possessions—the things a husband gets together with his wife— go to children.

Idrus Hakimy sacralizes Minangkabau matrilineality and the position of women by equating both with the practices of Islam. In another interview he said: "According to Al-Quran, women are the mast of the household and the mast of the state. If women are good, the household and the state are good. If women are faulty, the household and the state are damaged. For these reasons, Minangkabau trace descent through the mother."

The reconciliation between *adat* and Islam is also discussed by Abdullah, who claims that the acceptance of Islam gave new meaning to *alam Minangkabau* "as being the world that was supported by two sacred pillars, namely Islam and *adat*" (1985:153). This reconciliation is symbolically constituted by an agreement, called the Bukit Marapalam Agreement, which is said to have taken place "sometime in the past." This agreement reconciled the three components of Minangkabau history: royalty, *adat,* and Islam.

To conclude, the relationship between matrilineal *adat* and Islam is reconciled by placing traditional matrilineal institutions in a sacred frame of reference. It is by reference to the transcendental that the Minangkabau both harmonize contradictions and provide an ideology that legitimizes both sides of the contradiction. This method for legitimizing contradictory principles is most clearly expressed in the following tale of the exploits of the legendary queen, Bundo Kanduang. In this tale we see how, in popular discourse, matrifocal and androcentric subplots are deployed to perpetuate *adat* on the one hand and to preserve political boundaries on the other. This tale demonstrates the use of accommodating and integrative strategies to preserve both the moral and the political orders in the face of divisive forces. Since this kind of experience has characterized Minangkabau history, the tale provides a model *of* and *for* the Minangkabau response to potentially divisive historical forces.

Harmonizing Contradictions: Kaba Cindur Mata

Kaba Cindur Mata is a popular drama, which Abdullah (1970:3) calls "a state myth *par excellence* and a standard reference work for Minangkabau *adat* theoreticians and guardians." It is told as a tale and enacted as a drama. The tale introduces Bundo Kanduang, the mythical Minangkabau queen; her son, Dang Tuanku; her emissary, Cindur Mata, who may also be her son but is described as the son of her servant; and Putri Bungsu, who marries Dang Tuanku and is described as the replacement for Bundo Kanduang. In the story, Bundo Kanduang is presented as a model for proper behavior according to *adat,* as well as a symbol of female power and authority. Her behavior illustrates how *adat* precepts are passed from an authoritative mother to the next generation. The exploits of Dang Tuanku and Cindur Mata, on the other hand, constitute a male-oriented subplot illustrating how male behavior, at times subversive, at times responsible, maintains the political order. Female behavior is also depicted as being both subversive and responsible. On the whole, however, exemplary female behavior maintains the moral order while male behavior protects the moral and defends the political order.[8]

Kaba is derived from the Arabic word *achbar* and means message or news. *Kaba* and *tambo* are the two most important types of Minangkabau prose literature. *Tambo* generally treat the development of the Minangkabau world and its *adat,* while the *kaba* are usually stories about the inhabitants of this world and concentrate on local traditions and the ideal conduct of life. *Kaba Cindur Mata* relates the tradition of Minangkabau royalty and could be considered a *tambo* in that the major figures also narrate the develoment of Minangkabau *adat.*

Numerous versions of the story have been published since 1891.[9] The references to Islam in all of the versions suggest that it describes events after the cultural institutionalization of Islam, which probably began sometime in the sixteenth century. Early seventeenth-century reports on Minangkabau indicate that the process of Islamization was well developed by that time. Abdullah thinks it is possible that the story could present a model for the Minangkabau state of the seventeenth or early eighteenth century. Court life depicted in the story, for example, is similar to that witnessed in 1684 by Tomas Dias, the first European to enter the Minangkabau heartland. Abdullah (1970:12) tentatively concludes that the Kaba reached its present form "no earlier than the later seventeenth or early eighteenth century."

The story begins with a description of Bundo Kanduang, who lives in the royal palace in Pagarruyung. She is a queen, "one of the original royal line, who stood on her own, equal in fame to the Kings of the Land of Rum, the land of China, of the Seas, and of a four-branched lineage." She was entrusted with "the magical cloth that spread out as wide as the world and folded to the thickness of a fingernail," with the magical knife, a magical shield, drums, and other sacred objects. Her son, Dang Tuanku, is also described in metaphors alluding to magic: he gives forth a "varicolored light" and is a person of "great magical powers." Thus, the royal pair of mother and son, rulers of the Minangkabau world, are sacralized by being placed within a magico-religious realm.

The power and authority of the senior female are reflected in the personage and actions of Bundo Kanduang.[10] The story begins with a statement of the authority of Bundo Kanduang, who holds the insignia of power placing her at the level of famous kings.

A major theme of the story is the transition of authority from Bundo Kanduang to Dang Tuanku, Putri Bungsu, and Cindur Mata. In the beginning of the story most of the queen's actions display her power and authority; at its end she is more passive as she has turned her power over to her ministers and her authority over to Dang Tuanku and Cindur Mata. This transition occurs in response to external threats to local *adat*. Abdullah (1970) says that *Kaba Cindur Mata* describes an orderly, balanced world where every aspect of life follows the principles of *adat*. Tragedy occurs because the protagonists ignore these principles. The plot unfolds in response to a series of actions breaking the rules of *adat*.

When the story opens Putri Bungsu is betrothed to Dang Tuanku, her cross-cousin, an ideal marriage according to matrilineal *adat*.[11] Putri Bungsu, the daughter of Raja Muda, Bundo Kanduang's younger brother, is introduced as "no ordinary sort of person, but one who if weighed would be heavy, if tested would be as red, as our lord in Pagarruyung. She is the treasure of the east, the pride of Kampungdalam, the jewel of the valley of Sikelawi." Putri Bungsu is said to look exactly like Bundo Kanduang, "not even a little different." The marriage is essential because only she is considered suitable to govern within the great palace as a replacement for Bundo Kanduang. Relative to her father, Putri Bungsu has superior power and authority as an advisor. Bundo Kanduang is also described in terms denoting her superiority to Raja Muda. The superiority of the sister is also reflected in the actions of another woman, the sister of Imbang Jaya.

The plot of the story unfolds around the actions of Raja Muda, who breaks the *adat* of betrothal by arranging his daughter's marriage to the foreigner Imbang Jaya, despite her betrothal to Dang Tuanku. This violation of *adat* law leads to a series of violations. Imbang Jaya breaks the *adat* of peace between the countries by stationing thieves along the border. Dang Tuanku breaks the *adat* of consensus by sending Cindur Mata to bring Putri Bungsu to Pagarruyung in opposition to his mother's agreement with her ministers to overlook her brother's transgression. Ignoring *adat* principles brings death to the main protagonists, thus conveying the importance of following the ways of *adat*.

Throughout the story, but especially in its beginning, Bundo Kanduang is concerned with teaching Dang Tuanku the rules of behavior according to *adat* and explaining the structure of the Minangkabau government. These discussions are generally focused on how to respond if someone has broken the rules of *adat*. Breaking the rules, such as happened in the case of Raja Muda and Imbang Jaya when they broke the *adat* of betrothal, causes Bundo Kanduang to experience anger and a feeling of shame and humiliation. Her initial response is to follow her emotions and go to war. However, the value attached to harmonizing opposing forces makes this an unacceptable response, and Bundo Kanduang is persuaded by her ministers to accept the course of events and send Cindur Mata to Raja Muda as a token of her official acceptance of the marriage.

In her persona Bundo Kanduang embodies the dual aspect of nature. She symbolizes both the seed and full growth. Like a mother she encourages orderly growth according to the rule of *adat*, calling those who break the rules weak and immature, people whose growth is stunted. About Raja Muda and Imbang Jaya she says they are "children without shame," who cannot judge—selfish children who cannot grow up and who should be exiled. About Dang Tuanku, whose opinion she opposes, she tells her ministers that his judgment "is not yet as much as a mite, his wits are not yet as much as a grain of rice." She accuses Dang Tuanku and Cindur Mata of playing night and day, flying kites, and being unmindful of the day. When Cindur Mata does not respond to the request of the ministers to explain his bringing Putri Bungsu, she accuses him of being a child "who won't grow up, a child who doesn't do as he is taught."

As much as the story is about following the rules of *adat,* it is also about resisting external forces that challenge the orderly reproduction of the Minangkabau world. It is significant that Dang Tuanku and Cindur Mata secretly arrange to bring Putri Bungsu back despite the formal charge of Bundo Kanduang to honor her intended marriage to the foreigner. Bundo Kanduang makes this charge only after she has been persuaded by much discussion; her first inclination is to break *adat* and punish her brother. She agrees to follow *adat* and send Cindur Mata bearing gifts to her brother. Thus *adat* is followed "outwardly," but there is an inner agenda in Cindur Mata's trip when he secretly persuades Putri Bungsu to come back with him, arguing that Bundo Kanduang is getting old and must be replaced by means of her marriage to Dang Tuanku. Once they arrive back in Pagarruyung (the home of Bundo Kanduang), the marriage between Dang Tuanku and Putri Bungsu is agreed upon after *adat* rules have been rationalized to permit the event. However in the larger plan of the story, self-interest loses because Imbang Jaya is killed and Bundo Kanduang, Dang Tuanku, and Putri Bungsu are forced to leave the earth and ascend into the seventh heaven. They flee in order to avoid fighting the father of Imbang Jaya, who is determined to avenge the death of his son.[12] Thus, by their flight open conflict is avoided.

By their ascension into the seventh heaven, the triumvirate of mother, son, and niece together with the *adat* they embody receives permanent symbolic legitimation. Cindur Mata, on the other hand, lives out his life in the world and gradually widens the political boundaries of the Minangkabau kingdom. In so doing, he repeatedly breaks the rules of *adat* by engaging in actions that solidify Minangkabau political borders. Both his actions and those of Bundo Kanduang, who solidifies *adat* by fleeing to the seventh heaven, can be seen as forms of resistance to external political events.

The assumption into heaven of the divine threesome guarantees them and all they stand for a place in eternity. Ostensibly they represent matrilineal succession because Bundo Kanduang's power is passed on to her son and his wife, who is also Bundo Kanduang's niece. However, there is much in the story suggesting that the threesome represent mother, son, and daughter. Putri Bungsu is clearly more than a wife—she is "no ordinary person." The similarities drawn between the two women suggest that they represent senior and junior generations of the same line. Indeed, it has been suggested that Minangkabau royal succession was endogamous (Andaya 1975). These three figures in their being synthesize divine and human attributes. They personify royal and local *adat*, the eternal and the mortal, androcentric and matrifocal power and authority. Together with Cindur Mata and Raja Muda the three also represent the major positions of Minangkabau kinship. The authoritative role of Bundo Kanduang legitimizes matrifocality. In addition to presenting a uniquely Minangkabau ideology, *Kaba Cindu Mata* also represents a particular philosophy of history in its emphasis on the synthesis rather than the opposition of contradictory elements.

Discussion

Bloch (1987:330–31) has argued that contradictory representations of women among the Merina of Madagascar can be explained as "an inevitable part of the process of the production of ideology," the attempt to build a transcendental order. He describes two egalitarian representations of gender classes and a third representation in which women "are categorically inferior." The third representation builds a transcendental order by devaluing women in order to legitimize the authority and cohesion of the patrilineal descent group. In the latter representation, he suggests that the Merina are preoccupied with transcending the biological realities of lowly birth and messy death in order to establish an enduring connection with ancestors in the stone tomb.

For the Minangkabau, in contrast, biological realities are not something to be transcended. On the contrary, in their ideology there is emphasis on following the "unfurling of growth in nature" as a model for behavior. Tales like the story of Bundo Kanduang and of the two half-brothers demonstrate that the concern of the Minangkabau is with preserving political boundaries on the one hand and *adat* ideology on the other. In the story of Bundo Kanduang we see that continuity of the matrilineal descent group is achieved by transcending political squabbles and merging the divine threesome—mother-son-daughter (the replacement for the mother)—into an eternal undifferentiated unity.

Tales like the story of Bundo Kanduang and of the two half-brothers employ different strategies to ensure the continuation of the ideology of Minangkabau matriliny and matrifocality. One strategy "mythologizes" matrifocality, the other "historicizes" matriliny. Both strategies have been effective in preserving a distinctive Minangkabau ideology in the face of competing historical forces.

Stories about women like Bundo Kanduang and Putri Bungsu sacralize the moral authority of women in their dealings with men and the political system. Such stories are mythologies in Barthes's (1972:129) sense of myth as a discourse that transforms history into nature by taking events out of the realm of political acts in the here and now and placing them in the realm of the eternal and sacred, where nothing can be questioned or challenged. The story of Bundo Kanduang sacralizes the principles of matriliny and matrifocality in a dramatic format just as *adat* experts sacralize these principles in contemporary rhetoric by equating them with practices of Islam and the teachings of Al-Quran.

Folk historical tales such as the story of the two half-brothers, on the other hand, "historicize" the matrilineal principle of descent. Such tales are deployed to "legalize" the matrilineal rule of inheritance. The legal code laid down by the two half-brothers also included numerous rules codifying a legal and governmental system, which still operates to some extent despite the national governmental forms that are also followed. This code also included lengthy lists of clans that were to be brought into the rule of law. Today, throughout West Sumatra and beyond, village leaders conceive of their origins in terms of the actions of these two men. Thus, what we see here is the codification of an indigenous law and a federated ethnic enclave joined by the observance of this law. By claiming a common name and a common set of founders, the group that came to be known as the Minangkabau no doubt protected villages from being wiped off the ethnic map by immigrant forces.

Thus, in popular tales and contemporary rhetoric, matriliny is associated either with natural law or with a historically situated ideology. The first genre is matrifocal while the second is androcentric. It is difficult to assess the date when these contradictory gender templates first appeared in popular discourse. For the purposes of this paper I am interested in their contemporary value as reference points for expressing Minangkabau ethnic identity at a time when contemporary political forces in Indonesia, particularly modernization and nationalization, undermine indigenous ethnic practices.

For example, the tale of the two half-brothers masks the contemporary powerlessness of Minangkabau men in their titled roles in an era marked by the hegemony of national governmental forms and the demise of traditional forms beyond the level of kin group affairs. On the positive side, the symbolic allegiance to these half-brothers marks and celebrates the distinctiveness of Minangkabau ethnic identity and in doing so puts up a barrier to change. Matrilineal "mythologies," on the other hand, guard matrilineal inheritance from the destructive effects of "sacralized" patrilineal influences contained in Islam. By historicizing and mythologizing matriliny, the Minangkabau propagate *alam Minangkabau*, at least conceptually, in opposition to the political forces that would destroy it. No matter where they live in the world, those who identify with this conceptual world think of themselves as Minangkabau.

Conclusion

Contradictions in Minangkabau gender representations are best explained in terms of the historical preoccupation of these people to consolidate and protect their matrilineal identity in the face of external political and religious threats. Contradictions in the actual expression of male and female power and authority are not so puzzling viewed in the light of the complex history and contradictory gender representations that have been described. In everyday life, as I observed in many villages, there is considerable room for both sexes to maneuver. Moral and jural authority for both men and women is legitimized by *adat* ideology. Although men occupy lineage political roles, women make key economic decisions.[13] Although their realms of authority are separately defined, in fact the sexes influence one another. As F. von Benda-Beckmann notes (1979), a forceful *mamak* or *penghulu* wields considerable influence with his female relatives. But a forceful senior woman has equivalent power.[14] In addition, there is considerable room for manipulating *adat* behind the scenes and to draw on magical power to further particular self-determined goals or to provide direction for others.[15] However, these facts of everyday life are best interpreted as short-term moves, in comparison with the elaborate *adat* ceremonies and proverbs in which the long-term plan of Minangkabau culture unfolds as it is reproduced.

Women play leading roles in the long-term plan. The importance of their role is represented by the meaning of ceremonial food prepared by women according to elaborate *adat* recipes and arranged on plates to represent a harmonious display in all *adat* ceremonies. A plate that is not properly arranged can theoretically bring all ceremonial proceedings to a halt. Ceremonial food concretizes the Minangkabau worldview, providing a model *of* and *for* the value attached to blending all the various ingredients of existence into a harmonious whole in accordance with the recipes codified by *adat*.

In social life the blending and integration occur between geographical areas aligned with *alam Minangkabau* and between the ancient codes of *adat* and the more recent codes of religion. Males and females form inseparable dyads in the working out of this harmony—neither sex becomes an idiom for the oppositions or the status relations that evolved in the complex historical development of the Minangkabau world. Although the inevitable strains of harmony and integration in a complex culture like the Minangkabau are evident in the description of the relationship between such figures as Dang Tuanku and Bundo Kanduang, in the end they also are harmonized in their joint ascent into the seventh heaven.

Neither at the level of general ideology nor at the level of specific context is there any evidence that the categories of male and female are placed in a relationship of negation. The story of Bundo Kanduang shows how the construction of the ideological does not necessarily depend, as Bloch claims (1987:334–35), "on the creation of a nightmarish image of the world, such that . . . the irreversible processes of life—birth, conception, and death—can then be devalued and transcended" (for more on negation see discussion in the volume introduction). The split between the divine and the real created by this story was a split, not along sex lines, but between ideal *adat* practices and the realities of political tensions. To this day the divine threesome still live in the seventh heaven, and all over West Sumatra one occasionally hears stories about their appearance to confer power on blessed individuals, or about individuals who are considered their living descendants. In a village buried in the south of the province of West Sumatra, a group of these reputed living descendants proudly displays three Islamic graves, which they claim to be the final resting place of the divine threesome.

Thus, in the case of the Minangkabau we cannot speak of dialectical progression by negation or antithesis. The dialectical struggle most characteristic of Minangkabau history has been the struggle of the Minangkabau to maintain their unique identity not only as an ethnic enclave in the sea of Indonesian ethnic groups but as a matrilineal people. This struggle has been marked by integration and synthesis, not by opposition and subordination. It is ironic that defining themselves as a "matriarchate" gives Minangkabau male intellectuals what they most need—a specific angle to gain an edge in a larger ideological battle to maintain their uniqueness during a time when modernization and national integration exercise other pulls. It is ironic because by excluding women from their debate there is the danger that these men will drain "vitality" and the "potency" from the role of Bundo Kanduang.

Acknowledgments

I chose the Minangkabau for study in 1981 after completing a cross-cultural study of the sociocultural context of female power, male dominance, and rape (see Sanday 1981a, 1981b). My reasons for moving from cross-cultural research to intensive ethnographic fieldwork in a society like the Minangkabau were several. First, I wanted to study gender questions unmediated by the work of other ethnographers and I wanted face-to-face contact with informants. Second, I wanted to study the worldview and the character of interpersonal relations in a matrifocal and, I assumed, rape-free society, an assumption that was borne out by subsequent research (see Sanday 1986).

This paper has benefited significantly from talks with Minangkabau friends and colleagues and by a longtime association with Suwati Kartiwa. Many of the thoughts presented in this paper come from talks with Ibu Ellie, Ibu Idar, Pak Endri of Belubus, and Pak Sambas of Candung. The writings of Taufik Abdullah and talks with Idrus Hakimy Dt. Rajo Penghulu have significantly formed the overall theoretical approach. Ruth Goodenough and Sandra Barnes read drafts of the paper and helped me clarify my thinking. I am also grateful for the work of Nancy Tanner, which inspired me to go to West Sumatra in 1981. Finally, I wish to thank the Lembaga Ilmu Pengetahuan Indonesia (LIPPI) for granting me permission to engage in fieldwork in West Sumatra.

Notes

1. The discussion is based on fourteen months of research carried out in the province of West Sumatra between 1983 and 1985. In the early stages of fieldwork I learned that the Minangkabau connect matrifocality and concepts of creative power

(in their reverence for women and nature) with the fertility of their environment. Indeed, one informant speculated that the patrilineality of the neighboring Batak was probably due to the historical harshness of the Batak environment. Despite the early support for theoretical propositions developed on the basis of the cross-cultural research I reported elsewhere (see Sanday 1981a), such propositions obscure the important ideological bases for Minangkabau matriliny reported here.

The field research was conducted in selected villages in the Bukit Tinggi, Payakumbuh, and Batu Sangkar areas, the center of traditional Minangkabau culture. I also spent several weeks in the south of the province of West Sumatra observing two important ceremonial occasions in the house complex where Bundo Kanduang is believed to be buried and her descendants still live. In addition to my own fieldnotes, I rely on the work of Minangkabau and Western scholars published in the last decade.

2. A definition of ideology is presented in the introduction to this volume as a system of thought that guides and legitimates social action or attempts to create a transcendental order by legitimating the power of that order. By gender representations, also defined in the introduction, I mean the images, symbols, stories, social discourses, and practices that refer to males or females, the masculine or feminine.

3. Tanner and Thomas (1985:48) refer to Willinck's observation that the oldest common ancestress actually stands above the *mamak*. F. von Benda-Beckmann (1979:82–83) notes that each group must have a leader and this rule finds its expression in the notion of "mamakship," which denotes group leadership and "involves authority over the group members and the representation of the group or the individual group members in inter-group relationships." Mamakship is generally invested in the male sex, but von Benda-Beckmann refers to the work of Korn (1941), who recorded many instances of female *mamaks*. In my fieldwork I also encountered the phenomena of the female *mamak* in some villages.

Prindiville (1985:39) explains the variation in male and female authority in the system of village authority somewhat differently. She focuses on the "role of the procedural element." Looking at decision making as a procedural process, Prindiville lists three procedures that yield different conclusions regarding male and female power and authority. For example, an egalitarian model is suggested by the procedure for *developing* decisions, which necessitates the cooperation of *both sexes*. However, a male dominance model is suggested by the procedure for *affirming* and *validating* decisions, which is the responsibility of *males predominantly*. Finally, a matrifocal model is suggested by the procedure for *implementing* decisions, which is the responsibility mainly of females.

4. In Indonesian the phrase—*Mamak, ibu, adat menjadi satu; tidak bisa berpisa, sama-sama*—was repeated many times, denoting that it was impossible to split males, females, and *adat* because, as one informant said, they were joined as skin and nail to finger. This discussion of the relationship between the sexes applies to lineage and ceremonial affairs. Affairs connecting the village to state or national government functions or officials are handled predominantly by men, a situation that is probably due to the Dutch colonial policy of interacting with men. For example, several authors have noted that in hearing land disputes the Dutch colonial courts insisted that the person claiming to represent the lineage as owner appear in court

represented by the senior *mamak*. This meant that women who often went to court bringing land grievances were not heard because of an unwilling *mamak*. K. von Benda-Beckmann (1984:56), who studied the contemporary state courts, the legacy of the Dutch, notes that the cases of women who came to court every day to sue for the return of a plot of rice land, claiming that it is their ancestral property despite someone else's working it, were never heard.

5. See Sanday and Kartiwa (1984) for a discussion of the relationship between traditional textiles and *adat* philosophy.

6. According to Abdullah, the two main determinant factors in the continuity of the matrilineal system are "Islam as the legitimating value and *rantau* as an outlet as well as a structural solution" (1985:155). An interesting discussion of the contemporary economic forces threatening the stability of the matrilineal inheritance rule can be found in F. von Benda-Beckmann (1979:381).

7. It is interesting to note that this civil war pitted *adat* leaders of one Islamic strain against Islamic leaders of a more militant persuasion who were more concerned about instituting orthodox Islamic practices than with preserving *adat*.

8. The story is very popular. In August 1983 the story was lavishly produced with a cast of nearly 100 in celebration of the opening of the first annual week-long provincial cultural exhibition. This performance, which I attended, had all of the characteristics of an elaborate Broadway musical. I have also seen the story performed in a village in the form of sung narrative drama.

9. The following analysis is based on one version published by A. Dt. Madjoindo in 1951. Dt. Madjoindo was born in 1896 in Supayang, Solok, and educated in the Raja's School in Bukittinggi. He notes in the introduction that he stayed as close as possible to the original text of Cindur Mata, adding to it what he was able to learn from experts of Minangkabau *adat*. He adds, however, that his rendering of the story is a considerably shortened version of the original story and that he has rearranged its composition (A. Dt. Madjoindo 1951:12).

According to Dt. Madjoindo there is hardly a person in West Sumatra who does not know the story, or who has not heard it. Whenever the story is performed (usually in the form of sung narrative drama), the desire to hear it attracts many people. In one village where I paid to have it performed the whole village attended to watch the all-male performance (traditionally men performed dramas because women were not supposed to travel at night to other villages for performances).

10. A count of the number of times Bundo Kanduang initiates action as opposed to acting at someone's request shows that 69 percent of her actions demonstrate her superior authority.

11. De Josselin de Jong says that matrilateral cross-cousin marriage is "the really ideal marriage and the one that underlies the Minangkabau social structure" (see discussion by F. von Benda-Beckmann 1979:299 of this statement and his disagreement with it).

12. It is interesting to note that other versions of the story include further incidents in which the male and female children of Putri Bungsu and Dang Tuanku go back to earth to rule. The male child breaks the *adat* of marriage payment in his marriage to the daughter of the king of Atjeh. He is punished by being forced to surrender the western *rantau* to the king of Atjeh (Abdullah 1970:9).

13. In the capital city of Padang, modernization and nationalization have resulted in a gradual erosion of the female traditional role while the concept of the male *adat* leader has been retained. It must also be noted that in villages more modern sources of power and authority are available to those who participate in the national system of schooling and local government.

14. As I was completing this paper, Laurie Schwede sent me a chapter from her Cornell Ph.D. dissertation (Schwede 1989) surveying authority patterns in two villages near the kingdom with which Bundo Kanduang was associated. According to her survey, in husband-present, nuclear family residences, men and women list the husband as having the most authority over the family group. In most husband-absent residences, the wife lists herself as having the most authority. In the multi-family dwellings there was a higher likelihood for a woman to be listed as the residence group authority figure, regardless of presence or absence of husbands. These results appear to indicate the effect of modernization since in the past, one assumes from numerous sources, multifamily dwellings were the norm. The importance of the husband at the level of ideology needs further investigation. In my research on Minangkabau ideology for this paper, I found that the husband or father was usually relegated to a peripheral role.

15. My experience throughout West Sumatra in many villages was that in addition to the traditional sources of power already discussed, another important source is held by those who are endowed with magical powers. I did not discuss the importance of magical power in this chapter, because magical power is outside of the body of codes found in *adat* and religion. Even so, the relevance of magical power is evident in behavior I have observed in villages and in popular discourse I have mentioned here. For example, Bundo Kanduang's insignia of power include a "magical cloth," a "magical keris," a "magical shield of drums," and other magical objects. Her son, Dang Tunaku, is also described in metaphors alluding to magical powers. My hunch is that magical powers constitute the oldest source of power in Minangkabau, probably dating to the earliest of times. A discussion of the role of magic in supporting the authoritative styles of men and women will be considered in another publication.

Bibliography

Abdullah, Taufik. 1966. "Adat and Islam: An Examination of Conflict in Minangkabau." *Indonesia* 2: 1–24.

———. 1970. "Some Notes on the Kaba Tjindua Mato: An Example of Minangkabau Traditional Literature." *Indonesia* 9: 1–22.

———. 1985. "Islam, History, and Social Change in Minangkabau." In *Change and Continuity in Minangkabau*, Lynn L. Thomas and Franz von Benda-Beckmann, eds., pp. 141–56. Athens, Ohio: Monographs in International Studies Southeast Asia Series Number 71.

Andaya, Leonard. 1975. *The Kingdom of Johor, 1641–1728*. Kuala Lumpur: Oxford University Press.

Barthes, Roland. 1972. *Mythologies*. New York: Hill and Wang.
Benda-Beckmann, F. von. 1979. *Property in Social Continuity*. Verhandelingen van het Koninklijk Instituut voor Taal-, Land- en Volkenkunde 86. The Hague: Martinus Nijhoff.
Benda-Beckmann, K. von. 1984. *The Broken Stairways to Consensus*. Verhandelingen van het Koninklijk Instituut voor Taal-, Land- en Volkenkunde. Dordrecht-Holland: Foris Publications.
Benda-Beckmann, K. von, and F. von Benda-Beckmann. 1985. "Transformation and Change in Minangkabau." In *Change and Continuity in Minangkabau*, Lynn L. Thomas and Franz von Benda-Beckmann, eds., pp. 235–78. Athens, Ohio: Monographs in International Studies Southeast Asia Series Number 71.
Bloch, Maurice. 1987. "Descent and Sources of Contradiction in Representations of Women and Kinship." In *Gender and Kinship*, Jane F. Collier and Sylvia J. Yanagisako, eds., pp. 324–40. Stanford: Stanford University Press.
Hakimy, H. I., Dt. Rajo Penghulu. 1984. *1000 Pepatah-Petitih Mamang-Bidal Pantun-Gurindam*. Bandung: Remadja Karya CV.
Jordanova, L. J. 1980. "Natural Facts: A Historical Perspective on Science and Sexuality." In *Nature, Culture and Gender*, Carol MacCormack and Marilyn Strathern, eds., pp. 42–69. Cambridge: Cambridge University Press.
Kato, Tsuyoshi. 1982. *Matriliny and Migration*. Ithaca: Cornell University Press.
Korn, V. E. 1941. "De vrouwelijke mama' in de Minangkabausche familie." *Bijdragen tot de Taal-, Land-, en Volkenkunde* 100: 301–38.
Madjoindo, A. Dt. 1951. *Cindur Mata*. Jakarta: Balai Pustaka.
Manggis, M. Rasjid, Dt. Radjo Panghoeloe. 1982. *Minangkabau*. Jakarta: Mutiara.
Nasroen, M. 1957[1971]. *Dasar Falsafah Adat Minangkabau*. Djakarta: Bulan Bintang.
Prindiville, Joanne. 1985. "Mother, Mother's Brother, and Modernization." In *Change and Continuity in Minangkabau*, Lynn L. Thomas and Franz von Benda-Beckmann, eds., pp. 29–44. Athens, Ohio: Monographs in International Studies Southeast Asia Series Number 71.
Sanday, Peggy Reeves. 1981a. *Female Power and Male Dominance*. New York: Cambridge University Press.
———. 1981b. "The Socio-Cultural Context of Rape." *Journal of Social Issues* 37: 5–27.
———. 1986. "Rape and the Silencing of the Feminine." In *Rape: A Collection of Essays*, Roy Porter and Sylvana Tomaselli, eds., pp. 84–101. London: Basil Blackwell.
Sanday, Peggy Reeves, and Suwati Kartiwa. 1984. "Cloth and Custom in West Sumatra." *Expedition* 26: 13–29.
Schwede, Laurie. 1989. *Family Strategies of Labor Allocation and Decision Making in a Matrilineal, Islamic Society*. Ph.D. diss., Cornell University, Ithaca.
Tanner, Nancy. 1974. "Matrifocality in Indonesia and Africa and Among Black Americans." In *Women, Culture and Society*, M. Rosaldo and L. Lamphere, eds., pp. 129–56. Palo Alto: Stanford University Press.
———. 1982. "The Nuclear Family in Minangkabau Matriliny: Mirror of Disputes." *Bijdragen tot de Taal-, Land-, en Volkenkunde*, 1138 (13): 129–51.

Tanner, Nancy, and Lynn L. Thomas. 1985. "Rethinking Matriliny." In *Change and Continuity in Minangkabau,* Lynn L. Thomas and Franz von Benda-Beckmann, eds., pp. 45–72. Athens, Ohio: Monographs in International Studies Southeast Asia Series Number 71.

The people of Vanatinai occupy a large island 225 miles southeast of mainland New Guinea. As Maria Lepowsky describes the culture of this previously unstudied group, a markedly egalitarian ethos is evident. Beginning at birth, when girl and boy infants are welcomed equally, by both men and women, and continuing throughout the life cycle, the Islanders exhibit a respect for individuals regardless of age or sex.

Among these people there is no ethic of male dominance. The activities of women and men are held to be equally valuable, and there is considerable overlap in what they do. This holds true not only in the ordinary details of daily life but for the most important arena where personal prestige and influence over others is acquired, namely, in traditional exchange relationships and in the mortuary ritual context.

Other aspects of the culture are consonant with this overriding egalitarian ethos. Both men and women have access to supernatural power through communication with ancestor spirits, for example, and both are privy to the same magical lore. There is no ideology requiring male separatism or initiation rites, or one of female pollution. If they earn the respect of others, women as well as men may be referred to as strong, wise, or generous.

Lepowsky describes in some detail the social system, the elaborate exchange system, and the child-rearing practices that mesh with this overall ethic of egalitarianism. In doing so she presents a picture that challenges the concept of the universality of male dominance and the idea that the subjugation of women is inevitable in human societies. A final section of the chapter deals with the impact of recent contacts, including missionary activity, pacification, and central governance on the egalitarian ethos of these people.

Maria Lepowsky

7 Gender in an Egalitarian Society: A Case Study from the Coral Sea

Male dominance has been described as universal in human societies by many influential writers on gender, sex roles, and the status of women in cross-cultural perspective (for example, Beauvoir 1953; Rosaldo 1974, 1980; Ortner 1974; Ortner and Whitehead 1981). Such a universality implies that female subordination either results directly from human biology or is inherent in human cultures due to the constraints of human biology, and therefore perhaps unchangeable.

The independent nation of Papua New Guinea, the eastern half of the island of New Guinea, contains over 700 different linguistic and cultural groups. They, and other Melanesian societies, have frequently been described by anthropologists as egalitarian because almost all lack chiefs, nobles, or systems of ascribed rank, unlike the societies of the Polynesian culture area to the east. But, without specifying that they were writing about only half the society being observed, most anthropologists have described egalitarian social relations among men and not between men and women. Many of the cultures in the interior of New Guinea are well known for their strong ideologies of male dominance and beliefs in the polluting qualities of women (for example, Meggitt 1964; Brown and Buchbinder 1976; Poole 1981; Meigs, this volume). Yet New Guinea is also known for the great diversity of gender role patterns found in its many distinctive cultures (for example, Mead 1935).

Vanatinai, a small, remote island southeast of the main island of New Guinea, has its own language and culture and had never previously been studied by an anthropologist. Vanatinai is a sexually egalitarian society. There is no ethic of male dominance, the roles and activities of women and men overlap considerably, and the actions of both sexes are considered equally valuable. This overlap extends to the most important arena for the acquisition of personal prestige and influence over others, the traditional exchange and the mortuary ritual complex, in which both women and men participate. Both sexes have access to supernatural power through communication with ancestor spirits, who are believed to be the basis of all human prosperity, good fortune, and health. The prominent position of women in the island's social life is reflected in local gender ideology and myth.

This chapter focuses on the relationship between gender roles and cultural ideology in a sexually egalitarian society, placing both in the context of overall social relations. I will examine the roles and activities of women and men on Vanatinai in various aspects of social life, comparing them with local gender ideology and symbolism and with constructions of gender in island mythology. I will apply a variety of arguments and hypotheses about male dominance and gender equality to Vanatinai to see if, by their specific criteria, the island is an ethnographic example of an egalitarian, or a non–male-dominant, society and whether their predictions about gender roles and ideology hold for the Vanatinai case. I will also discuss the implications of the existence of egalitarian societies for the study of gender roles and ideology in cross-cultural perspective and for change in gender relations in societies that are not egalitarian.

Schlegel (this volume) distinguishes between a culture's "general," abstract gender ideology and its multiplicity of "specific" gender meanings defined through their location within social structure or "field of action." She points out that in human societies general versus specific meanings of maleness and femaleness, as well as different situationally distinct specific gender definitions, frequently seem to contradict each other. On Vanatinai both the general, most abstract forms of gender ideology and the great majority of specific gender meanings derived from everyday and ritual life are congruent, reflecting an ethic of egalitarian relations between women and men and among all individuals.

The Vanatinai case challenges the concept of the universality of male dominance and the idea that the subjugation of women is inevitable in human societies. Definitions of male dominance vary greatly, and assessments of its universality sometimes vary according to which criteria are used to define it (for example, Sanday 1981:163–79). Some authors refer primarily to the differential access of men versus women to prestigious activities and therefore to power over others (for example, Friedl 1975:164; Ortner and Whitehead 1981). Others focus on control of key resources or means of production (for example, Sacks 1974; Leacock 1978:252). Rosaldo (1980) discusses the universality of "sexual asymmetry." Divale and Harris (1976) highlight social structural asymmetries in kinship, marriage, and

Gender in an Egalitarian Society   173

residence systems, the sexual division of labor, and leadership roles. They see institutionalized warfare and a corollary cultural emphasis on male aggression as the primary cause of the "male supremacist complex." Similarly, Meigs (this volume) relates the "chauvinistic" ideology of Hua men to the male role as warriors. Sanday's (1981:164) definition of male dominance stresses "exclusion of women from political and economic decision making" and male aggression against women, measured by expectations of male aggressive personality traits, men's houses, wife abuse, institutionalized or regular occurrence of rape, and raiding other groups for wives. Ortner (1974) suggests that women are associated with nature and men with "the high ground of culture" in the gender symbolism of all human societies and that women are therefore universally devalued (compare Beauvoir 1953; Lévi-Strauss 1969a). Rosaldo and Atkinson (1975) see as a cultural universal the symbolic opposition of woman the life-giver and man the life-taker, related to the woman/nature to man/culture opposition, which in all cultures indicates asymmetry in the status of women versus men.

Vanatinai women have access to economically and ritually essential and prestigious activities and thus to power over others, equal access to resources, the advantages of matriliny and bilocal residence, a largely overlapping sexual division of labor, and access to the society's most significant "leadership role," that of *gia*, literally "giver," or "big man/big woman." There are no men's houses, respect for the warrior is focused on his ability to defend the community rather than to attack others, and rape and wife abuse are extremely rare and strongly disapproved. Gender ideology and mythology associate women as well as men with key domains of culture. Women are explicitly said to give life while men kill, which is the rationale for why women do not kill enemies in war, practice sorcery, or hunt with spears. Life-giving is also explicitly said in this context to be "more important" than killing. But women actually participated in decisions to make war or seek peace, accompanied brothers onto the field of battle, and knew important war magic. They also do occasionally learn and practice sorcery and are sometimes said to possess the destructive power of witchcraft. Finally, women do hunt: they just do not hunt with spears. Different levels of Vanatinai gender ideology and practice are here contradictory, but the overlap of male and female domains and the high value placed on female powers and activities are clear.

Few anthropologists have attempted to define or characterize sexual equality (compare Atkinson 1982; Strathern 1987). Leacock (1978:247) sees women as "autonomous in egalitarian society" because they hold "decision-making power over their own lives and activities to the same extent that men did over theirs." Lamphere (1977:613) focuses on control of others, stating that in a "situation of sexual equality . . . all men and women . . . could and actually did make decisions over the same range of partners and people, that is, exercise the same kinds of control." She also cites and criticizes what she calls the "complementary but equal" argument suggested by Schlegel for the Hopi and Briggs for the Inuit, where males and females control different, but not larger, spheres consisting of "their persons, property, or activities" (Lamphere 1977:616). Sanday (1981: 170) points out that these definitions of equality may refer to either "sameness" or "interdependence and balance" and suggests using the term sexual symmetry. Her definition of sexual equality is the converse of her definition of male dominance: it is when "males do not display aggression against women and women exercise political and economic authority or power" (Sanday 1981:165). Etienne and Leacock (1980:9) discuss societies with "egalitarian relations of production," where the division of labor is entirely by sex, the sexes reciprocally exchange goods and services, and all adults participate directly and equally in production, distribution, and consumption, having equal access to resources. The Vanatinai case meets the criteria of all of these definitions of an egalitarian society.

There are significant differences in status and prestige among individuals on Vanatinai, despite the island's egalitarian ideology. These are mutable, and they fluctuate over the lifetime of the individual. But Vanatinai society is egalitarian in that at specific stages in the life cycle, females and males have equivalent autonomy and control over their own actions, equal opportunity to achieve both publicly and privately acknowledged influence and power over the actions of others, and equivalent access to valued goods, wealth, and prestige. Its gender ideology stresses that both women and men should strive to be strong, wise, and generous, and the highly valued quality of generosity is explicitly modeled after parental nurture. Women are not viewed as polluting or dangerous to themselves or others in their persons, bodily fluids, or sexuality.

Vanatinai, which means both "motherland" and "mainland," is the indigenous name for the island which is usually called Sudest or Tagula on maps and charts. At 50 miles long by about 8 to 15 miles wide, it is the largest piece of land for over 200 miles and the largest island in the Louisiade Archipelago, a chain of islands that separates the Solomon Sea from the Coral Sea. Vanatinai belongs to what scholars since the late nineteenth

Gender in an Egalitarian Society   175

century have referred to as the Massim culture area (for example, Hamy 1888; Haddon 1894; Seligman 1909, 1910). The most famous portion of the Massim to the outside world is the Trobriand Islands, whose culture was described as it appeared seventy years ago in the extensive writings of Bronislaw Malinowski, probably the single most influential individual in shaping modern anthropology. Vanatinai lies about 300 miles southeast of the Trobriand Islands and about 225 miles southeast of the New Guinea mainland.

A "high status of women" has been described as a diagnostic feature of the Massim culture area by Malinowski (1929:28), Fortune (1963:257), and other writers (Haddon 1894:255; Armstrong 1928:100; Young 1971:54; Chowning 1973:30). But before the 1970s and the restudy by Annette Weiner (1976) of the Trobriand Islands, no ethnographer had offered any systematic description of what this "high status" consists of or an analysis of the relative positions of men and women in any Massim society as related to other significant aspects of social organization. Malinowski himself, who once issued a criticism of ethnographers who repeat without documentation "generalities and stock phrases such as that . . . 'the status of the wife is high'" (1962:18), is the only partial exception. In *The Sexual Life of Savages in North-Western Melanesia,* he includes a brief chapter titled "The Status of Women in Native Society," in which he discusses the position of women in the descent group, the customs applying to women of rank, and "women's share in magic" and in ceremonial activities among the Trobriand Islanders of the northern Massim (1929:28–49).

The research on which this chapter is based was designed to determine the range of roles and behavior deemed culturally appropriate for women and men throughout the life cycle of the individual on an island in the southern Massim region whose culture had never before been described. The research also was intended to relate local notions of gender-appropriate behavior to cultural ideology and to economic, political, and religious life, particularly to traditional interisland exchanges of ceremonial valuables and other goods.

During my residence on Vanatinai in 1978–79, I learned not only that women figure prominently in traditional exchange activities but that they also participate in the same arena of exchange as men, exchange with both men and women, and compete with men to acquire the same ceremonial valuables. In the Trobriands and on other Massim islands such as Panaeati (Berde 1974), women have their own separate domain of exchange, in both cases a major part of the essential series of mortuary ritual events following the death of each individual, and women have their own valuables—skirts and yams, respectively—which they generate by their own labor. On Vanatinai the exchange activities of women are largely integrated with those of men. Women participate alongside men in all of the many types of intra- and interisland exchanges practiced on Vanatinai. Individual women as well as men may gain area-wide prestige and renown for their success in accumulating valuables such as shell-disk necklaces, greenstone axeblades, shell currency pieces, and pigs, and in giving them away to other men and women in public acts of ritual generosity (Lepowsky 1981, 1983, 1989a).

The exchange activities in which both sexes participate on Vanatinai are the local equivalent of *kula*, the famous form of traditional exchange where shell-disk necklaces circulate clockwise among island groups while armshells circulate counterclockwise, documented by Malinowski (1922) based upon his residence in the Trobriand Islands. The *kula* in the Trobriands is described by Malinowski and by Weiner (1976) as an exclusively male activity, although the participation by women in *kula* exchanges has been reported for Kitava Island in the northern Massim (Damon 1980: 275) and for Normanby Island (Roheim 1950:184) and Tubetube Island (Macintyre 1987:210) in the southern Massim. Young women from Gawa Island in the northern Massim sometimes accompany their fathers on *kula* voyages without participating directly in exchanges (Munn 1986).

Exchanges on Vanatinai that involve the same shell-disk necklaces and greenstone axeblades that circulate in the *kula* region to the northwest as well as other valuables (armshells are not used in the Vanatinai region) are the island's most important means of acquiring prestige and influence over others. Women's freedom to enter into these most important and prestigious areas of public life on the island is a significant indicator of the sexually egalitarian nature of Vanatinai society.

The participation of women in traditional exchange activities has rarely been stressed in the ethnographic literature, but the Trobriand example suggests that women's exchange activities may in some cases have been underreported by anthropologists. Furthermore, the ethnographic evidence for women's exchange activities that does exist has been largely overlooked in analyses of social organization.[1] The traditional exchange activities performed by women in many societies clearly belong to the "public" rather than the "domestic" domain. Various authors have suggested either that there is a universal sexual asymmetry in the tendency for men to be prominent in the public domain while women's roles are largely domestic, or that the exclusion of women from public activities and their restriction to the domestic domain is strongly correlated with women's lower status relative to men in specific societies (Rosaldo 1974; Sanday 1973, 1974; Hammond and Jablow 1973; Sacks 1974; Bacdayan 1977; Leacock 1978).

Ortner and Whitehead (1981) argue that the significance of the public domain for understanding the cultural construction of gender is that it is dominated by men and that it is the locus of a culture's prestige structures. They suggest that "cultural notions of the genders and sexuality will vary from culture to culture in accordance with the way in which women, the woman-dominated domestic sphere, and cross-sex relations in general are organized into the base that supports the larger (male) prestige system" (Ortner and Whitehead 1981:19). The principal Vanatinai prestige system is the traditional exchange and mortuary ritual complex, but it is not restricted to men. Participation of island women in this and other arenas of prestige such as ritual expertise, production of garden surpluses, and the rearing of healthy and hard-working young matrilineage members (a primary concern of both men and women) shapes and is shaped by egalitarian Vanatinai gender constructions, as Ortner and Whitehead predict. The prominent positions of women in Vanatinai exchange and other extradomestic activities then should reflect generally egalitarian relations between women and men in Vanatinai culture according to the argument that women's exclusion from the public domain, a culture's locus of power and prestige, is related to women's lower status relative to men.

Gender and Social Structure

I suggest that societies that are sexually egalitarian tend to place little emphasis on other forms of social stratification such as class, rank, or age-grading (compare Leacock 1978; Etienne and Leacock 1980). Holding regional cultural ideologies of interpersonal relations constant, non–gender-based forms of stratification are more likely to arise in societies with dense populations. Thus some, but not all, small-scale foraging and horticultural societies are among the most socially and sexually egalitarian societies in the world. Vanatinai has only four persons per square mile of territory. Unlike the densely settled Trobriand Islands, also part of the Massim culture area, Vanatinai has no chiefs or other categories of ascribed rank and no division of lineages into noble and commoner.

Vanatinai and the rest of the Massim are unusual in Melanesia in having no men's houses, no male cult activities, and no initiation ceremonies for either males or females (compare Allen 1967). The institution of the men's house, where adult men either sleep apart from their wives and children or congregate regularly, limits women's participation in political, economic, and ritual life in much of Melanesia. The men's house, male initiation, and male cult activities concentrate both power over others and social prestige in the hands of adult males, and they group women, boys, and young children in a subordinate social position.

Characterizing Vanatinai society as egalitarian does not imply that there are no status differences among individuals on the island. Some islanders hold more rights to land, food trees, and reef areas than others, and some inherit more ceremonial valuables, pigs, and potential exchange partners from maternal kin or fathers. Some have more kin and more affines who can potentially offer aid, while others are disadvantaged in accruing prestige by chronic poor health. Morauta (1981) correctly points out that status inequalities in lowland Papua New Guinea societies have often been underreported by ethnographers.

Nevertheless, Vanatinai society has an egalitarian ethic. It offers every adult, regardless of sex or kin group, the opportunity of excelling at prestigious activities such as participation in traditional exchange or ritual functions essential to health and prosperity. With hard work and the appropriate magical knowledge, anyone may achieve the gender-blind title of *gia*, or "giver," and this status is not limited to one individual per hamlet or even per household. The result is a continuous competition for status and influence involving a large number of men and women who choose to make the extra effort necessary to acquire prestige among a wide group of peers. This state of competition and flux is inevitable precisely because Vanatinai society is egalitarian and without ascribed positions of status.

The low population density of Vanatinai largely negates the advantage that people with rights to more land hold over others, since the right to garden, hunt, fish, and make sago on particular tracts of land is always granted by the owners to their neighbors within the same district of the island. If population density were to reach the same alarming level as on Kiriwina in the Trobriand Islands, rights of ownership and usufruct of fertile garden lands, the fundamental basis of wealth and surplus on the high islands of the Massim, would probably be far more tightly controlled, with owners receiving formal tribute and perhaps even evolving into a chiefly or "noble" class.[2]

A low population density probably also contributes to an ethic of respect

Gender in an Egalitarian Society   179

for the individual, since if a serious conflict arises, one party has the option of moving to another location. This describes the Vanatinai situation. Since a hamlet will dissolve if its population drops, due to conflict, sorcery accusations, and resulting migration, below a certain minimum necessary to carry out subsistence tasks (which has happened on Vanatinai), individuals must learn to tolerate each other's idiosyncrasies of behavior and outlook or go their separate ways. The notion of individual autonomy, along with the idea that individuals vary greatly in their personalities and temperaments, is a key aspect of Vanatinai cultural ideology. The most common explanation for markedly unusual behavior is a flat and nonjudgmental statement, "She or he wants to/doesn't want to," or, "It is her or his way." There is a wide latitude of normal or acceptable behavior. The most significant means for regulating individual behavior, the fear of arousing anger or jealousy in a sorcerer or witch or of violating a taboo attached to a particular place by its guardian spirit, is based on an ideology of individual supernatural power rather than on a social body such as a council of elders.

Sanday (1973) suggests that the status of women is higher in societies where the domestic and the public spheres of activity are overlapping, and Schlegel (1977:9) proposes that "if the household is a central institution (women's) impact on major societal decisions may be very great" (compare Leacock 1978:147). Small-scale societies, where the community is composed largely of people related by ties of kinship and affinity, are likely to be centered around the household, and the distinction between domestic and public action will be blurred. This is the situation in the hamlets of Vanatinai.

In a small population where kin and fictive kin groups largely overlap the community of coresidents, as on Vanatinai, the opinions of women and young people are voiced in public debate. Key decisions affecting the lives and well-being of community members are made locally and as needed. Political authority is not delegated to a restricted number of adult male representatives who convene formally in a distant place for efficiency of communication and social control as in a large-scale society. Children, old people, and women are all more likely to be respected as individuals in a small-scale society, even though the predominant ideologies of social relations may hold women and children inferior to men and elders.

Descent on Vanatinai is matrilineal. A society that traces descent through women does not necessarily accord women a high status (compare Richards 1950; Schneider and Gough 1961; Schlegel 1972). But societies where women own and inherit land, may live with their own kin after marriage, and not only produce but allocate culturally valued resources, controlling their distribution beyond the household, tend to treat men and women more equally (Brown 1970a; Hammond and Jablow 1973; Sanday 1974; Friedl 1975). These conditions, more likely in a matrilineal society due to its typical structures of inheritance, residence, and economic organization, characterize Vanatinai society and ensure the prominence of women in all aspects of island life.

Vanatinai women inherit land, pigs, and ceremonial valuables from their mothers, their mothers' brothers, and sometimes from their fathers equally with men. They control the land and valuables they inherit or possess just as men do. They, along with men, produce staple garden foods, such as yams, sweet potato, and taro, and raise pigs. They have ultimate jurisdiction over the distribution of the fruits of their labors. Women are said to be the "owners" or "bosses" (*tanuwagaji*) of the gardens, although men, too, spend much of their time working in gardens. It is the women of the hamlet who must decide whether in a particular year there is a sufficient surplus of garden produce to exchange with outsiders for other goods, such as clay cooking pots or pandanus-leaf sleeping mats, or to host a major feast to commemorate a death.

"Wife-centered" postmarital residence has been suggested as a key variable that positively affects the status of women (Richards 1950; Ember and Ember 1971; Schlegel 1972; Divale and Harris 1976). The postmarital rule on Vanatinai is bilocal residence. A similar pattern was reported by Fortune (1963) for Dobu Island, also part of the Massim culture area, where couples reside in alternate years with the lineage mates of each spouse. The ideal arrangement on Vanatinai is for a married couple to reside alternately during the year in the natal hamlet of the wife and that of the husband, making gardens on the matrilineage lands of both spouses and assisting the kin of each with subsistence tasks. Each spouse has equivalent rights and obligations when living with affines. A newly married couple resides with the wife's parents for at least several months, and the husband is supposed to "work for his mother-in-law."[3] Some longer-married couples may choose to reside permanently or most of the time with the kin of either spouse depending on their personal preference, but even so active ties are maintained with the hamlet of the other spouse through visits for subsistence and social purposes.

The shift between residing with the kin of the wife and the kin of the husband allows each spouse the security of living with relatives for at least part of every year. Neither one is expected to give up the opportunity to participate in the important decisions of the natal kin group, and neither spouse, by virtue of absence, loses the right to use garden land, food trees, and territory belonging to the matrilineage. By living alternately with kin and affine, each spouse is in a good position to cultivate or maintain personal exchange ties with individuals belonging to both groups.

Vanatinai social structure is egalitarian overall in having no chiefs, no system of ranking, no delegation of political authority, and no fixed role specialization beyond the sexual division of labor. Its small scale and low population density promote respect for individual autonomy. Matrilineal descent and inheritance and bilocal postmarital residence provide both women and men with access to and control over land and goods and with the opportunity to activate equivalent ties of kinship and affinity. Vanatinai women and men both see women as autonomous beings who perform a constellation of culturally valued activities.

The Sexual Division of Labor

The sexual division of labor on Vanatinai features a marked overlap between the tasks considered appropriate for men and for women. Sanday (1974) hypothesizes that where men and women contribute equally to subsistence, women's status will be higher, and she suggests that the mingling of the sexes in the tasks of daily life works against the rise of male dominance (1981). Similarly, Bacdayan (1977) sees "task interchangeability" between the sexes as an important correlate of a high status of women in a particular society. Both Vanatinai women and men tend and harvest yams (the most highly valued cultigen), sweet potato, taro, manioc, banana, and other garden crops, and individuals of both sexes know various forms of garden magic, including the magic used in the annual yam-planting ritual. By contrast the analogous magic for growing yams is known only to men in the Trobriand Islands (Malinowski 1935).[4]

Vanatinai men cut tall forest trees to clear land for new gardens, but the work party is comprised of men and women, and the women cut the smaller trees and shrubs and supervise the burning of the forest cover. Men normally loosen the soil to form mounds for planting yams using eight-foot digging sticks, but I have observed women performing this task. Women generally do the actual preparation and planting of seed yams. Men cut sago palms and do most of the pounding of the sago pith to extract the starch, which is a major dietary staple, but again the work party is usually mixed, and women supervise the drying of cakes of sago starch over a low fire. Both women and men forage for a wide variety of wild nuts, legumes, tubers, fruits, and leaves in the rainforest, although women generally spend more time at this task than most men.

Hunting with spears for wild pigs and crocodiles is a male monopoly, as is using spears to hunt dugongs or to fish. But Vanatinai women hunt game such as possum and fruit bats by climbing forest trees or tall coconut trees to sneak up on the slow-moving nocturnal creatures. They also hunt monitor lizards, which grow to four feet in length, by climbing tall mangrove trees or by setting traps for them. Female hunting is relatively rare, but it has been reported among foragers and horticulturalists in various parts of the world, such as Australian aborigines of the Kimberleys and of Melville Island (Kaberry 1939; Goodale 1971), the Agta of the Philippines (Estioko-Griffin and Griffin 1981, 1985), and the Ojibwa, Montagnais-Naskapi, and Rock Cree of Canada (Landes 1938; Leacock 1978; Brightman n.d.).

In many parts of the Pacific, women are not supposed to climb trees, but on Vanatinai women climb not only to hunt but to obtain coconuts or betel nuts. Women fish using a fishing line or derris root, a fish poison. Formerly both sexes fished using nets woven by men of the fibrous aerial root of the wild pandanus palm. Both women and men gather shellfish in streams and along the fringing reef. Both dive in the lagoon for giant Tridacna clams. More rarely women dive for the blacklip or goldlip pearlshell, which may be sold to traders, or for the red-rimmed oyster-like shells, which are made by both men and women into the shell-disk necklaces that circulate throughout the Louisiade Archipelago and the *kula* ring as far as the Trobriand Islands.

Killing human beings with spears or greenstone axes was a former monopoly of men as well. But Vanatinai mothers and sisters accompanied the warriors, carrying spears and retrieving the wounded from the field of battle. They also gave the signal both to begin an attack and to make peace, which in both cases was to remove their outer coconut-leaf skirt and wave it or put it on the ground. It is said, for example, that if a sister wished to stop her brother from killing someone, she took off her outer skirt and threw it before him. If he then threw his spear at his enemy, he would symbolically be committing an act of incest and would therefore be "ashamed" to attack. This explanation also reveals the phallic association of the spear, another reason why women should not use it.

Men do most of the work of building houses. Women participate by collecting sago leaves for roofing and by weaving sago leaves for one type of wall. They must also provide the builders with cooked food. Men make outrigger paddling canoes and, more rarely, sailing canoes, but both men and women paddle and sail them. Although men more frequently crew sailing canoes, some women are expert sailors.

Men carve ceremonial axehandles and limesticks of wood and delicate tortoiseshell limesticks. Both men and women may manufacture shell-disk necklaces. Women weave pandanus sleeping mats, fine coconut-leaf betelnut baskets, and coconut-leaf skirts. All these items circulate in interisland exchange and during mortuary feasts.

Daily cooking, washing, fetching water and firewood, and sweeping are primarily female tasks, but men occasionally perform each of them. Men and women both fetch water and firewood and cook during feasts and other communal occasions, such as roofing or yam planting. Men butcher and boil pork, scrape coconut meat, and prepare the boiled sago and green coconut pudding. Women prepare the stone oven for roasting vegetable food.

The care of young children is primarily the responsibility of women. But men are frequently seen carrying around their offspring or maternal nieces or nephews and take older boys and girls with them to the garden for the day. People say that the reason why a father's matrilineal kin must be compensated with valuables when one dies is that the deceased excreted on the father as an infant and the father cleaned it up uncomplainingly.[5]

One man active in exchange activities was almost always accompanied by his nine-year-old daughter, who had already sailed around Vanatinai three times with him to look for valuables or attend feasts. Many adults have never seen the opposite end of the island.

In 1978–79 less than half of island children, boys and girls in equal number, attended the small, mission-run primary boarding schools, and most of these left school after a few years. Boys as well as girls are drafted as babysitters of younger siblings, although girls spend more time at this task.

Either a man or a woman may be a hamlet leader (*tanokau* if male and *yola* if female), an informal position of authority on matters of subsistence or custom. This person is usually the one who leads the hamlet's yam-planting ritual.

Both men and women learn and practice most forms of magic, which are based upon communication with ancestor spirits and other supernatural beings, upon whose goodwill all human prosperity, good fortune, and health are believed dependent. Magical practice in many cases might better be described as a religious act consisting of a prayer or petition to the ancestors. Both sexes know garden magic and the magic for finding wild food in the forest or an abundance of sago starch in a particular palm. Both know healing magic and a vast array of plant substances used in curing, the magic of exchange, war, fishing, and hunting, although a few types of hunting magic are restricted to men. Weather magic, the ability to make rain or wind or to end them, is restricted to a few men. Both women and men know love magic and the magic said to make one invisible. Sorcery is almost always practiced by men. A few women have been adept, but they dressed in the male traditional dress, an incised strip of woven pandanus leaf drawn between the legs and held up by a cord around the hips, when they practiced their nefarious trade. The islanders say that sorcery became more prevalent after the cessation of warfare, stating that, "Before we killed with spears, but now we kill with sorcery." The association with warfare may explain why sorcery is virtually a male monopoly. Witchcraft, on the other hand, is usually practiced by women, although some men too have learned it (see below). Women and men both know the magic of counter-sorcery.[6]

The sexual division of labor on Vanatinai meets criteria predicted for an egalitarian society by featuring a large degree of overlap and of complementarity between the roles and activities of women versus men, female control of valued commodities, and participation by women in prestigious activities in the public domain. It enables women to participate in publicly recognized ways in political, economic, and ritual decision making. In combination with an ethic of respect for individual autonomy, it also facilitates differences in people's activities. Individual women and men vary in the kinds of work they find congenial or distasteful and are therefore likely to do on a daily or seasonal basis.

Women and Traditional Exchange on Vanatinai

I once asked an elderly woman, then in poor health and spending her days sitting by the fire in her son's house, if she had ever been on a trading expedition, or *ghiva,* in quest of ceremonial valuables. She drew herself up proudly and answered, "Yes, I have traded" (*Aghiva*). Her father had died when she was a young married woman with children, she explained. She had dressed herself in the long mourning skirt of coarsely cut, dried coconut leaves and covered her face and body with the black mourning pigment of burnt coconut husk. Then she had set off by outrigger sailing canoe around the island of Vanatinai to the north coast to ask her trading partners for the shell-disk necklaces, axeblades of polished greenstone, huge tusked pigs, and other forms of wealth that are necessary for holding the great feast that commemorates a death and releases survivors from their mourning taboos. She had returned with large quantities of valuables. "Did your husband come with you?" I asked. "*Imuyai*," she replied, "He accompanied me," or literally, "He followed me."

Every adult on Vanatinai, both male and female, is expected to contribute valuables to the series of elaborate feasts that are held after the death of each individual. The pressure to host a feast, or to contribute extensively to a feast, is greatest at the death of a kinsperson, a father, or a close affine. The bulk of the wealth contributed is given in a public ritual, the *mwagumwagu*, to the matrilineal heir of the deceased's father, the patrilateral cross-cousin of the deceased (Lepowsky 1989a). This heir may be a woman or a man and is someone who has had a special exchange relationship with the deceased during life. The gender of the deceased's heir and mortuary feast hosts bears no relation to whether the dead individual was male or female.

In order to hold a feast, the hosts must accumulate large quantities of yams, sago starch and other vegetable foods, pigs, and ceremonial valuables such as shell-disk necklaces (*bagi*), greenstone axeblades (*tobotobo*), orange shell currency pieces (*daveri*), and ceremonial lime spatulas of carved tortoiseshell and tropical hardwood (*wonamo jilevia* and *ghenaga*). These ceremonial valuables are known collectively as *ghune*, a cognate of the term *kula*, made famous by Malinowski (1922) as the system of exchange linking the Trobriand Islands with other islands stretching to the south and east as far as the northern Louisiade Archipelago. Many of the same types of valuables and, in fact, the same individual necklaces and greenstone axeblades, circulate from Vanatinai to the Trobriand Islands, three hundred miles to the northwest. The shell-disk necklaces are manufactured, by both sexes, on Vanatinai and the neighboring islands of the East Calvados Chain to the northwest and by men only on the non-Massim island of Rossel to the northeast. They travel by traditional exchange links from these southeastern islands to the "Kula Ring" islands to the northwest.

But the rules of exchange differ on Vanatinai and the neighboring East Calvados region. In the "Kula Ring," shell-disk necklaces are passed by individual trading partners in a clockwise direction among the islands, while armlets of decorated Conus shell are circulated in a counterclockwise direction. Armshells are not exchanged on Vanatinai and neighboring islands, and there is no "ring" pattern to the exchange of valuables in the Louisiade Archipelago. Instead, both women and men have large numbers of overlapping personal exchange networks composed of men and women, kin, affines, and unrelated exchange partners.

The primary stimulus to an exchange journey is the obligation to provide valuables to an upcoming mortuary feast and thereby increase one's own personal prestige and reputation for generosity as well as that of one's matrilineage. On Vanatinai both women and men who have many exchange partners, possess substantial amounts of ceremonial valuables, and have hosted or contributed generously to many feasts are known as *giagia*, or "givers."

A person who is active in exchange activities or known to have accumulated ceremonial valuables will receive a large number of requests for contributions of valuables so that an exchange partner may satisfy a personal or ceremonial obligation. The persistent pressure to redistribute valuables is a leveling mechanism that keeps a class of especially wealthy individuals from arising. The giver is rewarded by her or his growing reputation for generosity, by having a large network of individuals indebted to her or him to be asked for labor or goods as needed in future, and by a reputation for wisdom and influence over the lives of others.

The degree to which an individual chooses to exceed the minimum demands of custom in hosting or contributing food and valuables at feasts and thereby increase her or his reputation for wealth and generosity is dependent upon individual personality rather than gender. There are more men than women who are extremely active in exchange, as women in early and middle adulthood tend to be more focused on child care and garden supervision. But there are some women who own more ceremonial valuables and more pigs and who give them away at memorial feasts far more than the majority of men. This difference among individuals is ascribed by Vanatinai people to differences in individual personality and desires. Both men and women are most likely to leave home in search of valuables after the death of father or affine or to assist a close associate with exchange obligations resulting from a death.

Hosting mortuary feasts is normally the responsibility of the surviving spouse. Women as well as men may host memorial feasts, receive large quantities of ceremonial valuables as the deceased's heir (the person who "eats" the feast), or make major contributions to assist the feast host. By giving away valuables, an individual places the recipient in his or her debt. He or she may call on the recipient at any later time in order to request the return of an equivalent valuable when it is needed. Through building a network of exchange debts and obligations an individual becomes wealthy and influential, able to satisfy not only personal ritual obligations but also those of close associates.

Both women and men may leave children, spouses, and subsistence tasks behind and lead an expedition by sailing canoe to the far side of Vanatinai or to distant islands in quest of ceremonial valuables, pigs, and foodstuffs. In addition to mortuary feasts, valuables are used to purchase garden land and pay a nonobligatory tribute or rent to the owners of garden or village land that one is using, pay a builder of a house or sailing or paddling canoe, or contribute bridewealth or "childwealth" to a kinsperson (see Lepowsky 1983, n.d.b). Some exchange journeys to destinations on Vanatinai are made on foot by women, men, or mixed groups, with each individual visiting personal exchange partners. Exchange partners are of both the same sex and the opposite sex. Success in obtaining valuables is believed to be impossible without knowledge of the proper magic that, drawing on the power of ancestor spirits, affects the mind of the exchange partner, making him or her *negenege*, or dizzy with desire, and anxious to give away precious and carefully hoarded valuables. Exchange magic is taught to both women and men, usually by matrilineal kin or fathers. The idiom of seduction is used regardless of whether the exchange partner is the same or the opposite sex.

Vanatinai is remarkable for the degree to which women are physically mobile. Ardener (1975:6) has suggested that the generally greater physical mobility of men in human societies is a significant factor in their higher status relative to women, as they negotiate and regulate relationships with outside groups. On Vanatinai women travel with their families to live with their own kin and then the kin of their spouse, make journeys in quest of valuables and to act as healers or as food or garden magicians, and attend memorial feasts in other districts and on other islands. Women's mobility is not generally restricted by cultural ideology or taboo, unlike on nearby Rossel Island, which is culturally and linguistically distinct, and where the status of women and young men is lower.[7] Vanatinai women build their own far-ranging personal networks of social relationships that may be activated as needed by the woman for the benefit of her kin or hamlet group.

The Vanatinai case is also remarkable for the extent of female participation in the public, ritually, economically, and politically significant prestige-generating activities, the same activities in which men are involved. In this society with no chiefs or indigenous system of formal political authority, the means of gaining personal renown and influence over the actions of others are visible success in accumulating foodstuffs and ceremonial valuables through one's own labor and through activating a personal network of exchange links, then giving away goods in acts of public generosity. This avenue to prestige and influence is used by both women and men.

Gender and the Life Cycle

It is impossible to gauge the degree of personal autonomy and of social influence deemed culturally appropriate for women in a particular group without examining the institutions and beliefs that shape the life course of the individual. It is also essential to contrast the ideologies, roles, and customs that shape the lives of females with those affecting males of the same age. This contrast of a society's gender constructs has been largely absent from the anthropology of gender literature since the pioneering work of Margaret Mead (1935).

Consideration of sex roles requires the understanding of age roles as well (compare Linton 1940, 1942). Local ideology concerning the transitions to biological and social adulthood and to old age are especially revealing of attitudes about gender. Focusing on the life cycle illustrates the restrictions and the opportunities facing individuals of both sexes.

Vanatinai society lacks a permanent political leader and has a strong egalitarian ethic that disapproves of the accumulation of wealth without redistribution of goods to those who request it. While cooperation among individuals is extolled and indeed is necessary for continued existence in a small-scale subsistence society, the culture's egalitarian outlook is revealed by the emphasis on personal autonomy and an ethic of respect for the will and the idiosyncrasies of the individual. This respect extends from the treatment of infants to the treatment of the aged and enjoins tolerance of a wide range of character traits and behaviors by women and men of all ages. Respect for others is enforced by the need to cooperate in daily life or suffer the sanction of having neighbors choose to live elsewhere on the island, but it also is enforced by strong beliefs in the destructive powers of others manifested in sorcery and witchcraft (see below).

People say that an infant must never be left crying or else he or she "might become angry and leave us" or, in other words, might die. Child treatment on Vanatinai is extremely permissive, and girls and boys receive equivalent treatment. Infants and young children are nursed on demand until about three years of age and allowed to explore their environment with minimal interference from adult or child caretakers, even manipulating sharp knives and firebrands as they wish. Both men and women welcome the birth of a girl as well as that of a boy and sometimes openly wish for a girl, who will give birth to future matrilineage members (compare Schlegel, this volume, for the matrilineal Hopi). Fathers, mothers, and their close kin are loving and indulgent to children, carrying them proudly around the hamlet and taking them along on subsistence tasks when older. Boys may accompany their mothers and girls their fathers to the garden or the shore, but children are not taken on hunting trips. By the age of about six, many children have learned to build a fire and boil tubers or roast sago cakes. Accompanying adults and older children on foraging expeditions into nearby forests, they have begun to learn to gather wild fruits and nuts and to gather shellfish and fish with lines from shore. Children cook fish on the shore and share it with each other. If they have more than enough fish or gathered foods, they graciously offer the surplus to adult kin and neighbors, emulating the adult pattern of sharing and generosity.

Toddlers are sometimes left in the hamlet in the care of older siblings while mothers go to their gardens, which may be one to three miles away. The children are patient and indulgent caretakers, stoking the fire and cooking food when the little one is hungry and then inducing her or him to sleep on a mat afterward while they play quietly nearby. Mothers may also take a young child to the garden, leaving an older sibling to watch the toddler in the garden shelter and returning to nurse the toddler on demand. Boys and girls spend approximately the same amount of time assisting their families with household and subsistence tasks until the approach of adolescence.

Adolescents are expected to work hard at gardening, gathering, fishing, and domestic chores in order to demonstrate their industriousness. Women and men alike say that the most important quality to look for in a potential spouse is willingness to work hard. Some adolescent boys work diligently at gardening and sago-making, but others do not. Parties of youths may roam the forest looking for signs of wild pig. Their success in hunting is appreciated by the entire hamlet both because the taste of wild pig is highly prized and because pigs often raid gardens and dig up tubers.

Certain youths may be criticized for not helping their families. After one incident where a respected thirty-five-year-old woman had publicly admonished a group of youths and young unmarried men for having a "spear"-throwing contest in the forest with shafts of tough grass, instead of working in the gardens, one of their leaders argued that throwing "spears" was important practice for hunting valued game, an argument with which the woman was unimpressed. Later that evening, an old man told me privately, in a nostalgic tone and laughing at the memory, that when he was a youth he and his friends had been similarly criticized by adults for holding "spear"-throwing contests.

Children from birth to about puberty are described by the gender-blind term *gama* (child). An adolescent girl is called *gamaina*, and an adolescent boy is called *zeva*. All kin terms for adults are sex-specific except the term for grandparent.

There are no ceremonies that formally mark puberty or physical maturation for either sex. Menstruation, called *wakinie*, which is also the adverb meaning "behind" or "in back," subjects a woman to few taboos. A menstruating woman should not work in or go near a food garden because, it is said, wild pigs and birds will eat the crop. Unlike on nearby Rossel Island (Armstrong 1928), there is no menstrual hut or period of seclusion at menstruation and childbirth. A woman may spend days of her menstrual period gathering in the forest or looking for shellfish on the reef, or she may choose to remain in the hamlet, wearing many layers of her oldest coconut-leaf skirts, weaving a basket or mat or merely relaxing and chewing betel nut.

Women consider their menstrual periods a pleasant interlude when they are free from garden work. They continue to cook food for their husbands and children, and there is no belief that they are polluting or dangerous to others. They also may have sex with men. When I asked whether it was all right to sleep with a man while menstruating, my female friends said, "Of course! Why do you ask?" I answered weakly that I had heard that in the New Guinea Highlands women could not sleep with their husbands while menstruating because they would make the men sick. The women laughed, and one asked, jokingly, "What kind of 'sickness' do they get? The same kind we have [that is, menstruation]?"

Neither a menstruating woman nor a person of either sex who has had sexual intercourse within the last two or three days should participate in the communal planting of a new yam garden, or else the yams will not grow properly. In this case the bodily fluids of both women and men are inimical to the growth of yams.

Adolescence is regarded by young and old alike as a time of relative freedom from domestic responsibilities and as a time to indulge in love affairs. Sexual activity on Vanatinai is regarded as a pleasurable activity appropriate for men and women from adolescence to old age. It is not believed to be dangerous or depleting of vital essence for either men or women, unlike in many other parts of Melanesia. Young people vary in the age at which they become sexually active, but it is usually in the mid-teens. Parents may tell their daughters that they are "too young" to have sex, as did the mother of one fifteen-year-old when she began to be courted by a young man of whom the mother disapproved because he was an orphan "with no parents to help him." On the other hand, some parents feel concerned if their daughters are not receiving lovers by the time they are in their late teens. Either sex may take the initiative in arranging a rendezvous either by speaking privately with the object of affection or by sending a verbal message through a third party, often a cross-cousin or a younger sibling. Couples may meet in isolated places in the forest, or the man may creep into the family home after everyone is asleep and quietly awaken the woman. If she is not interested, she may send him away either in silence or by rousing her parents with her loud, indignant protests, an incident that will lead to amused gossip the following day. Success is believed due to the strength of the love magic used by either party. The couple may be politely ignored by the rest of the family, and the man will slip away before dawn. Rape and other forms of sexual assault are completely unknown on the island.

Young girls say that two or more acts of intercourse with the same man are necessary for conception. In order to avoid pregnancy, they say that it is prudent to sleep with a number of different men rather than one. The child of an unmarried mother is enthusiastically welcomed as a new member of her matrilineage and is not stigmatized, but people feel sorry for the child because he or she has no father.

Men and boys may give gifts of tobacco, betel nut, or shell valuables directly to their lovers. If a couple is discovered sleeping inside a house, the mother or mother's brother may place a basket filled with ceremonial valuables and other goods near the man's head and then retreat. When the man awakens, before dawn, he must take this basket with its goods, called *buwa,* with him. He is not supposed to keep the valuables but must return them to the woman's mother and mother's brother along with equivalent valuables that he must request from his own kin. This presentation of valuables may be public and dramatic if, for example, the rendezvous has taken place during a feast. Afterward, the man is free to sleep with the woman for as long as is mutually agreeable. People stress that *buwa* is not a marriage payment. It goes to a woman's kin because they "worked hard to feed her." Lovers of prominent older divorced or widowed women may also give *buwa* to the woman's kin or to the woman herself, sometimes a shell-disk necklace, a valuable gift that is a source of pride to the woman. *Buwa* "is paid to the house" and may not be demanded if a couple meets in the forest, a strategy that is therefore favored by many young men.

The people in the three settlements that comprise the central dialect area of Vanatinai encourage their children to court and marry one another. They have therefore agreed not to "put out the basket" when their young men come to sleep with the young women of the region. The people of the small islands of the East Calvados Chain northwest of Vanatinai speak a different language and are culturally distinct from Vanatinai people, whom they frequently visit by sailing canoe for purposes of traditional exchange. These people have no custom of *buwa,* and their young men explain that they are afraid to sleep with Vanatinai women during their visits because they might have to ask their families to help them pay *buwa.* If they do not pay they risk attack by sorcery. The custom of *buwa* therefore helps to promote district and island-wide endogamy.[8]

There is no ritual or institutional homosexuality on Vanatinai. When after a long period of residence on Vanatinai and adjacent islands I had heard nothing about individual acts of or dispositions toward homosexuality (although I had heard of rare cases of other unconventional sex such as incest), I asked some trusted friends if there were any men or women who slept with members of their own sex. They seemed sincerely puzzled and amused at the idea and asked me why anyone would bother when intercourse with the opposite sex was so enjoyable. By contrast, homosexuality is institutionalized for young males in some Papua New Guinea societies with an ethic of male dominance where it seems to be a concomitant of an extreme ideology of female pollution and the resulting danger of heterosexual activity (for example, Herdt 1981, 1982; Schieffelin 1976).

Women and men are free to choose their own marriage partners. Kinfolk may express approval or disapproval of an individual or ask for (or not ask for) *buwa,* but no marriage will endure unless the couple is personally compatible. The act of marriage consists of the new husband's staying in the house with his wife after dawn and cooking the breakfast his bride prepares. Unmarried couples do not eat together. Afterward the husband goes to work in the garden of his wife's kin under the supervision of his mother-in-law. If he is lazy, his in-laws will lobby to have him leave. Name avoidance is practiced by affines. A man is usually addressed by his wife's kin as "*X*'s husband" (literally "*X*'s man"). A woman is usually called "*Y*'s wife" (literally, "*Y*'s woman"). Both may later be called "*Z*'s mother" or "*Z*'s father." Thus, both sexes are referred to symmetrically in terms of their relationship to one another.

Bridewealth, which normally consists of a shell-disk necklace and one or several greenstone axeblades, is not paid to the wife's kin unless it seems clear that the marriage will last. Often the wife is pregnant or has already borne children. The wife's kin give garden produce to the kin of the husband and may kill a pig to distribute when the bridewealth, or *vazavó*, is paid. Some men never pay bridewealth, and this may be a source of friction in marital quarrels. One woman, when she was angry with her husband, used to shout for the whole hamlet to hear, "You never gave my parents any *tobotobo* (greenstone axeblades) for me!" This woman seems to agree with John Ogbu's (1978) argument that bridewealth enhances female status by legitimizing marriage.

Bridewealth on Vanatinai is merely the opening round in a series of reciprocal affinal exchanges, which continues even beyond the deaths of the married couple, ending only with the completion of the mortuary ritual sequence at the deaths of a couple's children (see Lepowsky 1981, 1989a). At the birth of a firstborn child, the wife's kin are supposed to make a small feast and give ceremonial valuables to the kin of the husband in gratitude for his having sired a new member of their matrilineage. This "childwealth" payment flows in the opposite direction from the bridewealth and consists of the same types of valuables. Affines of either sex and their kin bear an equal obligation to assist the spouse and kin on request with gifts of labor, food, and valuables. Affines are normally one's most important exchange partners. People say that this is why polygyny is rare: a man with two or more wives has two or more sets of affines, and he must assist them as requested or face their potentially deadly wrath as they take revenge through sorcery or witchcraft.

Divorce may be initiated by either husband or wife. Bridewealth is supposed to be returned by the wife's kin to the husband no matter who initiated the divorce or who had offended the other spouse, because it is said that the husband will need the bridewealth again when he remarries. According to gossip, the wife's kin in certain cases will argue for reconciliation because they do not want to return the bridewealth, which was usually given long ago to other exchange partners to satisfy other exchange obligations. If a man and woman live separately but still call themselves husband and wife and still assist their affines as requested, they are still considered to be married, and any children borne by the woman are considered the offspring of the husband. This describes the living arrangement of at least one couple during my residence on Vanatinai. Adultery is disapproved of, but if discovered, the offender may be forgiven by the spouse, although sometimes an angry quarrel ensues. There is no disparity in cultural ideology or actual practice in treatment of male versus female adulterers. Gossip attributes acts of adultery to both sexes in approximately equal numbers.

Sanday's (1981:164–65) definitions of male dominance and gender equality include the presence or absence, respectively, of male violence against women. In Schlegel's (1972) cross-cultural study of matrilineal societies, "matrilocal residence," "positions held outside the home," and "absence of punishment of the wife" are found to be strongly correlated with "High Female Autonomy." The presence on Vanatinai of bilocal residence and of women's prominence in public political, economic, and ritual affairs has already been discussed. I heard of no cases, past or present, of rape. Wife-beating is rare and is strongly disapproved. In one case, about two generations ago, when a man assaulted his wife and seriously injured her head, her kinsmen in retribution killed almost every single member of the husband's lineage, which today consists of only a few people. In 1978–79 one husband hit his wife in the face and broke her jaw after accusing her of infidelity. His action was considered reprehensible. Husband abuse is also rare but also takes place. During the same year a jealous young wife broke her husband's wrist and burned his chest with a firebrand. In both of these cases village gossip held that the violent spouse had in fact been committing adultery and that the injured spouses were innocent. Both spouse abuse victims remained married for several more years, during which there were no further acts of violence, but both couples were divorced when I returned to the island in 1987.

All but a few adults marry. Most of these few have some kind of physical deformity but may still be sexually active. Adult women and men alike may gain a reputation as an individual who is a proficient gardener, food collector, hunter or fisher, or they may become known as healers or garden ritual experts. Most young adults become involved in traditional exchange activities by obtaining ceremonial valuables from their parents' exchange partners and other kin and then presenting them at memorial feasts as appropriate for members of their kin group. People have personal exchange partners of both the same and the opposite sex. It is up to the individual man or woman to decide whether the reward of area-wide renown and influence is worth the danger to oneself and one's family from retaliatory sorcery or witchcraft if he or she becomes exceptionally active and visible in exchange activities.

People in their thirties to early sixties tend to be most widely known for their wealth, skill, and knowledge about traditional exchange. Not only the mothers but the fathers of young children are inhibited by the fear that envious sorcerers or witches may take revenge by injuring or killing their children. Parents of young children may also refrain from extensive exchange activities because of their extra subsistence and child-care obligations.

The men and women of Vanatinai exhibit a wide range of temperaments and personality traits. Individual personality rather than gender determines whether a person chooses to exert extra effort to become known as an excellent gardener, a healer, a ritual expert, or a *gia* who has many exchange partners and ceremonial valuables and has hosted or contributed generously to many feasts. Experts in exchange, healing, or gardening must be "strong," whether they are male or female, because they must be willing to engage in persistent hard work beyond the demands of subsistence. They must seek out and learn the magic or ritual knowledge without which they will not succeed. They must also expose themselves and their families to the risk of illness or death through the sorcery or witchcraft of envious competitors.

In an egalitarian society like Vanatinai, there is no cultural discontinuity between the position of the premenopausal and postmenopausal woman (Lepowsky 1985a). There is no marked rise for some or all women to a higher or more "man-like" status once a woman has passed the age of childbearing the way there is in societies that emphasize the danger of female sexuality to the social order or the polluting qualities of the premenopausal female (compare Simmons 1945:63–5; Meigs 1976; Poole 1981; Brown 1982). The treatment of elderly women on Vanatinai parallels the treatment of elderly men. The terms *laisali* and *mankwesi,* which are synonymous and mean "old woman," are terms of respect that are used to address important women who are as young as twenty-five or thirty.

Both women and men may remain active in subsistence tasks until extreme old age, walking miles over rough terrain to gardens and maintaining ties with kin in other parts of the island. The needs of the elderly for food, water, and firewood are provided without complaint by kin and neighbors. Old people are respected for their knowledge and wisdom and for being close to ancestorhood. They may also be feared for their potential retaliation through knowledge of witchcraft or sorcery if their needs are not met and because of the possibility that after they die and join the other ancestor spirits they might refuse to aid their living descendants who treated them badly in their last years. Widows and widowers must undergo an equally onerous period of mourning that ends after the final memorial feast in honor of the deceased spouse, usually several years later. The deaths of a man and a woman receive equal ritual attention (Lepowsky 1989a).

As predicted for an egalitarian society, the degree of personal autonomy and influence over others is remarkably parallel for Vanatinai women and men at specific points in the life cycle. Individuals generally gain in power and prestige as they age. Differences in behavior, activities, and personal wealth are attributed to individual personality and knowledge, practical and magical.

Gender Ideology

There is no publicly or privately voiced ideology of male dominance on Vanatinai. Women are not characterized as weak, inferior, polluting, or dangerous. Men speak admiringly of female associates as "strong," "wise," and "generous." Significantly, these same qualities are also most highly valued in men. Generosity, or giving to others, is the most highly valued personal characteristic in Vanatinai culture. It is explicitly likened to parental nurture.

In some societies of the New Guinea Highlands and Highlands fringe, where gender opposition is marked, gender constructions are conceptualized as changeable or transitional, dependent in part upon human actions (for example, Meigs 1976; Kelly 1976; Poole 1981; Herdt 1981, 1982). On Vanatinai gender is ascribed at birth and remains immutable. Each sex follows its own developmental path and its prescribed part in begetting and giving birth to new people. The life cycle is not punctuated by critical periods such as puberty, marriage, or menopause when ritual action may be taken to change or validate male or female status. Passage through the life cycle from one age-sex category (Linton 1940, 1942) to the next is a gradual process across blurred boundaries.

Vanatinai also differs from societies of New Guinea and elsewhere with marked gender opposition in not sharing their tendency to project a dualistic symbolism upon the environment. When the domains and activities of males and females show considerable overlap, there is less cultural logic in categorizing the world into objects and actions with male versus female qualities. Although some in fact are so categorized on Vanatinai, such dualistic symbolism is much less pervasive than in many other Melanesian societies.

Ortner (1974) has suggested that an association of women with nature and men with culture is universal in human gender ideologies, the "male" domain of culture being more highly valued and thus male dominance itself universal. This dichotomy does not manifest itself in Vanatinai gender ideology. An association of femaleness with key domains of culture is revealed by Vanatinai mythology.

Sanday (1981) argues that gender ideology is shaped by the relationship of males and females to "sacred symbols of creative power" in a culture's mythology or sacred writings. She sees origin myths and the sex of the creator as being particularly significant in describing and validating concepts of power and gender relations, stating that "when the female creative principle dominates or works in conjunction with the male principle, the sexes are either integrated and equal in everyday life . . . or they are separate and equal" (Sanday 1981:33).

On Vanatinai the creator spirit is believed to be a male being named Rodyo who sometimes takes the form of a snake. He lives on Mt. Rio, the highest peak on Vanatinai, with his two wives and with the spirits of all the island's dead. Rodyo is said to have created the world simply by thinking of it and to have assigned clan names and animal and plant totems to the first people. Rodyo thus conforms to Sanday's (1981:58) prediction that male creators will be associated with the sky (in this case a cloud-shrouded mountain peak) and create through magic, while female or couple creators create from the body or from other natural substances. But if Sanday is correct in stating that origin myths are significant reflections of a culture's "sex-role plan," then why does an egalitarian society like Vanatinai have a male creator? The existence of a male creator on Vanatinai does not seem to reflect the influence of Christian missionaries who have worked intermittently on the island since 1947; an early white resident, a goldminer and pearlshell trader, wrote in 1892 that the "Great Chief" named "Rodes" lives on Mt. "Reo" with his wives and gardens and appears "like mist" to the human eye (White 1893). But the Vanatinai creation myth is culturally unelaborated, contains few details, and is rarely recounted by the islanders and not, apparently, because it is a particularly sacred myth. When it is told, the narrator usually launches immediately afterward into the story of Alagh, a supernatural who left Rodyo's community taking with him all the valuable goods that now belong to Europeans. Often narrated alone, this "cargoistic" explanatory myth is obviously more compelling to present-day islanders than the story of Rodyo's creation of the world (Lepowsky 1989b). The myth I was most frequently told concerns the origin of the most important aspect of Vanatinai culture, the exchange of valuables. This first exchange takes place between two female beings (see below).

In Sanday's cross-cultural analysis of 112 creation stories, she finds 50 percent allude to masculine symbolism, 32 percent to mixed male and female, and 18 percent to feminine symbolism. She notes that the largest percentage of "feminine tales" is found in the Insular Pacific region, where there are very few "masculine tales," and comments that the finding of "many feminine origin tales" is consistent with the "ritual focus on female reproductive functions" in this region (1981:60). However, most of the Pacific societies whose rituals are concerned with female reproduction are societies with an explicit ideology of male dominance and female pollution where "ritual emulation by men of female reproductive functions," as Sanday phrases it, seems to symbolize male efforts to control or appropriate female reproductive power. Couple or feminine origin myths in these Pacific societies may therefore symbolize not an egalitarian ideology of gender but male preoccupation with female power and the ritual means through which it may be assimilated by men, who thereby become ideologically dominant over women and children.

Although Sanday sees couple creators in mythology as being generally found in more sexually egalitarian societies, as the female creates by giving birth or shaping people, animals or natural objects, many New Guinea Highlands societies with couple creators also feature sexual segregation, concern with female pollution, and an ethic of male dominance (for example, Glasse 1965:33; Berndt 1965:80; Meggitt 1965:107; Meigs, personal communication 1983).

On the other hand, in the generally sexually egalitarian Massim culture area, there are a variety of origin myths. On Vanatinai there is a male creator, and the world comes into existence through his magical thought. People emerge from a hole in the ground, symbolically analogous to the act of birth, in the matrilineal Trobriand Islands (Malinowski 1922:305) as well as on nearby patrilineal Goodenough Island (Young 1971:12–13). An androgynous creator named Enak gives birth to "the first mortal ancestor," creating birth, death, and human artifacts on Sabarl Island (Battaglia 1983:294), one of the Calvados Chain Islands just to the northwest of Vanatinai. The Bimin Kuskusmin of the Highlands fringe, with a strong ideology of female pollution, also have an androgynous creator (Poole 1981:159). We must therefore be cautious in asserting that a culture's origin mythology directly reflects its gender ideology.

Origin myths can illuminate cultural constructions of gender if we

Gender in an Egalitarian Society 199

examine them in relation to other significant myths in the same culture and focus on the complexity and the possibly contradictory nature of their relationships to other aspects of gender-related thought and action. Even within the same myth, particular motifs may be emphasized by different tellers in different versions. Indigenous exegeses may vary among individuals and over time, providing ideological foundations for explaining or validating quite different aspects of the environment or the behavior of humans, animals, or supernatural beings.

Rodyo, the Vanatinai creator spirit, is primarily associated by Vanatinai people today not with his ancient act of creation but with the spirits of the dead, for he sends his canoe to pick up the spirits of the newly dead and takes them to live in his hamlet on the summit of Mt. Rio, where he is usually in the form of a snake. Rodyo is also one of the two supernatural patrons of sorcery. The other, Tamudurere, who lives at an unspecified place in the sea, is also male. Sorcery is virtually a male monopoly, replacing killing through warfare as a male activity. All of this is consistent with the Vanatinai belief that women are the givers of life, discussed below.

Vanatinai has a large number of myths that explain the origins of particular features of the landscape and of various cultural institutions. The myth of the origin of exchange is the most frequently told on the island and is one of the most detailed. To summarize it briefly, a female snake named Bambagho decided to leave Goodenough Island (Mwalatau) where it had been living. After a long journey it finally took refuge in a cave on Vanatinai. There it was discovered by an old woman, who fed it secretly. Every morning she would bring it a big platter of sago and green coconut pudding (a delicacy usually served at mortuary feasts). Every morning the snake would in gratitude give the old woman a piece of its excrement. The snake's excrement was *daveri,* or orange shell currency. This was the first time that any kind of ceremonial valuable had ever been seen on Vanatinai. The snake also taught the old woman the first magic of exchange, called *une* or *ghune,* cognates to the Tubetube *kune* and Trobriand *kula.* But the old woman had two grandsons who could not understand why the bundles of sago starch they had made kept disappearing. They spied on the old woman, followed her to the cave, and saw her give the snake sago pudding and receive excrement/shell currency in exchange. Furious, they drove the snake off the island using branches of two trees that bear edible nuts. Angry and hurt, the snake fled to nearby Rossel Island (Rova or Yela), where it lives today on a mountain peak.[9]

The islanders who tell the myth today usually comment at its conclusion about the foolish action of the young men in driving away the snake who gave shell currency for sago pudding in the prototypical first exchange. They hold as a moral exemplar the wise old woman whose generosity with a valued food was rewarded by her acquiring not only the first shell valuables but the knowledge of how to obtain more from human beings through the use of exchange magic. Because the snake now lives on Rossel, they say, that island now has thousands of shell currency pieces in circulation.[10]

In this myth a female being teaches another female the peaceful exchange with off-islanders of surplus food for ceremonial valuables. Similar exchanges are the most important and valued aspect of Vanatinai culture. The myth not only indicates the association of females with the domain of culture but provides a mythological charter (Malinowski 1922) for the exchange activities of island women, their right to learn the magic of exchange, to own valuables, and to dispose of the surplus production of both men and women. It emphasizes that generosity is rewarded, perhaps in unexpected ways, portraying the unselfish action of the old woman, initially ignorant of the value of shell currency, in nurturing the stranger. The old woman takes the sago produced by her kinsmen, a semen-like substance, and feeds it to the snake, who "gives birth" through excretion to wealth and then generously gives away its excrement. Perceived by the young, selfish males as the ultimate worthless object, this excrement is supernaturally revealed to the old woman as the ultimate token of value, and symbol of culture, shell currency. This element of the myth echoes the Freudian equation of money or wealth with excrement. Similarly, Róheim (1950:195) recounts two myths from Normanby Island in the southern Massim in which *kula* shell-disk necklaces and armshells are found in a sow's belly in place of excrement, and Dundes (1979:401) documents "the association of wealth, in the form of copper, with feces" in the potlatches of the Indians of the Pacific Northwest.

The motif of the wise woman is common in Vanatinai myths. A female supernatural named Emuga (*mumuga* means "custom") is at first the only being to know the secret of fire and how to cook food, another example of the association of females with the "cooked" domain of culture as opposed to the "raw" domain of nature (contrast Lévi-Strauss 1969b). In other myths, mothers and sisters assist their kinsmen by giving them magical—and cultural—knowledge of how to slay tyrannical beasts and giants that menace the islanders.

There is no explicit or implicit opposition of "natural woman" to "cultural man" in Vanatinai gender ideology (compare MacCormack and Strathern 1980). Ortner (1974:73–74) does not argue that men are perceived as exclusively cultural and women exclusively natural but that women are universally seen as "closer to nature than men." In Vanatinai gender ideology both sexes simultaneously embody natural and cultural attributes to the same degree. In myth both females and males bring key aspects of culture. In ritual, the aspect of human activity that Ortner (1974:72) perceives as quintessentially cultural in portraying human action on "the givens of natural existence," women participate equally with men. In fact, as discussed below, one woman must represent her matrilineage in the climactic moment of the final mortuary feast in order to ensure the reestablishment of social order following the disintegration induced by death. Thus Vanatinai ideology holds women responsible for both cultural and biological reproduction (compare Weiner 1982).

The people of Vanatinai say explicitly that women give life while men kill, offering this statement as an explanation for why killing in war and sorcery are specializations of men. But death as well as birth belongs to the domain of nature as opposed to culture (compare Sanday 1981:5). Associations of the female with life and the male with death have been suggested as universal in the gender symbolism of human societies (for example, Beauvoir 1953; Rosaldo and Atkinson 1975). They are extremely widespread cross-culturally (for example, Sanday 1981:5; Schlegel, this volume). It is hard to imagine a society that would not give symbolic weight to women's biologically ordained role as the sex that gives birth and lactates. In all known human societies men are the primary, if not the exclusive, defenders of the group and killers of game (compare Brown 1970a; Brightman n.d.). The opposition of female/life to male/death, however, is not universal at every level of gender ideology in a given society. For example, Strathern (1980:204, 206) notes that the people of the Mt. Hagen area of the New Guinea Highlands associate the male with life and with the cults that assure the continuity of life and the female with death and pollution: "Through the perpetuity of the clan, ancestor worship and their spirit cults, males represent social continuity, whereas females are said to have brought death into the world."

On Misima, Panaeati, and the Calvados Chain Islands, the Misima and Saisai language areas that lie to the northwest of Vanatinai, people say that witches, the destroyers of life, are usually women, and healers, who counteract the power of witchcraft, are usually men, a reversal of the Vanatinai concept of the usual supernatural division of labor by sex. The Vanatinai ideal that women are life-givers fails to take into account the fact that even on that island many deaths are attributed to the witchcraft of women from both Vanatinai itself and the islands to the northwest. Similarly, there are many widely known, powerful male witches in the Misima and Saisai language areas. Both men and women in the Vanatinai region have the power to destroy (Lepowsky 1981:423–68, 1989b).

The association of maleness on Vanatinai with death, war, and sorcery is reflected in the fact that the supernatural patrons ("owners") of sorcery, witchcraft, and warfare are male. The "owner" of healing, Egoregore, is a female being who lives on Mt. Rio, but on the other hand, the "owner" of illness is her sister Ediriwo. There is one male and one female owner of hunting, an activity sometimes carried out by women (without spears). The female owner is a pigeon, the totem bird of a local matrilineage. Totem birds are sometimes addressed respectfully as "my mother" when seen in the forest. Two owners of garden fertility, the sisters Jinrubi and Eurubi, are female, and the third, Mwaoni, is male. Mwaoni is also one of several male owners of exchange. A female owner, the snake Bambagho, migrated to Rossel Island. Human women and men may both learn the magic pertaining to all of these aspects of island life, usually from their mother or mother's brother, less often from father, spouse, or an unrelated person who is paid in ceremonial valuables. Women are usually not taught certain types of weather and hunting magic, although they do know some powerful hunting magic and formerly could acquire war magic. Men and women each teach individuals of the opposite sex. Possession of magical knowledge, which depends primarily for its efficacy on spells that communicate with ancestor spirits, of both sexes, and supernatural beings such as those mentioned here is a primary means, in local belief, of obtaining prosperity, success, and power over others.

The Vanatinai gender ideology that associates women with life and men with death is contradicted by indigenous beliefs in the destructive power of female witches and the few female sorcerers and by the reality that women do hunt; they just do not hunt wild pigs, dugongs, or crocodiles with spears. Beliefs about the supernatural patrons of death and illness on the one hand and healing, fertility, and abundance on the other show no clear-cut sexual division of labor among supernatural beings. These aspects of Vanatinai sexual meanings are ambiguous and contradictory, and thus perhaps islanders may interpret and use them differently for their own ideological reasons. Yet there is no overall division of kinds of positive and negative supernatural power into male and female domains.

Collier and Rosaldo (1981:275–76) express surprise at the lack of ritual emphasis on female fertility and maternity in the anthropological literature on hunter-gatherer and hunter-horticulturalist societies, finding that women's rituals "have much less to do with the creation of life than with health and sexual pleasure." In the two instances on Vanatinai when women are singled out for special ritual treatment, the value of female fertility and of women as mothers of present or future matrilineage members is emphasized. The occasions are the birth of a firstborn child and the death of a spouse or affine. Both associate woman with the "natural" domain, but in both cases the natural event requires cultural elaboration to ensure human continuity.

Birth is not seen as polluting: husbands, fathers, and kinsmen as well as kinswomen may be present and may perform magical spells to ease the birth. After a first child of either sex is born, the mother remains in seclusion in the house where she gave birth for up to several months, leaving only to eliminate and then covering her head and shoulders with a coconut-leaf skirt. This seclusion is supposed to protect her child and herself from the destructive gaze of jealous sorcerers that might otherwise cause illness or death. The period of seclusion probably does protect the mother and child from greater exposure to various infectious diseases.

The new father too is supposed to remain close to the hamlet and to provide food for his wife and child. Both he and his wife are to observe the same set of food taboos in order to protect the health of their infant (Lepowsky 1985b). The mother emerges from seclusion at a feast that her kin organize where ceremonial valuables are given to her husband's kin to show gratitude at his having sired a new member of the mother's matrilineage. After subsequent births, the mother only remains in seclusion for up to a few weeks.

At the death of a spouse or a person related by marriage, a woman of the affinal matrilineage must represent her kin group and their mourning by undergoing a form of temporary social death. Like the new mother of a first-born, she remains in the house, leaving only to eliminate and then covering her head and shoulders with a coconut-leaf skirt. She also wears the ankle-length mourning skirt and blackens her body with charcoal. She is not allowed to touch her hands to her lips and must be fed by the kin of the deceased until the first mortuary feast is made, when she is also released from this strict seclusion. When a husband dies, his wife is the principal mourner who represents the affinal matrilineage. When a wife dies, her husband undergoes this same form and period of mourning, but he is joined in mourning by one designated kinswoman.

Undertaking this mourning is regarded as an honor and a means of accruing prestige for one's matrilineage. The mourners and their exchange partners accumulate ceremonial valuables, pigs, and foodstuffs to present to the kin of the deceased and to the person who represents the matrilineage of the deceased's father in order to "clear" their mourning taboos at the final mortuary feast several years after the death. On this occasion when mourners are socially reborn, the representatives of the matrilineage of the deceased or of his or her father bathe, oil, dress, and decorate the erstwhile mourners and send them to dance publicly for the first time since the death. The mourning spouse is then free to remarry (Lepowsky 1981, 1989a).

Birth and death are both events when there is a threat to the continuity and fertility of the matrilineage. The islanders have observed that firstborn infants have a higher mortality rate than others. The new mother is therefore expected to sacrifice temporarily her freedom and mobility to protect her child from harm. Not only sorcerers of unknown identity but her husband's kin may be jealous because she has given birth to a child whom their kinsman will help to grow but who does not belong to them. Her kin therefore compensate her husband's kin with valuables. This childwealth is also perceived as being part of the ongoing exchange between affines initiated by bridewealth. Bridewealth therefore does not lead to a permanent asymmetry between affinal lineages that might lead to an asymmetry in the status of husband and wife (compare Divale and Harris 1976:523–24). The wife is then socially reborn in her new status as mother and returns to normal life. The mother is acting for the social good: the survival of the infant represents the future of the matrilineage.

Similarly, the principal female mourner undergoes a social death and is placed under the control of the deceased's kin for the social good. Vanatinai custom places suspicion on spouses and affines of having caused a death through sorcery or witchcraft or of benefiting from a death because at the close of the mortuary feast sequence, the affines will be free of their obligations to contribute valuables, food, and labor to the deceased's kin. Affinal relations are marked overtly by respect and covertly by tension and competition. The mourning spouse and/or principal female mourner are symbolically held hostage by the deceased's kin during the liminal period until the final feast in order to compensate the kin for the loss of a lineage member. At this final feast the kinswomen of the deceased, or his or her father's kinswomen, present the female affinal mourners with new coconut-leaf skirts, and the mourning women give new skirts to the kin of the deceased or of his or her father.

The cultural theme of skirt exchanges between affinal women during the mortuary ritual sequence is far more highly elaborated in the Trobriand Islands, as reported by Weiner (1976). On Vanatinai this skirt exchange represents the good wishes of each matrilineage for the future fertility of the other now that the crisis of death and the resulting threat of retaliatory sorcery and further deaths have been satisfactorily resolved through mortuary exchanges. The exchange of fine new skirts also symbolizes the willingness of matrilineages to continue in future the peaceful exchange of men in marriage (contrast Lévi-Strauss 1969a), which is necessary to produce new members of each kin group. Thus both at the birth of an infant and at the death of an affine a woman is regarded as acting unselfishly for the benefit of her matrilineage. Vanatinai gender ideology differs therefore from that of the Mt. Hagen region of the New Guinea Highlands, where Strathern (1981) reports a belief that males act for the good of the larger community, while females act out of self-interest.

Vanatinai gender ideology, as manifested in general statements, mythology, beliefs about the supernatural bases of power, and ritual practice, does not separate out female versus male domains of power or privilege one gender over the other. Females are as cultural, and as natural, as males and are just as essential to the construction and continuity of the human and supernatural worlds. The culture's gender ideology thus parallels its social structure and sexual division of labor in being egalitarian and valorizing the power and autonomy of individuals of both sexes.

Gender and Social Change

Vanatinai has had six generations of intermittent contact with Europeans, but in many respects island life has changed little. Per capita income is still well under 20 dollars per year. The island was brought gradually under the control of first the British and then the Australian colonial governments, and since 1975 it has been part of the independent nation of Papua New Guinea. The major change that the islanders note is one with a likely impact on female status, the cessation of warfare and raiding. This was not fully accomplished until 1943, although the British colonial government had been under the impression that the region was completely "pacified" by the late 1880s, the time of a brief goldrush on the island. Peaceful conditions have meant an expansion of interdistrict and interisland trading and exchange and greater mobility for both men and women.

Vanatinai men were formerly admired for their prowess in warfare, but according to local belief the islanders fought primarily to defend themselves rather than to attack others or gain territory or goods. Population density on Vanatinai, an island consisting primarily of precipitous mountain slopes, malarial sago, and mangrove swamps, is very low and was probably low a hundred years ago, judging from the reports of early European visitors. There is and probably was ample land to make gardens and collect food, especially given that until about fifty years ago people relied far more heavily on sago-making and the collection of wild foods and less on cultivation than they have in recent years (Lepowsky 1985b).

It is worth noting that the people who were the most persistent raiders of Vanatinai came from small and infertile coral islands in the Calvados Chain and near the New Guinea mainland that even today find it difficult to support their dense populations. The raiders often appeared on Vanatinai after the annual yam harvest and carried off yams and other foodstuffs. Oral tradition asserts that there was an increase in raiding by off-islanders on Vanatinai hamlets and gardens in late precolonial times and that settlements were moved from the shore to steep, defensible ridge-tops along the central mountain range (Lepowsky 1983, n.d.b). Although people from the various districts on Vanatinai occasionally raided one another, these engagements are seen by their descendants as having been in retaliation for an offense such as fishing without permission on reefs belonging to another matrilineage or even assault on a wife, as described above.

Killing for revenge or defense was valued and celebrated by ritual cannibalism and an accompanying presentation of ceremonial valuables. A man with a reputation as a great fighter was known as *asiara*, or champion. Generally Vanatinai males were esteemed not for their aggressiveness but for their ability to defend the hamlets. Success in obtaining valuables from an exchange partner because of one's cleverness and magical knowledge was more highly valued, the islanders say, than obtaining similar goods through warfare and plunder. This relative lack of a cultural value of male aggressiveness for its own sake distinguishes Vanatinai from many societies of the New Guinea Highlands. In the latter, a high population density, a relative shortage of suitable garden land, a high value accorded to men for their prowess in warfare, and the segregation of males from females in order to protect males from the polluting and depleting females who might impair their ability to fight enforce a social emphasis on male solidary groups that dominate political, economic, and ritual life.[11]

On Vanatinai people say that male killing in warfare has been replaced by male killing through sorcery, an analogous form of social control. But women may know counter-sorcery or witchcraft and in these fashions influence the lives and deaths of others.

The male specialization in defense in precolonial times meant that men were more likely to meet strangers visiting the island in case they planned to raid instead of trade, but the islanders say that even in early times women went on exchange voyages. The prominent position of women on Vanatinai is said to be part of *taubwaragha*, the customs of the ancestors. The earliest recorded visitors to the island, the men of the British survey ship H.M.S. *Rattlesnake*, who arrived in 1849, were at first only approached by canoes full of men until trade relations had been established, after which women also came alongside the vessel in canoes to engage in trade (Huxley 1935; Macgillivray 1852). Captain Owen Stanley observed women in canoes on Sudest Lagoon and noted in his diary, "Some of the Women in the Canoes seemed to have a certain amount of command; and some respect was shown to them, but those we have yet seen in Shore have been employed carrying Baskets on their heads" (Stanley 1849:18). The British had arrived in July, the peak of the present-day yam harvest, and soon arranged a trade of massive quantities of yams in exchange for pieces of iron and iron axes. The women carrying baskets were probably then, as now, regarded as the "owners" of the yams they brought and had decided to trade them to the strangers.

Changes during the colonial and national government periods have placed men in the position of relating to the administration and to outsiders with interests in the island. Although the island's migration rate is very low, about 3 percent, some men have left the island for a few years in search of work as crews of coastal vessels, on plantations or in towns and then returned, some speaking a bit of English. Under the Australian colonial government and, since 1975, the national government of Papua New Guinea, official local authority is supposed to belong to a local government councillor elected from each district of the island. Those from Vanatinai have all been male. Two prominent middle-aged women who were nominated, by men, on one occasion that I witnessed withdrew their names in embarrassment. People said it was because they, like almost all adult Vanatinai women, do not speak English. A few men have learned some English from migrating elsewhere in Papua New Guinea to work. The islanders explain that the local government councillor is expected to receive, organize meals for, and converse with the government officer-in-charge or other government officials on their rare visits to the island villages. These individuals were formerly mostly Australians and are now almost all Papua New Guineans from other parts of the country. Since there are over 700 different languages in Papua New Guinea, these officials must try to communicate in English, one of the nation's three official languages, since the other two, Pidgin and Motu, are spoken by very few people in the Vanatinai region.

The yearly census throughout the country records a person's given name and then uses the father's name as a surname, even in matrilineal areas such as Vanatinai.

The Roman Catholic Mission of the Sacred Heart and the United Church (Methodist) Mission have both attempted to convert the islanders since 1947 with only partial success. Since then, Australian priests, along with Australian nuns, have lived on nearby Rossel and Nimowa Islands. The first Papua New Guinean priest, from a Calvados Chain island, was recently ordained. Nine women from the Calvados Chain, where Catholic influence is far stronger than on Vanatinai, became nuns, but all of them had quit by 1978. Catholic lay catechists are all male, as are United Church ministers and pastors, many from Misima Island, seventy miles to the northwest, who are posted temporarily to some of the Vanatinai settlements. During United Church services, men always sit on the right and women on the left, "so that they won't say bad things to each other during the service." Church and government officials, who are male, expect to deal with Vanatinai men. Women are supposed to form clubs (mostly inactive on Vanatinai) to weave mats for church and for government rest houses, to bake scones in a clay cooking pot over a fire to sell for money for club projects, to assist the elderly and ailing with their daily chores, and to assist on government works projects. The United Church also organizes Women's Fellowship chapters (again mostly inactive on Vanatinai), which are supposed to meet for prayers, good works, and laboring on the church, grounds, and pastor's house and garden.

Several recent writers on the anthropology of gender have stressed the changing nature of gender roles and ideology and the necessity of evaluating the historical context of gender relations in a particular society (for example, Etienne and Leacock 1980; Gewertz 1981, 1983). The evidence from Vanatinai seems to corroborate aspects of Leacock's (1978) hypothesis that women's position relative to men is eroded in small-scale societies that come under colonial domination. New, formalized systems of power have been imposed by government and mission, and their roles are filled exclusively by men, with Vanatinai village constables, local government councillors, pastors, and lay catechists themselves subordinate to outside authority held exclusively by men, formerly whites and now mostly Papua New Guineans from societies with an ideology of male dominance. The autonomy of all individuals on Vanatinai, male and female, has declined with pacification and the hegemony of laws, courts, district officers, priests, and mission boards. Females are effectively shut out of new avenues to power and prestige in the public domain, and in this sense, Vanatinai society seems to be less egalitarian than it was in precolonial times.

It is too simplistic, however, to argue that colonization inevitably and in every aspect of social life has a negative impact on the social position of women; Leacock's stance is too monolithic. In one New Guinea case, Gewertz (1981, 1983) shows that for the Chambri (Tchambuli), Australian colonial hegemony in the 1920s and 1930s resulted in regional pacification, a return from exile, a new cash economy, men's departure as migrant laborers, attrition of male exchange partnerships, and intensified female control of subsistence production and of barter. These factors strengthened women's economic position and personal autonomy enough so that Margaret Mead (1935) could describe the Tchambuli as a society where women were dominant, and, according to Gewertz, their position was stronger around the time of Mead's 1933 visit than at any time before or since due to various historical factors.

In the Vanatinai case, warfare formerly was an avenue to prestige and influence for men, who could achieve the title of *asiara*. Institutionalized or frequent warfare and a consequent tendency to reward male aggression and prowess in killing are likely to reflect and reinforce a cultural ideology of male dominance and female inferiority. Divale and Harris (1976:521) "identify warfare as the most important cause" of "the male supremacist complex" (compare Sanday's [1981:164] definition of male dominance). Vanatinai women were prominent in warfare and diplomacy, participating publicly in decisions to wage war or make peace, entering the field of battle, and possessing knowledge of critical forms of war magic, both according to oral traditions and in island mythology. This prominence is quite unusual in the cross-cultural literature (but compare Macintyre [1987] on Tubetube, also a southern Massim society; and Brown [1970b] on the Iroquois, another matrilineal, horticultural society). Still, the domain of warfare on Vanatinai was one in which men could achieve renown in ways that were barred by custom to women, who were forbidden to use spears. This aspect of traditional life privileged men and may have contributed to some degree of sexual asymmetry in precolonial times. Pacification contributed to a greater mobility for both men and women and a greater volume of interisland exchange journeys without fear of attack. It is likely that Vanatinai women are more involved in long-distance ceremonial exchange than they were in the late precolonial period, during which warfare and raiding had intensified (Lepowsky 1983, n.d.b).[12]

Despite government and mission influence that promotes the roles of men in communicating with these bodies, Vanatinai women and men both continue to take part in public discussions on community matters and in private discussions on kin group matters. Women also operate in traditional systems of relationships between lineage groups such as exchange partnerships and take a prominent role in mortuary feasts. They may achieve area-wide renown as experts in healing or garden ritual. Although women are highly valued for their ability to give birth to new matrilineage members, they are not restricted by their biologically ordained tasks of bearing and nursing young to the domestic or inner sphere of social life while men monopolize the public or outer sphere, despite the traditional male role of community defense, formerly through warfare and now through sorcery and counter-sorcery.

Conclusion: Lessons from an Egalitarian Society

Vanatinai is a matrilineal society where women are by definition central to the kin group, the most significant social unit on the island. They have equal rights to postmarital residence with their own kin, to inheritance, and to use and distribution of land and other valuable resources. This is a situation in which female autonomy and cultural ideals of the value of women are likely to be high (compare Schlegel 1972 and on the Hopi, this volume; Sanday on the Minangkabau, this volume; Nash 1987). In contrast, a patrilineal social structure inherently places women at a disadvantage in terms of rights, roles, and privileges and thus probably in terms of autonomy and control over their own actions and those of others (compare Divale and Harris 1976; Schlegel, this volume).

Vanatinai is also a small-scale, loosely structured and fluid society with a low population density where people have the option of removing themselves to another area where they have land rights if social conflicts arise. Its small scale, fluidity (compare Collier and Rosaldo 1981), and mobility, in combination with its matrilineal social structure, are conducive to egalitarian social relations between men and women and old and young. It promotes an ethic of respect for the individual that must be integrated with the ethic of cooperation essential for survival in a subsistence society. Conflict must be worked out through face-to-face negotiation or else existing social ties will be broken by migration or by death through sorcery or witchcraft. Vanatinai society values the same qualities in both women and men: strength, wisdom, and generosity. If possessed of these qualities, an individual woman or man will act in ways that bring prestige not only to the actor but also to the kin and residence groups to which he or she belongs.

Current writings on the anthropology of women, in an effort to assess degrees of female power and influence, frequently focus on the disparity between the ideal sex role pattern of a culture, often based on an ideology of male dominance, and the real one, manifested by the actual behavior of individuals, in order to uncover female social participation in key events and decisions and to learn how women negotiate their social position (for example, Rogers 1975; Collier and Rosaldo 1981). This focus on social and individual "action" or "practice" is prominent in cultural anthropological theory of recent years (Ortner 1984). Schlegel (this volume) points out that there are multiple levels and social contexts of gender ideology in a given society and that different levels of ideology are often contradictory (compare Meigs, this volume; Sanday's chapter on Minangkabau gender constructions, this volume). In the Vanatinai case, gender ideology in its multiple levels and contexts emphasizes the value of women and provides a mythological charter for the degree of personal autonomy and freedom of choice manifested in the lives of individual women. Cultural ideal and real sex role patterns are largely congruent.

Current social science theory emphasizes "the centrality of domination" and the analysis of "asymmetrical social relations" as the key to understanding a particular social system (Ortner 1984). This focus on asymmetry and domination may distort analyses of male and female roles and of gender ideology in societies with a tradition of egalitarian social relations. There is no ideology of male dominance on Vanatinai. Unlike in many cultures where men stress women's innate inferiority, such as the Hua (Meigs, this volume) and the Mendi (Lederman, this volume) of New Guinea or the Mundurucú of Brazil (Murphy and Murphy 1974), gender relations on Vanatinai are not "contested," in Lederman's terms, or antagonistic, and there are no male-versus-female ideologies that vary markedly or directly contradict each other. Vanatinai mythological motifs, beliefs about supernatural power, cultural ideals of the sexual division of labor and of the qualities inherent to men and women, and the customary freedoms and restrictions upon each sex at different points in the life course all provide ideological underpinnings of sexual equality.

Vanatinai is not a perfectly egalitarian society, either in terms of a lack of difference in the status and power of individuals or in the relations between men and women. More men than women are highly active in traditional exchange activities, even though some women surpass almost all men in their acquisition and distribution of ceremonial valuables. Women in young and middle adulthood are likely to spend more time on child care and supervision of gardens and less on building reputations as prominent transactors of ceremonial valuables. The average woman spends more of her time sweeping up the pig excrement that dots the hamlet due to the unfenced domestic pigs that wander through it. The average man spends more time hunting wild boar in the rainforest with his spear (although some men do not like to hunt). His hunting is more highly valued and accorded more prestige than her daily maintenance of hamlet cleanliness and household order. The ideal and real sexual division of labor on Vanatinai is slightly asymmetrical, despite the tremendous overlap in the roles of men and women and the freedom that an individual of either sex has to spend more time on particular activities—gardening, foraging, fishing, caring for children, traveling in quest of ceremonial valuables—and minimize others. Yet the average Vanatinai woman owns some of the pigs she cleans up after, and she presents them publicly during mortuary rituals and exchanges them with other men and women for *kula* shell-disk necklaces, long axeblades of polished greenstone, and other valuables. She thereby gains status, prestige, and influence over the affairs of others, just as men do and as any adult does who chooses to make the effort to raise pigs, grow large yam gardens, and acquire and distribute ceremonial valuables. Vanatinai is an equal opportunity society, and women who achieve prominence and wealth through the distribution of yams, pigs, and ceremonial valuables and thus the ability to mobilize the labor of others are highly respected by both sexes. An overview of the life course and the sexual division of labor on Vanatinai reveals the striking lack of cultural restrictions upon the autonomy of women as well as men and the openness of island society to a wide variety of life-styles.

Vanatinai gender ideology and sex role patterns must be placed into historical context. Key changes include increases and decreases in the frequency of warfare and raiding, the build-up of population (closely related to warfare patterns in the precolonial period), the resulting scarcity of key resources and the potential for increasing political hierarchy, the introduction of new forms of religious ideology with the advent of missionization, and the imposition of colonial and then national political authority on a previously autonomous island society. Vanatinai society has lost one source of sexual asymmetry, the male opportunity to obtain power and influence through a reputation as a champion fighter, and women may have benefited even more than men from the increased mobility for everyone made possible by pacification. But the impact on women's authority and influence of the absorption of Vanatinai into colonial and national polities have probably been negative overall. The new political and religious systems emphasize hierarchical authority controlled by distant outsiders with a few local adult males chosen to exercise control over the rest of the population as local government councillors, policemen, and pastors. The new systems directly oppose the traditional ethic of egalitarian relations among autonomous individuals and exclude women from the new positions of authority.

Recently anthropologists have criticized the widespread practice of writing about "the status of women" as if it were a single, straightforward, and uncontradictory phenomenon unaffected by historical forces, social context, or multiple and conflicting forms of gender ideology (for example, Meigs, this volume). Strathern (1987:299) states, "No blanket classification of 'the relationship' between the sexes, and thus no summary conclusion about equality, can be offered" for a given society. She cautions against generalizing from individual actions and relationships and warns that "none of the single terms—complementarity, dominance, separation—will in the end do, because there is no single relationship." There is of course no single relationship between the sexes on Vanatinai. Power relations and relative influence vary with the individuals, sets of roles, situations, and historical moments involved. Gender ideologies embodied in myths, beliefs, prescriptions for role-appropriate behavior, and personal statements sometimes contradict each other or are contradicted by actual behavior of individuals. Nevertheless, I refer to Vanatinai as an egalitarian society because of its absence of an ideology of male dominance and the way its various levels of gender ideology and individual action are congruent in expressing gender equivalence, complementarity, and overlap.

What can people in other parts of the world learn from the example of a traditionally egalitarian island society? The fact that it is small in scale facilitates Vanatinai society's emphasis on face-to-face negotiations of interpersonal conflicts without the delegation of political authority to a small group of middle-aged male elites. It also leaves room for an ethic of respect for the will of the individual regardless of age or sex. A culture that is egalitarian and nonhierarchical overall is more likely to have egalitarian relations between men and women.

Vanatinai society exhibits a large amount of overlap between the roles and activities of women and men, with women occupying public, prestige-generating roles. Women control the production and the distribution of valued goods and inherit property. Women's role as nurturing parent is highly valued and is the model for the generous men and women who gain renown and influence over others by accumulating and then giving away valuable goods.

These same social characteristics are also possible in large-scale industrial and agricultural societies. The Vanatinai example suggests that sexual equality must be accompanied by an overall ethic of respect for and equal treatment of all categories of individuals, the decentralization of political power, the inclusion of women and of ethnic minorities in public positions of authority and influence, greater role overlap through increased integration of the workforce, increased control by women and minorities of valued goods—property, income, and educational credentials—and increased recognition of the social value of parental care. The example of Vanatinai shows that the subjugation of women by men is not a human universal and is not inevitable, and that sex role patterns and gender ideology are closely related to overall social systems of power and prestige.

Acknowledgments

This chapter is a revised version of a paper presented in Chicago at the 1983 Annual Meetings of the American Anthropological Association in the session titled "Cultural Constructions of Gender and Female Status," organized by Peggy Sanday and Anna Meigs. I am grateful to session participants and audience members for their comments. Parts of this chapter were presented in the Departments of Anthropology of Columbia University, the University of California at San Diego, and the University of Southern California, as well as in the Departments of Anthropology and Women's Studies Programs of the University of Wisconsin, Madison, and the University of Iowa. I would also like to thank members of these groups for their comments. Peggy Sanday, Robert Brightman, and two reviewers for University of Pennsylvania Press have provided helpful criticisms and suggestions. The research upon which the chapter is based was carried out on Sudest Island (Vanatinai), Papua New Guinea, primarily in 1978 and 1979, with financial support from the United States National Science Foundation and from the Chancellor's Patent Fund and the Department of Anthropology of the University of California, Berkeley. Support during the writing of earlier drafts of this chapter was provided through a United States National

Gender in an Egalitarian Society   215

Institutes of Health Public Health Service Fellowship. All of this financial support is gratefully acknowledged. I returned to the island in 1981 and 1987.

Notes

1. For example, for documentation of women's roles in exchange in the Pacific see Feil (1978) for the Enga of the New Guinea Highlands, Gewertz (1983) for the Middle Sepik of Papua New Guinea, Weiner (1986) for Samoa, and Parmentier (1984) and Margold and Bellorado (1985) for Belau. For Africa see Wiessner (1982:70) for the !Kung and Hoffer (1974:174) for the Mende. In Native North America see Reichard (1934:241, 1969:122–23) for the Navaho, and for women's participation in potlatch exchanges of the Pacific Northwest Coast see Barnett (1968:70–71) and Rosman and Rubel (1971:60–62) for the Haida, Barnett (1968:70) and Drucker and Heizer (1967:105–7) for the Kwakiutl, Rosman and Rubel (1971:94–100) for the Nootka, Barnett (1968:70) and Olson (1936:213) for the Tlingit, and Rosman and Rubel (1971:24–25) for the Tsimshian. See also Mintz (1971) for a comparative discussion of women and trade in nonsubsistence economies. For a fuller discussion of women, exchange, and trade in cross-cultural perspective see Lepowsky (n.d.a).

2. Population density is extremely high on the coralline islands of the Massim, as is true of such islands, when inhabited, in much of the Pacific. But low islanders in the Massim, who are generally not self-sufficient in cultivated or wild vegetable foods, have adapted culturally by intensive fishing and exploitation of marine resources, trading and, formerly, raiding high islands for food (Lepowsky n.d.b). Control of garden land therefore does not become the primary determinant of differential status.

3. Collier and Rosaldo (1981:278–79) argue that hunter-gatherer and horticulturalist societies may be divided into "brideservice" and "bridewealth" societies based on their customary marriage arrangements, with each type exhibiting a characteristic pattern of gender roles, politics, ritual, ideology, and social organization. But Vanatinai society has strong traditions of both brideservice and bridewealth. The Vanatinai case therefore suggests that such societies might better be conceptualized as forming a continuum ranging from those where only brideservice is found to those where only bridewealth is customary, with Vanatinai being in the middle and sharing some attributes of each ideal type.

4. On Vanatinai, which differs in soil type, topography, and climate as well as culture from the Trobriand Islands, the long yams, or *kuvi*, which are grown by Trobriand men particularly for display and exchange purposes (Malinowski 1935), are never grown. The smaller and better-tasting yams, called *taytu* in the Trobriands and *lailu* on Vanatinai, are the Vanatinai staple, and it is the magic for growing *lailu* that is known to some women as well as some men on the island.

5. The association of shell valuables with excrement is also found in the most frequently told myth on Vanatinai.

6. Following both indigenous Massim and anthropological traditions, I dis-

tinguish between sorcery, called *ribiroi* on Vanatinai, as a conscious, malevolent act involving the manipulation of objects, and witchcraft (*wadawada*), as resulting from "an inherent quality" (Evans-Pritchard's phrase, 1937:21, 387) of the witch, whose acts are unconscious or involuntary and do not involve the use of spells or magical objects. On Vanatinai, though, it is said that witchcraft may be learned as well as inherited (Lepowsky, in press).

7. The Rossel Islanders restrict women to special small houses during menstruation and during and after childbirth. Women were traditionally forbidden to travel in the type of canoes reserved for "chiefs" and could not visit offshore Loa Island and various other sacred sites (Armstrong 1928). During my own several weeks of residence on Rossel, I learned that women are still forbidden to visit various sites on and near the island such as, for example, a particular stretch of reef just off Jinjo Village on the north coast. Menstrual and childbirth restrictions are still followed.

8. Malinowski (1935:301) notes that in the Trobriand Islands "the payment given for erotic services is called buwana, and this name is, I think, derived from the word for betel nut, Buwa." He does not describe the nature, content, or direction of this payment. On the northern Massim island of Gawa, the gifts of food given to a child's spouse by his or her kin are called *buwaa* (Munn 1986). *Buwa* is a cognate of the reconstructed Proto-Austronesian term for betel nut, *buNah (Conklin 1958:2). The Vanatinai term for betel nut is *ghelezi* or *eledi*, depending upon dialect. Betel nut is often given to a lover and is sometimes first bespelled with love magic (Lepowsky 1982). It is possible that *buwa* on Vanatinai is a loan word that originally derived from the word for betel nut in many present-day Austronesian languages.

9. Young (1983a, 1983b) identifies the "theme of the resentful hero," who offers wealth but is rejected and abandons the place where the rejection takes place, as a motif common to the mythology of many parts of the Massim culture area. One wealth-producing resentful hero of patrilineal Goodenough Island is a male snake (Young 1987:236). In the Vanatinai case, the snake protagonist who offers wealth but is driven off the island is female. Similar mythical accounts of a female snake from whose body shell wealth is produced and who also departs resentfully for Rossel Island after being attacked by a human male have been recorded for matrilineal Duau (Normanby Island) in the southern Massim (Róheim 1950:202; Thune 1980; cited in Young 1987:236–37).

10. However, Vanatinai also has thousands of these shell currency pieces circulating in traditional forms of exchange. Known as *daveri* on Vanatinai and *ndap* on Rossel Island, the valuables are used differently on each island. They were made famous to scholars as "Rossel Island shell money" by Armstrong (1928). Their extensive use on Vanatinai was first documented by the present writer (Lepowsky 1981, 1983, 1989a).

11. A positive value of male aggression in certain contexts in the Vanatinai past is suggested by the reports of present-day islanders that in the period just before European contact enemy skulls circulated in traditional exchanges more frequently than ceremonial valuables. Also, islanders say that shell-disk necklaces (*bagi*) of the kind used in exchange both in the Vanatinai region and in the *kula* area to the northwest, which are manufactured on Vanatinai, were originally decorated human

skulls transformed into necklaces, with white shell substituting for the skull nowadays in what is referred to as the "head" of the *bagi* (Lepowsky 1983, n.d.b).

12. Similarly, Macintyre (1987:227) speculates that the involvement of Tubetube women in *kula* is a postpacification phenomenon. The locally famous story of Dulubia's combined trading and raiding expedition from Kwaraiwa, an island adjacent to Tubetube, to Vanatinai and nearby islands around 1910 indicates that some women from the Engineer Group of islands did make long-distance journeys during this unsettled period before colonial authorities managed to suppress warfare in the Massim (Lepowsky 1983).

Bibliography

Adams, John W. 1973. *The Gitksan Potlatch: Population Flux, Resource Ownership and Reciprocity*. Toronto: Holt, Rinehart and Winston.

Allen, M. R. 1967. *Male Cults and Secret Initiations in Melanesia*. Melbourne: Melbourne University Press.

Ardener, Edwin. 1975. "Belief and the Problem of Women." In *Perceiving Women*, Shirley Ardener, ed., pp. 1–18. London: Malaby.

Armstrong, W. E. 1928. *Rossel Island: An Ethnological Study*. Cambridge: Cambridge University Press.

Atkinson, Jane. 1982. "Anthropology." *Signs* 8: 236–58.

Bacdayan, Albert. 1977. "Mechanistic Cooperation and Sexual Equality Among the Western Bontoc." In *Sexual Stratification: A Cross-Cultural View*, Alice Schlegel, ed., pp. 270–91. New York: Columbia University Press.

Barnett, Homer. 1968. *The Nature and Function of the Potlatch*. (Originally Ph.D. diss., 1938.) Eugene: Department of Anthropology, University of Oregon.

Battaglia, Debbora. 1983. "Projecting Personhood in Melanesia: The Dialectics of Artefact Symbolism on Sabarl Island." *Man* (n.s.) 18 (2): 289–304.

Beauvoir, Simone de. 1953. *The Second Sex*. New York: Alfred A. Knopf.

Berde, Stuart. 1974. "Melanesians as Methodists: Economy and Marriage on a Papua and New Guinea Island." Ph.D. diss., Department of Anthropology, University of Pennsylvania.

Berndt, R. M. 1965. "The Kamano, Usurufa, Jate and Fore of the Eastern Highlands." In *Gods, Ghosts and Men in Melanesia*, P. Lawrence and M. J. Meggitt, eds., pp. 78–104. Melbourne: Oxford University Press.

Brightman, Robert. n.d. "Woman the Non-Hunter: Ideologies of Foragers and Anthropologists." Manuscript.

Brown, Judith. 1970a. "A Note on the Division of Labor by Sex." *American Anthropologist* 72: 1073–78.

———. 1970b. "Economic Organization and the Position of Women Among the Iroquois." *Ethnohistory* 17 (3–4): 151–67.

———. 1982. "Cross-Cultural Perspectives on Middle-Aged Women." *Current Anthropology* 23 (2): 143–56.

Brown, Paula, and Georgeda Buchbinder, eds. 1976. *Man and Woman in the New Guinea Highlands*. Washington, D.C.: American Anthropological Association.

Chowning, Ann. 1973. *An Introduction to the Peoples and Cultures of Melanesia.* Addison-Wesley Module in Anthropology no. 38. Reading, Mass.: Addison-Wesley.
Collier, Jane, and Michelle Rosaldo. 1981. "Politics and Gender in Simple Societies." In *Sexual Meanings: The Cultural Construction of Gender and Sexuality,* Sherry Ortner and Harriet Whitehead, eds., pp. 275–329. Cambridge: Cambridge University Press.
Conklin, Harold. 1958. "Betel Chewing Among the Hanunoo." Special reprint paper no. 56. Proceedings of the Fourth Far-Eastern Prehistory Conference. National Research Council of the Philippines.
Damon, Frederick. 1980. "The Kula and Generalised Exchange: Considering Some Unconsidered Aspects of the Elementary Structures of Kinship." *Man (N.S.)* 15: 267–94.
Divale, William, and Marvin Harris. 1976. "Population, Warfare, and the Male Supremacist Complex." *American Anthropologist* 78 (3): 521–38.
Drucker, Philip, and Robert Heizer. 1967. *To Make My Name Good: A Reexamination of the Southern Kwakiutl Potlatch.* Berkeley: University of California Press.
Dundes, Alan. 1979. "Heads or Tails: A Psychoanalytic Study of Potlatch." *Journal of Psychological Anthropology* 2 (4): 395–424.
Ember, Melvin, and Carol Ember. 1971. "The Conditions Favoring Matrilocal Versus Patrilocal Residence." *American Anthropologist* 73 (3): 571–94.
Estioko-Griffin, Agnes, and P. Bion Griffin. 1981. "Woman the Hunter." In *Woman the Gatherer,* Frances Dahlberg, ed., pp. 121–52. New Haven: Yale University Press.
———. 1985. "Woman Hunters: The Implications for Pleistocene Prehistory and Contemporary Ethnography." In *Women in Asia and the Pacific: Towards an East-West Dialogue,* Madeleine Goodman, ed. Honolulu: Women's Studies Program, University of Hawaii.
Etienne, Mona, and Eleanor Leacock, eds. 1980. *Women and Colonization: Anthropological Perspectives.* New York: Praeger.
Evans-Pritchard, E. E. 1937. *Witchcraft, Oracles and Magic Among the Azande.* Oxford: Oxford University Press.
Feil, D. K. 1978. "Women and Men in the Enga Tee." *American Ethnologist* 5 (2): 263–79.
Fortune, Reo. 1963[1932]. *Sorcerers of Dobu: The Social Anthropology of the Dobu Islanders of the Western Pacific.* New York: E. P. Dutton.
Friedl, Ernestine. 1975. *Women and Men: An Anthropologist's View.* New York: Holt, Rinehart and Winston.
Gewertz, Deborah. 1981. "A Historical Reconsideration of Female Dominance Among the Chambri of Papua New Guinea." *American Ethnologist* 8: 94–106.
———. 1983. *Sepik River Societies: A Historical Ethnography of the Chambri and Their Neighbors.* New Haven: Yale University Press.
Glasse, R. M. 1965. "The Huli of the Southern Highlands." In *Gods, Ghosts and Men in Melanesia,* P. Lawrence and M. J. Meggitt, eds., pp. 27–49. Melbourne: Oxford University Press.
Goodale, Jane. 1971. *Tiwi Wives.* Seattle: University of Washington Press.

Haddon, A. C. 1894. *The Decorative Art of British New Guinea*. Dublin: The Academy House, University Press.

Hammond, Dorothy, and Alta Jablow. 1973. *Women: Their Economic Role in Traditional Societies*. Reading, Mass.: Addison-Wesley.

Hamy, E. T. 1888. "Etude sur les Papouas de la mer D'Entrecasteaux." *Revue D'Ethnographie* t. vii: 503–19.

Herdt, Gilbert. 1981. *Guardians of the Flute: Idioms of Masculinity*. New York: McGraw-Hill.

———. 1982. "Fetish and Fantasy in Sambia." In *Rituals of Manhood: Male Initiation in Papua New Guinea*, Gilbert Herdt, ed., pp. 44–98. Berkeley: University of California Press.

Hoffer, Carol. 1974. "Madam Yoko: Ruler of the Kpa Menda Confederacy." In *Woman, Culture and Society*, Michelle Rosaldo and Louise Lamphere, eds., pp. 173–88. Stanford: Stanford University Press.

Huxley, Julian, ed. 1935. *T. H. Huxley's Diary of the Voyage of H.M.S. Rattlesnake*. London: Chatto and Windus.

Kaberry, Phyllis. 1939. *Aboriginal Woman: Sacred and Profane*. London: Routledge.

Kelly, Raymond. 1976. "Witchcraft and Sexual Relations: An Exploration in the Social and Semantic Implications of the Structure of Belief. In *Man and Woman in the New Guinea Highlands*, P. Brown and G. Buchbinder, eds., pp. 36–53. Washington, D.C.: American Anthropological Association.

Lamphere, Louise. 1977. "Anthropology." *Signs* 2 (3): 612–27.

Landes, Ruth. 1938. *The Ojibwa Woman*. New York: Columbia University Press.

Leacock, Eleanor. 1978. "Women's Status in Egalitarian Society: Implications for Social Evolution." *Current Anthropology* 19: 247–76.

Lepowsky, Maria. 1981. "Fruit of the Motherland: Gender and Exchange on Vanatinai, Papua New Guinea." Ph.D. diss., Department of Anthropology, University of California, Berkeley.

———. 1982. "A Comparison of Alcohol and Betelnut Use on Vanatinai (Sudest Island)." In *Through a Glass Darkly: Beer and Modernization in Papua New Guinea*, Mac Marshall, ed., pp. 325–42. Monograph 18, Boroko, Papua New Guinea: Institute of Applied Social and Economic Research.

———. 1983. "Sudest Island and the Louisiade Archipelago in Massim Exchange." In *The Kula: New Perspectives on Massim Exchange*, Jerry Leach and Edmund Leach, eds., pp. 467–501. Cambridge: Cambridge University Press.

———. 1985a. "Gender, Aging and Dying in an Egalitarian Society." In *Aging and Its Transformations*, Dorothy Counts and David Counts, eds., pp. 157–78. Association for Social Anthropology in Oceania Monograph Number 10. Washington, D.C.: University Press of America.

———. 1985b. "Infant Feeding and Cultural Adaptation on Vanatinai (Sudest Island), Papua New Guinea." *Ecology of Food and Nutrition* 16 (2): 105–26. (Also in *Infant Care and Feeding in the South Pacific*, Leslie Marshall, ed. New York: Gordon and Breach Science Publishers, 1985.)

———. 1989a. "Death and Exchange: Mortuary Ritual on Vanatinai (Sudest Island)." In *Death Rituals and Life in the Societies of the Kula Ring*, Frederick

Damon and Roy Wagner, eds., pp. 199–229. De Kalb: Northern Illinois University Press.

———. 1989b. "Soldiers and Spirits: The Impact of World War II on a Coral Sea Island." In *The Pacific Theater: Island Representations of World War II*, Geoffrey White and Lamont Lindstrom, eds., pp. 205–30. Pacific Monograph Series Volume 8. Honolulu: University of Hawaii Press.

———. (in press). "Sorcery and Penicillin: Treating Illness on a Papua New Guinea Island." *Social Science and Medicine.*

———. n.d.a. "Fruit of the Motherland: Gender and Exchange in an Egalitarian Society." Unpublished manuscript.

———. n.d.b. "Kula and the Resilience of Culture." Unpublished manuscript.

Lévi-Strauss, Claude. 1969a. *The Elementary Structures of Kinship*. Rodney Needham, ed. Tr. J. Bell and J. von Sturmer. Boston: Beacon Press.

———. 1969b. *The Raw and the Cooked*. Tr. J. Weightman and D. Weightman. New York: Harper and Row.

Liep, John. 1983. "Ranked Exchange on Rossel Island." In *The Kula: New Perspectives on Massim Exchange*, Jerry Leach and Edmund Leach, eds., pp. 503–25. Cambridge: Cambridge University Press.

Linton, Ralph. 1940. "A Neglected Aspect of Social Organization." *American Journal of Sociology* 45: 870–86.

———. 1942. "Age and Sex Categories." *American Sociological Review* 7 (5): 589–603.

MacCormack, Carol, and Marilyn Strathern, eds. 1980. *Nature, Culture, and Gender*. Cambridge: Cambridge University Press.

Macgillivray, John. 1852. *Narrative of the Voyage of H.M.S. Rattlesnake. Commanded by the Late Owen Stanley, R.N., F.R.S. and During the Years 1846–1850. Including Discoveries and Surveys in New Guinea, the Louisiade Archipelago, etc.* 2 vols. London: T. and W. Boone.

Macintyre, Martha. 1987. "Flying Witches and Leaping Warriors: Supernatural Origins of Power and Matrilineal Authority in Tubetube Society." In *Dealing with Inequality: Analysing Gender Relations in Melanesia and Beyond*, Marilyn Strathern, ed., pp. 207–28. Cambridge: Cambridge University Press.

Malinowski, Bronislaw. 1922. *Argonauts of the Western Pacific*. New York: E. P. Dutton.

———. 1929. *The Sexual Life of Savages in North-Western Melanesia*. New York: Harcourt, Brace and World.

———. 1935. *Coral Gardens and Their Magic: A Study of the Methods of Tilling the Soil and of Agricultural Rites in the Trobriand Islands*. 2 vols. New York: American Book Co. (Reprinted 1978 in one volume. New York: Dover Publications.)

———. 1962. *Sex, Culture and Myth*. New York: Harcourt, Brace and World.

Margold, Jane, and Donna Bellorado. 1985. "Matrilineal Heritage: A Look at the Power of Contemporary Micronesian Women." In *Women in Asia and the Pacific: Towards an East-West Dialogue*, Madeleine Goodman, ed., pp. 129–52. Honolulu: Women's Studies Program, University of Hawaii.

Mead, Margaret. 1935. *Sex and Temperament in Three Primitive Societies*. New York: William Morrow.

Meggitt, M. J. 1964. "Male-Female Relationships in the Highlands of Australian

New Guinea." In *New Guinea: The Central Highlands,* James B. Watson, ed., pp. 204–24. Washington, D.C.: American Anthropological Association Special Publication 66 (4, pt. 2).

———. 1965. "The Mae Enga of the Western Highlands." In *Gods, Ghosts and Men in Melanesia,* P. Lawrence and M. J. Meggitt, eds., pp. 105–31. Melbourne: Oxford University Press.

Meigs, Anna. 1976. "Male Pregnancy and Reduction of Sexual Opposition in a New Guinea Highlands Society." *Ethnology* 15: 393–408.

Mintz, Sidney. 1971. "Men, Women, and Trade." *Comparative Studies in Society and History* 13: 247–69.

Morauta, Louise. 1981. "Social Stratification in Lowland Papua New Guinea: Issues and Questions." Mimeograph of paper prepared for seminar on Social Stratification in Papua New Guinea, May, Department of Political and Social Change, Research School of Pacific Studies, Australian National University, Canberra.

Munn, Nancy. 1986. *The Fame of Gawa: A Symbolic Study of Value Transformation in a Massim (Papua New Guinea) Society.* Cambridge: Cambridge University Press.

Murphy, Yolanda, and Robert Murphy. 1974. *Women of the Forest.* New York: Columbia University Press.

Nash, Jill. 1987. "Gender Attributes and Equality: Men's Strength and Women's Talk Among the Nagovisi." In *Dealing with Inequality: Analysing Gender Relations in Melanesia and Beyond,* Marilyn Strathern, ed., pp. 150–73. Cambridge: Cambridge University Press.

Ogbu, John. 1978. "African Bridewealth and Women's Status. *American Ethnologist* 5: 241–62.

Olson, Ronald. 1936. "Some Trading Customs of the Chilkat Tlingit." In *Essays in Anthropology Presented to A. L. Kroeber in Celebration of His Sixtieth Birthday,* pp. 211–14. Berkeley: University of California Press.

Ortner, Sherry. 1974. "Is Female to Male as Nature Is to Culture?" In *Woman, Culture and Society,* Michelle Rosaldo and Louise Lamphere, eds., pp. 67–88. Stanford: Stanford University Press.

———. 1984. "Theory in Anthropology since the Sixties." *Comparative Studies in Society and History* 26 (1): 126–66.

Ortner, Sherry, and Harriet Whitehead. 1981. "Introduction: Accounting for Sexual Meanings." In *Sexual Meanings: The Cultural Construction of Gender and Sexuality,* Sherry Ortner and Harriet Whitehead, eds., pp. 1–27. Cambridge: Cambridge University Press.

Parmentier, Richard. 1984. "Gendered Wealth: Male and Female Valuables in Belau Mortuary Exchange." Paper presented at the American Anthropological Association Annual Meeting, Denver, Colorado.

Poole, Fitz. 1981. "Transforming 'Natural' Woman: Female Ritual Leaders and Gender Ideology Among Bimin Kuskusmin." In *Sexual Meanings: The Cultural Construction of Gender and Sexuality,* Sherry Ortner and Harriet Whitehead, eds., pp. 116–25. Cambridge: Cambridge University Press.

Reichard, Gladys. 1934. *Spider Woman: A Story of Navajo Weavers and Chanters.* New York: Macmillan.

———. 1969[1928]. *Social Life of the Navajo Indians.* New York: AMS Press.

Richards, Audrey. 1950. "Some Types of Family Structure Among the Central Bantu." In *African Systems of Kinship and Marriage*, A. R. Radcliffe-Brown and Darryl Forde, eds., pp. 207–51. London: Oxford University Press.

———. 1956. *Chisungu: A Girls' Initiation Rite Among the Bemba of Northern Rhodesia*. London: Faber and Faber.

Rogers, Susan C. 1975. "Female Forms of Power and the Myth of Male Dominance: A Model of Female/Male Interaction in Peasant Society." *American Ethnologist* 2: 727–56.

Róheim, Geza. 1950. *Psychoanalysis and Anthropology: Culture, Personality and the Unconscious*. New York: International Universities Press.

Rosaldo, Michelle. 1974. "Woman, Culture and Society: A Theoretical Overview." In *Woman, Culture and Society*, Michelle Rosaldo and Louise Lamphere, eds., pp. 17–42. Stanford: Stanford University Press.

———. 1980. "The Use and Abuse of Anthropology: Reflections on Feminism and Cross-Cultural Understanding." *Signs* 5 (3): 389–417.

Rosaldo, Michelle, and Jane Atkinson. 1975. "Man the Hunter and Woman: Metaphors for the Sexes in Ilongot Magical Spells." In *The Interpretation of Symbolism*, Roy Willis, ed., pp. 43–75. New York: John Wiley.

Rosman, Abraham, and Paula Rubel. 1971. *Feasting with Mine Enemy: Rank and Exchange Among Northwest Coast Societies*. New York: Columbia University Press.

Sacks, Karen. 1974. "Engels Revisited: Women, the Organization of Production, and Private Property." In *Woman, Culture and Society*, Michelle Rosaldo and Louise Lamphere, eds., pp. 207–22. Stanford: Stanford University Press.

Sanday, Peggy. 1973. "Toward a Theory of the Status of Women." *American Anthropologist* 75: 1682–1700.

———. 1974. "Female Status in the Public Domain." In *Woman, Culture and Society*, Michelle Rosaldo and Louise Lamphere, eds., pp. 189–206. Stanford: Stanford University Press.

———. 1981. *Female Power and Male Dominance: On the Origins of Sexual Inequality*. Cambridge: Cambridge University Press.

Schieffelin, Edward. 1976. *The Sorrow of the Lonely and the Burning of the Dancers*. New York: St. Martin's.

Schlegel, Alice. 1972. *Male Dominance and Female Autonomy: Domestic Authority in Matrilineal Societies*. New Haven: HRAF Press.

———. 1977. "Towards a Theory of Sexual Stratification." In *Sexual Stratification: A Cross-Cultural View*, Alice Schlegel, ed., pp. 1–40. New York: Columbia University Press.

Schneider, David, and Kathleen Gough, eds. 1961. *Matrilineal Kinship*. Berkeley: University of California Press.

Seligman, C. G. 1909. "A Classification of the Natives of British New Guinea." *Journal of the Royal Anthropological Institute* 39: 246–75, 314–33.

———. 1910. *The Melanesians of British New Guinea*. Cambridge: Cambridge University Press.

Simmons, Leo. 1945. *The Role of the Aged in Primitive Society*. New Haven: Yale University Press.

Stanley, Captain Owen. 1849. Unpublished journal. Photocopy in New Guinea Collection, Library of the University of Papua New Guinea.

Strathern, Marilyn. 1980. "No Nature, No Culture: The Hagen Case." In *Nature, Culture and Gender,* Carol MacCormack and Marilyn Strathern, eds., pp. 174–222. Cambridge: Cambridge University Press.

———. 1981. "Self-Interest and the Social Good: Some Implications of Hagen Gender Ideology." In *Sexual Meanings: The Cultural Construction of Gender and Sexuality,* Sherry Ortner and Harriet Whitehead, eds., pp. 166–91. Cambridge: Cambridge University Press.

———. 1987. "Introduction." In *Dealing with Inequality: Analysing Gender Relations in Melanesia and Beyond,* Marilyn Strathern, ed., pp. 1–32. Cambridge: Cambridge University Press.

Thune, Carl. 1980. "The Rhetoric of Remembrance: Collective Life and Personal Tragedy in Loboda Village." Unpublished Ph.D. diss., Department of Anthropology, Princeton University.

Weiner, Annette. 1976. *Women of Value, Men of Renown: New Perspectives in Trobriand Exchange.* Austin: University of Texas Press.

———. 1982. "Sexuality Among the Anthropologists: Reproduction Among the Informants." In *Sexual Antagonism, Gender, and Social Change in Papua New Guinea,* Fitz Poole and Gilbert Herdt, eds. *Social Analysis* (special issue) 12: 52–65.

———. 1986. "Forgotten Wealth: Cloth and Women's Production in the Pacific." In *Women's Work: Development and the Division of Labor by Gender,* Eleanor Leacock and Helen Safa, eds., pp. 96–110. South Hadley, Mass.: Bergin and Garvey Publishers.

White, David. 1893. "Descriptive account by David L. White, Esquire, of the customs, etc. of the natives of Sudest Island." British New Guinea Annual Reports, Appendix U, pp. 73–76.

Wiessner, Polly. 1982. "Risk, Reciprocity and Social Influences on !Kung San Economics." In *Politics and History in Band Societies,* Eleanor Leacock, ed., pp. 61–84. Cambridge: Cambridge University Press.

Young, Michael W. 1971. *Fighting with Food: Leadership, Values and Social Control in a Massim Society.* Cambridge: Cambridge University Press.

———. 1983a. "The Theme of the Resentful Hero: Stasis and Mobility in Goodenough Mythology." In *The Kula: New Perspectives in Massim Exchange,* Jerry Leach and Edmund Leach, eds., pp. 383–94. Cambridge: Cambridge University Press.

———. 1983b. *Magicians of Manumanua: Living Myth in Kalauna.* Berkeley: University of California Press.

———. 1987. "The Tusk, the Flute and the Serpent: Disguise and Revelation in Goodenough Mythology." In *Dealing with Inequality: Analysing Gender Relations in Melanesia and Beyond,* Marilyn Strathern, ed., pp. 229–54. Cambridge: Cambridge University Press.

In the company of the ethnographic essays that make up the rest of this volume, Ruth Goodenough's contribution presents a change of focus and scale. Dealing with the transient cultures of small groups rather than with a stable, historical society, her study of sexism at the kindergarten level offers insight into the kinds of social situations that may generate antagonism toward females.

The groups studied are from American middle-class society. That one group should show a strongly egalitarian bent and the other a chauvinistic one is attributed by the author to features of stress in the situation of the more sexist one.

The more sexist group is marked by hierarchy, control, male separatism, dominance behaviors, exaggerated male bonding, rejection of dependency, devaluation of things female, and repression of feminine input. These features are largely absent from the other group, which is marked instead by an ethic of respect for the individual and a positive valuation of nurturance. The reader will find parallels between the characteristics of the egalitarian group and the social ethos of the Vanatinai and the Minangkabau, described by Lepowsky and Sanday, respectively, in this volume.

Ruth Gallagher Goodenough

8 Situational Stress and Sexist Behavior Among Young Children

Using ethnographic case studies, other authors in this volume have been chipping away at the assumption of universal domination of women by men. Schlegel, Lepowsky, and Sanday, for example, provide visions of alternative gender arrangements as they describe societies, such as the Hopi, the Vanatinai, or the Minangkabau, that are fashioned on egalitarian models. In these societies the prevailing ideology tends to incorporate the values of cooperation, harmony, and life-giving rather than those of control, competition, and dominance, which we associate with patriarchy. From studies such as these we learn that women in more egalitarian societies control important resources and enjoy commensurate status and respect.

That egalitarian arrangements are less common, however, and presumably at greater risk, can hardly be denied. More often than not, external conditions appear to reinforce a possible tilt toward the subordination of women that may be embedded in certain features of our sexual dimorphism. Harsh physical and social environments, for example, have been shown by Sanday and others to foster the emergence of societies that are sex-stratified and authoritarian,[1] just as, in the literature of personality development, certain kinds of harsh psychological environments provide the milieu for the development of authoritarian personalities in individuals.[2]

At the societal level it appears that where food supplies are particularly scarce or unreliable, or where enemies habitually threaten the group, women are more likely to find themselves debased and relatively powerless within a culture that is elaborated essentially on male terms. Moreover, since entrenched male dominance, like other social power systems, sees to its own survival, it is difficult for a society to shift back to a more egalitarian mode. The rigidities of this form of social organization (again perhaps like the rigidities of authoritarian personality structure) are particularly resistant to change.

In a study of sexism among children of kindergarten age in the United States,[3] I found echoes of some of these macrosocietal forms and processes. In the intimate setting of small classroom groups and within a time frame of months, discrete peer-group cultures evolved that mimicked certain historical cultural adaptations, producing minireplicas of both sexist and egalitarian social systems.[4] It is my intention to describe and explore some of these parallel adaptations in cross-sex interaction with particular emphasis on the role of situational stress in the emergence and persistence of sexist forms in small group organization.

For this chapter I shall describe two of the four groups of the original study, the kindergarten-level ones identified as K1 and K2. These two not only were the most intensively studied of the original four but also were the most comparable in all but the nature of their cross-sex interactions. They were kindergarten classes from a small private school where, for reasons of educational philosophy, children were permitted considerably more freedom of expression and choice than usually prevails in standard public school settings. The children involved were middle-class American five and six year olds. All of them were white with the exception of two black children in one of the groups. In social background the parents were largely college-educated professional or business people. Given the nature of the school to which they were sending their children, the parents could perhaps be presumed to be somewhat more liberal in their attitudes toward sexual equality than others of their socioeconomic class and age.[5]

The classes we will be looking at were small, with fifteen children in K1 and nineteen in K2, all of whom attended for the full school day (8:30 to 3:00). Although atypical in these and perhaps other ways from standard kindergartens, for our purposes the two groups were appropriate for study because they provided a rich field of spontaneous boy-girl interactions at the kindergarten level. It was also important for purposes of comparison that the head teacher—an experienced, capable, and intelligent woman—was the same for both groups.

I participated in the daily affairs of both classes for a significant part of the school year, monitoring play and work groups as well as the activities of isolated children. I kept counts of seating and association choices, records of spontaneous responses to teachers' questions in whole group settings, and records of access to areas and materials. For both groups I used a projective test at year's end that employed models of the play area and school room, followed, in the case of K1 girls, by a short interview with each on the subject of existing boy-girl relationships.

Sexist Behavior Among Young Children

TABLE 8.1. Ratios of Negative to Positive Response

Group		Boys to boys Neg.	Pos.	Boys to girls Neg.	Pos.	Girls to boys Neg.	Pos.	Girls to girls Neg.	Pos.
K1	Responses	87	20	124	4	25	8	22	7
	Ratio	4.4 to 1		31.0 to 1		3.1 to 1		3.1 to 1	
K2	Responses	80	32	32	51	17	46	19	44
	Ratio	2.5 to 1		0.6 to 1		0.37 to 1		0.43 to 1	

In the analysis of the data, items of interpersonal behavior were labeled as positive or negative. As negative behaviors I included aggressive acts, verbal put-downs, tauntings, and rejections; positive behaviors included helpful acts, compliments, acts of affection or consideration, and expressions of liking. To compare the groups, I converted the total output of recorded negative and positive behaviors to ratios within four categories of interaction.[6] In Table 8.1 we see for both classrooms the ratio of negative to positive where boys and girls are directing their behavior either to same sex or to opposite sex targets.

By the evidence of Table 8.1 it is clear that the climate of interaction for the two groups was widely different. In every category the boys and girls of K1 showed more negative than positive responses, but the figures of greatest significance appear in the category of behavior directed by boys to girls. If a ratio of 1 to 1 may be considered cross-sex neutral, the 31 to 1 ratio of K1 indicates an extremely negative cross-sex atmosphere—a powerfully sexist one by any definition. In dramatic contrast, the boys of K2 generated almost twice as much positive as negative behavior toward the girls of their class. At the level of mature societies this suggests an order of difference such as Sanday (1981), for example, found between the Yanamamo Indians of South America and the Semang of the Malay Peninsula, one that similarly represents opposite poles of accommodation to male-female differences.

When we speak of male-female differences in the context of this work, we need to be clear that we are talking about those that are relevant to the problem of sex stratification at ages five and six. Quite obviously these are a special subset within the larger picture of male-female differences.[7] At birth and shortly afterward these differences are limited to those of anatomy, size, and the relative maturity of the infant nervous system. By the age of five or six, when such biological differences have radiated out into social behavior, the spread is wide enough that for some purposes we may treat girls and boys of our own culture as two distinct populations. Cultural expectations, physical maturation, and the channeling of experience along the lines of gender identity account for differences in behavior that show up in the familiar overlapping bell curves of psychological studies. By kindergarten age, such studies show boys of our culture to be more aggressive and girls more nurturant; additionally, boys are more competitive, impulsive, and attention-seeking than girls, who tend toward greater cooperativeness, empathy, and compliance.

Close contact between groups divided by psychological differences such as these might reasonably be expected to lead to some inequalities of status and power. Unless met by strong counter-measures to promote equality and mutual interdependence, one might expect that the more aggressive, competitive group would be at an advantage in obtaining power and privilege over the more nurturant, cooperative one. With the kindergarten age population, additional thrust is given to such a possibility in the emergence of certain developmental differences that encourage male antagonism toward females.

The first of these is the familiar problem in identity formation that confronts boys as a consequence of being mothered by a member of the opposite sex. Developmental psychologists point out that boys, as biological "others" in this elemental dyad, must overlay their primary female identification with a later masculine one, whose achievement and maintenance are always then at some risk.[8] In the uncertainties and inevitable stress of this identity process lie a number of possible distortions, including the gratuitous assumption of hostility toward girls and women.[9]

To judge by the literature of psychoanalysis, boys of five or six are perhaps at the height of this process. At this age, they are particularly concerned to validate their identity as males, and some of them find it easier to do so by rejecting and denigrating girls. If parents encourage such a stance as a sign of being a "proper" boy, or if the identity process is compromised by the lack of an appropriate male model or by dependency weaning that is harsh or inappropriate, the boy may be particularly vulnerable to feelings of inadequacy and shame, and his rejection of girls may therefore take an exaggerated form. Moreover, as we shall see, even those boys whose masculine identity may be at relatively low risk can be drawn into these kinds of over-compensating behaviors under conditions of stress or if status among their peers seems to hinge upon it.

Related developmental differences that contribute to the rejection of girls by their boy peers originates with the girls. A conjunction of biology and social training, as well as their more straightforward identification with mother, results in a stronger affinity between girls and various dependency situations than boys normally exhibit. That girls find infancy and dependency appealing is obvious to any parent of daughters; most girls play freely at both sides of the dependency relationship far longer than boys do. Even in real-life situations they tend to cling to some immaturities of speech or behavior, with or without parental approval, that boys more readily forswear. On the other hand, their identification with the mother role often makes them irritatingly precocious moralists. Young boys of kindergarten age, working hard to come to terms with dependency and maternal control in a way that they think will be acceptable in the eyes of men and other boys, may find these propensities of girls particularly trying.

All in all, the differences we have described would seem to make cross-sex conflict or avoidance, if not actual sexism and male dominance, a likely outcome in the kindergarten. But of course there is more than just mutual uneasiness, with its potential for discord and rejection, at work here. What we have not yet factored into the situation is the powerful countervailing force of cross-sex attraction. Although they can seem alienating or threatening, male-female differences also exert a power of attraction at this age, even as they do later. Girls of five and six, when not put off by too much roughness, may like and admire boys and find their antics amusing; similarly boys are often drawn to the attractiveness of girls and to their nurturing ways. From a biological perspective it would seem rather inevitable that this should be so, but it is a feature of young life whose importance adults tend to underplay or forget. Paradoxically, this kind of attraction may itself be a source of stress for five and six year olds. Boys may be threatened by evidence of cross-sex attraction for which they feel unprepared, or which exposes them to critical judgment by their peers; girls may find the boys' attentions unwelcome if they are of the unpleasant pigtail-pulling variety.

To see how these forces of attraction and rejection may work out in concrete social settings we turn now to the descriptions of our two kindergarten groups, K1 and K2.

The K1 Group

In the fall term K1 had fourteen children, nine of them boys. Two of the fourteen were black children, a boy and a girl; the others, as we have seen, were from white, suburban, middle-class backgrounds. The two black children left in December to attend first grade, and another white girl joined the group at the beginning of January. In a situation that was highly unusual for this school, all of the girls and the majority of the boys of the group were new, not only to the school but to each other. Despite the disturbed social environment reflected in the skewed ratios of Table 8.1, seen as individuals there were no discernibly disturbed boys or girls in K1.

The few boys who had been at the school the previous year would hardly have seemed qualified to act as an organizing focus, yet three of them quickly assumed leadership roles in the first days of the term. They built on previous acquaintance and their knowledge of the scene to establish themselves as an in-group that set the tone for the new kindergarten boys. All of the incoming girls were strangers; without a comparable leadership base, they were at an initial disadvantage vis-à-vis the boys. As we shall see, this disadvantage grew worse with time.

The two black children, Elena and Kurt,[10] by virtue of a somewhat different cultural background and perhaps a defensiveness about their minority position in the group, tended to be more aggressive than their white classmates. Indeed their role in the class for the three months of their stay was anomalous in a number of ways. They maintained an attitude of rather belligerent disdain for their white peers and chose to play with each other much of the time. When they did play with the other children they often intimidated them. These two undoubtedly contributed to the generally aggressive profile of the group and to its initial stress level, but because they managed to dominate both the girls and the boys, their behavior ran counter to the sexist trends of the white majority. Kurt, unlike his white peers, was equally aggressive with both boys and girls, while Elena had the white boys so intimidated that they treated her with wary respect. Because they were with the group for less than half the year, and operated in a sense beside it rather than fully within it, the adaptations of this pair lie somewhat outside the main focus of the present study. What follows is weighted toward a description of the cross-sex interaction within the white majority of the class, much of it taking place after the withdrawal of the two black children.

THE BOYS' CROSS-SEX INTERACTION

If none of the children could be singled out as a serious behavioral problem by any of the usual classroom standards, the same could not be said for the group culture that they set in motion. In the judgment of the adults who dealt with them, as well as in the evidence of Table 8.1, there was excessive antagonism from the boys to the girls of K1. The boys dominated or discriminated against the girls regularly, rarely using force, but relying on small harassments and verbal put-downs. They excluded girls from choice play or sitting areas. They openly rejected their hands in circle games and pointedly resisted sitting next to them at snack or lunch time. They paid little or no attention when the girls spoke in whole-group sharing time and on several occasions held their ears rather than listen. A boy holding a pet snake was seen to thrust it repeatedly in the faces of the girls to make them flinch; others, seeing a girl write her name on the board, scribbled over it.

With "I hate girls" as a sometimes explicit watchword, they scapegoated the girls for things that went wrong and equated them jokingly with monsters: "Dracula did it! No, Kathleen did it!" They chortled over the real or imagined discomfiture of girls and made up songs or stories that associated them with nastiness. "Her ears were full of yellow diarrhea" or a chorus of "She went pee and pooh in her pants" were five-year-old bathroom-humor attempts at the sort of thing we associate with locker-room humor among adult males.[11]

The boys of K1 frequently resorted to tones of superiority to intimidate the girls. They refused permission for instance when Jill announced that she wanted to join a group of boys in the prized loft area, telling her with exaggerated patience, "Can't you see we're having a *conference,* Jill?" Another girl, who tried to climb up at the same time, was simply jostled off the ladder. They spoke of "wars" or "science" projects with the same air of importance and the same implication that girls were naturally to be excluded from these lofty concerns.[12]

The boys exploited the belongings and the territory of the girls while jealously guarding their own. In one example, a boy snatched a toy from a girl and then made a face at her. When she objected, he told her coolly, "I'll give it to you when we're done with it." Another appropriated a musical toy from a girl's locker and passed it around among his friends as she watched somewhat anxiously from a distance. Only when the boys tired of it did she venture to retrieve it. In contrast, when one of the boys saw the girls playing with a toy he mistakenly thought belonged to a friend, he shouted angrily at them, "Hey, girls! I call on you girls to get this back! It belongs to Tom!"

The girls attempted to buy their way into favor by bringing treats and games from home to share with the boys, but the brief détentes that followed, where boys and girls would sit together amicably, would last about as long as the treat did. If the girls would play service roles or fetch and carry for the boys, they were sometimes allowed to play, but the tones of voice used and the orders given—"Pick that up!" or "What are you doin' in my seat?"—made it clear that they were there on the boys' sufferance.

In the most common form of cross-sex activity, the boys defined themselves as baddies, whose role was to disrupt the girl's play. Characteristically, the girls would be busy with some sort of domestic play when the boys would descend on them, looking for things to "steal" or ways to pester. They might pretend to set a fire, or leap down on the scene from an overhead rope, then run off with mock-villainous laughs as they regaled each other with what they had done. The girls, trying to ignore or play around these interruptions, would be drawn half-reluctantly into the boys' scenarios. They would go along, perhaps threatening to "call the police," or trying to recover their belongings in exasperated forays. But what had begun as quiet family play would often end as a hurly-burly requiring teacher intervention.[13]

The activities of the boys, on the other hand, were almost never disrupted by the girls. Their space-war games and building projects went on without interference, no matter how much of the room or its equipment they monopolized. As we have seen, they surrounded their own activities with a forbidding atmosphere of importance, often adopting deepened voices and an air of command. One such play started with Tom's announcement to Carl, "Let's play World War I. I'm General Howe, and you're one of my men!" They arranged themselves in hierarchies, where self-appointed leaders gave orders to various underlings, or fathers instructed their sons. One boy wrapped it up with, "I'm the father. That means I'm the captain, and I tell you what to do!"

In an alternative form of organization the boys defined themselves as comrades or buddies. Groups of boys would sit or walk with their arms across one another's shoulders, seeming to rejoice in prototypical male bonding. When the mood was on them they liked to sing strongly cadenced songs together and sway in exaggerated unison. Despite frequent clashes and disagreements among themselves, they had an obvious sense of identity as an all-boy group. To maintain it they sternly guarded a code of manly behavior. "You're scared!" was a charge that drew instant denials; "You're a girl!" was another. Lesser embarrassments lay with babyish mispronunciations, or not knowing the "in" vocabulary of a popular war or space play. A couple of the boys erred when they showed their liking for the most popular lad in the class by kissing him. He reacted with immediate disgust and scrubbed away at the offending spot on his face.

DEPENDENCY

Correlated with their rejection of girls and their strong sense of identity as an all-boy group went a consistent rejection of dependency. A familiar start for a play, for example, was "Pretend our parents are dead." They showed little interest in caring for the classroom guinea pigs, nor did they pretend to be baby animals themselves. Human babies and babyhood were a source of unease and ambivalence;[14] if they pretended to be babies at all, the boys burlesqued it by acting silly, and saying "goo-goo, gaw-gaw." They reacted with "oooh, sick!" at hearing of a nurse changing a new-born infant, and they became increasingly restive during a short film showing the bathing of a baby. In the follow-up discussion, when their teacher asked, "Do you think you liked it when your mother or father bathed you when you were little?" the boys answered with a defiant chorus of "I hated it!" On the way back from seeing this film several of the boys dogged the steps of one of the girls, chanting derisively "Kathleen is a gir-rul, a pretty little gir-rul!" underlining the words with scorn as she hurried back to the classroom. (On the other hand, in a situation divorced from their particular classroom ethos, a group of these same kindergarten boys gently rescued a four-year-old girl when she turned up crying on the playing field, and returned her to her teacher. Indeed their solicitude was such that they came back the next day to check that she was all right.)

CROSS-SEX ATTRACTION

If within their own classroom the boys' macho values were incompatible with dependency or other reminders of their own recent pasts, these same attitudes produced conflict about activities that pointed toward more mature heterosexual relationships. Circle games were often painfully embarrassing, while light-hearted games of chase between the boys and girls, like those we will encounter in K2, were compromised by the boys' rejections of the girls in other contexts. As teases, the boys of K1 came off as heavies; locked into the pattern of the ethos already set in motion, the best they could do was to be the baddies who disrupted what the girls in their group were doing. Understandably, both sexes in K1 looked with some envy at the carefree chases of the then four-year-old nursery group. Some of the kindergarten boys occasionally slipped off to join them, and in similar fashion the oldest boy in the group would sometimes join the first-graders in one of their boy-girl chase games. When Kurt and Elena got a kind of disco-dancing scene going one day, the girls joined in, but the boys largely held back. One of them said to a friend, "Pretend this is on TV, and we're just watchin' it."

In summary to this point, the boys of K1 frequently rejected and denigrated the girls of their class. They denied dependency in themselves and suffered conflict in showing heterosexual interests. Concentrating their attention on what they saw as traditional masculine pursuits, they enforced conformity with their image of masculinity and exalted male comradeship. All of the boys participated in the development of this hyper-masculine ethos, but five of the nine were the most vocal in rejecting the girls and the most vigilant in holding the other boys to the line.

THE GIRLS

We have seen that Elena was exempt from the harassments that the boys directed at the white girls of the class. She daunted them with the menace of her tongue: "Shut up! You need to learn manners!" she would say, perhaps following it up with a scornful "Your mother is ignorant!" But she was also ready to back up threats with action. If she got into a fight with one of the boys, it was he who would usually report the episode, sometimes tearfully, to the teacher, for Elena did not pull her punches. She disassociated herself from the other girls with scorn—"God, Kathleen, you so babyish!"—or mocked what she saw as their prissiness by devilishly repeating it. Thus Elena successfully dealt with real or perceived slights, whether based on sex, race, or social class. When she left the school at the beginning of the Christmas holidays, her self-esteem appeared to be quite intact.

We turn now to the very different situation of the remaining girls of the class. These five, including Wendy, who joined the group in January, suffered in varying degrees the excessive sexist dominance that we have described. Despite their high ratios of negative to positive behavior both with the boys and among themselves, however, their teachers rated none of them individually as aggressive or difficult children.

Table 8.2 shows the distribution of cross-sex negative behavior generated and received by these individual girls. Although three of them received by far the largest share of negative behavior from the boys, the table shows little correlation between what they received and the amount they generated. To appreciate the reflexive nature of the girls' negative responses we must look more closely at the cross-sex interaction of individual girls.

In comparison with the others, Jill's scores in both columns of Table 8.2 are high. From these alone one might assume that she was unusually contentious and suspect that the boys were responding appropriately in their strong reaction to her. A closer look reveals that her negative behavior to the boys consisted almost entirely of verbal responses to negative inter-

TABLE 8.2. Cross-Sex Negative Behavior

	Given	Received
Jill	17	49
Wendy	2*	44*
Kathleen	4	20
Karen	2	12
Susan	2	11

*Because she was with the group for one term only, Wendy's score was doubled to make comparison possible.

changes that they initiated. Jill was in fact an agreeable, outgoing girl. Perhaps unfortunately, she was attracted to the boys' activities and tried, at least in the beginning, to join them. When they rejected her or put her down, she compounded the problem by trying in a ladylike way to stand her ground. It did not take the boys long to learn that her defenses were ineffectual, and her efforts to defend herself often became a springboard for fresh baiting, as shown in the following incident, which catches the flavor of their interactions:

> Jill is at the sandbox with four boys. They have just taunted her, and Jill chooses to ignore it. She hums a tune. Adam, coming back to the attack, says, "That's a dumb song!" and Tom echoes him. Jill responds with her favorite ploy, "You're verrry, verrry smart, and you are too." Tom says with scorn, "I'm smarter than you!" Carl flies his plane close to her head, causing her to duck. Jill retaliates with, "I'm not going to invite you to my birthday party!" Tom answers complacently, "Good! you have yukky parties." Adam, "Yeah!" Carl threatens again with his plane. Jill tries her mollifying tack once more, but can't sustain it, "Well, I *am* gonna invite you to my birthday party, you creeps!" Tom, in the same complacent one, "Good!" Jill, near tears, says, "Excuse me!" and leaves. Adam turns to Carl, who, despite his hectoring, is suspected of liking Jill, and asks innocently, "Who's your best girl friend?" Carl walking into the trap, says, "Jill." Adam looks at him unbelievingly, "You must be sick!" Carl quickly retreats with "My *mom* is my best girl friend."

By the second term some of Jill's ebullience was gone and she began to show signs of anxiety about the boys. In the year-end interview she confessed that their rejections made her "nervous," and she wished, somewhat plaintively, that the boys liked her.

Table 8.2 shows that Wendy accumulated negative reactions from the boys at an even greater rate than Jill, but also that she rarely if ever paid them back in kind. Curiously, these rejections followed a period of initial acceptance. Coming into the group after the departure of Elena and Kurt, she was warmly welcomed by both the boys and the girls. In an unusual show of gallantry, for example, the boys invited Wendy up into the loft, one of them even helping her to climb up. They structured the play to include her: "Let's pretend we're little boys," suggests Adam, and Tom adds, "And Wendy can be a little girl." On another day, Peter, one of the more confirmed misogynists, announced during sharing time that Wendy was coming to his house after school. Wendy was gracious in accepting these attentions, but had trouble deciding what boy she liked best. She favored John, whom she invited to her home, but also liked Tom, whose head she patted lovingly during story time, and Adam, whose company she sought out at rest time.

Within a month this honeymoon atmosphere had dramatically changed, and most of the boys now singled her out for vehement rejection. When a teacher remarked on how well Wendy had played the piano in assembly, Peter and Adam shouted, "We hate how she played!" John, referring to a situation in which Wendy was barely involved, said angrily, "That's why I hate her!" and Peter appeared to go out of his way to push or hit her, sometimes making her cry. Perhaps jealousy, with its potential threat to their solidarity, was at the root of it, but in any event the boys began an almost unrelieved campaign of derogation and rejection that continued for the rest of the year. From Wendy's point of view the shift in the boys' attitude was incomprehensible. Her manner, which had been one of easy confidence, began to change. When playing with the girls she took to defining herself as sickly or lame. When questioned late in the term about her feelings, she responded, "I feel very sad, 'cause they make fun of me, 'cause they don't like me . . . all except Tom."

Kathleen got less than half as much negative response from the boys as Wendy and Jill, but since she tried to avoid confrontation at all costs, that much seems disproportionate. She too was a secure child, but more reserved than the others. Pretty, and always attractively dressed, she was popular with the girls, among whom she played the role of peacemaker.

Yet Kathleen was the one the boys would spin on the merry-go-round long after she begged them to stop, the one whose quiet efforts at sharing time they pointedly ignored or even shut out by holding their ears. She was the one they taunted with being a "gir-rul, a pretty little gir-rul." Suppressed attraction and even envy would appear to have been part of the boys' problem with Kathleen; they worked hard at denying her appeal, at times blocking out even the sound of her voice. The derogatory songs they made up about nameless girls may have come from the same conflicted motivation, blocking out appeal or value by associating it with excrement or abasement. In the interview at year's end, Kathleen claimed that the boys were "just too fighty" and she hoped that when they grew up they would be more "polite." In her words, "I know a friend, twenty years old, who didn't get polite, but some people do."

The remaining two girls suffered the least antagonism from the boys, although it was still much more than they themselves returned. Karen, unlike Jill, made a point of avoiding the boys. She appeared to be uninterested in their play, and did not present images of vulnerable femininity or excessive motherliness or tenderness as perhaps Wendy or Kathleen did. Susan appeared to have few illusions about boys her own age and had set her sights on the later dating scene. Her play fantasies leaned in the direction of clothes, shopping, and entertaining, and were largely absorbed by play in the girl group.

Neither of these girls reported feelings of anxiety about the boys in the year-end interview, but we cannot assume that they escaped altogether the negative fall-out from the boys' hostility. They, along with the other girls, stayed unusually close to grown-ups while at school, and restricted their activities to avoid confrontation. The classroom participation of all the girls suffered as they became less and less willing to speak up when the boys were around. During question periods the boys gave almost all the answers. When the children were choosing activities for a free period, the girls invariably waited quietly for the boys to announce their choices and even to move off the scene before venturing to name their own.

There is little doubt that the playing out of the boys' antagonism reined in the spontaneity and limited the participation of the girls. But the ratios of Table 8.1 show a further possibility. The rate of negativity in the girl to girl category is at least six times what it is for K_2. Even if we allow for the presence of the feisty Elena for three months, the rate remains high. It would not be stretching the facts to suggest that the girls of K_1, unwilling or unable to fight back against the boys' harassment, tended to displace their frustration inwardly or upon each other.

THE TEACHERS

The teacher and her assistant were deeply concerned about the sexist attitudes of the boys. Whenever they heard a boy call the girls dumb, or weird, or fatheads, they rebuked him. A boy who made a vomiting gesture when a girl chose him in a circle game was firmly told that he would be removed from the game if he repeated it. They reprimanded boys for refusing to listen to girls and held discussions about hurting the feelings of others, but to little avail. The boys continued their attacks on the sly or simply shrugged off the mild rebukes.

The teachers resorted to seating and resting charts that included cross-sex pairings, but these failed as the boys found graphic ways to show their distaste for girl partners and the girls came to dread the charts because of the hatefulness they engendered. When the boys were off the scene, the teachers encouraged the girls to speak out in discussion sessions. This was useful as far as it went, but the girls clammed up again when the boys returned. At mid-year the teachers greatly expanded the dress-up corner to offer alternatives to the stereotyped games of space and war. At the same time they increased activities like cooking and exercise sessions that involved everyone. Despite these and other creative attempts to deal with the situation, the end of the year found the teachers discouraged by the persistence of the boys' sexist attitudes. In this group the boys had hardened their behavior into a sexist stance that even the teachers were not able to change materially.

The K2 Group

As kindergarten groups from the same private school, K1 and K2 shared a number of common background features. Along with the same teacher and curriculum they had a similar socioeconomic profile, that of the children who made up the majority of the school's population. K2, with eleven girls and eight boys, was a larger group, however, and its sex distribution ratio reversed that of K1.

We already know from Table 8.1 that the two groups were very different in the quality of their boy-girl interactions. The figures in the ratios, however, as dramatic as they are, hardly prepare us for the differences in tone between them. The emotionally restrictive, male-dominated atmosphere of K1 stands in sharp contrast to the easy egalitarianism of K2, where it was commonplace for girls and boys to show that they liked one another, and for the girls to be as free and independent in their behavior as the boys.

Although something of the difference in tone between them no doubt reflects the relatively greater number of boys in K1 and of girls in K2, the overt sexism of the one and the lack of it in the other cannot be attributed simplistically to such numerical imbalances. In the original study from which these descriptions are taken, the group identified as K4 was the least sexist of all,[15] yet its boys outnumbered the girls by more than 2 to 1. A more promising circumstance to investigate, as we look more closely at K2, lies in the size and nature of its core group, that is, the group of children who were already acquainted when kindergarten began. The core group of K2 (although closely parallel to that of K4) differed significantly in size, experience, and sexual composition from that of K1.

Close to 60 percent of the boys and girls of K2 had been together at least one full year before entering kindergarten, with most of these having been in the school's nursery program since they were three. As preschoolers they had been part of a well-knit group that included equal numbers of boys and girls. Although their play might include any combination of these children, three social groupings made up an enduring pattern of association. The most cohesive group was a central threesome made up of Michelle, Jonathan, and Bruce, who charged about as superheroes (including Wonder Woman) or pretended to be members of real or animal families, wrestling and chasing each other in high good humor. The five remaining girls specialized in more elaborate family plays, often based on characters from the then still-popular sitcom, *The Brady Bunch*. The rest of the boys, when not playing at boy-type games with each other, fit in and around the activities of the girls or the mixed-sex threesome.

Among the strengths of the core group of K2 must be counted their long-standing affection for one another, as well as the social skills they had developed for minimizing conflict within their group. Although they were a strong-minded bunch, in two years of nursery school they had picked up useful strategies that allowed them to work out differences rather than prolong them. As a result the general tone of the class, if not always without friction, was easygoing and pleasant. These patterns of association and behavioral resources were part of the culture that the core group carried over into kindergarten; they proved to be strong enough to absorb and shape the behavior of a sometimes difficult assortment of eight newcomers into the prevailing group culture.

The aspects of the culture that had to do with cross-sex interaction differed at every point from those that characterized K1. In months of observation, one never heard "I hate girls" or any other put-down in terms of sex. Disagreements between a girl and a boy could arise, but they were context-specific and were dealt with as such. Boys did not monopolize prized areas or toys; girls were not bullied or ordered around in service roles. These boys did not disrupt girls' activities or see themselves as baddies with a mission to harass the girls.

Although boys and girls tended to clump together in same-sex groups for particular kinds of play, just as they had in preschool, members of the opposite sex were not excluded. In a fairly typical example, when a number of boys were building with large blocks, Kevin called to a girl who was standing on the sidelines, "We've got plenty of room, come on and build with us."

In this group, children frequently hugged or patted each other, and it was common to see friends of the opposite sex sitting or resting next to one another. One boy, seeing the chart for rest-time placement, said, "Good, I get to rest next to a girl." His friend, checking the list, noted, "Oh, me too!" The hand-holding games and dances that caused grief in K1 were not a problem in K2. There were nearly always combinations of boys and girls who wanted to be partners.

DEPENDENCY

With K1 we saw that the boys rejected symbols of dependency as being incompatible with their masculine image. In contrast, the boys and the girls of K2 spent a great deal of time holding and petting the classroom rabbits, and K2 boys showed interest rather than embarrassment when a visiting baby brother underwent a diaper change. Some of them still played that they were in animal or human families, either as babies or parents, and these roles sometimes slid over into real life, as in this episode from a music class:

> The children are playing a guessing game and Michelle wants to go out as Jonathan's partner. She can't, it's Laurie's turn. She looks unhappy, then puts her head in Bruce's lap. He pats it. Soon she recovers and sits up again. Later, Bruce cannot have a turn for the same reason. He says, "Oh shucks, Baby!" and hugs Michelle, who hugs him back.

CROSS-SEX ATTRACTION

In the realm of cross-sex attraction and rudimentary courting games, K2 boys and girls were predictably more at ease than those of K1. This was true for circle games and dances, but it was also apparent in the way they could think about more serious cross-sex attachment. The three friends, Bruce, Michelle, and Jonathan, were sometimes caught up in the question of which of the boys was to marry Michelle:

Bruce turns to Michelle and asks, "You gonna marry me, Michelle?" She answers, "Yes." Bruce continues, "You're not gonna marry Jonathan?" Michelle, "No." Bruce turns and says, "Jonathan, she's gonna marry me, and not you." Jonathan looks unhappily at Michelle, "You're not gonna marry me?" Michelle says lamely, "I'm sorry, Jonathan, I can't help it. I *was* gonna marry my cousin."

That the field is open, and that others can play the game is clear from a later episode:

> Michelle has the record player. Bruce reaches across the table and tries to grab it. She laughs and grabs it back. Bruce explains, "It's not yours, it's the school's!" Michelle just laughs. Cathy, sitting next to Bruce, says something to him, ending in "Bruce, honey." Laurie, sitting across the table and enjoying it all says, "That's your honey," and she laughs. Then she adds mischievously, "Your honey had to rest next to me yesterday."

In another pairing, Andrea and Michael, one of the new boys, formed an attachment early in the year. Thanks to Andrea's persistence and sense of the dramatic, the affair lasted several months, running through various femme fatale and Sleeping Beauty episodes. Some of these entailed the cooperation of half the class, whose job it was to lure Michael in from his affairs outdoors to awaken the "sleeping" Andrea. Everybody knew what was afoot, including Michael, who allowed himself to be drawn into these grand awakenings to everyone's amused satisfaction.

Although fewer than half the children were involved in explicit attractions of this sort, most of them could vicariously enjoy them. When it came to games of pursuit between the boys and girls, however, no one held back. The classic "Kissing Girls" game of first and second graders at the school involved a chase whose ostensible but rarely achieved purpose was the kissing of a captured boy. The girls of K2 substituted perfume or chapsticks, often as not brought to school by the boys, and in their version of the game the chase could go either way, as this excerpt shows:

> The girls are chasing the boys to put perfume on them. Four boys come running breathlessly around the corner of the building and compare experiences. One of them says, "Get Michael! Get Michael to help us!" (Michael is in shop.) Steve says, "They almost got me!" Jonathan adds, "They almost got me, but I got away!" Apparently Jonathan has captured the perfume, for they sneak over and try to hide it in the tall grass. The girls appear by now, and seeing what is going on, one says firmly, "Jonathan, it's Cathy's!" Jonathan says, "I'll give it back to you if you stop chasing us!" Cathy answers, "We will,

we're havin' a little break." Jonathan passes the bottle back, but then, seeing that this promises to put an end to the game, he asks, "Can I have it back?" Cathy gives it to him and Laurie says, "Now it's the boys chase the girls!" They happily change roles and the girls take off, with the boys in pursuit.

INDIVIDUAL STYLES OF ACCOMMODATION

The various strands that made up the nonsexist ethos of K2 were represented in the behavioral styles of particular children, each of whom contributed to the successful bridging of the differences between the two sexes. The common bridging roles are those that minimize such differences or capitalize on them in a culturally acceptable way. One thinks of the roles of "tomboy" or of "boyfriend-girlfriend" as examples of these; but simply being friends, or treating each other as siblings, or taking a caring parental role are forms of bridging that are possible in an environment where children feel secure with one another. The following short descriptions are of seven children who successfully played bridging roles in K2. They represent some of the possible styles of cross-sex accommodation that occurred, but by no means exhaust them.

Michelle, with a tomboy sturdiness and an attractive, open personality, took equally to the rough play of the boys or the domestic play of the girls. As Wonder Woman, Baby, or Disco Girl, and at all times secure in the affection of Jonathan and Bruce, she made attachment between the boys and girls seem both easy and desirable.

Andrea's cross-sex interests formed another successful bridge between the worlds of the boys and the girls. She concentrated on romance and courtship, bringing presents of pennies and gum for her new conquest, wearing her prettiest clothes for him, and figuring out ways to involve him in her romantic schemes. We saw that the others enjoyed these fantasy plays, which provided a safe look at some of the allurements and clichés of romantic attachment.

Maureen, the most loving and maternal child in the group, bridged the differences between the sexes with an unfailing supply of smiles and affectionate gestures, which the boys accepted unself-consciously:

> After her turn at holding the visiting baby brother, Maureen says to Andrea, "I hugged him and I kissed him, like this," and she kisses Bruce, who is now holding the baby. Bruce accepts the kiss on his cheek without comment, while Maureen and Andrea smile at each other over his head.

Among the boys, Bruce and Jonathan showed the widest range of bridging skills. They were affectionate and protective, particularly of Michelle, but they also played the courtship game with gusto. As large, sturdy boys they enjoyed the company and activities of other boys, yet they were genuinely interested in the activities of the girls.

> As one of the girls demonstrates her newly acquired skill at knitting, Bruce and Jonathan lie on the floor watching. Bruce asks in a tone of some awe, "How did you learn to do it?"

Michael, even as a newcomer, jumped into the cross-sex games with enthusiasm. He played Prince Charming in Andrea's romance, but his attachments were broader than this. He combined unmistakably macho ways with an open liking for girls, which many of them reciprocated. Although it was his first year in the group, he established himself as a hearty fellow with both the boys and the girls, and did nothing to subvert the nonsexist atmosphere of the class despite his tough-guy masculinity.

Finally, Marcus played a more gentle role. As an affectionate older brother in real life, he often initiated light-hearted, brotherly kinds of play with the girls. In a typical instance, he and Kate spent a happy half hour changing each other and anyone else they encountered into green mushrooms; in another, where he was seen marching with a friend, he explained away the stick "guns" they were carrying: "We're not baddies. We're guards, really. We're guarding Andrea, 'cause she's the Queen."

SUMMARY FOR K2

In K2, boys and girls treated each other with virtually twice as much positive as negative behavior. In such a group one would expect that both sexes would show fewer signs of stress than we encountered in K1. To this observer, the boys of K2 appeared less anxious and self-protective than those of K1; they were less critical of one another and their play was less stereotypical. The greater difference in security level, however, lay with the girls, who showed far more spontaneity than the girls of K1, and unlike them, were free to play or sit or rest where, how, and with whom they pleased. Significantly, when teachers addressed questions to the whole group, these girls answered as freely and as frequently as the boys. As one might also expect, in their freedom from rejection and domination by the boys they generated very little negative interaction among themselves.

Analysis and Conclusions

To those of us who share the cultural background of these children, the forms they chose for encapsulating their gender interactions are familiar. As widely different as the resulting classroom cultures of K1 and K2 were, we recognize them as possibilities within the multiple gender ideologies that our culture embraces. Children absorb these multiple and often conflicting ideologies not only from their own family circumstances but from all the gender representations that come to them through television and other windows on the larger culture. The sexism of K1 undoubtedly has an American accent, just as does the egalitarian ethos of K2.

Yet for those who are interested in the general problem of social stratification by sex, the descriptions of K1 and K2 also suggest parallels with the social-structural arrangements of cultures other than our own and provide useful insights into their genesis. The cross-sex accommodations of the boys and girls of K1 show many of the classical features of patriarchal societies or other male-dominated groupings. On the side of the boys we saw the characteristic rejection, exclusion, and intimidation of the girls, as well as the exploitation of their property and services. We saw the emergence of early scenarios where girls are cast as scapegoats, monsters, or victims. In the boys' chants and jokes we saw the creation of images that, although immature in content, were reminiscent of the well-developed ideologies of female pollution that mark many societies featured by male dominance.

The boys of K1 reverted to Spartan relationships that increased their sense of power and control. Bonding together in ways that reduced competition among themselves, they sometimes exalted comradeship, at other times relished hierarchies of prestige and power. They developed a code of masculinity that rejected dependency, and policed each other for signs of defection. Their preoccupation in play was with games of war, combat, and space in which Good Guys endlessly did battle with Bad Guys. In the play they initiated most commonly with the girls, they cast themselves as baddies and marauders. All these are childish replications of elements common to sexist societies.

Looked at from the standpoint of the girls, we found a lowering of spontaneity and participation, and a familiar silencing. One feels the impoverishment of a system that effectively muffled the voices of so many of its members.

By contrast, the culture of K2 was built on the full participation of both sexes. In the absence of the boys' need to control and dominate we found a more relaxed, egalitarian atmosphere, marked by tolerance for the needs and differences of others. Things that were subjected to control or suppressed in K1 found a comfortable home in K2. The children of K2 were as unconflicted about nurturance and dependency as they were about heterosexual attachments. Members of both sexes were free to play in same- or mixed-sex groupings, and the traditional play of either sex was not out of bounds to the other. It is hardly a coincidence that the observer's notes for K2 contain frequent references to laughter and smiles.

If we look for a key to the differences between the two groups it would have to be in the word *control*. The boys of K1 constrained the activities of the girls in all the ways they could think of, and those of K2 did not. Since we know that humans mobilize to exert control when they feel threatened, we must identify, if we can, some of the kinds of threat that the boys of K1 felt in their kindergarten situation, and see how these triggered the emergence of a full-blown sexist response.

As we have seen, Sanday (1981), in dealing with historical cultures, has located the source of threat in environments made harsh by uncertain food supplies and hostile neighbors. One could argue that even at the societal level, such external or structural conditions are ultimately felt by individuals as ego threats, or as things that put the self in jeopardy. When dealing with the problem at the level of kindergarten children, however, we must look to both structural and psychological explanations; we must look, that is, for situational hazards that impinge on the self within the processes of identity formation.

In the original study, from which our accounts of K1 and K2 are taken, the background feature that most clearly differentiates the nonsexist groups from the others is the extent to which the children knew one another before entering kindergarten. As one would expect, the groups with the least sexism had the most substantial core of well-acquainted children. Where more than half of both sexes had been together in nursery school for a year or longer there was a large, associated reduction in negative cross-sex behavior.

The nonsexist culture of K2 was the product of long association in nursery school, a rich mix of cross-sex interactions that went back to when many of its members were barely three. These boys and girls had come together at an age when they still felt free to give open expression to the dependency needs that were high on their personal agendas as they entered the newly forming nursery school group. They came up through a family-like atmosphere where they played and worked, ate, napped, toileted, and made jokes together much as a set of siblings might. As very young children they had seen each other in intimate and occasionally vulnerable situations that had bred support and trust among them. As three year olds, each of them had known feelings of sadness, fatigue, or hurt when only tears, or the teacher's lap, or one's own thumb in the mouth would serve. The management of such dependency needs was something they had shared. Now, as kindergarten children, an occasional outcropping of need on somebody's part was still felt as no big thing. The boys could be comfortable with the familiar, ongoing nurturance of the girls as well as with the emergence of attachments that pointed to more mature heterosexual interests. With these girls, and in this familiar setting, their vulnerability to feelings of adequacy or shame was minimal. Whatever their identity needs, they were not at risk in the ambience of K2.

With K1 we have seen that due to an unusual attrition of students at the end of nursery school (specifically the lack of any carryover of girls), there was no such pre-existing culture of accommodation to soften the entry into kindergarten. Placed in a situation where they were expected to play, eat, and nap with strangers during a long school day, these five- and six-year-old boys and girls, by this time more self-conscious and with strong self-protective needs, might well find it initially stressful. The boys, with shaky masculine identities to protect against the pulls of dependency and the threat of more mature cross-sex attraction, would find it especially so. When we add to this the presence of the two black children, with their own defensive needs and their own ways of coping, we round out a picture of initial strain for all the children of K1, but particularly for the boys, whose identity concerns called for cool and manly behavior, however shakily buttressed.

The small handful of boys who had been in the nursery school before had experienced the kind of cross-sex intimacy we have described for K2, but the girls with whom they had established trusting relationships were gone. As kindergarteners they faced the ten newcomers with only the resource of their prior acquaintance and a certain amount of bravado; but this, as it turned out, was enough. The new boys looked eagerly to the small group of "old hands" for leadership, and with this move tapped into the latent power of male bonding. It may have been largely bluff at first, but the small group of incumbents responded with the most macho behavior they could command[16] and set the sexist course of the year in motion.

The white girls, all of them strangers, and under siege from the start from both Elena and the boys, drew back into the defensive formations that they occupied most of the year. (Their situation was not unlike that of the in-marrying wives of the Hua, as described by Anna Meigs in this volume, where the practice of village exogamy introduces women as strangers into a male-dominated culture.) The boys of K1 saw these girls increasingly as an alien lot and worked to find rationalizations for rejecting them. From the safety of their newly won male comradeship, they scorned the dependency they associated with the girls and rejected anything that suggested intimacy and heterosexual attachment. That they knew other ways of behaving is clear from their initial treatment of Wendy and their behavior in relation to younger children outside the class. But within the bounds of their own classroom these behaviors were cognitively dissonant with the burgeoning macho culture, and the boys did not sustain them. Perhaps the rewards of power and the vision of themselves as superior provided positive reinforcement, helping to override the latent sympathy or attraction they might feel for the girls. In the reassurance of their bonding with one another, they were relatively impervious to the corrective strategies and appeals of the teachers.

All these children were under the stress of having to form new relationships in a situation with high potential for embarrassment. At an age when masculine identity concerns dominated their personal agendas, the five- and six-year-old boys among them drew upon familiar masculine resources, including the flawed ones based on identity conflict, to create a society with familiar patriarchal outlines. Although it was only weeks in the making, once crystallized it endured for the whole school year, despite the efforts of adults to change it. Like genuine patriarchal arrangements, the system of controls set up by the boys of K1 had a rigidity that effectively ruled out change to a softer or less sexist mode. The girls, under these constraints, occupied the diminished physical and social space left to them, and variously endured.

Without the external stresses we have identified for K1, the boys and girls of K2 continued to build a culture based on equality that they had started as three year olds. The gender identity problems of the boys found resolution in an unbroken transition from dependency to more mature heterosexual interests that they and the girls worked out together. At no point did these identity needs become the organizing focus for the boys' behavior in relation to the girls. Like the males in nonsexist historical cultures, the boys of K2 kept in touch with dependency and learned to extend it in nurturance. In like manner they kept in touch with their positive feelings toward the girls and learned to extend them toward real attachments in play.

Thus, as small as our kindergarten groups were, they offer productive insights into the way humans, even very young ones, deal with sex and gender differences. The possibilities for male dominance are there, given the (generally) greater size, aggressiveness, and competitiveness of males, and compounded by their frequently more precarious identity development. But these possibilities can be muted or even overridden in situations where stress is at a minimum and the positive attractions and mutual interdependence between the sexes have room to flourish. If we are to bring the problem of sex stratification under more rational control and reduce its cost in the loss of human potential, it will be because we more fully understand the kinds of stress that breed it and the life-history crisis points at which gender differences are most likely to produce emotional conflict.

Notes

1. See Sanday (1981) and Chafetz (1984).
2. Adorno et al. (1950).
3. R. Goodenough (1987).
4. For a theoretical and analytical treatment of culture construction among nursery school children see Corsaro (1985).
5. Aside from identifying these most general characteristics, however, no effort was made to study the individual children in their family settings. As valuable as such information might have been, its gathering was well beyond the scope and resources of the study as it was initially undertaken. The focus of this chapter remains at the level of social interaction within small-group cultures, not at the level of individual biography.
6. For chi-square tests of significance see R. Goodenough (1987).
7. For thorough reviews of the extensive literature see Maccoby and Jacklin (1974) and Pitcher and Schultz (1983).
8. Stoller (1974) and Chodorow (1978).
9. W. Goodenough (1963).
10. Fictitious names have been substituted for real names throughout.
11. This echoes the attribution of pollution to females in ethnographic accounts of male-dominated societies. See Meigs, this volume.
12. In his study of younger children, Corsaro (1985) identifies two recurring but conflicting interactive patterns that are obviously at work here. The first is based on children's needs for social participation, the second on their need to preserve what he calls their "interactive space" (ongoing play or social relationships). In his experience, resistance to access attempts falls off to about a 50 percent level as children settle in to established relationships over time. (Although, curiously, in his raw data [127] boys resist the access of girls 75 percent of the time.) What we see with the boys of K1, however, is a far more determined and consistent resistance to girls' access attempts. They are in fact so successful at it that the girls largely give up trying.
13. For a sensitive description of this kind of interaction in a less negatively charged atmosphere, see Paley (1984).

14. That boys at all ages show less interest in infants than girls do is reported by Blakemore (1981). It seems clear, however, that the aggressive rejection of infancy by the boys of K1 was more than a matter of reduced interest.

15. R. Goodenough (1987).

16. The boys' response was not unlike that resorted to by some young college men or new recruits to the service, who, under some of the same kinds of stress and with the support of other males in the same position, may come up with virulently sexist attitudes and behavior.

Bibliography

Adorno, T. W., E. Frenkel-Brunswick, D. J. Levinson, and R. N. Sanford. 1950. *The Authoritarian Personality*. New York: Harper.
Best, R. 1983. *We've All Got Scars: What Boys and Girls Learn in Elementary School*. Bloomington: Indiana University Press.
Blakemore, J. 1981. "Age and Sex Differences in Interaction with a Human Infant." *Child Development* 52: 386–88.
Chafetz, J. 1984. *Sex and Advantage: A Comparative, Macro-Structural Theory of Sex Stratification*. Totowa, N.J.: Rowman and Allanheld.
Chodorow, N. 1978. *The Reproduction of Mothering: Psychoanalysis and the Sociology of Gender*. Berkeley: University of California Press.
Corsaro, W. 1985. *Friendship and Peer Culture in the Early Years*. Norwood, N.J.: Ablex Publishing.
Eisenhart, M. A., and D. C. Holland. 1983. "Learning Gender from Peers: The Role of Peer Groups in the Cultural Transmission of Gender." *Human Organization* 42: 321–32.
Goodenough, R. 1987. "Small Group Culture and the Emergence of Sexist Behavior." In *Interpretive Ethnography of Education at Home and Abroad*, G. Spindler and L. Spindler, eds. Hillsdale, N.J.: Lawrence Erlbaum Associates.
Goodenough, W. 1963. *Cooperation in Change*. New York: Russell Sage Foundation.
Maccoby, E. E., and C. N. Jacklin. 1974. *The Psychology of Sex Differences*. Stanford: Stanford University Press.
Paley, V. 1984. *Boys and Girls: Superheroes in the Doll Corner*. Chicago: University of Chicago Press.
Pitcher, E. G., and L. H. Schultz. 1983. *Boys and Girls at Play: The Development of Sex Roles*. New York: Praeger.
Sanday, P. 1981. *Female Power and Male Dominance: On the Origins of Sexual Inequality*. Cambridge and New York: Cambridge University Press.
Stoller, R. J. 1974. *Sex and Gender*. New York: Jason Aronson.

In a society like the Yoruba, where deference and power flow along the multiple channels of age, gender, seniority, wealth, and political position, the relative empowerment of women vis-à-vis men may be crosscut and even reversed, as Sandra Barnes describes in her essay. Analyzing the situation of urban African women, Barnes shows that property holding opens the door to power and authority as well as to the public world of urban politics.

She investigates what she terms "the structure of opportunity," particularly as it applies to women in the city of Lagos. She examines the processes by which women move from being without property and dependent on others to being owners who can co-opt the productive labor of others. It is this that enables them to reach the economic independence necessary to engage in competitive transactions in the political arena.

Yoruba ideology supports both the subordination of women and the contradictory position that "men and women are equally capable of performing society's valued and essential tasks." The urban women of Lagos (perhaps like urban women across tropical Africa generally), elect not to contest the terms of this contradiction so much as to exploit it. Despite the structural conditions that hinder their entry into the status of house owner they are achieving it, and by virtue of their effort are trading domestic subordination for domestic autonomy, with attendant access to positions of public power.

Sandra T. Barnes

9 Women, Property, and Power

Scholars are struck by apparent contradictions in beliefs and behaviors surrounding women and their holding of power. Among the Yoruba-speaking peoples of West Africa, a population that approaches 20 million, women in some contexts appear to subordinate themselves to their husbands, male family elders, employers, and public office holders to the extent that they kneel, feign ignorance, and give them great deference,[1] but in other contexts they are assertive, independent, and powerful. Indeed, they are well known as the organizers, controllers, and leaders of markets and extensive systems of trade.[2] Yoruba ideology strongly supports both of these postures. The notion of male dominance/female subordination is firmly in place, especially in domestic and familial settings. Yet it is contradicted by the equally prevalent notion that women are as capable as men in undertaking economic and political endeavors. To quote a popular proverb, "Whether the man or the woman kills the snake is immaterial; the essential thing is that it is gone."[3] The message of this proverb—that men and women are equally capable of performing society's valued and essential tasks—makes it difficult to reconcile the markedly subordinate behavior that women display in certain contexts. How do these West African women wield powers that women in few societies wield, yet consistently defer to authority figures, the majority of whom are male? The goal of this essay is to resolve this seeming contradiction, because doing so helps us understand how it is that some women, in the face of an almost universal imbalance in men's and women's presence in public political bodies, can in fact use their powers to assume positions in those same bodies.

The way that ideologies of gender inequality reinforce or mask the material conditions of power has been approached from many directions (for example, Sanday 1981; Schlegel 1977; and Strathern 1987). The approach taken here is to focus on the context within which the ideology of inequality seems most strongly expressed and to determine why this is so. Where the ideology is strong—in this case, the domestic context—the stakes may be high. Where dominance is vigorously expressed or acted out, it may well be part of the apparatus for maintaining control over particular resources and relationships that have significant rewards. An ideology of dominance clearly acts as a self-serving mechanism for one gender in its effort to gain advantage over the other, particularly when the rewards to be gained from being the dominant figure in a particular context are the same for either gender.

In Yoruba-dominated cities of southwestern Nigeria, one kind of control that leads to important societal rewards is derived from house ownership. Control gains greater significance as urban property, because of rising costs or spatial limitations, becomes more scarce. On the surface, house owning appears to be a pragmatic aspect of everyday life, but for Yoruba owners it means authority over a domestic unit. As such, house owning encompasses economic, social, and political relationships and facilitates their expansion. For these reasons it is important to understand the way in which ownership occupies a critical position in the social system, how it comes about, and how, ideology notwithstanding, it can work to the advantage of women. What, in other words, does control of domestic space have to tell us about the pragmatics of women's quest for power?

The evidence for addressing these questions comes from metropolitan Lagos,[4] where women from many Yoruba-speaking subgroups exercise public political powers by participating in neighborhood affairs, making decisions that affect others, and even controlling the actions of others. In many localities, these powers are exercised informally, but in a few neighborhoods informal powers have been converted into formal, titled offices. Women do not participate in neighborhood affairs in large numbers, although their participation is unquestioned and in some instances even solicited or encouraged. The reason for low levels of female participation is that the structure of opportunity, that is, the economic, social, and legal conditions that affect an individual's modus operandi in the public domain,[5] is less favorable to women than to men. The point is that women do not seek or use power in ways different from men. Rather the difference between men and women, insofar as the quest for power is concerned, lies not in the way they go about that quest but in the structure of opportunity as it applies to each gender.[6]

Two issues are meaningful if we are to understand the structure of opportunity as it applies to women and power—security and independence. Security can be found under the protective umbrellas of marriage and kinship, and a dependence on them for economic well-being, or security can be found in one's own independent abilities to be economically self-sufficient. This does not mean that independence is separated from marriage: many economically independent women are married. Neither does it mean that independence is separated from kinship obligations: virtually all women are heavily encumbered by kin ties. Indeed, economic independence often brings about more social involvements than dependence does. There is a difference, however, between being dependent on others and being involved with others. My interest is in women who find security not through their dependence on others but through economic independence—women who, if they choose, can provide their own food, shelter, clothing, and care in old age, and can make most decisions about the use of their own time, energy, and resources. A subtle shift takes place when women do not have to *depend* on others but, instead, can *use* others—people who depend on them—in order to meet their needs for security. The more one is able to use the services, labor, or support of others, the more one is able to accumulate wealth and invest it in the kinds of social and material items that make participation in community affairs possible. But as the evidence from Lagos shows, the structure of opportunities is such that women, to a far greater extent than men, find it difficult to control their lives in ways that help them gain independence.

Accordingly, as a way of tracing the route to public power among contemporary Lagos women—and, I suspect, in many other urban places in tropical Africa—one must first examine three meaningful aspects of women's lives: the reasons for African women's preoccupations with security, the strategies that lead to their getting it, and the structure of opportunities as it affects women. Then one can turn to questions of power. What do security and independence do for women in terms of the kinds of powers that accrue to them? Are these powers expandable and, if so, in what contexts do women exercise them? Finally, what are the consequences of women exercising power in these contexts?

Economic Independence

Studies of urban African women since the 1950s stress their preoccupation with security.[7] Little sums up women's predicament in this way:

> . . . the urban economy does not provide women as a whole with the safeguards and security they traditionally enjoy in most rural systems. In the

latter milieu, with all its drawbacks, women have groups of their own, including age sets, secret societies, initiation schools and other associations which, as well as playing their part in the general life of the village, engender an *esprit de corps* among its female members. Also, many wives are able to support themselves and their children through horticulture; and although in the rural system women depend for protection upon their families and husbands, both on the farm and in the home the women's cooperation is, in turn, essential to men. (1973:29)

As already indicated, one way of seeking security, with stress on material well-being, is through dependence relationships: marriage, descent, and extended family ties. But dependence presents problems. Many urban women are migrants and consequently are separated from their natal homes and all of the security that comes from living close to their descent and affinal groups. The ability to utilize kin ties effectively depends, to a large extent, on proximity and habitual interaction. Whether they are married or single, women and men who are new to a city find that when they have pressing problems, their attempts to find immediate assistance are impeded if the core of their support system resides elsewhere. Furthermore, they find that time erases memories and estranges kinsmen and kinswomen from one another, in relative proportion to the distance of the tie. Except for the closest relationships, people must be active in keeping their kin ties alive in some way—conventionally with visits, gifts, fostering hometown family children, or offering hospitality to members when they visit the city—otherwise they find it difficult to ask for help. Both men and women find that keeping up with kinship obligations requires monetary investments. Although rejection is rare, I was nevertheless told repeatedly that there is no warm welcome for the poor. The point is that urban women migrants cannot automatically look homeward for security, but must work toward keeping their security options open. Indeed, women who leave their home towns, if they wish to return to them in the future, are faced with a dilemma: they must engage in the kinds of reciprocal exchanges that indicate to others that they are meeting the obligations expected of kin group members, but in order to do so, and to lay claim to their rights to be protected, women must be relatively economically successful under conditions in which they have the least amount of kinship support, that is, when they are away from home.

Husbands are not a sure source of long-term economic support. Marriage does not necessarily last for a woman's lifetime, and this is especially true for the nonelites. The literature on African women repeatedly testifies to the fragility of marriage, the causes of which include mistreatment, polygyny, abandonment, or poverty. Polygyny in an urban setting (where descent group backing is often minimal) creates insecurity for women on several counts. For one, there are incompatibilities among wives. For another, husbands sometimes fail to earn enough, or do not have enough resources to support several wives and all of their children. Women are conventionally expected to contribute some of their earnings to their own and their children's upkeep. When there are several wives, each with several children, women may be relied on to contribute heavily to household expenses. Inasmuch as women are eager to benefit their own children, they feel that providing monetary assistance to the household is warranted unless it is out of proportion to other members' contributions or if they are neglected in comparison to other family members, especially other wives. Women who are unduly deprived are likely to terminate their marriages if they can improve their positions by doing so. The same holds true for women who are outstandingly successful and from whom too much is expected.

The life cycles of women are different from men, and this works to the disadvantage of women. Conjugal relationships are most salient for women in their twenties and thirties, and less so for the rest of their lives (see Sanjek 1983:340). If women divorce during their child-producing decades, they are likely to remarry, usually older men—particularly affluent ones—who attract them precisely because of their relative success, but who are quite likely to leave them as widows with young children. (I found a substantial number of men in their sixties married to women in their twenties and thirties.) Otherwise, middle-aged women, whether or not they remain with their spouses after child-bearing years, move from roles that place emphasis on reproducing and parenting into roles that place more stress on grandparenting and caring for the aged. Such women are considered undesirable conjugal partners and frequently are labeled as "used cargo." The exceptions are wealthy women who remain sexually active and maritally desirable well into their middle years, but (and I will return to this point) whose husbands rarely reside with them. Men, on the other hand, maintain conjugal relationships into old age, stressing parent and husband roles. If they do not remain married to the same person, they consistently remarry, serially or polygynously. Furthermore, they co-opt the time and labor of sexually active wives to carry out household tasks for them, although they do not demand these same services of older wives nor do they closely control their movements and domestic work.

At this point in their lives, older women, whether or not they reside with a spouse, must acquire sufficient economic power to attract and support their own dependents whose energies and labors they can co-opt if they are to acquire the same kind of domestic support that their husbands can command. Increasingly women find in their middle years that incentives to remain with their spouses decline. For some, the security of having a place to live is sufficient to keep them in their spouse's residence. For others, housing alone is not a sufficiently compelling reason to keep them with their spouses. An added reason for residing separately is that there is, in this day and age, little security offered to women through the institution of widow inheritance. This resource is disappearing, thanks to the prohibitive costs to survivors of supporting widows as well as the inexpandability of city housing that rarely is large enough to accommodate large, extended families. For these and other reasons, it appears that marriage offers many women temporary security, particularly during childbearing years, but not necessarily thereafter.

Children, too, are not necessarily a dependable form of security for old-age care. For one thing, adult children who are themselves at the low end of the income scale are of little benefit to their mothers—even when the children intend to care for them. For another, the average urban dweller rents only one room, and the addition of a parent to that room places great stress on the conjugal household. One of the dilemmas for Yoruba women is that customarily children are to remain with their fathers if the parents divorce. This may weaken mother-child contact. Informants consistently justified their loyalty to one parent or the other, and to the descent group of the primary parent, by saying: "They did the most for me. They trained me. They brought me up." Realizing that they may not be a primary parent in such terms, some women remain with their husbands for the sake of developing a close mother-child relationship, even though they might prefer to leave them or enter into a new union. Others effect compromises. The compromise I found most frequently was that fathers keep male children and allow mothers—knowing how important it is for a woman to have the services and support of a child—to keep and raise a daughter or daughters.

One consequence of the practice of relying on children for security in old age is that the burden for providing it falls mainly on women. One of the most significant findings, in this respect, of a study of women in central Accra is that they are more likely to care for aged parents than men are (Robertson 1984:207–12). The same is true of Mushin, where household

TABLE 9.1. Average Household Size of Men and Women Household Heads (Yoruba-speaking respondents only)

	Female owners* (n = 20)	Female nonowners** (n = 14)	Male owners* (n = 51)	Male nonowners** (n = 39)
Household size	6.8	4.4	7.5	4.9
Number of children	3.6	3.4	4.5	3.1
Number of spouses in residence			1.4	1.1
Number of foster children	2.3	1.4	2.0	1.6
Number of generations	2.3	2.3	2.2	1.9

*Owners are automatically heads of their households.
**Figures refer only to rent-paying tenants who are heads of households.
Source: author's survey, Mushin, 1972.

heads who are women are more likely than men to accommodate three generations, that is, a parent, themselves, and a child or children. Table 9.1 compares the number of generations housed by male and female household heads. But numbers do not tell the whole story. The greatest responsibilities still fall on women, be they daughters, daughters-in-law, or granddaughters, because the division of labor is such that females are expected to care for the aged when they are incapacitated, particularly if the aged are financially dependent. During their middle years, as already indicated, men are marrying, reproducing, and facing the accompanying responsibilities: as they age, and perhaps need care, their younger wives provide it. This means that people who are sufficiently free to care for members of their extended families are middle-aged women who frequently support aged parents, especially their mothers. This duty places extra burdens on women, because their middle years are precisely the critical period during which they are sufficiently free of domestic obligations to work most intensively to establish some kind of financial security for themselves.

A highly informative study from Sierra Leone shows that many older women do find security through children, but not necessarily their own (Bledsoe and Isiugo-Abanihe 1989). They do so by fostering young children—mainly those of a relative—thereby placing them and their parents in their debt. The same pattern exists in Kinshasa, where women often educate a brother's child in order to build up "a claim on him and his father for the future" (LaFontaine 1974:107). Younger parents, who have crushing economic responsibilities in their childbearing years, rely on older women to raise and educate their children. As the parents' economic burdens diminish, the parents then move into a position to help the older women in their declining and less productive years when they need it most. Nevertheless, it is imperative that foster parents have some type of income, usually acquired from trade or other entrepreneurial occupations, during the time they care for dependent children. It is incumbent on these women to educate their own or their foster children to the highest possible levels, since the better educated they are, the higher the children's incomes and the more help they can eventually offer their sponsors.[8] The obligation to repay an educational debt is one of the most compelling obligations I found among Lagos residents, for the beneficiaries are acutely aware of the rewards of receiving a good education and feel particularly bound to their benefactors.

Given all of their problems, urban women are impelled to find safeguards of their own. Real security comes with economic independence. But this goal is more easily envisaged than reached. Women are at a disadvantage in an economy that places a premium on specialized skills, for their education has lagged markedly behind that of men. Unable to compete for many wage-earning positions, much of women's economic endeavors must be devoted to exploiting the informal economy, largely through self-employment, where average income levels are so low that they can usually only supplement the earnings of a domestic group.[9] Recent studies from Abidjan and Lusaka indicate that the structure of employment in both places is forcing younger women increasingly to look to their husbands for most of their financial security because they are systematically excluded from competing in the skilled job market (Etienne 1983:316; Hansen 1980: 845). Elsewhere in Sub-Saharan Africa, women seem less constrained in their economic endeavors.

Women employ a variety of tactics to establish a secure economic base. In Central Africa some women marry late as a way of securing their futures before they become encumbered with family responsibilities (Hansen 1980:844). In West Africa women can acquire economic assets by contracting a series of advantageous marriages or becoming lovers of prominent men (Hoffer 1974:187; Pittin 1983:294). In East Africa and other places where women do not have a traditional foothold in the marketplace, dispensing sexual favors in many forms is a common tactic for making a living (Bujra 1975:213; Obbo 1980:98; Pittin 1983:292; Schuster 1979:91). In parts of southern Nigeria, up to 70 percent and more of adult women work on their own in trade, crafts, or services, such as sewing, hair dressing, or preparing food. Small-scale commerce, perhaps the trademark of West African women, makes important contributions to their sense of self-reliance and individual identity—women characteristically include in their formulaic greetings an inquiry as to how business is faring—but it rarely leads to total economic independence. Instead, trade and other forms of self-generated work are partial answers to the problem of establishing lifelong economic security. Total independence means that a woman establishes little by little a relatively permanent source of income that is sufficient to support herself and some dependents. This kind of economic independence may come from trading in highly valued and expensive commodities such as cloth; from contracting; from producing and manufacturing commodities; or more significantly from owning a shop, income property, or, in the case of highly educated women, a private school. None of these endeavors is mutually exclusive inasmuch as highly successful women and men engage in several. Contracting, trading, and owning property, for instance, are one common combination.

Obbo's description (1975:291) of a Kampala woman's struggle for independence is a classic example of a woman who used small-scale means to achieve large-scale ends. Obbo's informant sold cooked food to industrial workers, from which she made about 800 shillings (about 112 US dollars) per month. With savings she bought a ten-room rental house that nearly doubled her income. The woman did not reveal her income to her husband—indeed, there was some question as to whether he knew she owned a house. In the local parlance she had become *nakyeyombekedde,* a woman who is not male-dependent and who is set apart from those who are (Obbo 1980:88ff.).

Owning income-producing real estate appears to be one of the most common strategies for establishing real economic independence. In the crowded and mushrooming cities of the continent, urban shelter is a scarce and valuable resource. Women owners are prominent in cities such as Accra, Katsina, Abidjan, Dakar, Kampala, Mombasa, Kinshasa, and small towns in Liberia.[10] They have owned property in central Lagos (Mann 1985:118) and other West African cities such as Freetown since at least the nineteenth century (Steady 1976:230), and in Nairobi since the earliest years of this century. More than 40 percent of the housing in Nairobi's oldest section was owned in the 1940s by women—many of whom acquired it originally from proceeds earned from prostitution (Bujra 1975:216). A similar situation exists in the northern Nigerian city of Katsina, where three-fifths of that city's houses of prostitution were purchased by women from proceeds earned in that profession, but whose entrepreneurial interests turned to trade or selling prepared food once they were established as owners (Pittin 1983:295).

In metropolitan Lagos, where an estimated 15 percent of house owners are women, purchasing real estate, usually from proceeds earned from trade, is a highly valued strategy. The houses are intended to accommodate the owner, her dependents, and rent-paying tenants who usually occupy single rooms (see Barnes 1986:55–61). Given the almost automatic income-producing quality of urban real estate, it is one of the key indicators of economic independence. For both women and men, to be *ominira*, independent, is to be free from the constraints of institutional employment, free from a fixed and, therefore, not readily expandable income, and most important free from the authority of someone else in the workplace. When wage earners, other than the elites, purchase property they almost always leave their jobs and move to self-employed occupations.[11] Thus 95 percent of women owners are self-employed, whereas 79 percent of nonowners (women) are self-employed.

The independence felt by women owners across the continent is best assessed through their own words. "My house is my husband," a Nairobi woman reported (Bujra 1975:224). "What I celebrate the most," a Kampala landlady said, "is having an independent source of income" (Obbo 1975: 291). "When a woman has a house," a Liberian house owner stated, "she thinks she is the only woman, the most powerful woman on earth!" (Bledsoe 1980:130).

Clearly women who own houses become a privileged group and I shall discuss them in greater detail below. Here it is sufficient to say that the security and rental income derived from real estate allows women to invest in business enterprises, to take risks, and more important in this context, to devote their energies to activities that are not necessarily income-producing. It is difficult in the extreme to reach a point of having discretionary time over and above that spent in domestic or subsistence-producing endeavors. While many women would like to own property and reap its benefits, most of them find their abilities to acquire this kind of asset are severely restricted.

The Opportunity Structure

At the beginning of this essay I proposed that there is an opportunity structure that is not the same for women as for men. The opportunity structure consists of legal, economic, and social factors, that, in the case presented here, hinder or help individuals with respect to their securing economic or political power in their communities. In Lagos, as in most societies, the opportunity structure, as it appeared in the 1960s through 1980s among Yoruba-speaking residents, was more heavily weighted against women than men. There are several reasons for this imbalance.

The domestic hierarchy is structured in favor of men. To begin with, marriage is patrilateral. A woman moves into her husband's household and, should they also live with his relatives, automatically places herself under his and his kinsmen's authority—since he, or they, are the "owners" of the property and responsible for all people who reside within it. The household structure is hierarchical, just as all social relationships in Yoruba societies are hierarchical. Members of domestic groups are ranked according to such factors as their age, gender, birth order, time of arrival in a household, or status as an owner or renter/leaser of residential property. This ranking determines the kind of behavior one household member displays toward another, to whom they must act in subordinate ways, and over whom they can exercise authority in situations that require it. Inasmuch as wives usually move into their husbands' households, they are automatically junior to them in the domestic hierarchy. In general, they are also junior to wives who arrived before them, to children who were born before their arrival, and so on.

The fact that household status is assessed according to several criteria means that ranking in the hierarchy is not entirely fixed, but is subject to manipulation, debate, and negotiation. Put another way, ranking is dependent on context and the evaluations, by those concerned, of a host of variables. A subordinate in one context or according to one evaluation of criteria may be dominant in another context. So long as the original purchaser of a house is alive, the one element that rarely, if ever, is manipulated, however, is ownership. A person who purchases real estate automatically is the senior person in the household hierarchy. The irrevocability of this status is reinforced by the fact that the purchaser is remembered and propitiated after death by his or her heirs as the "founding ancestor" of the house. However, once a purchaser dies the inheritance of real estate does open doors to manipulation of senior status, since heirs—who, according to customary law, must be junior siblings or children of the purchaser—are usually multiple. Unless a female heir is relatively wealthy, charismatic, or powerful in other ways, the senior role in the domestic hierarchy will usually devolve upon a male co-heir, continuing down through succeeding generations.

Inheritance rules favor men in other ways. Rights to use descent-group land are routinely passed to all male agnates. Men who live in urban places, such as Mushin, retain their rights to rural or hometown property, even though many never activate these rights. Wealthy men sometimes hire tenants to farm the land that they are entitled to use while they reside elsewhere. Furthermore, men share the proceeds of land sales or cash cropping, if they are collectively managed, even though, again, they may live elsewhere. Urban women rarely farm or share in the proceeds of their descent groups' agricultural endeavors on distant farms. If they or their sons wish to use their descent group's land they must make a special appeal to do so, though it is rarely denied. Women and men do, however, inherit urban real estate with equal rights shared among all siblings, and they inherit rights to use rooms in their natal homes whether rural or urban.

Perhaps the most significant aspect of inheritance customs, and the one that works most unfavorably for women, is the fact that spouses cannot inherit property from one another unless a specific provision is made in a written will.[12] Unlike in the Western world, a house is not jointly held as property between husband and wife, except for a few elite, Westernized, monogamous couples who have jointly purchased property and legally protected the surviving spouse's rights to inherit it. Instead, a house is held singly until the owner dies, and then it passes down to his junior relatives and not to his wives or older relatives such as senior siblings, parents, parents' siblings, and so on. A woman, furthermore, cannot conventionally acquire a house as a divorce settlement. A lover may be given a house, or a wife may be given a house by a very wealthy husband. But these are rare instances. Wives of men who purchase property, therefore, are in the main dependent on their children's sense of responsibility to care for them and house them after the death of such spouses.

In the domestic hierarchy, the one area in which wives are not subordinate to their husbands is in their occupational endeavors. The monetary affairs of husbands and wives are strictly separated, each managing his or her own income and expenditures. This works to the advantage of women since what they earn is their own, to be used as they decide. This is a primary factor in making women independent. Women who have no incomes and do not contribute to household expenses have no sanctions imposed on them. Women who do have an income usually choose to contribute to household expenses because it is in their own and their children's interests to do so. The one disadvantage, that women must spend on children who, legally, belong to their husbands, is offset by the fact that children do respond emotionally and in time of need to a parent who has contributed to their well-being. Men, in the long run, have more overt sanctions placed on them than women do if they choose not to contribute to housing and feeding their families, for failure to do so can be used as grounds for divorce.

It is the ability of women to be independent in their occupations and with their income that gives them the chance to achieve some form of financial security. Like men, they, too, save small sums, borrow additional sums, and eventually make down payments on houseplots, usually 50 by 100 feet in size. Once a person has made a down payment, kinsmen and friends tend to rally round and contribute cash toward completing the purchase. For the most part, however, the payments come from the purchaser alone. Once a purchaser owns a piece of land, it usually takes several years to save additional cash for building a house on it. Some owners do this in piecemeal fashion; others save enough to do it all at once—strategies vary considerably. The size of the structure, its location, and the building materials used are generally in accordance with the relative affluence of the builder. Low-income owners use traditional mud bricks for one-story structures; high-income owners build multistoried concrete dwellings.

Although women have opportunities to become independent, men have an automatic economic head start over women. They are assisted in contracting marriages, and by virtue of this, gain access to the reproductive and productive powers of women. Securing bridewealth for a first marriage is the collective responsibility of a man and his kinsmen; the bulk of the bridewealth ideally comes from the groom's kin and in turn it goes, not to the bride, but to her kin. Women do not have this automatic start in building up a domestic establishment and therewith the services of others. It is conventional, however, that if a woman's parents or husband are sufficiently affluent they provide her with some capital to start her own business. In this matter a woman is dependent on the relative wealth of those above her to give her an economic start, if and when they choose; a man receives his economic boost—by way of acquiring a domestic household—almost without question, although eventually he is expected to help those who come after him in similar ways.

To men, the productive role of wives is within the domestic sphere. Wives prepare food for their husbands, their children, and others senior to them in household. They bear and raise children who in time also provide domestic labor. They care for clothing, clean the quarters, and shop for provisions. To a large extent, the time and domestic labor of wives during their reproductive years is controlled by their husbands or by others senior to them in the household. The allocation of household tasks follows the domestic hierarchy from top to bottom, with the relatively senior being able to direct the relatively junior. The head of the household, the most senior individual, has ultimate control over other members and has the right to be served and cared for first. Given the ideological and economic advantages men have in gaining this senior status, they are in a position to appropriate the greatest amount of household labor to their own ends, and to use it in ways that free them to pursue extradomestic endeavors, especially income-producing endeavors.

Older women who gain sufficient flexibility to achieve some measure of economic affluence are still at a disadvantage. Wealth may indeed bring women influence within their residences and kin groups, and this is expressed in several ways. Some husbands give older wives their "freedom," indicating that they are free from conjugal obligations and free to go about their occupational interests as they like. Other husbands actually assign a section of the house or compound to a successful wife if there is sufficient space. She then acts as a head of that subsection, but not of the entire house. Thus, the overall domestic hierarchy stays in place with subordinate members of a household, or of subsections of a household, still junior to the owner in the full domestic context and in that position unable to make certain critical extradomestic connections.

In Lagos, the senior member of the residential unit is its representative in neighborhood and community affairs. This person is the owner, or member of a group of co-owners who have inherited the property. Until a woman achieves owner status, her opportunity to play a part in public affairs, as these affairs are open to owners, is restricted.

House Owners

When women own houses they benefit in many ways. The principle that the owner is the senior authority figure in the domestic context is constant, whether the owner is male or female. Hence, there is a significant transformation in the structure of opportunities for women once they own real estate and they can control and allocate domestic resources in ways of their own choosing.

As property owners, women, like their male counterparts, have rights over their own households, to some extent over their clients' households if clients reside with them, and to a very small extent over tenants' households. The rights vary in each case. As head of her own immediate household, a woman owner has the right to command the obedience of junior household members and to direct their labors. One of the reasons a husband does not like to live with a wife in a house that she owns is that he loses seniority and is subject to the authority of someone (his wife) he is conditioned to view as subordinate in that context. Men are not opposed to having wives who own houses; in fact, they are attracted to affluent women. But they prefer to live separately and to be the senior person of a separate establishment on a day-to-day basis and to visit their wives, or vice versa, for conjugal purposes (compare Bledsoe 1980:129–30).

The principle of owner seniority also applies to domestic clients—people who are neither rent-paying tenants nor relatives but who reside in a house at the owner's behest and who interact with the owner in an idiom of kinship. In the few Mushin houses where this is the case, the clients, regardless of their sex or age, pay the same deference to a female owner that they pay to a male owner. This involves gestures of subordination and observing the owner's rules concerning household behavior, such as meeting a curfew. Clients, it should be added, are usually given their own rooms.

The relationship of female owners to rent-paying tenants varies from house to house. There is an average of ten tenant households in each dwelling. Most tenants rent one room, a few two. Each tenant-headed household (as in an apartment house or block of flats) is autonomous internally, but only the owner of the dwelling has rights to represent that residence in external, community affairs. Tenants and owners do not interact in an idiom of kinship unless the relationship is long-standing; in most cases there is no relationship, and no service or labor is exchanged. Nevertheless, owners often establish house rules, help resolve tenants' domestic disputes, or otherwise monitor tenant behavior to a greater degree than in Western society. The scarcity of housing, coupled with owners' abilities to evict uncooperative or disputatious tenants, make for their compliance.

Much of the interaction among owners and tenants is occasioned by the layout of the houses themselves. The common arrangement is that a large, rectangular house is bisected by a common corridor on each side of which are rooms whose doorways open onto the corridor. Owners usually live at the front, using one room for sleeping and another as a parlor. Common cooking, washing, and lavatory areas are generally at the back. Verandahs and stoops are at the front; they are used by women for trading and by both sexes for socializing. Given the small size of rooms (for example, 12 by 12 feet), many household tasks take place outside and in association with co-residents. Children move freely between rooms. There is, as might be expected, considerable common knowledge about one another and considerable occasion for conflict. The owner is the acknowledged resolver of conflict and is considered the authority to whom co-tenant or neighbor-to-neighbor disputes are taken. Together with his or her role in other neighborhood affairs, the household leadership role establishes owners as local authority figures. Needless to say, a great deal of leadership experience is gained in the role of owner.

Among the advantages gained by women owners is their ability to control space. They are able to attract and provide shelter to more dependents than average tenant household heads (male or female) because they can allocate accommodations (see Table 9.1). In a census taken in 1972 of 155 houses in Mushin, I found that owners usually use two rooms, tenants one. Owners accommodate more children and foster children than nonowners. Women owners have larger households, 6.8 people compared to 4.9 for male tenants or 4.4 for female tenants. Male owners, however, have households averaging 7.5 persons; the difference is explained by the fact that almost all men have one or more wives living with them—an average of 1.4—whereas almost all women owners either live separately from their husbands, are widows, or are divorced.

The woman owner can put others to work and profit from their labors. Members of her household who are subordinate to her (excluding tenants) are expected to cook, keep the quarters clean, and perform myriad other tasks that free women from mundane domestic responsibilities. It is important that self-employed women have dependents, usually children, who can run errands, purchase and collect goods, make sales, or tend shop. By having labor at their command, entrepreneurial women can profit from the surplus value of that labor. A virtue of ownership is that women can expand the numbers of people who are dependent on and thus subordinate to them and from whom they can extract a wide range of services and thereby expand their opportunities to increase their own earnings in other ways.

Perhaps one of the greatest benefits for a house owner is that she controls her own time. She is able to organize her life, not necessarily in the service of others, but in conjunction with her own needs and wishes. Time probably acts as one of the greatest constraints on women (compare Peil 1983: 276), who, if they are subordinate to others or are unable to acquire the services and labor of others, rarely gain sufficient free time from imposed or

TABLE 9.2. Activities of Women: Owners and Nonowners Compared (Yoruba-speaking respondents only) (in percentages)

	Female owners ($n = 20$)	Female nonowners* ($n = 25$)
Voluntary association membership		
none	29	43
one	47	29
two	12	12
three	12	7
TOTAL	100	100
Political party membership	20	7

*Heads of households only.
Source: author's survey, Mushin, 1972.

subsistence-level responsibilities to participate in activities of their wider communities.

House owning makes it possible for women, as well as men, to establish many connections and expand their opportunities for economic and political advancement.[13] In extensive surveys in Nigerian cities, it was found that women (very few of whom were owners) have a much narrower range of contacts than men, but that their connections expand when they become relatively affluent or participate intensively in the labor force (Peil 1983: 275–76). Women house owners have a more extensive involvement in voluntary associations and political parties than women who do not own property (see Table 9.2), but still not as extensive as men (see Table 9.3). The most significant expansion in community connections for owners begins in their neighborhoods.

Owners interact with one another. Above all else, they have a vested interest in their neighborhoods and communities, and it is incumbent upon them to enhance and protect those interests. I have discussed elsewhere in greater detail the steps that individuals take in Lagos in order to acquire real estate (Barnes 1977, 1979, 1986). Suffice it to say here that purchasing real estate is fraught with legal and financial difficulties—to say nothing of difficulties in simply finding available land that is for sale. Each and every step in this process from acquiring land to building a structure requires assistance: establishing networks of people who will help a prospective owner locate houseplots; establishing contacts in order to secure reliable

TABLE 9.3. Activities of Men: Owners and Nonowners Compared (Yoruba-speaking respondents only) (in percentages)

	Male owners (n = 51)	Male nonowners* (n = 39)
Voluntary association membership		
none	5	21
one	35	66
two	37.5	10
three	22.5	3
TOTAL	100	100
Political party membership	51	5

*Heads of households only.
Source: author's survey, Mushin, 1972.

builders; establishing ties with neighboring owners to help new purchasers protect property before it is developed, since landstealing, in various forms, is an abiding threat; or joining neighborhood groups in order to protect property once it is built. Even financing real estate ventures draws women into extensive monetary transactions, and for the sake of loans (from neighbors, friends, or local moneylenders) one must establish creditworthiness. The latter comes with being known, having well-placed contacts, and in some demonstrable way, being accountable to others.

Women owners are active residents in the neighborhoods I studied. Five landladies I know established themselves as clients (in a political, not residential sense) to important community leaders, who were almost invariably owners themselves. They asked them for help with the following problems:

—*solving boundary disputes*
—*collecting rent from delinquent tenants*
—*securing government variances to build shops on houseplot premises*
—*seeking help in lowering property taxes*
—*settling family quarrels over property inheritance rights*
—*settling neighborhood disputes over placement of fences*
—*intervening with judges over sanitation violations*
—*seeking legal help in order to prove purchases were legitimate*

The point is that in order to deal with property-related problems, owners must interact with people who have wide political and governmental networks. It is unusual, in fact, for owners not to make contact with community leaders. In seeking and getting help, owners create debts. Marcel Mauss's (1954) theory of exchange can be fruitfully applied to the Mushin case: a favor given means a favor to be repaid. Owners in Mushin incur political debts when they seek help in solving property problems. They become clients to leaders who ask them to repay their debts in direct and indirect political ways. Once there is a transaction, there is a relationship; once there is a relationship, there is a permanent tie that can be activated by either party when or if it is necessary. With ownership, then, comes an almost inevitable layer of involvement with political activists that draws one into community affairs in some way.

Women owners in some neighborhoods go beyond their informal one-to-one client involvement with community leaders and participate in formal political groups.[14] One type of group is the neighborhood landowner association. Such groups are known to lobby government for improvements, settle disputes between owners and tenants, or hire night guards to protect residents. Another type of group is the political party. In some cases, during civilian regimes, owner groups and parties overlap. The political goals of women who join these groups vary. One woman joined a landowner association to make connections with important people. In fact, she became its assistant secretary because she was afraid that if she declined the position—urged on her by an influential neighborhood leader—she would not receive his help in arranging transactions with local government functionaries or court officers when she needed it, as she frequently did. Another woman joined a similar association with the explicit intention of gaining influence in her community. She drew attention to herself and her keen interest in local problems by contributing heavily to the landowner association. She was repaid by fellow owners with a neighborhood chieftaincy title. It was an informal title in the eyes of government officials, but it was salient in the woman's neighborhood where owners and tenants alike looked to title holders as authority figures—the kinds of people who took neighbors as clients and helped them with their problems. A third woman showed her interest in political affairs by joining the neighborhood branch of a national political party. She became a successful campaigner in elections and was eventually given a party office in the branch. The formal political participation of women owners in associations and parties is considerably lower than that of men owners (as Tables 9.2 and 9.3 indicate). Still, many community groups with political agendas have at least one woman title or office holder.

Property owning is an important part of the urban economy. In metropolitan Lagos, property taxes constitute the single most lucrative source of internally generated revenue for local government budgets. At least 99 houses out of 100 are privately owned and taxable. Owners, therefore, are a vocal and potentially mobilizable source of influence and pressure at the local government level. Almost all political activity at the local level, in fact, is generated by owners either as individuals or as groups, and most appointments to advisory bodies are from the owner stratum of the city and its suburbs.

Property ownership is by no means the only power basis for women. Throughout coastal West Africa, markets are mainly run by women (since most but not all traders are women) and it is well known that holding high office in a market organization is a significant political position in any community. Women's secret societies elsewhere in West Africa also are active and influential. Officers of both types of groups have large constituencies and opportunities, by virtue of holding office, to organize political support, pressure, or protest. There are only a few women, however, who hold offices in these groups, and who, as a result, have meaningful political connections outside them compared with the numbers of women who are property owners and who are thereby entitled to act as authority figures and establish wider political connections.

One of the interesting things about seeing house owning as a basis for gaining political power is that it opens up a relatively unexplored realm for examining the ways contemporary urban African women gain influence in public affairs. No doubt there are many other ways that are yet to be explored. Focusing on housing provides an alternative to what is sometimes a bias toward seeing marketing or solidarity groups as women's "route to power."[15] Certainly these outlets provide significant opportunities for women to exercise leadership in public arenas, and they are important in providing role models for female office holding. Yet, important as they may be in the social fabric of community, their existence is not a precondition for women's exercise of public power, in either a collective or an individual sense. It is more important that women have access to statuses in the community, such as house owner, that are open to individual achievement, that are *not* necessarily in short supply, and that give them an entrée into politically influential circles, than it is for them to belong to gender-exclusive or other groups whose offices *are* in short supply and whose activities may or may not be directed to their interests.

It is important to draw attention to property owning among women for many reasons. Because urban houses are designed to accommodate owners and tenants, property is a source of economic security—a regular income that eventually serves as a kind of pension. Property frees the owner from subordinating herself to the authority of another person in domestic matters. It places her in a position of authority over others and in a position to form social relationships in the wider community that are politically significant. Property owning legitimates her entry into the public domain. Indeed, being the head of a self-owned domestic domain virtually necessitates a woman's entry into the public domain.

In entering the public world of urban politics women are not entering a man's world or creating a political arena of their own. Rather they are entering a public sphere that is, as Sudarkasa stresses, a world of both genders (1981:50–55). How extensively women owners exercise the powers available to them once they enter this world is another matter. In a sense, property ownership is one of the ways women as well as men reach a threshold of community involvement. Moving from that threshold into active political affairs is linked to personal style, connections, and a host of other factors that lie outside the scope of this chapter. It is inevitable that a new set of constraints and opportunities, and different configurations in the opportunity structure, come into play at this point.

Conclusion

Sacks (1974) reminds us of Engels's proposition that the difference in the position of women and men was accentuated when capitalism created private property and made owners the rulers of households. Although it is questionable that capitalism alone is responsible for this state of affairs or that it is exclusive to capitalist economies, the principle that property ownership accentuates the dependence of nonowners is a valid one. As Engels correctly observed, the unpropertied move to the propertied for security. Because they are dependent, the energies of the unpropertied can be relatively easily co-opted to enhance an owner's economic position and an owner's abilities to engage in competitive exchanges outside the household. The challenge, then, is to investigate the processes by which African women move from being propertyless and dependent on others for significant parts of their economic support to being owners who can co-opt the productive labors of others so that they can reach sufficient economic independence to engage in competitive transactions in civic arenas. In analyzing this process I have found it necessary to pinpoint the structural conditions that, on one side, hinder women but, on the other, allow them to bridge the gap between domestic subordination and public power.

In every society there are certain statuses or positions that, because they bridge domains, are in and of themselves political resources. The idea of "bridging" is conceptually important, because it is through this concept that we can see how people establish viable social relationships and connections that allow them to use the social or economic capital gained in one context to gain access to another context. Such statuses or positions are *threshold statuses*. An individual occupying a threshold status is poised on the edge of one domain and thus in a position, or eligible, to enter another one. To reach a political threshold means one has the legitimate rights and even obligations to enter into public affairs. In contemporary Lagos, the status that exists at the threshold between domestic and public space is the status of owner. Hence it is a valuable resource. And this is why, to return to the seeming contradiction with which I began, individuals wish to be dominant in the domestic context and why the ideology of male dominance/female subordination in the household is a strong ideology. It excludes, or tries to exclude, a certain amount of competition for these valuable statuses. The custom that wives move into the dwellings of their husbands reinforces the status quo and at the same time provides tangible support to the ideology of male dominance. But, in fact, as the evidence here shows, the principles governing the hierarchy of domestic dominance are not gender specific. All members of a dwelling are subordinate to the owner whether the owner is female or male.

The power that both women and men acquire in the domestic context, if they own and thereby control that context, acts as a natural bridge to the public realm. Inasmuch as public participation can derive from domestic control, these two domains must be seen as interdependent. Among the Yoruba, as in most African cases for which we have information, women and men are on the same footing once they are at the top of a domestic hierarchy. The question, then, is not whether women have the capacity to gain power and perform effectively in positions of authority, but under what conditions they can transcend the social, economic, and legal obstacles that stand in the way of their achieving domestic dominance. For these reasons, ownership must be seen as a threshold for women in their desire to gain economic independence and security, because once they reach this point they automatically gain the rights to move further into the domain of public affairs.

Acknowledgments

The author thanks Arjun Appadurai, Caroline Bledsoe, Margaret Peil, and Peggy Sanday for their suggestions for improving an earlier draft of this essay. Research, based on a total of two years' work in metropolitan Lagos, was undertaken in 1971–72, under a grant from the National Institute of Mental Health; in 1975, under a grant from the University of Pennsylvania Faculty Fellowship Fund; and in 1986 under a Fulbright Research Fellowship and Basic Research Grant from the National Endowment for the Humanities. I am also indebted to the Institute of African Studies, University of Ibadan, where I have been a Research Associate on each of these occasions.

Notes

1. See also Fadipe 1970:112–13, Lloyd 1965:565–66, and Sudarkasa 1973:109 for women's domestic posture.
2. See also Baker 1974:223–43, Barnes 1986:159–80, and Sudarkasa 1973:65–86 for women's public posture.
3. *Bi okunrin rejo, bi obinrin pa, ki ejo saa maa ti lo.* I wish to thank Dr. Bolanle Awe for bringing my attention to this proverb, also found in Abraham (1958:106).
4. The time period under consideration, unless otherwise noted, is roughly 1960 to 1986.
5. "Domain" is used here, not as a predetermined comparative or theoretical construct, but as a social unit, the content of which fluctuates according to time and place (Comaroff 1987:83–84).
6. The structure of opportunity is an analytic construct connoting the constraints and opportunities that surround humans as social beings. The factors that are involved in any structure of opportunity are, of course, more complex than can be represented, even replicated, in a brief study of this nature.
7. See, for example, Bledsoe and Isiugo-Abanihe (1989), Bujra (1975), Hansen (1980), LaFontaine (1974), Obbo (1980), Robertson (1984), Steady (1981), and Ware (1983).
8. Ware reports that a survey of Yoruba groups indicates 98 percent of the respondents feel that educating children is the best investment for securing their old-age care (1983:26).

9. Average earnings of self-employed persons and wage-earning laborers in Lagos in the mid-1970s were less than $500 per annum (see Fapohunda 1978:92).

10. See Bledsoe 1980:128, Etienne 1983:314, Grandmaison 1969:150, Halpenny 1975:282, Kilson 1974:30–31, LaFontaine 1974:107, Obbo 1980:89, Pittin 1983:295, Robertson 1984:51, Smock 1977:196, and Stroebel 1979:67.

11. Several studies from West Africa and the Caribbean discuss the high value women place on trade because of the independence it provides in contrast to wage-earning and salaried jobs. They are discussed in Bourguignon (1980:11).

12. An exception was that during the early years of the colonial era, couples who married under a civil marriage ordinance did, in the absence of a will, inherit rights to use the deceased spouse's property for life (Mann 1985:167 n.32).

13. House ownership is also used as a base from which to build political power by Liberian men and women (Bledsoe 1980:131).

14. A more complete description of political careers and of strategies for moving from neighborhood to metropolitan governmental circles is provided in Barnes (1986).

15. For other concerns about these approaches see Bledsoe 1984:455 and Lewis 1977:161.

Bibliography

Abraham, R. C. 1958. *Dictionary of Modern Yoruba*. London: University of London Press.

Baker, P. H. 1974. *Urbanization and Political Change: The Politics of Lagos, 1917–1967*. Berkeley: University of California Press.

Barnes, S. T. 1977. "Political Transition in Urban Africa." *Annals of the American Academy of Political and Social Science* 432 (July): 26–41.

———. 1979. "Migration and Land Acquistion: The New Landowners of Lagos." *African Urban Studies* 4 (Spring): 59–70.

———. 1986. *Patrons and Power: Creating a Political Community in Metropolitan Lagos*. Manchester: Manchester University Press and Bloomington: Indiana University Press for International African Institute.

Bledsoe, C. 1980. *Women and Marriage in Kpelle Society*. Stanford: Stanford University Press.

———. 1984. "The Political Use of Sande Ideology and Symbolism." *American Ethnologist* 11 (3): 455–72.

Bledsoe, C., and U. C. Isiugo-Abanihe. 1989. "Strategies of Child Fosterage Among Mende Grannies in Sierra Leone." In *African Reproduction and Social Organization*, R. Lestahaeghe, ed. Berkeley: University of California Press.

Bourguignon, E. 1980. *A World of Women*. New York: Praeger.

Bujra, J. 1975. "Women 'Entrepreneurs' of Early Nairobi." *Canadian Journal of African Studies* IX (2): 213–34.

Comaroff, John. 1987. "*Sui genderis:* Feminism, Kinship Theory, and Structural

'Domains.'" In *Gender and Kinship: Essays Toward a Unified Analysis*, J. F. Collier and S. J. Yanagisako, eds., pp. 53–85. Stanford: Stanford University Press.
Etienne, M. 1983. "Gender Relations and Conjugality Among the Baule." In *Female and Male in West Africa*, C. Oppong, ed., pp. 303–19. London: George Allen & Unwin.
Fadipe, N. A. 1970. *The Sociology of the Yoruba*. Ibadan: Ibadan University Press.
Fapohunda, O. J., et al. 1978. *Lagos: Urban Development and Employment*. Geneva: ILO.
Grandmaison, C. 1969. "Activities Economiques des Femmes Dakaroises." *Africa* XXXIX: 138–51.
Halpenny, P. 1975. "Three Styles of Ethnic Migration in Kisenyi, Kampala." In *Town and Country in Central and Eastern Africa*, D. Parkin, ed., pp. 276–87. Oxford: Oxford University Press for International African Institute.
Hansen, K. T. 1980. "When Sex Becomes a Critical Variable: Married Women and Extra-Domestic Work in Lusaka, Zambia." *African Social Research* 30: 831–49.
Hoffer, C. P. 1974. "Madam Yoko: Ruler of the Kpa Mende Confederacy." In *Woman, Culture and Society*, M. Rosaldo and L. Lamphere, eds., pp. 173–87. Stanford: Stanford University Press.
Kilson, M. 1974. *African Urban Kinsmen: The Ga of Central Accra*. New York: St. Martin's.
LaFontaine, J. S. 1974. "The Free Women of Kinshasa: Prostitution in a City in Zaire." In *Choice and Change*, J. Davis, ed., pp. 89–113. New York: Athlone.
Lewis, B. C. 1977. "Economic Activity and Marriage Among Ivoirian Urban Women." In *Sexual Stratification*, A. Schlegel, ed., pp. 161–91. New York: Columbia University Press.
Little, K. 1973. *African Women in Towns*. Cambridge: Cambridge University Press.
Lloyd, P. C. 1965. "The Yoruba of Nigeria." In *Peoples of Africa*, J. L. Gibbs, Jr., ed., pp. 549–82. New York: Holt, Rinehart and Winston.
Mann, K. 1985. *Marrying Well: Marriage, Status and Social Change Among the Educated Elite in Colonial Lagos*. New York: Cambridge University Press.
Mauss, M. 1954. *The Gift*. Tr. I. Cunnison. London: Cohen and West.
Obbo, C. 1975. "Women's Careers in Low Income Areas as Indicators of Country and Town Dynamics." In *Town and Country in Central and Eastern Africa*, D. Parkin, ed., pp. 288–93. Oxford: Oxford University Press for International African Institute.
———. 1980. *African Women: Their Struggle for Economic Independence*. London: Zed Press.
Peil, M. 1983. "Urban Contacts: A Comparison of Women and Men." In *Female and Male in West Africa*, C. Oppong, ed., pp. 275–82. London: George Allen & Unwin.
Pittin, R. 1983. "Houses of Women: A Focus on Alternative Life-Styles in Katsina City." In *Female and Male in West Africa*, C. Oppong, ed., pp. 291–302. London: George Allen & Unwin.
Robertson, C. C. 1984. *Sharing the Same Bowl: A Socioeconomic History of Women and Class in Accra, Ghana*. Bloomington: Indiana University Press.
Sacks, K. 1974 "Engels Revisited: Women, the Organization of Production, and

Private Property." In *Women, Culture and Society,* M. Rosaldo and L. Lamphere, eds., pp. 207–22. Stanford: Stanford University Press.

Sanday, P. R. 1981. *Female Power and Male Dominance.* Cambridge: Cambridge University Press.

Sanjek, R. 1983. "Female and Male Domestic Cycles in Urban Africa: The Adabraka Case." In *Female and Male in West Africa,* C. Oppong, ed., pp. 330–43. London: George Allen & Unwin.

Schlegel, A., ed. 1977. *Sexual Stratification.* New York: Columbia University Press.

Schuster, I. M. 1979. *New Women of Lusaka.* Palo Alto, Calif.: Mayfield.

Smock, A. C. 1977. "The Impact of Modernization on Women's Position in the Family in Ghana." In *Sexual Stratification,* A. Schlegel, ed., pp. 192–214. New York: Columbia University Press.

Steady, F. C. 1976. "Protestant Women's Associations in Freetown, Sierra Leone." In *Women in Africa,* N. J. Hafkin and E. G. Bay, eds., pp. 213–37. Stanford: Stanford University Press.

———. 1981. "The Black Woman Cross-Culturally: An Overview." In *The Black Woman Cross-Culturally,* F. C. Steady, ed., pp. 7–41. Cambridge, Mass.: Schenkman.

Strathern, M., ed. 1987. *Dealing with Inequality.* Cambridge: Cambridge University Press.

Strobel, M. 1979. *Muslim Women in Mombasa 1890–1975.* New Haven: Yale University Press.

Sudarkasa, N. 1973. *Where Women Work: A Study of Yoruba Women in the Marketplace and in the Home.* Anthropological Papers, No. 53, Ann Arbor: Museum of Anthropology, University of Michigan.

———. 1981. "Female Employment and Family Organization in West Africa." In *The Black Woman Cross-Culturally,* F. C. Steady, ed., pp. 49–63. Cambridge, Mass.: Schenkman.

Ware, H. 1983. "Female and Male Life-Cycles." In *Female and Male in West Africa,* C. Oppong, ed., pp. 6–31. London: George Allen & Unwin.

Caroline Bledsoe's chapter, set in modern Sierra Leone, deals with the conjugal and career options of young Mende girls of school age. In a work documented by contemporary newspaper references as well as field observation, Bledsoe details the intricate maneuvering of girls, their parents, and possible suitor-patrons over the issue of the payment of school fees. Western-style schooling increasingly is viewed by the Mende as a path of escape from constraints of village life. For young girls, access to the greater wealth and personal autonomy of the urban, modern world hinges on school fees and the question of who pays them.

Bledsoe's focus on practice and potentialities allows her to highlight contradictions and conflicts that the various social actors encounter as they pursue their strategies—yet the world she describes is firmly set in the framework of local custom. The processual nature of African marriage—what she calls "conjugal testing"—is of particular interest, as it forms the traditional backdrop for prolonged negotiation and maneuver among all the participants. What emerges in this study is a richly detailed picture of social change in the making.

Caroline Bledsoe

10 School Fees and the Marriage Process for Mende Girls in Sierra Leone

Introduction

The last decades have undermined comfortable ways of understanding gender. Notions of female subordinance and conjugal roles, far from being given, are increasingly recognized as the outcomes of complex political and ideological processes by which people seek to shape culture (see Collier and Yanagisako 1987 for a useful review). In questioning previous frameworks of knowledge, we inevitably expose as problematic issues that previous generations of scholars took for granted. The construct "the subordination of women" has provided an attractive question for a generation of work. Far more challenging are attempts to understand how people try to craft and legitimize definitions of important gender categories that broaden or constrain women's choices. This paper takes the category of "school girl" among rural Mende people in Sierra Leone as an entry into the problem of gender identity formation. It asks how girls, parents, and suitors seek to control definitions of women and women's conjugal options through their attempts to define school fees.

The category of school girl (in Mende, *suku* [a loan word] *nyahɛ-lopoi*—literally, "school woman child") initially appears an odd choice to investigate the cultural subtleties of gender construction in rural Sierra Leone, because it does not represent the "normal" Mende woman. A school girl is not a woman, and most rural girls in Sierra Leone do not even go to school, much less graduate from primary or secondary school.

The choice of school girls, however, is surprisingly useful. First, the apparent oddities themselves of the school girl category mirror the "normal" social world, provoking people to comment on "normal" assumptions, predicaments, and possibilities for reconstrual. In Sierra Leone, where education is not compulsory for girls, but conjugal life almost inevitably is, people view with ambivalence the gradual intrusion of formal schooling into what they see as the normal marriage process. Their responses throw into sharp relief the social forces that increasingly bear on girls as they progress toward conjugal age. Second, the notions of both school and girl place strong emphasis on process: in this case, the making of a social identity. People in both categories—that is, school children and girls—are culturally recognized as undergoing formative processes from which numerous kinds of people could emerge.

This latter issue of social construction extends much more broadly. Concerns with process have been raised across a number of disciplines as social scientists have turned increasingly from static views of culture that do not account for achievement or negotiation toward theories of action that "see people not simply as passive reactors to and enactors of some 'system,' but as active agents and subjects in their own history" (Ortner 1984:143). The work of Bourdieu (1977) and Gramsci (1971), among others, suggests that power operates less through force than by subtly shaping the contexts in which people negotiate the definition of events (see also Collier 1988:6). Within such frameworks, scholars are raising new questions of how people try to use, create, and negotiate cultural categories, rather than respond passively to norms, as they continually reshape culture afresh. Analyzing the category "school girl" draws special attention to processes by which all important cultural categories are continually shaped.

The Marriage Process in Africa

In this view of relationships as being constantly adjusted, material transactions become critical junctures that can mark the state of the relationship or rechannel it. How marriage and bridewealth transactions structure African women's lives has, in fact, occupied considerable anthropological thought. Marriage and, in many societies, bridewealth are generally acknowledged to transfer legal rights in an African woman's labor and sexual and reproductive services from her natal lineage to that of her husband (Radcliffe-Brown 1950), bringing about little change in her subordinate legal status, especially if she enters a polygynous household as a junior wife. We now know, however, that despite the formal statuses that economic transfers would appear to confer on them, African women can carve out areas of considerable autonomy in conjugal units, especially if they have several children who can help support their economic enterprises. For example, Guyer (1981) and several contributors to Hafkin and Bay (1976) point out that spouses often separate their incomes and expenditures, making many women quite independent of their husbands economically. Others show that, under certain conditions, women spend considerable time trying to extricate themselves from marriage (for example, Cohen 1971; Bledsoe 1980).

We usually take as our focus "married" women's efforts to cope with the constraints of conjugal life or to gain independence. Yet central to understanding women's options is the processual nature of African marriage. "Getting married" is rarely a single event. Rather, it extends over a period of months or even years (see, for example, Comaroff and Roberts 1977; Aryee and Gaisie 1979; Brandon and Bledsoe 1988). During this time, potential partners and their families engage in what we might call "conjugal testing": working cautiously toward more stable unions. Because marriages evolve gradually, a girl—sometimes with her family's implicit permission— may test out relationships with several partners before establishing a long-term one. At some point in the process, cohabitation and sexual relations begin and children are born, but these events do not necessarily coincide with marriage rituals or with transfers or bridewealth and gifts, which can precede cohabitation and signify continued intent thereafter. For many a girl, youth consists of preparing for life with a man with whom her family actually began affinal negotiations when she was a toddler or even before birth, while her "married" life may be marked by periodic disputes about outstanding bridewealth debts or charges of adultery.

Emphasizing marriage as an extended process of conjugal testing highlights the fact that we know little about how a young woman as well as other people try to shape her conjugal or career potentials in the long stretch of marital processing. This becomes even more important in light of one of the most significant trends in contemporary Africa: the advent of formal Western schooling. Most women in Africa have had little or no education, and most school girls must drop out well before completing secondary school because of marriage and pregnancy. Still, many rural girls see education as a ticket to leaving the village and becoming urban career women and monogamous wives. (See Oppong 1973; Harrell-Bond 1976; Mann 1985; Obbo 1987, among others, for insightful treatments of marriage among educated urban women.)

Whereas rural girls view education as a step toward greater independence, their families view it ambivalently. Although educating a girl can improve her family's economic well-being through her remittances, they view it as a potential waste of valuable female subsistence labor if her school career, like that of many others, is terminated by a pregnancy. Education can also erode the family's control over her marital rights by giving her more economic options to fall back on if she refuses to marry the man her family has earmarked as a choice son-in-law.

Although a generation of concerted work on gender issues has exposed the problems in treating women only as wives, we need to re-examine the meaning of African marriage for rural women in these rapidly changing times. We can do so most fruitfully by returning to the old question of economic transfers that surround marriage. Here I accept Gluckman's (1965) general premise that African social relations are created and symbolized through transfers of property. In Sierra Leone, for example, frequent gifts of money are crucial symbolic markers of social relationships, including those between kin and between patrons and clients. For women of childbearing age, however, economic transfers have specific meaning. Any transfer by an unrelated man for, or to, a young woman—a loan, a ticket to a dance, or even sustained trading transactions—can signal marital or sexual intent.

Capturing the purpose of economic transfers for women in Africa, Comaroff (1980:37) points out that "prestations transform mating, which in itself may have no intrinsic social value, into a socially meaningful process, and thereby locate it in a universe of relations" (see also Parkin 1980). Yet as Comaroff and others have stressed, the processual nature of marriage creates enormous opportunity for manipulation. A girl's parents may acknowledge the money given by a man at one point as a marriage payment. But they may try to redefine it later as a gift unrelated to the marriage or as a payment for a previous debt, should the marriage plans dissolve.

Because marriage payments and transactions take different forms under different historical and economic conditions, we need to take a fresh look at new forms of marital transfers in the context of greater opportunities for education. I ask how people attempt to define the economic transactions that permit a Mende girl from a family of limited means to attend school. I refer here to adults' contributions to school fees (tuition) in particular, and secondarily to costs such as room and board, uniforms, and books.

School fees have become a key symbol of contemporary young people's aspirations toward what is culturally termed "civilized." But beyond the apparently straightforward Western notion of school fees, the Mende place deeper layers of meaning on them, particularly for girls. Like more conventional notions of payments for women, school fees—when paid by outside men on behalf of girls—can signal marital or sexual interest. What, then, are the implications for girls' conjugal lives as well as their chances of continuing in school?

This paper shows that rural girls' efforts to obtain an education must be understood against the indigenous model of marriage. It suggests that by manipulating the definition of material transactions for women, Mende actors try to channel or restructure each others' options and constraints. The paper draws on material from 1981–82 and 1985 fieldwork in eastern Sierra Leone and from archival work on recent Sierra Leone newspapers, which contain rich statements of cultural ideology and pose pithy dilemmas.

Ethnographic Background

Numbering about a million, Mende speakers live primarily in the eastern and southeastern hinterland of Sierra Leone, although schooling and employment have drawn them increasingly to the Freetown metropolitan area on the coast. I worked in a town with a population of 4,500 in the Eastern Province, an area producing coffee, cocoa, and diamonds, along with subsistence rice. Since the town had several schools, many households contained the children of rural relatives or acquaintances who were fostered in to attend school in exchange for household or marketing labor.

The Mende profess patriliny and allow polygyny. Many rural families now say they allow their daughters to choose whom they wish to marry, but they usually exert strong pressure to influence these choices: families may forbid certain choices outright and demand others. A girl is eligible for marriage after joining the Sande, the female secret society (see, for example, MacCormack 1979; Bledsoe 1984), which ritually initiates her reproductive life by reputing to teach her the secrets of reproduction and wifely skills.

It is important to the analysis of Mende marriage as a process to point out that Sande initiation is the most critical requirement for initiating sexual life. It is far more important, even, than rituals or economic transfers more directly related to marriage: a fact that helps explain why prospective suitors are expected to contribute heavily to Sande initiation. Sande leaders insist on separating initiates during their liminal phase (during which their sexual identity is ritually created) from secular scrutiny. Engaging in sex before initiation smears the girl's character and exposes her to the risk of infertility. Becoming pregnant and bearing a child is even worse because it upstages the Sande's role in ritually facilitating reproduction.

Although the Sande maintains its ritual importance in marking a girl's transition to womanhood, it is losing ground to formal schooling in many of its training functions. Schooling is said to impart skills important to modern women: an ability to speak and write English and the training and contacts to get a white-collar job and to marry a man with one. Conteh (1979:175) points out that in the Kono District of Sierra Leone, for example, men made wealthy by the diamond-mining industry compete for educated wives who may get jobs as company clerks. Along with these changes, bridewealth per se has become less important than the understood obligations of a man toward his wife's family to help educate their other children and to help them with food and medical problems.

Changes in economic transfers for women also operate against a broader cultural context of patron-clientelism (see also Richards 1986). Under the British colonial regime, local polities in Sierra Leone were drawn into a system of chieftaincies within the national parliamentary and presidential system. Within this national structure, jobs, scholarships, and other valued resources trickle down through personal ties to powerful brokers who can intervene with national institutions (see Murphy 1981 and Handwerker 1987 for Liberian cases). While the modern world offers opportunities for wealth and advancement, it has its dark side as well. Court cases that strip people of land, property, and dependents are commonly trumped up against those known to have weakly developed patronage support. Within this political climate of uncertainty and instability, obtaining services of virtually any kind—jobs, legal assistance, scholarships, medical support, or even food in times of hardship—necessitates having well-placed patrons with access to resources and to powerful members of the business and civil service bureaucracy.

Illiterate rural people are especially vulnerable. They need outside resources obtainable only through influence, yet suffer from heavy-handed government officials who demand unnecessary tariffs and pressure them for "contributions" to building projects that benefit the administrative elite. With precipitous recent declines in the national economy, people have even greater need for patrons well connected to the urban and government bureaucracies to bypass cumbersome bureaucratic channels during shortages of food, money, and petrol, and to provide them with crucial ties to the international world: for travel, jobs, and access to hard foreign currency.

As this suggests, having educated patrons is seen as critical to families' economic and political well-being. Even illiterate rural villagers now try to educate some of their children to broker for them with the threatening modern world or to gain the status to marry into powerful patronage networks. Investing in students' educations entails risks and expenditure, but it establishes claims on the pupil's future (Bledsoe, 1990). Indeed, successful children come under enormous pressure to share property and money freely with those who financed their educations—to pay their hospital bills, educate their own children, give them a place to live—in short, everything, and more, that was done originally for the students themselves during their own dependence.

The Quest for Civilization

The "village" or the "bush" versus "civilization" is the dichotomous national idiom—relic, to a large extent, of the country's colonial history—that contemporary Sierra Leoneans themselves invoke (for a parallel discussion of Liberia, see Moran, forthcoming). A "villager" (*fula-hu mɔi*—"village-in-person") is cast as a low-status subsistence farmer who languishes in the "bush" (*lɔi*). Villagers are stereotyped as living in a "closed place," illiterate and ignorant of the outside world. They work barefoot in the dirt, bear telltale calluses and cutlass scars, have little cash, wear dirty and unironed clothes, and cook meals without the benefit of processed foods such as dried fish and bouillon cubes. Although in some contexts young people respect rural villagers as the source of valued traditional knowledge and life-styles, calling someone a villager is grounds for a lawsuit.

Young people yearn to be civilized (*pu*—"modern," "civilized"; *pumɔi*—"civilized person"): to live in "open places" where knowledge of the outside world is said to uplift society and promote "development" (*tɛɛ-guloma*—"to go forward"). Most young people want to be literate; wear clean, well-tailored Western-style clothes; speak English and Krio (the national lingua francas, known locally as *pu-woo*—"civilized words"); and entertain important visitors with foods prepared from civilized ingredients. They also desire employment in a civil service or business job where they can sit down, earn cash on a regular basis, deal with paperwork, and so on. Eventually, they hope to acquire urban property (see Barnes, this volume) and use other means to gain permanent footing in the city. Young people also want to buy cigarettes and attend modern cinemas, "amplifier" dances, and nightclubs. To them, this is not trivial conspicuous consumption. It is meant to impress upwardly mobile peers, community leaders, and teachers, who are respected as the possessors of civilized knowledge—as well as for their roles as critical brokers for scholarship recommendations for higher education.

Especially for girls, civilization also connotes monogamy. Although affairs with "outside" partners are common, most men with a secondary school education have only one legal wife at a time. Given a choice, most young women say they prefer monogamous marriage, which they believe will liberate them from the domination of senior wives and give them greater control over the household's resources as well as more leverage with their husbands.

Above all other means of becoming civilized and shedding villager status is formal Western education. The ability to pay school expenses, particularly tuition ("school fees"), has come to symbolize for children—and the benefactors who help finance them—a new life in the civilized modern world (see also Caldwell 1980; Berry 1985; Obbo 1989). However, supporting an education is a large undertaking. Students need money for room and board, uniforms, books, school supplies, and application and examination fees. School fees themselves, even at the primary level, range from several leones a year for government schools (in April 1986 one leone was worth about $0.20 officially) to several hundred leones for more prestigious schools. Because of the investment required to educate especially a secondary student, parents as well as students themselves often turn to outside benefactors, relatives as well as nonrelatives, for help.

Rural Girls' Chances for Education and Civilization

For girls, the most important manifestations of the civilized/village distinction are two role potentials: urban career woman versus dependent wife of a rural polygynist. Before education was available to her, a rural girl was clearly destined as the latter: a rural wife. All her early training was directed toward her roles as a wife, co-wife, and bearer and caretaker of children. Such a marriage obviously confined women geographically and economically, and channeled their potentials into things of a reproductive character: health concerns, sexuality, physical labor, cooking, and so on.[1] Life is surprisingly difficult even today for the wife of a powerful chief. Because of increasing tensions over succession rights to chieftaincy, children's legitimacy can be exposed to intense public scrutiny. A woman whose grown son runs for the chieftaincy against his agnates, as well as candidates from other lineages, can be taken to task for her hour-long absence from the compound on a certain afternoon about nine months before her son was born. As a result, chiefs' wives are confined ever more tightly to the compound, knowing that some potential rival faction will almost certainly keep written records on their unaccounted-for absences from the compound.

Increasingly, however, rural girls seek civilized urban careers. To this end, many rural girls go to primary school, and a few go on to secondary school. Almost without exception, girls who make it to secondary school want professional careers of their own. The twenty-six girls in a rural secondary school I surveyed (which had 112 boys) wanted to be lawyers, doctors, nurses, bank managers, teachers, and accountants. All wanted to go on to college. Many wanted Ph.D's and M.D.'s. Despite these ambitions, considerably fewer girls than boys in Sierra Leone (as in Africa as a whole) complete secondary school. Although the number of girls and boys beginning primary school is now roughly equal, these proportions decline rapidly, especially as girls approach puberty and their families begin to give sons priority for higher degrees (see also Pellow 1977:116, 120).

FAMILY AMBIVALENCE TOWARD GIRLS' EDUCATIONS

Among the most difficult barriers to a girl's education is her own family's ambivalence. Although most school girls maintain high educational and career aspirations for themselves, their families' perceptions of their potentials are less clear. In the past, family opinion was largely negative. Twenty or thirty years ago, as a man related, "When I was growing up, there was an attitude that parents did not want to pay the educational expenses of girls. They felt that the girl was going to grow up to be a housewife anyway, so they didn't want to waste resources on her—unlike a boy, who could get a job after he got an education. Also, most of the positions were open to men: even clerical work and civil service jobs."

Nowadays, many rural families do support their daughters' ambitions, for they know that more professional opportunities are open to women. An older rural woman with no schooling asserted, "If a girl is ambitious for book learning, we force her to do it. Tomorrow she will be somebody reliable.... Today we are seeing so many educated girls working in big offices. That is what makes most people educate their girls nowadays, because they will bring some benefit to the home."

Families recognize that professional daughters can help support them. A local school principal related that one woman, herself an uneducated farmer, hoped desperately for her daughter to succeed educationally: "The mother prayed that her daughter would finish school and begin to work so that she would be released of this heavy work. The mother goes to the farm; even now they are harvesting. So she wants to rest [stop farming] if the daughter gets a job. . . . The mother will say, 'Let my child finish school and then I will begin to enjoy [have a better life] now.'"

Nonetheless, most rural parents support their daughters' advanced educational goals with mild enthusiasm at best, because young women provide far more daily labor to a household than boys. An illiterate older woman explained:

> Girls start being an advantage to you and helpful to you when they are matured and join the Bundu [Sande] society and are given to a husband. Then she can benefit you. . . . When my daughter was 12, I gave her to a husband and started getting benefit from her. She wasn't educated. . . . With boys, it depends on the education. At about the age of 21 and over, when the boys might have completed schooling, picked up jobs and started earning money, they will be able to give support to the parents.

Families also see a daughter as underwriting her brothers' education, by her work in the home but especially by marrying early and marrying a man who will help her brothers who wish to attend school.

These ambivalences belie a more basic view of women and marriage as currency for patron/client hierarchies. Since young women bear valued children and provide most subsistence and household labor, giving them in marriage has long comprised the cornerstone of families' efforts to create obligations toward both potential patrons and clients (for example, Kopytoff and Miers 1977; Bledsoe 1980). Family members fear that an educated woman, filled with her own importance, will become an arrogant wife who disobeys her husband, quarrels with the co-wives with whom she may have to live, and refuses subsistence farm work, if such becomes necessary. Ultimately, such behaviors could drive away a son-in-law whose allegiance the family has cultivated.

Because education for girls interferes with the long span of marital processing, elders also fear losing control over a girl left in school for a prolonged period, or the possibility of an unwanted pregnancy. Yet they recognize that the longer she remains in school, the more desirable she will be to a civilized man or a man in the rural chieftaincy hierarchy. Therefore, a family may play off leaving a girl in school as long as possible against the chance that she will get pregnant or choose independently a man of whom they do not approve.

Some parents try to resolve these conflicting pressures by exploiting the civilized auras that their daughters acquire through a few years of education and forging ties with men with connections to the civilized world who can give them money or political assistance. Such efforts are reflected in the complaints of a secondary school boy to the editor of a Freetown newspaper's column, entitled "Women's Corner":

> [My school girl sweetheart] told me to marry her while I am still a school boy. [But] her parents abuse [insult] and even drive her out of their home everytime for my sake [because of me]. The problem is that I am not working. . . . Her parents . . . wanted to give her to a man who is working at the Bank of Sierra Leone. You know some parents want their daughters to get married to millionaires because of their money. (*The New Shaft*, 13 May 1985)

PREGNANCY AND SEXUALITY AS IMPEDIMENTS TO A GIRL'S EDUCATION
Above all families' stated fears in allowing a girl to prolong her education is the fear that she may contract an untimely pregnancy, perhaps by a schoolmate with a highly uncertain future. Her purpose in contracting sexual alliances may appear to stem from little more than peer pressure to obtain nice clothes and sustain a civilized life-style. But as one student stressed:

> Girls need *money* to use for their . . . daily transactions . . . whenever they get sick or any other thing like that. So they would like money. So one of the *main* things with most of these girls is—why most of these girls become pregnated—is because of money. They need *money*. And in getting it, they have to be in line with somebody who has it. And you can't get such money unless you have to go into "friends" [have boyfriends]. And that person would like to make use of you, that his money going out is a reward for having intercourse with you. So if you are in love with [having an affair with] the man you like, that man will be doing everything for you. You will be sleeping with the man [his emphasis].

Ironically, therefore, the very thing that many parents fear may become a self-fulfilling prophecy: school girls needing money may turn to outside men, increasing their risks of pregnancy and the likelihood of dropping out of school.

Certainly pregnancy has an important effect on a school girl's subsequent life chances. Besides terminating her school career, it can undermine her chances for a desirable marriage. As a result, although returning to school after a pregnancy is now legal, unlike the situation in the colonial and early postcolonial period, a teacher stressed that: "The schools in Sierra

Leone do not generally admit girls who have given birth: mothers. She is not considered a school girl again."

Why is pregnancy so incompatible with continuing an education? The most obvious answer is that the time and money required to care for a baby do not allow a young mother to return to school. However, pregnancy by itself does not automatically end a girl's schooling. Many girls attempt abortion (for example, through large ingestions of presumed abortifacients, wire probes, or covert visits to surgeons), though this can entail considerable expense and risk. Others leave their babies with their mothers and return to school. But this is still difficult, for a girl's past pregnancy can be used to shame her, as a girl related:

> When you get pregnant, that is virtually the end of your schooling. Of course, you can now try to come back to the same school, but sometimes you will get mocked, making you very afraid to come back. . . . If a girl comes back to school, she will be mocked, especially while getting flogged or punished for some [other] reason. [Students frequently mock each other while they are getting punished, taunting them with embarrassing remarks.] Others will taunt her, saying *"koi-ma"* [a woman who has borne a baby].

To avoid censure, a girl who has borne a baby can enroll in a school in another town where she is not known. But potential guardians may refuse to take her in, fearing blame if she continues her past behavior. Even for a girl who does relocate, her guardians may be unforthcoming, forcing her to look to outside men for support. In such cases, explained a man,

> [For girls] living on their own while they are going to school: they may stay in the same compound with a relative, say, but they are not that much directly under the control of that relative. I would say that most of the high school girls live like that, and that might be the type of relationship they would have: with men, who help support them. Other girls, like those in Sixth Form, might rent a place with other girls. In many cases, they do have boyfriends who help support them.

Some girls undergo extreme duress. A young secondary school girl who was put to hard work in her guardian's household accidentally spilled some food before serving it. As a punishment, her guardians deprived her of food for four days, yet continued to demand that she perform her normal duties. She was able to bear this for two days, but finally sought help from a local shopkeeper in return for sex. Not surprisingly, she soon became pregnant and was forced to drop out.

Beyond the most obvious economic problems that young mothers face in returning to school is a more symbolic one: the incompatibility between childbearing and returning to school as a student. In fact, there are striking parallels between the cultural view of school and that of the Sande society's role in preparing girls for marriage. Among the Sande's most vital concerns is attempting to restrict all knowledge about sex and reproduction to initiated members. In doing so it creates distinctions between women who have experienced the secrets of childbirth and those who have not. Sande leaders also attempt to separate girls undergoing initiation—that is, girls in liminal initiation status—from their uninitiated peers.

Schools also try in theory to keep their own initiates uncontaminated by experience in, or knowledge of, reproduction. As a result, asserted a man, "Girls who get pregnant are generally discouraged from coming back to school. What I used to hear was that such a girl would be a bad influence." The awkward fact that some girls already know about sex and reproduction, whether through Sande initiation or other sources, is relegated to mutual silence, as an educated man asserted:

> The other thing was that pregnancy and childbirth were looked on as a mysterious science. Even the time I was going to school, men were not supposed to know about it [because of Sande influence]. It was taboo for a man to study reproduction in biology. So the whole idea of childbirth was that it should be left unspoken. So, possibly, here is a girl who has known these secrets. She has become a woman now. In a sense, she really didn't belong in school with the children. So this is why she was kept away from the schools.

One of the most important symbolic manifestations of the Sande's efforts to separate training and sexual life was the attire a girl wore. If she had to leave the sacred grove briefly on errands, she donned special ritual clothing and painted white chalk on her body to indicate that she was not at liberty to interact freely, especially with men, during her dangerous liminal state.

Like the traditional Sande attire, the school uniform has become an important symbol. Individually tailored in the school's official colors, the uniform is the most important outward manifestation of students' prospects for upward mobility and sets them apart from rural "villagers." Wearers are regarded with a mixture of respect and fear because of their potentials for achievement in the civilized world—potentials that are being developed by esoteric rituals and instruction. This was how a school principal characterized the symbolism of the uniform: "The reason for using the uniform: if you are in your uniforms, when somebody sees you, he will conclude you are a student. So you should be protected and treated in a special manner than the others that are not in uniforms."

A school uniform has additional connotations for a girl. First, it suggests that she is being prepared for marriage to a man of importance, and as such should be treated with respect. Second, like the special Sande attire, it marks her as occupying a liminal preparatory status, and sets her off limits to sexual advances. The association between wearing a uniform and being untouched by pregnancy and childbirth helps explain why public resentment at a pregnant school girl is often voiced in the image of a tarnished school uniform. An older girl with a dirty, torn uniform is suspected of having no one to "watch over" her properly, rendering her vulnerable to men who might tempt her with food and money in exchange for sexual favors that her family elders have not sanctioned. A teacher drew out these comparisons between school and initiations, focusing on the school uniform as a symbol of a child, inexperienced in, and allegedly ignorant of, childbirth, but allowed to retain a privileged position in society while attending school. He implied that being pregnant (or having been pregnant) and wearing a uniform are symbolically incompatible:

> The girl will still be in town and will feel ashamed to wear a uniform and return to school. . . . Legally, there is no problem with that, but the parents [of other students] would probably get upset. The students have to dress in uniforms. And here is a girl who has been pregnant here, attended clinic [antenatal clinic] here, and even goes through the market every time she wants to attend clinic, with a big stomach. . . . Other people might say that although she is very ambitious in returning to school, the school will be cast as a sort of "high school": *kpako-nyahei suku,* a "big women's" school. That is, instead of school for children, you have schools for mothers.

The Meaning of School Fees in the Marriage Process

Obstacles such as pregnancy at inappropriate times, family worries about marrying well, and symbolic incompatibility between childbearing and student status suggest that girls' schooling must be seen against the indigenous model of marriage. In this model, Mende marriage is a long, attenuated process marked by labor or political support from a prospective husband, or by bridewealth, gifts, and (especially) Sande initiation fees, that assist the parents in, or compensate them for, raising the woman and preparing her for marriage.

Just as more indigenous marital transactions contain numerous ambiguities that are constantly reshaped over time, a school girl's status as a student as well as a wife is fraught with uncertainty. To retain as much control as possible over the long, ambiguous stretch of education, family elders draw on indigenous tenets about rights in women, as defined by economic transactions. These tenets hold that a woman's sexual and domestic labor services are inseparable, and that they are controlled by her family and, eventually, her husband. The model therefore restricts, at least in theory, a young woman's control over her own sexuality.

The indigenous model of marriage also restricts girls' freedom to engage in independent economic transactions to finance their educations, because these can imply an illicit exchange of sex for money. Whereas a boy can ask an unrelated man for money for school fees, a young woman who does so implies sexual favors in exchange. Nor can she earn school fee money by performing domestic activities for an unrelated or distantly related man. The reason is that whoever controls a woman's domestic capacities is also assumed to control her sexual services. A girl's elders can forbid her to work independently for a man to obtain her school fees if there is not a mature woman in his household to whom she may be attached as a ward or servant. As a woman explained, "It would imply she was 'loving to' him." (Bleek 1976:250 notes that many young Ghanaian men look for a sexual partner under the pretext of seeking a woman to cook for them.) Moreover, whereas boys can exploit several sources of support simultaneously, all of whom may know about each other, girls do so at greater risk. Since a woman should have only one male partner at a time, a man who discovers that his school girl lover is getting assistance from another man is likely to terminate his support. However, given the realities imposed by the patronage system, both boys and girls must obtain help—whether school fees or recommendations for scholarships—to complete their educations. In return they face demands, in one form or another, for reciprocity.

In some cases, families' worries about the association between sex and earning money prove useful to girls. Such families prioritize school fees for their daughters, letting the boys fend for themselves, as a man recalled from his own childhood: "For girls, in my own family's case, when it came to things like school fees, they always took care of the girls first. Even my older sister would contribute first to the school fees of my younger sisters before mine. This was because I could easily fend for myself. But the older sisters and brothers, they would always make sure that the younger girls had what they needed."

Family elders can also utilize to their own advantage the indigenous model of marriage that counts any expenses paid on behalf of a woman as statements of conjugal interest. They may obtain assistance for their daughter's schooling from a man they would like as a son-in-law, and treat this as a preliminary marriage payment, thus taking advantage of the long, ambiguous intersection between marriage and education. As a man put it:

> When a man pays the school fees for a girl, that . . . means that he has interest in her. The phrase they use for it is, "You [the man] put a string on their daughter's hand. . . ." That has a traditional background. A man in the old days would give the parents some gifts even when the girl was small, pay her initiation fees, and so on. So similarly, a man may be paying her school expenses with the expectation that she eventually marry him.

Although the extent to which this happens is difficult to estimate, a teacher in the local secondary school told me, perhaps with some exaggeration: "Most of the girls in this school are in fact married or engaged. Even [X] is married to the Paramount Chief. With these girls, the man has given the dowry [bridewealth]."

As in earlier eras, sexual relations and reproduction are not conditional on a final marriage ceremony, but can be commenced while a suitor is putting a girl through school, as long as she has undergone Sande initiation. Therefore the family may allow her to begin a sexual relationship with the man who begins to help the parents support her while she is still a student. They may even insist on it, as a woman explained: "If the parents accept the money, they will find a way for the girl to accept the man, willing or not." If pregnancy results, the parents simply withdraw the girl from school and send her to live with the man who paid her fees.

Despite their overt disapproval of girls' sexual liaisons to obtain school assistance, therefore, parents are increasingly complicit in such cases, a trend some link to increasing economic hardship. In fact, a parent's refusal to pay a girl's school expenses may imply that the girl can continue her school career only if she can find an outside benefactor to assume her expenses. Indeed, some parents adopt an obverse strategy of withholding a girl's school fees to encourage her to obtain a boyfriend's support for her expensive secondary school education.

A family can even use school fees to force a girl's compliance with her family's marital choice. For example, a girl who had passed her Ordinary level exams upon completing secondary school with the highest results in the school was anxious to go on to college. Her parents, however, urged her to quit school to marry a rich though illiterate diamond dealer who wanted her. They even promised that the man would pay for her to study abroad if she agreed to marry him later. When she still refused, her parents, in desperation, consulted a Muslim ritual specialist who, according to the local story, made a potion that made her forget entirely about school and happily marry the man.

In another case, a rural girl who had made it to Form Five (last year in secondary school) had higher educational ambitions, so she refused to marry the local paramount chief who had asked for her. In response, her parents withdrew their financial support for her schooling and told her that if she wanted to finish, she would have to accept the chief's conditional offer of school fees with marriage. Seeing no other alternative, she consented in despair and moved into his compound where she was immediately reminded of her place as a junior wife and told that she could not leave the compound without proper escort. After she bore her first child, the chief put her off further, promising vaguely that if she bore him several children, he would send her back to school—a highly dubious outcome. Still, she refused to lose hope and accept everyone else's attempts to define her as a polygynous wife. She confided to me a secret plan that she had devised for trying to return to school and edge out of the restrictions imposed by her current marriage. After bearing her second child, with which she was currently pregnant, she planned to leave her two year old behind and use the excuse of going to relatives to get child care help while nursing the baby. The relatives she had in mind were carefully chosen. They were the ones who lived not in a rural village but in a large city with several good schools and professional colleges. She pointed out that they would be likely to be sympathetic with her plight since they themselves were educated and might, therefore, help her with school expenses.

As in the more indigenous model, of course, parents may change their minds about their daughter's marriage, after a suitor has spent considerable money. They may even intentionally mislead him from the beginning, implying that he can marry her when they have no such intentions. Moreover, national laws have eliminated, at least in theory, a family's obligation to reimburse a man's bridewealth if his wife leaves him or his wife-to-be changes her mind; families hope their daughters will gain as much education as possible from suitors' support.

Yet the very fact that school fees and bridewealth are closely associated makes parents reluctant to label school fees publicly as marital payments. Despite the legal changes at the national level, parents still fear that their local courts will rule that any expenses the man made must be refunded. Alternatively, the parents may entertain hopes of obtaining a better son-in-law eventually—after their daughter manages to get a good education through school fee support from her first suitor. Hence, parents hedge their bets by appearing to disapprove of the arrangement and construing it as an illicit one that their daughter has made without their consent.

In any case, the apparently simple act of paying a girl's school fees cannot necessarily be taken at face value, as an investment in furthering her education. By linking the acceptance of girl's school fees from outside men to the indigenous model of marriage, families define their own actions as within the approved cultural definitions of the conjugal process.

Are School Girls Students or Potential Wives? Girls' Attempts to Manipulate the Labels

Although a school girl would like to become civilized, having her school fees paid by an adult man, often with her parents' consent, places her in a precarious position. The same school fees that could mark her progress toward civilization can, if defined as conjugal preliminaries, trap her in the village as the wife of an illiterate polygynist. How school fees are defined, therefore, can determine her future life-style, whom she must marry, and when she must stop being a student and become a wife—a status that itself can remerge with student status, if the opportunity surfaces. Not surprisingly, girls struggle to define these payments in ways most advantageous to them: whether as marital payments or as more distant acts of patronage or friendship. It is not hard to understand why, then, girls continually attempt to maneuver for negotiating room within the cultural confines of marriage and the patronage system.

In some cases, a girl is happy for a man her parents chose to pay her school fees and pleased to marry him later. But in others, a girl has little choice and deeply resents the circumscription of what she saw as progress toward becoming civilized. A pregnancy by a village man, even a chief, who has paid her school fees is likely to terminate her school career, which she has envisioned in greater terms than the man of limited accomplishments whom her parents thrust upon her.

Depending on her options for support elsewhere, a girl can try to refuse to marry the man with whom her parents arranged school assistance, and try to deflect her parents' wrath. She can attempt secretly to abort his pregnancy that would force her to leave school and become his wife.

Here I stress that pregnancy, like marriage, is an ambiguous process that continually tests the relationship between the partners and their families. At any point, shifting relations among these parties could alter the definition of a pregnancy. Although a school girl is likely to abort a pregnancy by a man she does not want to marry and proceed with her schooling, she may try to get pregnant to bolster a wavering relationship to a man she wishes to marry. If he clearly loses interest, she may attempt abortion. But he may string her along with promises of marriage and the lure of material advantages, only to lose interest after the baby is born. The outcome of this pregnancy, then, may be a denial of the baby's legitimacy and its fosterage up-country with rural kin. Other solutions are possible also. I have heard of cases wherein an unwanted baby became sick and, because it was not treated, died.

As this suggests, an increasingly common alternative is for secondary school girls to create independent sources of support: many become girlfriends and sexual partners to outside men to pay their school fees—men with whom the parents have *not* negotiated marriage plans. In this sense, although the coupling of economic transfers with sexual relations resembles more indigenous marital processes, girls increasingly contract affairs independently of their families. Since they have more choice in the matter, their partners frequently include their own teachers. Teachers can provide money for school fees or negotiate with principals to delay or waive payment of school fees. (See Bleek 1976 for a fuller discussion of Ghanaian teachers' affairs with students.) A guest editor of a column titled "Mainly for Women" in a Freetown paper alleged that 90 percent of school girls' pregnancies resulted from affairs with teachers. He also identified the girls most likely to engage in these affairs:

> Attractive or sexy-looking school girls not sound academically are the easiest of victims. Then, the "nice looking ones" easy targets girls from very poor homes who can ill afford secondary school education without some financial supports from other members of the family, boyfriends or "outside" adults. Many male teachers exploit such girls to their hearts' desires! There are the mercenary (wild) school girls. . . . These girls become prey as they look at sex as extreme fun and accommodating interested teachers as a means of acquiring high marks after poor examination performances. (*Weekend Spark*, 27 September 1985)

However, as stated above, parents do not always oppose their daughters' affairs. The same columnist suggested that some parents even take advantage of the situation: "Some parents even connive with male teachers to conceal 'ownership' pregnancies [questions of paternity] from school authorities. They 'protect' teachers by not disclosing that they [the teachers] were responsible while the male teachers secretly promised to look after both the girl and the child and to further his pupil's education after delivery" (*Weekend Spark,* 27 September 1985).

Besides teachers, school girls can use their acquired civilized statuses to attract older, wealthy men who pay their school fees: urban sugar daddies with position and wealth, such as politicians and senior civil servants. A man explained: "Now there is a really rampant fear that girls turn to politicians, because they can give them money and scholarships, because they are the ones in the most visible positions, and they are the ones most likely to be living not just purely out of their salary [that is, through bribes and embezzlement]." Many of these men are married already and are committed to legal monogamy, which most educated urbanites, Christian as well as Muslim, hold out as the mark of advancement. They are lured by the prospect of being seen with prestigious young girlfriends to sustain their reputations as virile men (see also Harrell-Bond 1976). Public opinion on these affairs is mixed. Outrage occasionally flares into public controversy, as a man related:

> When I was in Freetown in 1982, I heard that was one of the biggest fears when they decided to build . . . [a big government building]. It was directly opposite a girls' [secondary] school. It was a hot issue. Most people were reacting against the government choosing that site to build it. They were arguing that it was going to create much temptation for the school kids and the civil servants, wherein they could easily get together during lunch time, and so on. The proximity was too much. There was a lot of discussion in the newspapers about it.

But private sentiments may support the liaison of a girl whose school career is in jeopardy. The editor's responses to letters in the "Women's Corner" reveal such ambivalences. When one girl who wanted to complete her education wrote for advice on how to resist her boyfriend's sexual advances, the editor, a man, moralistically applauded her virtue: "At this stage when many school going girls run after men they call sugar daddies to satisfy their worldly needs, you are thinking of your future" (*The New Shaft,* 16 January 1985). Yet when another girl emphasized the risk of her school career, the same editor was sympathetic with her economic plight and urged her to seek help from a boyfriend if other sources failed:

> I would have said that you go to a vocational Institution but for that again [also] you need money. If you had a boyfriend who is prepared to help you he could see you through school. My advice is that you first of all look around for a relative of yours who is willing to help and if that fails then you get a man to help you. He might have to marry you before he takes the chance lest you slip away. I wish you good luck. (*The New Shaft*, 1 November 1985)

Many girls' strategies, like those of parents and suitors, play on the inherent ambiguity of the meaning of school fees and of marital payments in general (see, for example, Comaroff and Roberts 1977; Comaroff 1980). A girl may try to define these payments later, after she has derived substantial benefit from them, as assistance of a nonmarital kind, and construe this as a patronage relationship, like one the man would have with her brother. She may also define these payments as gifts in exchange for her sexual favors. Such actions lead many men to suspect their girlfriends' motives, as the editor of the "Women's Corner" column warned one girl: "The only problem now is that men don't trust young girls. On several occasions men have gone all out to help young girls who have proved ungrateful [deserted the men who paid their expenses]" (*The New Shaft*, 1 November 1985).

As this suggests, many men who support their student girlfriends are serious about marriage and view school fees as an investment toward obtaining a prestigious, educated wife. Some girls clearly hope to marry the men who are supporting them, preferably through formal legal marriage to upwardly mobile young men. Also possible, although less satisfactory to a girl, is to marry an already-married urban man in the customary manner. This allows him to continue presenting a monogamous face to the urban public (Clignet 1987; Bledsoe n.d.; for a comparative West Indian case, see Smith 1987), while providing his rural wife with money to build a house (see Barnes, this volume, on the importance of owning houses), begin a cash crop plantation, and so on.

In sum, girls' efforts to obtain school fees from men cannot be explained away as irresponsible acts. Relationships with outside men, construed or accepted as part of the process of conjugal testing, comprise many girls' best hopes of obtaining an education that their families are unable, or reluctant, to provide. In this perspective, school girls' affairs are not deviant, irresponsible behaviors but attempts to prolong their school careers by accepting school fees from men. Hence, these young women may be attempting to maximize their chances simultaneously in the educational and marriage markets. They can utilize their own sexuality to obtain financing for schooling in ways that appear to contravene the strict model of indigenous marriage and rights in women, but that, in a deeper sense, are quite compatible with it. What has changed markedly is that many girls strike up relationships on their own, without permission from their families.

Conclusions

Although school fees appear to be unambiguously associated with civilization, far removed from the more indigenous marital model of rights in Mende women's sexual and domestic services, they may be construed as quite the opposite: marriage payments or claims for sexual favors. Whether a girl can leave village life to become a civilized career woman hinges on who pays her school fees and how these payments become defined. Success in defining the meaning of school fees is central to where she eventually falls out on the continuum between polygynous village wife and monogamously married civilized career woman. Under these circumstances, it should not be surprising that girls (and those who want to make claims on them) attempt to manage reproduction and the definitions of their marital status through definitions of school fees, a multivocal sign of the times.

One of the most important issues raised here, of course, is the impact of biology—that is, pregnancy—on a girl's prospects for achievement in the civilized world. It may appear that fickle school girls who enter heterosexual relations endanger their career prospects; they teeter precariously between educational success, on the one hand, and pregnancy and/or early marriage, on the other hand. One standard answer, for that matter, to why many African girls must drop out of school and forego professional careers is pregnancy. Biology apparently intercedes yet again, relegating a girl to the life of a rural polygynous wife or a cast-off "outside wife" of an elite man, while boys' freedom from the biological consequences of their sexual affairs allows them to pursue more valued career achievements in the outside world.

The conclusion that emerges forcefully from this discussion, however, is that although education is usually assumed to decrease fertility through raised consciousness of higher life goals, perhaps the reverse is more accurate: low fertility increases education. That is, those girls who manage to avoid pregnancy and childbirth can stay in school longer. Hence, instead of early participation in sex decreasing school girls' educational chances, it allows some girls to *avoid* early marriage and the concomitant disadvantages of early and frequent childbirth.

Further, a careful reading of the evidence reveals that school girls are more alert to the possible consequences of their actions than their behavior might suggest. Their efforts to play off the ambiguity of school fees as marriage payments or financial support for education to different audiences in different contexts attest to a keen capacity for what Giddens (1984:3) calls reflexivity: the monitored character of social life, wherein actors size up each other's intentions and try to use these interpretations as leverage in subsequent interactions. Giddens draws on the work of Willis (1977), who stresses actors' enormously sophisticated knowledge about the system, showing that although low-class boys in Britain frequently reproduce their own limited employment options by offending school authorities and having to drop out early, it is their very knowledge, rather than ignorance, of the school structure (contrary to popular belief) that brings this about.

Just as lower-class British boys exert more control than we assume over the possible consequences of their actions, Mende school girls, with little overt power in the traditional sense by which we have understood the concept, maneuver within the confines of their situations. They play off their own marital and educational prospects and try to avoid relations that would hamper their life prospects. At the same time they try to redefine confining circumstances as resources to use to their advantage.

The evidence also underscores the importance of taking fully into account the processual nature of creating gender definitions that was raised at the outset. The notion of "potentiality" is pivotal to the processual approach I have used. It implies a negotiable reality, meaning that any of a person's innumerable potentials might come to dominate his or her social image in different contexts or at changing points in the life cycle. This can take quite subtle forms, as individuals seek to bring about certain identity outcomes by "managing meaning" (see Comaroff and Roberts 1977).

Certainly the case cited earlier of the young woman who was forced to become a polygynous chief's wife bears important lessons. If ever any woman appeared to have a limited career potential, it was this one. The chief had paid a hefty bridewealth for her and because of his power no one was likely to suggest that this was an incomplete marriage, a stage along the marital process, within which she could maneuver. Moreover, as the wife of a chief, she was literally confined night and day to a compound where her rival co-wives and their relatives kept her under close scrutiny. But the woman's own depiction of her status and options revealed an image that was quite different. Her undiminished longing to resume her education and her covert plans to escape the compound on the pretext of obtaining help with child care from extended family members suggested that she saw her situation as one in flux: a temporary setback but one within which she was exerting unremitting effort to develop other sets of options. Hence, despite the apparent closure of marital options and a clear definition of roles that her marriage apparently created, she was treating the conjugal transactions that had occurred as elements of a continuously negotiated process in which she would have to pit her strategies against the simultaneous efforts of other people to channel her identity and obligations in ways most advantageous to them.

More important than the biological fact of pregnancy, therefore, are social and cultural processes of construal. Even relationships as apparently clear as husband-wife are not irrevocably locked at the outset of a marriage. Similarly, wifely identity and a conjugal career are not fixed by unitary events in time. Instead, they continually change, in convergence with other forces such as efforts to gain education, in ongoing processes that can be shaped by intelligent action.

Acknowledgments

I want to thank the following people for their help on various aspects of this paper: Sandra Barnes, David Cohen, John Comaroff, Kerry Knox, William Murphy, and Peggy Sanday. Thanks also to two anonymous reviewers for the University of Pennsylvania Press for their constructive comments.

Notes

1. This represented a potential quite close to Ortner's (1974) description of women's association with devalued things of nature—reproduction, feeding, and cleaning. But although the rural Mende generally associate women with children and reproduction and men with the world of extradomestic achievement, marriage and childbearing do not automatically associate women with nature. A fortuitous marriage or a good education allows a girl to live in a house with modern conveniences, shop for processed foods at the supermarket, buy imported leather shoes, and pass on messy tasks of child care to servants. Rather than link the categories of female and male a priori with nature (the village) or culture (civilization), I concen-

trate on how individuals apply these dichotomous attributes to women, and ask how young women strategically manage schooling and reproduction. (Critiques of biological determinism can be found in Rapp 1979, MacCormack and Strathern 1980, and several articles in this volume.)

Bibliography

Aryee, A. F., and Gaisie, S. K. 1979. "Fertility Implications of Contemporary Patterns of Nuptiality in Ghana." In *Nuptiality and Fertility. Proceedings of the IUSSP Seminar on Nuptiality and Fertility,* L. T. Ruzicka, ed. Bruges, Belgium: Ordina Editions.

Berry, Sara S. 1985. *Fathers Work for Their Sons: Accumulation, Mobility and Class Formation in an Extended Yoruba Community.* Berkeley: University of California Press.

Bledsoe, Caroline H. 1980. *Women and Marriage in Kpelle Society.* Stanford: Stanford University Press.

———. 1984. "The Political Use of Sande Ideology and Symbolism." *American Ethnologist* 11 (3): 455–72.

———. 1990. "The Social Management of Fertility: Child Fosterage Among the Mende of Sierra Leone." In *Births and Power: The Politics of Reproduction,* W. Penn Handwerker, ed. Boulder: Westview Press.

———. n.d. "The Politics of Polygyny in Mende Child Fosterage Transactions." In *Gender Hierarchies,* Barbara D. Miller, ed. (under review).

Bleek, Wolf. 1976. "Sexual Relationships and Birthcontrol in Ghana: A Case Study of a Rural Town." Ph.D. diss., University of Amsterdam.

Bourdieu, Pierre. 1977. *Outline of a Theory of Practice.* Cambridge: Cambridge University Press.

Brandon, Anastasia, and Caroline Bledsoe. 1988. "The Effects of Education and Social Stratification on Marriage and the Transition to Parenthood in Greater Freetown, Sierra Leone." Paper presented at the Workshop on Nuptiality in sub-Saharan Africa: Current Changes and Impact on Fertility, Paris.

Caldwell, John C. 1980. "Mass Education as a Determinant of the Timing of Fertility Decline." *Population and Development Review* 6 (2): 225–55.

Clignet, Remi. 1987. "On dit que la polygamie est morte: vive la polygamie!" In *Transformation of African Marriages,* D. Parkin and D. Nyamawaya, eds., pp. 199–209. Manchester University Press, Manchester.

Cohen, Ronald. 1971. "Dominance and Defiance: A Study of Marital Instability in an Islamic African Society." Anthropological Studies, No. 6, American Anthropological Association.

Collier, Jane F. 1988. *Marriage and Inequality in Classless Societies.* Stanford: Stanford University Press.

Collier, Jane F., and Sylvia J. Yanagisako. 1987. "Introduction." In *Gender and Kinship: Essays Toward a Unified Analysis,* pp. 1–13. Stanford: Stanford University Press.

Comaroff, J. L. 1980. "Introduction." In *The Meaning of Marriage Payments,* J. L. Comaroff, ed., pp. 1–47. London: Academic Press.

Comaroff, John L., and Simon Roberts. 1977. "Marriage and Extra-Marital Sexuality: The Dialectics of Legal Change Among the Kgatla." *Journal of African Law* 21 (1): 97–123.

Conteh, James S. 1979. "Diamond Mining and Kono Religious Institutions: A Study in Social Change." Ph.D. diss., Indiana University. Ann Arbor: University Microfilms.

Giddens, Anthony. 1984. *The Constitution of Society: Outline of a Theory of Structuration.* Berkeley: University of California Press.

Gluckman, Max. 1965. *Politics, Law and Ritual in Tribal Society.* Chicago: Aldine.

Gramsci, Antonio. 1971. *Selections from the Prison Notebooks of Antonio Gramsci.* Ed. and tr. Quentin Hoare and Geoffrey Nowell Smith. New York: International Publishers.

Guyer, Jane. 1981. "Household and Community in African Studies." *African Studies Review* 24 (2/3): 87–137.

Hafkin, Nancy J., and Edna G. Bay, eds. 1976. *Women in Africa: Studies in Social and Economic Change.* Stanford: Stanford University Press.

Handwerker, W. Penn. 1987. "Fiscal Corruption and the Moral Economy of Resource Acquisition." *Research in Economic Anthropology* 9: 307–53.

Harrell-Bond, Barbara. 1976. *Modern Marriage in Sierra Leone: A Study of the Professional Group.* The Hague: Mouton.

Kopytoff, Igor, and Suzanne Miers. 1977. "Introduction." In *Slavery in Africa: Historical and Anthropological Perspectives,* pp. 3–81. Madison: University of Wisconsin Press.

MacCormack, Carol P. 1979. "Sande: The Public Face of a Secret Society." In *The New Religions of Africa,* B. Jules-Rosette, ed., pp. 27–37. Norwood, N.J.: Ablex Press.

MacCormack, Carol, and Marilyn Strathern, eds. 1980. *Nature, Culture and Gender.* Cambridge: Cambridge University Press.

Mann, Kristin. 1985. *Marrying Well: Marriage, Status and Social Change Among the Educated Elite in Colonial Lagos.* Cambridge: Cambridge University Press.

Moran, Mary H. Forthcoming. *"Civilized Women": Gender and Prestige Among the Glebo of Cape Palmas, Liberia.* Ithaca: Cornell University Press.

Murphy, William P. 1981. "The Rhetorical Management of Dangerous Knowledge in Kpelle Brokerage." *American Ethnologist* 8: 667–85.

Obbo, Christine. 1987. "The Old and the New in East African Elite Marriages." In *Transformations of African Marriage,* David Parkin and David Nyamwaya, eds., pp. 263–80. Manchester: Manchester University Press for the International African Institute.

———. 1989. "Women's Autonomy, Children and Kinship." Paper presented at the African Studies Workshop, University of Chicago.

Oppong, Christine. 1973. *Marriage Among a Matrilineal Elite.* Cambridge: Cambridge University Press.

Ortner, Sherry. 1974. "Is Female to Male as Nature is to Culture?" In *Woman,*

Culture and Society, M. Rosaldo and L. Lamphere, eds., pp. 67–87. Stanford: Stanford University Press.

———. 1984. "Theory in Anthropology since the Sixties." *Comparative Studies in Society and History* 26: 126–66.

Parkin, David. 1980. "Kind Bridewealth and Hard Cash: Inventing a Structure. In *The Meaning of Marriage Payments*, J. L. Comaroff, ed., pp. 197–220. London: Academic Press.

Pellow, Deborah. 1977. *Women in Accra: Options for Autonomy*. Algonac, Mich.: Reference Publications.

Radcliffe-Brown, A. R. 1950. "Introduction." In *African Systems of Kinship and Marriage*, A. R. Radcliffe-Browne and D. Forde, eds. pp. 1–85. London: Oxford University Press.

Rapp, Rayna. 1979. "Review Essay: Anthropology." *Signs: Journal of Women in Culture and Society* 4 (3): 497–513.

Richards, Paul. 1986. *Coping with Hunger: Hazard and Experiment in an African Rice-Farming System*. London: Allen & Unwin.

Smith, Raymond T. 1987. "Hierarchy and the Dual Marriage System in West Indian Society." In *Gender and Kinship: Essays Toward a Unified Analysis*, J. F. Collier and S. J. Yanagisako, eds., pp. 163–96. Stanford: Stanford University Press.

Willis, Paul E. 1977. *Learning to Labour: How Working Class Kids Get Working Class Jobs*. Westmead, England: Saxon House.

Abu-Lughod's paper addresses the problem of power and how to define and track it through the resistance it generates. She inverts Foucault's assertion (1978) that "where there is power there is resistance" and uses her study of the resistances of Bedouin women to diagnose the nature of the power structure they resist.

Through her decade-long fieldwork among the Awlad ʿAli, a Bedouin group in Egypt's Western Desert, she is able to show how forms of resistance and power have changed with the encroachment of what she describes as "modern nonlocal networks of economic and institutional power." Using consumerism to resist their elders, young Bedouin women exposed to Egyptian national television and schooling also aspire to new styles of marriage that, ironically, may impose new forms of domination perhaps more restrictive than the old.

This chapter deals with complex and subtle issues, at both the descriptive and the analytic level. Abu-Lughod warns against the tendency to romanticize resistance. From the point of view of feminist concerns there is the reality that Bedouin women simultaneously support the traditional system of dominance by elder males while they subvert and resist it. Indeed they see their restricted women's world as a haven to be protected, not least of all because it is the institutional base for their often successful resistance and subversion of male authority. At the analytic level, this work is informed by subtleties of thought about issues of power that are the legacy of decades of study by behavioral scientists.

Lila Abu-Lughod

11 The Romance of Resistance: Tracing Transformations of Power Through Bedouin Women

Introduction

One of the central problematics in recent years within the human sciences has been the relationship of resistance to power.[1] Unlike the grand studies of peasant insurgency and revolution of the 1960s and early 1970s (for example, Paige 1975; Scott 1976; Wolf 1969), what one finds now is a concern with unlikely forms of resistance, subversions rather than large-scale collective insurrections, small or local resistances not tied to the overthrow of systems or even to ideologies of emancipation. Scholars seem to be trying to rescue for the record and to restore to our respect such previously devalued or ignored forms of resistance.

The popularity of resistance provokes a number of interesting questions that cannot be considered in this chapter. First, one might ask what is the relationship between scholarship or theorizing and the world-historical moment in which it takes place such that this is a moment in which scholars from diverse disciplines and with extremely different approaches are converging on this topic.[2] Second, one might ask what is the ideological significance within academic discourse of projects that claim to bring to light the hitherto ignored or suppressed ways subordinate groups have actively responded to and resisted their situations.[3] In this paper I want to consider a different question: What are the implications of studies of resistance for our theories of power?

At the heart of this widespread concern with unconventional forms of noncollective, or at least nonorganized, resistance is, I would argue, a growing disaffection with previous ways we have understood power, and the most interesting aspect of this work on resistance is a greater sense of the complexity of the nature and forms of domination. For example, work on resistance influenced by Bourdieu and Gramsci recognizes and theorizes the importance of ideological practice in power and resistance and works to undermine distinctions between symbolic and instrumental, behavioral and ideological, and cultural, social, and political processes.[4]

Despite the considerable theoretical sophistication of many studies of resistance, within and outside of anthropology, and their contribution to the widening of our definition of the political, it seems to me that because they are ultimately more concerned with finding resistors and explaining resistance than with examining power, they do not explore as fully as they could the implications of the forms of resistance they locate. In some of my own earlier work, like theirs, there is perhaps a tendency to romanticize resistance, to read all forms of resistance as signs of the ineffectiveness of systems of power and of the resilience and creativity of the human spirit in its refusal to be dominated.[5] By reading resistance in this way, we collapse distinctions between forms of resistance and foreclose certain questions about the workings of power.

I want to argue here for a small shift in perspective in the way we look at resistance—a small shift that will have serious analytical consequences. I suggest that we should use resistance as a *diagnostic* of power. In this, I am taking a cue from Foucault, whose theories, or as he prefers to put it, analytics, of power and resistance although complex and not always consistent are at least worth exploring. One of his central propositions, advanced in his most sustained discussion of power, in the first volume of *The History of Sexuality*, is the controversial assertion, "where there is power, there is resistance" (1978:95–96). Whatever else this assertion implies, certainly Foucault is using this hyperbole to force us to question our understanding of power as always and essentially repressive. As part of his project of deromanticizing the liberatory discourse of our twentieth-century so-called sexual revolution, he is interested in showing how power is something that works not just negatively, by denying, restricting, prohibiting, or repressing but also is something productive (of forms of pleasure, systems of knowledge, goods, and discourses).[6] He adds what some have viewed as a pessimistic point about resistance by completing the sentence just quoted as follows: "Where there is power, there is resistance and yet, or rather consequently, this resistance is never in a position of exteriority in relation to power."

This latter insight about resistance is especially provocative, but to appreciate its significance one must invert the first part of the proposition. This gives us the intuitively sensible statement, "where there is resistance, there is power," which is both less problematic and potentially more fruitful for ethnographic analysis, because it enables us to move away from abstract theories of power toward methodological strategies for the study of power in particular situations. As Foucault (1982:209, 211) puts it, when he himself advocates this inversion, then we can use resistance "as a chemical catalyst so as to bring to light power relations, locate their position, find out their points of application and the methods used." We could continue to look for and consider nontrivial all sorts of resistance, but instead of taking these as signs of human freedom we will use them strategically to tell us more about forms of power and how people are caught up in them.

In the ethnography of the Awlad ʿAli Bedouins that follows, I want to show how, in the rich and sometimes contradictory details of resistance, the complex workings of social power can be traced. I also want to show that these same contradictory details enable us to trace how power relations are historically transformed—especially with the introduction of forms and techniques of power characteristic of modern states and capitalist economies. Most important, studying the various forms of resistance allows us to get at the ways intersecting and often conflicting structures of power work together these days in communities that are gradually becoming more tied in with multiple and often nonlocal systems. These are central issues for theories of power that anthropologists are in a unique position to consider.

Forms of Resistance/Forms of Power

I will be taking as my case the changing situation of women in a Bedouin community in Egypt's Western Desert, not because I want to make an argument about women in particular, but because first, one does not usually study women when thinking about resistance; second, gender power seems to be one of the more difficult forms of power to analyze; and third, the circumstances of doing fieldwork in a sex-segregated society are such that I have from women more of the kind of rich and minute detail needed for this sort of analysis. The group of Bedouins I will be discussing are known as Awlad ʿAli and are former sheep-herders settled along the Egyptian coast from west of Alexandria to the Libyan border. Although sedentary, they describe themselves as Arabs and Bedouins, not Egyptians, and claim an affiliation with the Bedouin tribes of eastern Libya. They insistently distinguish themselves from the rural and urban Egyptians of the Nile Valley.[7]

By way of introduction to them, I should confess my own involvement in a complex romance of resistance. Since pastoral nomads have reputations within the popular and anthropological literature as proud and free, those who go to study them are often attracted by these qualities. Nevertheless, I was not prepared for the specific forms Bedouin resistance was taking when I arrived in the late 1970s to begin fieldwork. For example, when I returned from my first trip back to Cairo after having officially moved into a household, one of the first bits of news the women and girls gave me was that in my absence they had been visited by the local head of the Egyptian security police. The women were furious and protective, describing how they had refused to let him search my suitcases, lying to the government "son-of-a-dog," as they called him, by saying I had locked them and taken the keys. A couple of months after I had begun living with them, my host disappeared for a while. It turned out that he had been taken in for questioning about political ties to Libya and hash smuggling; people reacted only by denouncing the Egyptian government for harassment. Over the years that I lived with them, I got used to finding pistols under my mattress and rifles in my wardrobe, attending feasts to welcome home people who had been imprisoned for smuggling and crossing borders, knowing young men who disappeared into the desert with the herds to avoid conscription into the Egyptian army, hearing people talk about how to hoodwink officials or avoid paying taxes, and knowing individuals like one man whose temporary insanity took the form of a terror that the government was looking for him and would take him away because he had failed to register the death of a child whose name was still on his family identity card. This was not the diffuse kind of resistance by independent nomads I had fantasized about but rather particular resistances to the specific ways—inspection, conscription, detention, control of movements, registration, and taxation—through which the Egyptian state was seeking to "integrate" the Bedouins of the Western Desert into its domain at that time.

But what of women? Although I did not begin with any sort of interest in Bedouin women's resistance, I discovered various forms. Through these forms of resistance we can begin to grasp more clearly the traditional structures of power in this community. I will describe four types of resistance associated with women. Then I will go on to discuss some important transformations of both resistance and power in the larger world into which Bedouins are being incorporated.

The first arena for resistance, one I have described elsewhere (Abu-Lughod 1985), is the sexually segregated women's world where women daily enact all sorts of minor defiances of the restrictions on activities and movements enforced by elder men in the community. Women use secrets and silences to their advantage. They often collude to keep knowledge away from men; they cover for each other in minor matters, like secret trips to healers or visits to friends and relatives; they smoke in secret and quickly put out their cigarettes when children come running to warn them that men are approaching. These forms of resistance indicate that one way power is exercised in relation to women is through a range of prohibitions and restrictions applied to them that they both embrace, in their support for the system of sexual segregation, and resist, as suggested by the fact that these women fiercely protect the inviolability of their separate sphere where the defiances take place.

A second and widespread form of resistance is Bedouin girls' and women's resistance to marriages. Indeed, one of the major powers that families, and especially elder male relatives like fathers and paternal uncles, wield is control over the arrangement of marriages. Actual marriage arrangements are always complicated and involve many people, especially mothers and female relatives. Mothers sometimes successfully block marriages their daughters do not want, even though fathers or other male guardians are supposed to have control. For example, on my last visit to the Bedouin community I found out that my host's eldest unmarried daughter had just narrowly avoided being married off. Her father had run into some friends in the market and they had asked if their sons could marry his daughter and niece. Marriages are arranged between allies, friends, and kin and to refuse someone without a good excuse is difficult. He had agreed to it and then returned home to inform his wife.

She reported to me that she had been furious and had told him she refused to let her daughter marry into that family. They lived in tents in the desert and her daughter, who had grown up in a house and did not have many of the old Bedouin skills like taking care of tents or milking sheep, would find it a hard life for which she was not prepared. Moreover, the family that had asked for her was in trouble. The reason they lived in tents was that two of their members had gotten into a fight with someone and accidentally killed him. According to Bedouin customary law, they had to seek refuge with another family, leaving behind their homes and land. They lived in fear, knowing that the kinsmen of the man they had killed would want revenge. My host's wife did not want her daughter to be a widow. So she refused. Her husband got angry, she told me, saying, "What am I supposed to tell them? I already agreed." He then marched off to talk to his niece's mother, to enlist her support. But she too refused to let her only daughter marry into that family. The women suggested that he inform the men to whom he had promised the girls that the girls' male cousins had decided to claim them. This is a cousin's right, so he was able to save face and indeed the marriages did not go through.

When men are stubborn, however, or so caught up in strategies and relations of obligation with other men that they will not or cannot reverse a decision, the women may not succeed. Even then, they do not necessarily remain silent. One woman whose daughter was forced to marry a cousin sang a song as the groom's relatives came to pick up her daughter for the wedding:

> You're not of the same stature as these
> your true match is the man with the golden insignia . . .
> intī mā gadā hadhōl
> gadāk bū dabābīr yilihban . . .

The song was a taunt to them that suggested that her daughter was worthy of an officer, not the poor man who was getting her.

Neither are unmarried girls always silent about their feelings about marriages. Girls sing songs as they get water from the wells and publicly at weddings. Among the songs I heard about the men they did not want to marry were the following:

> I won't take an old man, not I
> I'll give him a shove and he'll fall in a ditch
> mā nākhudshī shāyib nā
> nzuggū yāgaʿ fil-ganāh

> I don't want the old fez on the hill
> what I want is a new Peugeot
> lubt il-ʿilwā nā ma nrīdu
> wuddī fī bājō jdīda

> God damn the uncle's son
> Lord don't lead me near no blood relative
> yikhrib bēt wlad il-ʿamm
> rabbī mā ygarrib lā dam

Significantly, the particular kinds of men they are objecting to are older men and their paternal cousins, two categories of men who tend to have binding claims on their fathers such that their marriage requests would be hard to refuse.

The most interesting cases are those where women themselves actually resist marriages that have been arranged for them. Their retrospective narratives of resistance are among the most popular storytelling events I heard. The following one was told to me and a group of her daughters-in-law and grandchildren by the old matriarch of the community I lived in. The events must have taken place at least sixty years before. She began by explaining that the first person to whom she was to have been married was a first cousin. His relatives came to her household and conducted the negotiations and even went as far as to slaughter some sheep, the practice that seals the marriage agreement. She went on:

> He was a first cousin, and I didn't want him. An old man and we were living near each other, eating out of one bowl [sharing meals or living in one household]. They came and slaughtered a sheep and I started screaming, I started crying. And my father had bought a new gun, a cartridge gun. He said, "If you don't shut up I'll send you flying with this gun."
>
> Well, there was a ravine and I went over and sat there all day. I sat next to it saying, "Possess me, spirits, possess me." I wanted the spirits to possess me, I wanted to go crazy. Half the night would pass and I'd be sitting there. I'd be sitting there, until Braika [a relative] came. And she'd cry with me and then drag me home by force and I'd go sleep in her tent. After twelve days, my cousin's female relatives were dyeing the black strip for the top of the tent. They were about to finish sewing the tent I'd live in. And they had brought my trousseau. I said, "I'll go get the dye for you." I went and found they had ground the black powder and it was soaking in the pot, the last of the dye, and I flipped it over—POW!, on my face, on my hair, on my hands until I was completely black.
>
> My father came back and said, "What's happened here? What's the matter with this girl? Hey you, What's the matter?" The women explained. He went and got a pot of water and a piece of soap and said, "If you don't wash your hands and your face I'll . . ." So I wash my hands but only the palms and I wipe my face, but I only get a little off from here and there. And I'm crying the whole time. All I did was cry. Then they went and put some supper in front of me. He said, "Come here and eat dinner." I'd eat and my tears were salting each mouthful. I had spent twelve days and nothing had entered my mouth.
>
> The next afternoon my brother came by and said to me, "I'm hungry, can you make me a snack?" I went to make it for him, some fresh flatbread, and I was hungry. I had taken a loaf and I put a bit of honey and a bit of winter oil in a bowl. I wanted to eat, I who hadn't eaten a thing in twelve days. But then he said, "What do you think of this? On Friday they're doing the wedding and today is Thursday and there aren't even two days between now and then."

> I found that the loaf I was going to eat I'd dropped. He asked, "Well, do you want to go to so-and-so's or do you want to go to your mother's brother's?" I said, "I'll. . . ." There was an eclipse, the sun went out and nothing was showing. I said, "I'll go to my maternal uncle's." I put my shawl on my head and started running. I ran on foot until I got to my uncle's. I was in bad shape, a mess.

She then went on to describe how her uncle had sent her back, with instructions to his son to send greetings to her father and to ask him to delay a bit, perhaps she would come around. She continued, "So I went home. After that I didn't hear another word. The trousseau just sat there in the chest, and the tent, they sewed it and got it all ready and then put it away in their tent. And autumn came and we migrated west, and we came back again. When we came back, they said, 'We want to have the wedding.' I began screaming. They stopped. No one spoke about it again." This old woman's narrative, which had two more episodes of resisted marriages before she agreed to one, follows the pattern of many I heard—of women who resisted the decisions of their fathers, uncles or older brothers and eventually won. Her story, like theirs, let others know that resistance to marriage was possible.

A third form of Bedouin women's resistance is what could be called sexually irreverent discourse. What I am referring to are instances when women make fun of men and manhood, even though official ideology glorifies them and women respect, veil for, and sometimes fear them. In this irreverence one can trace the ways the code of sexual morality and the ideology of sexual difference are forms of men's power. Women seem only too glad when men fall short or fail to live up to the ideals of autonomy and manhood, the ideals on which their moral superiority and social precedence are based, especially when such lapses occur through desiring women. They joke about certain men behind their backs and they also do it in general ways, as through folktales like one I recorded in 1987 in which a man with two wives is cuckolded by the younger one but foolishly rewards her and punishes his obedient and faithful senior wife. The folktale has many messages, but one of them is certainly that men are fools whose desires override their supposed piety and undermine their overt demands for women's sexual propriety and chastity. The kind of power this tale attempts to subvert, and thus diagnoses, is the power of controlling women's sexuality entailed by the Bedouin moral system.

Bedouin women's resistance also takes the form of an irreverence toward the mark of masculinity and the privileges this automatically grants. For example, Bedouin men and women express an avowed preference for sons, saying people are happier at the birth of a boy. Yet in one discussion, when I asked what they did when a baby turned out to be a boy, one old woman said, "If it's a boy, they slaughter a sheep for him. The boy's name is exalted. He has a little pisser that dangles." All the women present laughed. Another woman, commenting on the ending of a folktale she had told about the meanness of sons and the compassion of daughters, an ending in which the mean son was asked to slaughter a ram and produce its womb, explained, "You see, the male has no womb. He has nothing but a little penis, just like this finger of mine [laughingly wiggling her finger in a contemptuous gesture]. The male has no compassion. The female is tender and compassionate [playing on the double meaning of the Arabic root *rahama*, from which the words womb (*riḥm*) and the word compassion (*raḥma*) are formed]."

Here the usual terms are reversed and the male genitals are made the sign of a lack—the lack of a womb. An even clearer example of women's irreverence is a folktale I heard women and girls tell to children, which went as follows. An old woman and an old man traveled into the desert and set up camp in a lonely area where there were wolves. They had brought with them seven goats, a cow, a donkey, and a puppy. The first night a wolf came to the tent. He called out to all of them "Ho!" and then demanded, "Give me someone to eat for dinner tonight!" So the old man and woman gave him a goat.

He came the next night and called out the same thing, asking, "Who will you give me to eat for dinner tonight?" They gave him another goat. This went on night after night until the old couple had given the wolf all seven goats, their donkey, their cow, and their puppy.

Then they realized that they had no more animals to give him and that he would eat them. The old man said to his wife, "Hide me in a basket we'll hang from the tentpole. And you, hide in the big urn." So she hung up the basket with the old man in it and she hid inside the pottery urn.

When the wolf came that night, no one answered his call. He came into the tent and sniffed around. Then he looked up. Now the basket had a tear in it and the old man's genitals were showing, they were dangling out of the hole in the basket. The wolf kept jumping up trying to bite them. The old woman watching this started laughing so hard she farted. This split open the urn she was hiding in, and the wolf ate her. Then he nipped at the old man's genitals until he pulled down the basket and ate the old man too. And then he went to sleep in their little tent.

In the most recent version of the telling, the group of women and girls with whom I was sitting laughed hard. The storyteller teased me for having asked to hear this story and her final comment was, "The old woman was laughing at the wolf biting her husband's genitals." There is rich material here for a Freudian analysis and there is no doubt that male fears of castration and of being cuckolded could be read in this folktale and the one mentioned briefly above. The messages in both are complex. Yet it is important to remember that it is women who are telling the stories, women who are listening to them, and women who are responding with glee to the things men dread.

Folktales, songs and jokes among women are not the only subversive discourses in Bedouin society. Those I have just described, though, indicate the significance of the ideology of sexual difference itself as a form of power. Recently I analyzed what I consider to be the most important of the subversive discourses in Bedouin society—a kind of oral lyric poetry (Abu-Lughod 1986). This is the fourth type of resistance. These poem/songs, known as *ghinnāwas* (little songs), are recited mostly by women and young men, usually in the midst of ordinary conversations between intimates. What is most striking about them is that people express through them sentiments that differ radically from those they express in their ordinary-language conversations, sentiments of vulnerability and love, often about relationships with members of the opposite sex. These sentiments reflect on situations in their lives about which they otherwise respond with anger or denial of concern.

I argued that most people's ordinary public responses are framed in terms of the code of honor and modesty. Through these responses they live and show themselves to be living up to the moral code. Poetry carries the sentiments that violate this code, the vulnerability to others that is ordinarily a sign of dishonorable lack of autonomy and the romantic love that is considered immoral and immodest. Since the moral code is one of the most important means of perpetuating the unequal structures of power, violations of the code must be understood as ways of resisting the system and challenging the authority of those who represent and benefit from it. When examined for what it can tell us about power, this subversive discourse of poetry suggests that social domination also works at the level of constructing, delimiting, and giving meaning to personal emotions.

The Bedouin attitude toward this type of poetry and toward those who recite it returns us to some of the central issues about power and resistance. Like wearing veils, reciting poetry is situational. Poems are recited mostly in contexts of social closeness and equality. The only exceptions to this were, in the past, wedding festivities which, not surprisingly, dignified older men avoided. This avoidance, along with people's opinions that this type of poetry is risqué and un-Islamic, suggests their uneasy recognition of the subversiveness of the genre. On the other hand, for the Bedouins with whom I lived, poetry was cherished.

This ambivalence about poetry suggested to me that certain forms of resistance by the less powerful in Bedouin society could be admired, even by those whose interests the system supports. I argued that this attitude was connected to the Bedouin valuation of resistance itself, a valuation associated with the larger political sphere and men's activities, whether traditional and tribal or current and government-directed, as one can infer from the attitudes toward the state I described earlier. It is a value in contradiction with the structures of inequality within the family, where gender enters in. Women take advantage of these contradictions within their society to assert themselves and to resist. But they do so, most clearly in the case of poetry, through locally given traditional forms, which suggests that in some sense at least, these forms have been produced by power relations and cannot be seen as independent of them. I take this as a good example of what Foucault (1978:95–96) was trying to get at in suggesting that we not see resistance as a reactive force somehow independent of or outside of the system of power.

The everyday forms of Bedouin women's resistance described above pose a number of analytic dilemmas to our usual way of thinking about resistance. First, how might we have theories that give these women credit for resisting in a variety of creative ways the power of those who control so much of their lives without either misattributing to them forms of consciousness or politics that are not part of their experience—something like a feminist consciousness or feminist politics—or devaluing their practices as prepolitical, primitive, or even misguided? Second, how might we account for the fact that Bedouin women both resist and support power, the latter for example through practices like veiling, without resorting to concepts like false consciousness, which dismisses their own understanding of their situation, or impression management, which makes of them cynical manipulators? Third, how could we recognize that their forms of resistance, like folktales and poetry, might be culturally provided without immediately assuming that even though we cannot therefore call them cathartic personal expressions they must somehow be safety valves?[8] I struggled with some of these dilemmas in my earlier work and I find them in the work of others.

With the shift in perspective I am advocating, by asking not about the status of resistance itself but what the forms of resistance indicate about the forms of power that they are up against, we are onto new ground. In addition to questions such as whether official ideology is really ever hegemonic, or whether cultural or verbal resistance counts as much as other kinds, we can begin to ask what can be learned about power if we take for granted that resistances, of whatever form, signal sites of struggle. The forms I have described for Bedouin women suggest that some of the kinds of power relations in which they are caught up work through restrictions on movement and everyday activities; through elder kinsmen's control over marriage; through patrilateral parallel cousin marriage; through a moral system that defines superiority in particular ways (like autonomy) that men are structurally more capable of achieving; through a set of practices that implies that maleness is sufficient justification of privilege; and through the linking of sets of sentiments to respectability and moral worth. These are not the only things at work—there are also such things as elder kinsmen's or husbands' control over productive resources, which may or may not be resisted directly. But to discount the former as merely ideological is to fall into the familiar dichotomies that have kept people from looking at the most significant aspect of this situation: that power relations take many forms, have many aspects, and interweave. By presupposing some sort of hierarchy of significant and insignificant forms of power, we may be blocking ourselves from exploring the ways in which these forms may actually be working simultaneously, in concert, or at cross-purposes.

Transformations of Power and Resistance

The other advantage of using resistance as a diagnostic of power is, as I argued at the outset, that it can help detect historical shifts in configurations or methods of power. In this final section, I want to turn to the ways Bedouin women are living a profound transformation of their social and economic lives. From a careful look at what may initially appear to be trivial matters, something important can be learned about the dynamics of power in situations where local communities are being incorporated into modern states and integrated into a wider economy.

I will make three observations about resistance on the basis of recent fieldwork. The first concerns the fate of traditional subversive forms. Some of these, like folktales, seem to be dying out as Egyptian television and radio supplant young people's interest in such forms.[9] Others, like the kind of poetry described earlier, are being incorporated into other projects and appropriated by different groups. I had thought, when I left Egypt in 1980, that this form of poetry was also disappearing. In recent years, however, the new popularity of semi-commercial, locally produced cassettes has given traditional Bedouin poetry new life. At the same time, however, its social uses are changing. As I have shown elsewhere (Abu-Lughod 1990), these poem/songs, always before recited equally by women *and* young men, are becoming in their new form a forum for almost exclusively male resistance. Older women continue to sing the songs or to reminisce about how they used to sing them, but the major public occasions for singing have disappeared and young women do not develop the skills or habit of reciting them. Women and girls avidly listen to these low-budget commercial cassettes but they do not record them, because no modest woman would want her songs played in front of strangers or would be willing to sit in a recording studio with strange men.

As I argued (Abu-Lughod 1990), women seem to be losing access to this mode of resistance; this form of poetry is becoming increasingly associated with young men who now sing the songs, make the small profits, and use this kind of love poetry, in cassette form, to protest or resist the increasing power of older kinsmen. The latter's greater and more inflexible power is made possible by the Bedouins' involvement in the market economy in two ways: first, monetarization and the privatization of property, especially land, give patriarchs more absolute economic power; and second, as hierarchy in general is becoming more fixed and wealth differences between families more extreme, the tribal ideology of equality that limited the legitimacy of domination by elders is eroding. The shifting deployments of this poetic form of resistance are related to and reveal these complex changes.

The second observation about resistance is that new signs of women's resistance to restrictions on their freedom of movement are beginning to appear. On the one hand, I witnessed a number of arguments between older women and their younger nephews and sons about how harshly these young men were restricting the movements of their sisters and female cousins. Among themselves and in the presence of the young men, the older women expressed outrage and recalled the past, when they had freely gone off to gather wood and get water from wells, occasionally on the way exchanging songs and tokens of love with young men. For the first time in 1987 I also heard adolescent girls and young women complain that they felt imprisoned or that they were bored. On the other hand, I noticed increasingly frequent incidents of young wives or unmarried girls having to defend themselves, usually again with the support of their mothers, aunts, and grandmothers, against slanderous accusations usually initiated by their male kinsmen, that they had been seen someplace where they had no permission to go or had been talking to boys outside the family. This resistance to the restrictions on movement, and the smears of reputation intended to enforce them, do not index any new spirit or consciousness of the possibilities of freedom on the part of women. Rather, I would argue, they index women's sense of the new forms of the powers of restriction that have come with sedentarization and the more extreme division between men and women. In the span of the present generation the Bedouins have settled and built houses in permanent communities. Surrounded by neighbors who are not kin, in a social world where there has been no dilution of the modesty code, women have ended up having to spend far more time out of sight or veiled than in the desert camps, and they are subject to surveillance whenever they step out.

Third, a new and very serious form of resistance is developing in the women's world that, unlike the two just discussed, which widen the gap between women and men as groups, pits young women against older women and indirectly against their fathers and uncles, in alliance with young men of their own generation. These generational conflicts involve a deceptively frivolous issue: lingerie. Nine years ago I witnessed the following incident. Two of the adolescent girls in our community had bought negligees from a peddler. (Bedouins usually just sleep in their ordinary clothes.) The girls' grandmothers were furious and tried to make them sell them back by threatening to set them on fire. When the old women had some visitors, they demanded that one of the girls bring out the nightgown to show them. The women all touched it and pulled at it, and one old grandmother in the midst of hilarity put the sheer lime-green gown over her layers of clothing, danced around the room and made for the doorway, as if to go out and show the men. She was pulled back.

By 1987, it had become almost routine for brides to display nylon slips and negligees with their trousseaus. Most adolescent girls had bought such items for their marriages and their older female relatives no longer tried so hard to thwart them. Now the frontier has shifted to bras, cosmetics, and bobbypins. In the household in which I lived, for example, many of the tensions between one of the daughters and her mother was over the homemade bra the girl insisted on wearing. Her mother was scandalized by the way it drew attention to her chest and frequently criticized her. The daughter persisted, as Bedouin children nearly always do in the face of parental pressure, retaliating by criticizing her mother for having so many children and running such a chaotic Bedouin household. In her resistance to her mother's imposition of older Bedouin standards of modesty can be seen the beginnings of an ironic and crucial transformation of Bedouin life.

What the older women object to in the purchase of lingerie is not only the waste of precious money on useless items but also the immodesty of these emergent technologies of sexualized femininity to be deployed in the pleasing of husbands. Not that *they* had not worked to remain in their husbands' good graces; they had fulfilled their duties in maintaining the household and their moral reputations. But they had relied on their kinsmen for assurance of good treatment and redress of mistreatment by husbands. They had gained their right to support through their status as kinswomen or mothers and through the work they contributed to the extended household. What wealth women would get they got at marriage and after that, everyone had much the same things, grown, raised, or made in the household. This older generation, at least as I saw them, were at best dignified in their comportment, but usually loud, sure of themselves, and hardly what we would consider feminine. Some Bedouin men also commented on this.

Young women, in resisting for themselves the older women's coarseness by buying moisturizing creams and frilly nylon negligees are, it could be argued, chafing against expectations that do not take account of the new set of socioeconomic circumstances into which they are moving. Some of the girls with whom I spoke still, like their grandmothers, want to resist marriages. They do not object to the fact that marriages are arranged for them, but only resist particular matches, mostly those that do not promise to fulfill certain fantasies. What they say they want and often sing about in short public wedding songs, are husbands who are rich (or at least wage-earning) and educated (or at least familiar with a more Egyptian way of life), husbands who will buy them the things they want—the dressing tables, the beds, the clothes, the shoes, the watches, the baby bottles, and even the washing machines that would mean the end of back-breaking outdoor work. Sedentarized and more secluded, these girls aspire to be housewives in a way their mothers never were. Their well-being and standard of living now depend enormously on the favor of husbands in a world where everything costs money, there are many more things, large and small, to buy with it, and women have almost no independent access to it. That women's resistance to unfairness in the distribution of purchased goods, from blankets to bars of soap and boxes of matches, causes the most frequent conflicts in most households confirms this; men's powers now importantly include the power to buy things and to punish or reward women through withholding or giving these things.

As the veils they wear get sheerer and these young women become more involved with the familiar features of a sexualized femininity tied to the world of consumerism—if the comparatively small-time world of $5 nightgowns and 15-cent nail polish—they are becoming increasingly enmeshed in new sets of power relations of which they have little awareness. These developments are tied to their new financial dependence on men but at the same time are directed pointedly at, and as a form of resistance to, their elders of both sexes. If resistance signals power, then this form of resistance may indicate the desperation with which their elders are trying to shore up the old forms of family-based authority that the moral code of sexual modesty and propriety supported.

Like the older forms of women's resistance described earlier, these young women's forms are also culturally given, not indigenously as before, but rather through a borrowing from and emulation of (not to mention a buying from) Egyptian society. These resistances are again, therefore, not outside of or independent from the systems of power. Nevertheless, what is peculiar to these new forms of resistance is how they travel between two systems and what this can tell us about relations of power under such conditions. For instance, along with the lingerie and cosmetics goes a pleasure in listening to Egyptian rather than Bedouin songs, following Egyptian romantic soap operas on the radio, and watching Egyptian television. Their mothers impatiently scold the young women for wasting their time with that Egyptian trash, and some old Bedouin men refuse to allow televisions to enter their homes, even after they have acquired electricity. These Egyptian songs and stories, like the lingerie, are oppositional within the young Bedouins' strategies of resistance to their elders, but unlike the old forms of Bedouin poetry or even folktales, they are not oppositional discourses within their original social context, which is the context of middle-class Egyptian urban life, a way of life whose debts to the West are manifold and whose penetration by the state is pervasive.

Here the irony that sets in must be considered carefully. In taking up these Egyptian forms and deploying them against their elders, these young women are also beginning to get caught up in the novel forms of subjection such discourses imply. These novel forms are part of a world in which kinship ties are attenuated, companionate marriage, marital love based on choice, and romantic love are idealized, making central women's attractiveness and individual uniqueness as enhanced and perhaps necessarily marked by differences in adornment (hence the importance of cosmetics, lingerie, and differentiation in styles and fabrics of clothing). The contrast between this world and the Bedouin world is captured wonderfully in an incident I remember from some years ago, illustrating the two worlds coming together. An elderly aunt visiting the household in which I lived jokingly teased her nephew, my host, who was an extremely important man in the community. She said he lived a dog's life. There he was with three wives, all good Bedouins. His house was a mess, his clothes were wrinkled and not one of these women would budge when he called. Her son, on the other hand, had just married an Egyptian girl and he was living well these days. His bride, she reported, put on nice clothes whenever he came home, brought him special foods, and even ironed his handkerchiefs. Everyone present laughed at the time. Yet now young Bedouin women would be less scandalized by such behavior and may even be moving toward it.

Even more telling is what is happening to weddings. As I have argued elsewhere (Abu-Lughod n.d.), these are important sites for the production and reproduction of Bedouin sexuality and social relations. Weddings too are becoming a point of conflict for young and older women. While older Bedouin women are scandalized by the practices of Egyptian weddings, today's adolescents are intrigued with them and try to emulate what small bits of them they can. Older women find shocking the fact that an Egyptian bride comes dressed in make-up and fancy clothes and sits in public with her groom in front of the mixed-sex gathering of guests. They are more disturbed by the idea that she goes willingly to be with him privately at night to have sex.

They find Egyptian weddings distasteful because, much like our own, these weddings construct the couple as a separate unit of private desire, distinct from their families and gender groups. For Awlad 'Ali, proper weddings must involve at their center a public daytime defloration that is part of a dramatic contest between kin groups and between men and women. This central wedding rite, enacted in a homologous fashion on the bodies of the bride and groom and on the collective bodies of the gathered kin and friends, produces a sexuality that is public and focused on crossing thresholds, opening passages, and moving in and out as a prelude to the insemination that should eventuate in childbirth for the groom's kin group.

Through songs about the families of the bride and groom and about the investment of others in the bride's virginity, and even in the ritual movements themselves, identifications of individuals with their kin groups are reinforced. For example, a bride is brought from her father's household completely cloaked in a white woven cloth that belongs to the girl's father or some other male kinsman. Protected and hidden by her kinsman's cloak she is brought out of her father's domain and carried to her husband's kin group. In the past, she remained under her father's cloak until the defloration. Nowadays the woven blanket is usually removed once she gets to her marital room so the women can view the coiffed young bride made up with cheap smudged lipstick and cakey white face powder and wearing a white satin wedding dress and makeshift hair ornament, suggesting the new importance of individual attractiveness.[10]

Bedouin weddings also played out a contest between men and women as groups. There is still a formulaic struggle between the groom and his age-mates, on the one hand, and the bride and the women who surround her when the groom comes to the marital chamber to take her virginity, on the other hand. But older women deplore the change in weddings that has altered the balance of this ritual contest. It used to be that the night before the wedding a young kinswoman of the groom would go out to dance amidst a group of young men. Veiled and girded in the same kind of white woven men's cloak that the bride would arrive in the next day, she was serenaded by the men and would dance with a stick that the men tried to grab from her. Representing the bride and all women, the dancer enacted a challenge to men by inciting desire but eluding capture. Now all that is left is the men's invasion of the women's world on the wedding day when the groom as hunter takes his feminine bride as prey. Young people would prefer to dispense even with this remnant of the public rites of defloration that link the groom and bride with their respective gender groups.

In resisting the axes of kin and gender, the young women who want the lingerie, Egyptian songs, satin wedding dresses, and fantasies of private romance that their elders resist are perhaps unwittingly enmeshing themselves in an extraordinarily complex set of new power relations. These bind them irrevocably to the Egyptian economy, itself tied to the global economy, and to the Egyptian state, many of whose powers depend on separating kin groups and regulating individuals. For the Awlad 'Ali Bedouins the old forms of kin-based power, which the resistances described above allowed us to see clearly, are becoming encompassed and cross-cut by new forms, methods, and sources of subjection. These new forms do not necessarily displace the old. Sometimes, as in the case of the demands of sexual modesty and settling down, they run along the same tracks. Sometimes, as in the case of older men's greater control of resources and precedence in the political realm, they just catch up the old ones into larger nonlocal networks of economic and institutional power, something that gives them a new kind of rigidity. Some forms, however, such as the penetration of consumerism and the disciplines of schooling and other institutions of the state, with their attendant privatization of the individual and the family, are altogether new and just add to the complex ways that Bedouin women are involved in structures of domination.

Although their elders are suspicious of many of these new forms, the young women (and young men, I should add) do not seem to feel the ways in which their forms of rebellion against their elders are backing them into wider and different sets of authority structures or the ways their desires for commodities and separation from kin and gender groups might be producing a kind of conformity to a different range of demands. This raises a final question: do certain modern techniques or forms of power work in such indirect ways or seem to offer such positive attractions that people do not as readily resist them? There is some evidence for this, and it is a question worth exploring comparatively.[11] In the case of the Awlad ʿAli Bedouin, though, there seem to be new forms of resistance to just these kinds of processes. If that is so, then such resistances can be used as diagnostics as well.

One sign that these new forms of subjection *are* felt as such is that there has been a growing interest in the Islamic movement among those Awlad ʿAli who have become most involved with and have had most contact with secular Egyptian state institutions (especially schools) and cultural life (especially through television, radio, fashions, and consumerism), those for example living in major towns and the city of Marsa Matruh. Participation in the Islamic movement is signaled through adopting Islamic dress, engaging in Koran study, and shifting behavior, especially toward members of the opposite sex. If within the Arab world generally the Islamic movement represents a resistance to Western influence, consumerism, and political and economic control by a Westernized elite, within the Awlad ʿAli community it serves as a perfect response to, symptom of, and therefore key to understanding the kinds of contradictory sets of power relations in which they are currently caught. For young Bedouin women and men, it is a kind of double resistance to two conflicting sets of demands—on one hand, the demands of their elders and the system of face-to-face kin-based authority they represent, and on the other hand, the demands of the national Westernized state with a capitalist economy in which, because of their cultural differences, lack of education, and lack of ties to the elites, they participate only marginally and at the bottom. For young women, adopting modest Islamic dress has the added advantage of allowing them to distinguish themselves from their uneducated sisters and their elders while leaving them irreproachable in matters of morality.[12]

Like the other forms of resistance discussed above, participating in Islamic movements is a culturally shaped and historically specific response. It could not have been taken up by individuals in this community to resist the situation they found themselves in at this juncture unless it had already developed in Egypt and elsewhere in the 1980s. It is easy to see as well how rigidly fundamentalist practices involve participants in yet a third set of disciplines and demands and tie them to new transnational structures—of religious nationalism in the Islamic world—that are not isomorphic with the transnational structures of the global economy.

This may seem like boxes within boxes within boxes. But that is the wrong image. A better one might be fields of overlapping and intersecting forms of subjection whose effects on particularly placed individuals at particular historical moments vary tremendously. As I have tried to show, tracing the many resistances of old and young Awlad ʿAli, men and women, and those from the desert and the town gives us the means to begin disentangling these forms and to grasp that they interact and the ways in which they do. It also gives us the means to understand an important dynamic of resistance and power in nonsimple societies. If the systems of power are multiple, then resisting at one level may catch people up at other levels.

This is the kind of contribution careful analyses of resistance can make. My argument has been that we should learn to read in various local and everyday resistances the existence of a range of specific strategies and structures of power. Attention to the forms of resistance in particular societies can help us become critical of partial or reductionist theories of power.[13] The problem has been that those of us who have sensed that there is something admirable about resistance have tended to look to it for hopeful confirmation of the failure—or partial failure—of systems of oppression. Yet it seems to me that we respect everyday resistance not just by arguing for the dignity or heroism of the resistors but by letting their practices teach us about the complex interworkings of historically changing structures of power.

Acknowledgments

Reproduced by permission of the American Anthropological Association from *American Ethnologist* 17:1, 1990. Not for further reproduction.

I began this paper while a member of the Institute for Advanced Study and completed it while a Mellon Fellow at the University of Pennsylvania. I am grateful to both institutions for support. Fellowships from the National Endowment for the Humanities and Fulbright made possible my research in Egypt in 1986 and 1987, and gave me time to write. Joan Scott and Judith Butler gave especially helpful comments on early drafts, but the final version owes much to critical readings by Catherine Lutz, Timothy Mitchell, and four anonymous reviewers for *American Ethnologist*. Audiences at a number of institutions where the paper was delivered also forced me to clarify some crucial points. Finally, my gratitude to the people in the Bedouin community in which I lived grows deeper each year.

Notes

1. Terms like voices, subversion, dissidence, counter-discourse, and counter-hegemony, as well as resistance, key this interest and circulate through such widely diverse enterprises as French feminist theory (for example, Kristeva 1981; Moi 1986:163–64) and social scientific studies of specific subordinate groups. Among the latter figure studies of resistance among working-class youths in England (Willis 1981), slaves in the American South and on plantations in the Caribbean (Craton 1982; Gaspar 1985; Genovese 1974, 1979; Levine 1977), poor Southeast Asian peasants (Scott 1985; Scott and Kerkvliet 1986; Stoler 1985; Turton 1986), subaltern groups in colonial India (Guha 1983a, 1983b), marginalized black peasant-workers in rural South Africa (Comaroff 1985), Bolivian tin-miners and Colombian plantation-workers (Nash 1979; Taussig 1980), and various groups of women in both this country (for example, E. Martin 1987; Morgen and Bookman 1988) and elsewhere (Ong 1987).

2. This question has begun to receive some attention within and outside of anthropology. Marcus and Fischer (1986), Jameson (1984), and Haraway (1985) are especially concerned with the development of postmodernist theory in the post-colonial age of late capitalism. Foucault (1980:116) argues that the task of analyzing the mechanics of power "could only begin after 1968, that is to say on the basis of daily struggles at grass roots level, among those whose fight was located in the fine meshes of the web of power." I would credit a number of sociopolitical movements, including feminism, with shaking the hegemony of Marxism as radical discourse and opening up possibilities for rethinking power and resistance. Scott (1985:29) traces his own concern with everyday resistance more narrowly to his disillusionment with socialist revolutions.

3. O'Hanlon (1988) asks this question with regard to the *subaltern studies* group, and Rosaldo (1986) has made an interesting argument linking Evans-Pritchard's admiration of Nuer indominability to his role as anthropologist in a colonial setting.

4. Jean Comaroff (1985:263), for example, explicitly rejects the conventional division between the symbolic and the instrumental or religion and politics (distinctions, she argues, made by ethnocentric social science and Third World revolutionary intellectuals alike). James Scott (1985:292) refuses to accept the distinction between real and unreal resistance, defined in terms of the oppositions between individual and collective, self-indulgent and principled, *or* behavioral and ideological. The move within Marxian scholarship to explore more fully the Gramscian notion of hegemony, which, at least according to interpreters like Raymond Williams (1977:108–14), not only rescues ideology as a part of the apparatus of domination but actually breaks down the distinction between cultural, social, and political processes, is another kind of attempt to get at the complex forms of domination.

5. For a lucid discussion of the problems with humanism in the historiographical project of *Subaltern Studies,* see O'Hanlon's (1988) sympathetic critique. Some of her points apply as well to other projects on resistance.

6. A particularly clear statement of Foucault's view of power as productive is the following: "What makes power hold good, what makes it accepted, is simply the fact that it doesn't only weigh on us as a force that says no, but that it traverses and produces things, it induces pleasure, forms of knowledge, produces discourse. It needs to be considered as a productive network that runs through the whole social body, much more than as a negative instance whose function is repression" (1980:119). His position on resistance is more ambiguous. Despite his insistence that resistance is always tied to power, he occasionally implies the persistence of some residual freedom (Foucault 1982:225).

7. I went to live in one small Bedouin community first in 1978 and have returned several times since, most recently for fieldwork in 1987, on which the analysis in the final section is based.

8. Among the many problems with this last idea is that it assumes society is a machine and understands human actions as functions in this machine rather than recognizing that society is nothing but the collective practices of the people who compose it, a view developed most systematically by Bourdieu (1977).

9. Messick (1987) analyzes the dissolution of a North African women's alternative, if not subversive, discourse brought about by the capitalist transformation of weaving.

10. One wonders also what effect images of coiffed and groomed Egyptian urban women that young Bedouin men see on television, or the girls they flirt with in school, have on their desires.

11. Bourdieu (1977, 1979) and Foucault (especially 1977), among others of course, offer useful ways of thinking about the effects of new forms of power associated with modern states in a capitalist world because they attend to the micro-processes that affect individuals in seemingly trivial ways. Mitchell (1988) considers the effects of such political transformations in Egypt specifically.

12. See El-Guindi (1981) and Hoffman-Ladd (1987) for more on women in these movements.

13. Feminist theory has been especially receptive to the notion of multiple forms and sites of resistance because it has had to face the obvious inadequacy of any current theories about domination to account for gender power, the complex field of forces that produces women's situations and the manifold and subtle forms of their subjection. See B. Martin (1982) for an extremely helpful discussion of these issues.

Bibliography

Abu-Lughod, Lila. 1985. "A Community of Secrets." *Signs: Journal of Women in Culture and Society* 10: 637–57.
———. 1986. *Veiled Sentiments: Honor and Poetry in a Bedouin Society.* Berkeley and Los Angeles: University of California Press.
———. 1990. "Shifting Politics in Bedouin Love Poetry." In *Language and the Politics of Emotion,* Catherine Lutz and Lila Abu-Lughod, eds. New York: Cambridge University Press.
———. n.d. "The Construction of Sexuality: Public and Private in Bedouin Weddings." Paper presented at Cornell University, October 8, 1988.
Bourdieu, Pierre. 1977. *Outline of a Theory of Practice.* Cambridge: Cambridge University Press.
———. 1979. "The Disenchantment of the World." In *Algeria 1960,* pp. 1–94. Cambridge: Cambridge University Press and Maison des Sciences de l'Homme.
Comaroff, Jean. 1985. *Body of Power, Spirit of Resistance.* Chicago: University of Chicago Press.
Craton, Michael. 1982. *Testing the Chains: Resistance to Slavery in the British West Indies.* Ithaca: Cornell University Press.
El-Guindi, Fadwa. 1981. "Veiling *Infitah* with Muslim Ethic: Egypt's Contemporary Islamic Movement." *Social Problems* 28: 465–83.
Foucault, Michel. 1977. *Discipline and Punish.* New York: Pantheon.
———. 1978. *The History of Sexuality. Vol. 1: An Introduction.* New York: Random House.
———. 1980. *Power/Knowledge,* Colin Gordon, ed. New York: Pantheon.
———. 1982. "Afterword: The Subject and Power." In *Beyond Structuralism and Hermeneutics,* Hubert Dreyfus and Paul Rabinow, pp. 208–26. Chicago: University of Chicago Press.
Gaspar, David B. 1985. *Bondmen and Rebels: A Study of Master-Slave Relations in Antigua.* Baltimore: Johns Hopkins University Press.
Genovese, Eugene. 1974. *Roll, Jordan, Roll: The World the Slaves Made.* New York: Pantheon.
———. 1979. *From Rebellion to Revolution: Afro-American Slave Revolts in the Making of the Modern World.* Baton Rouge: Louisiana State University Press.
Gramsci, Antonio. 1971. *Selections from Prison Notebooks,* Quinten Hoare and Geoffrey Smith, eds. London: Lawrence and Wishart.

Guha, Ranajit. 1983a. *Elementary Aspects of Peasant Insurgency in Colonial India.* Delhi: Oxford University Press.

———. 1983b. "The Prose of Counter-Insurgency." In *Subaltern Studies II: Writings on South Asian History and Society,* Ranajit Guha, ed., pp. 1–42. Delhi: Oxford University Press.

Haraway, Donna. 1985. "A Manifesto for Cyborgs: Science, Technology, and Socialist Feminism in the 1980s." *Socialist Review* 80: 65–107.

Hoffman-Ladd, Valerie. 1987. "Polemics on the Modesty and Segregation of Women in Contemporary Egypt." *International Journal of Middle East Studies* 19: 23–50.

Jameson, Frederic. 1984. "Post Modernism, or the Cultural Logic of Late Capitalism." *New Left Review* 146: 53–92.

Kristeva, Julia. 1981. "Women's Time." *Signs: Journal of Women in Culture and Society* 7: 13–35.

Levine, Lawrence. 1977. *Black Culture and Black Consciousness: Afro-American Thought from Slavery to Freedom.* New York: Oxford University Press.

Marcus, George, and Michael M. J. Fischer. 1986. *Anthropology as Cultural Critique.* Chicago: University of Chicago Press.

Martin, Biddy. 1982. "Feminism, Criticism, and Foucault." *New German Critique* 27: 3–30.

Martin, Emily. 1987. *The Woman in the Body: A Cultural Analysis of Reproduction.* Boston: Beacon Press.

Messick, Brinkley. 1987. "Subordinate Discourse: Women, Weaving and Gender Relations in North Africa." *American Ethnologist* 14: 210–25.

Mitchell, Timothy. 1988. *Colonising Egypt.* Cambridge: Cambridge University Press.

Moi, Toril. 1986. *Sexual/Textual Politics.* London and New York: Methuen.

Morgen, Sandra, and Ann Bookman, eds. 1988. *Women and the Politics of Empowerment.* Philadelphia: Temple University Press.

Nash, June. 1979. *We Eat the Mines and the Mines Eat Us.* New York: Columbia University Press.

O'Hanlon, Rosalind. 1988. "Recovering the Subject: *Subaltern Studies* and Histories of Resistance in Colonial South Asia." *Modern Asian Studies* 22 (1): 189–224.

Ong, Aihwa. 1987. *Spirits of Resistance and Capitalist Discipline: Factory Women in Malaysia.* Albany: State University of New York Press.

Paige, Jeffrey. 1975. *Agrarian Revolution: Social Movements and Export Agriculture in the Underdeveloped World.* New York: Free Press.

Rosaldo, Renato. 1986. "From the Door of His Tent: The Fieldworker and the Inquisitor." In *Writing Culture: The Poetics and Politics of Ethnography,* James Clifford and George Marcus, eds., pp. 77–97. Berkeley and Los Angeles: University of California Press.

Scott, James C. 1976. *The Moral Economy of the Peasant.* New Haven: Yale University Press.

———. 1985. *Weapons of the Weak: Everyday Forms of Peasant Resistance.* New Haven: Yale University Press.

Scott, James C., and Benedict J. Tria Kerkvliet, eds. 1986. "Everyday Forms of

Peasant Resistance in South-East Asia." *Journal of Peasant Studies* (special issue) 13 (2): 1–150.
Stoler, Ann. 1985. *Capitalism and Confrontation in Sumatra's Plantation Belt, 1870–1979*. New Haven: Yale University Press.
Taussig, Michael. 1980. *The Devil and Commodity Fetishism in South America*. Chapel Hill: University of North Carolina Press.
Turton, Andrew. 1986. "Patrolling the Middle-Ground: Methodological Perspectives on 'Everyday Peasant Resistance.'" *Journal of Peasant Studies* 13 (2): 36–48.
Williams, Raymond. 1977. *Marxism and Literature*. London: Oxford University Press.
Willis, Paul. 1981[1977]. *Learning to Labour: How Working Class Kids Get Working Class Jobs*. New York: Columbia University Press.
Wolf, Eric. 1969. *Peasant Wars of the Twentieth Century*. New York: Harper and Row.

Contributors

Lila Abu-Lughod is Assistant Professor of Religion and Associated Faculty of the Department of Anthropology at Princeton University. She is the author of *Veiled Sentiments: Honor and Poetry in a Bedouin Society* (Berkeley and Los Angeles: University of California Press, 1986) and co-editor, with Catherine Lutz, of *Language and the Politics of Emotion* (New York: Cambridge University Press, 1990). Currently finishing a book on the social and cultural transformation of Bedouin women's lives that is also an experiment in ethnographic writing, she has begun research on Islam and public culture in contemporary urban Egypt.

Sandra T. Barnes is Professor of Anthropology at the University of Pennsylvania, where she has held a faculty appointment since 1973. Her research and publications have focused on African urbanism, religion, politics, and history. In addition to numerous articles on these subjects, she is the author of *Africa's Ogun: Old World and New* (Bloomington: Indiana University Press, 1989) and *Patrons and Power: Creating a Political Community in Metropolitan Lagos* (Bloomington: Indiana University Press, and Manchester: Manchester University Press for International African Institute, London, 1986). She is currently preparing a study of cultural diversity in precolonial West Africa.

Caroline Bledsoe is Associate Professor of Anthropology at Northwestern University. Her field research in Liberia and Sierra Leone has concerned marriage, fertility, child fosterage, and child mortality, as well as more general issues of economic development and qualitative approaches to demography and social stratification. She is the author of *Women and Marriage in Kpelle Society* (Palo Alto: Stanford University Press, 1980) and is currently writing a monograph on child fosterage.

Ruth Gallagher Goodenough is the author (with L. S. Cottrell, Jr.) of *Developments in Social Psychology 1930–1940*, Sociometry Monograph No. 1 (New York: Beacon House, 1941). She was engaged in attitude and opinion research for the War Department during World War II, has taught elementary school, and has published research on adoption in Truk, Micronesia, and on the behavior of children in kindergarten and first grade. Her most recent study was of the early school years in a Pennsylvania school, for the Carnegie Foundation for the Advancement of Teaching.

Alma Gottlieb is Assistant Professor of Anthropology at the University of Illinois at Urbana-Champaign. She is the co-editor, with Thomas Buckley, of *Blood Magic: The Anthropology of Menstruation* (Berkeley and Los Angeles: University of California Press, 1988) and has published articles on gender and kinship, mythology, and religion among the Beng. Her monograph, *Under the Kapok Tree: Identity and Difference in Beng Thought*, will be published by Indiana University Press.

Igor Kopytoff is Professor of Anthropology at the University of Pennsylvania. His published articles deal primarily with issues in African ethnology and focus especially on the relation between theoretical issues in anthropology, Western semantics, and African cultural macrosemantics. He has also written extensively on African indigenous slavery and is co-editor, with Suzanne Miers, of *Slavery in Africa: Historical and Anthropological Perspectives* (Madison: University of Wisconsin Press, 1977). Most recently, he edited *The African Frontier: The Reproduction of Traditional African Societies* (Bloomington: Indiana University Press, 1987). He is currently working on a general theory of magic and witchcraft.

Rena Lederman is Associate Professor of Anthropology at Princeton University. She has done field research in Highland Papua New Guinea on gift exchange and the practical articulation of gift and market relations, on local politics and political discourse, and on gender relations and constructions. She is author of *What Gifts Engender* (Cambridge: Cambridge University Press, 1986) and is completing a book on the meanings of "wealth" in Melanesia, *The Wealth of Tribes* (Berkeley: University of California Press, forthcoming), which also juxtaposes Melanesian and anthropological perspectives on "history," "comparison," and "value."

Maria Lepowsky is Assistant Professor of Anthropology and Women's Studies at the University of Wisconsin, Madison. She has published a variety of articles based on her field research on Vanatinai, Papua New Guinea, on such topics as traditional exchange, mortuary ritual, sorcery, traditional religion, the introduction of biomedicine, diet, health and cultural adaptation, child survival, betel nut use, and gender and aging. She is currently completing a book on gender in an egalitarian society.

Anna Meigs is Associate Professor of Anthropology at Macalester College. She is the author of a number of articles as well as a book (*Food, Sex, and Pollution: A New Guinea Religion*, New Brunswick, N.J.: Rutgers University Press, 1984) on gender and associated ideologies in regard to physical processes among a population of the Eastern Highlands of Papua New Guinea. She is currently doing research on women of the New Right in the United States.

Peggy Reeves Sanday is Professor of Anthropology at the University of Pennsylvania. She has had a long-standing interest in the application of anthropological theory and method to the study of social inequality. She is the editor of *Anthropology and the Public Interest* (New York: Academic Press, 1976). She has conducted cross-cultural research on rape, sex-roles, and cannibalism. This research is published in *Female Power and Male Dominance* (Cambridge: Cambridge University Press, 1981) and *Divine Hunger* (Cambridge: Cambridge University Press, 1986). In addition to conducting ongoing fieldwork in West Sumatra, she has conducted an anthropological study of rituals of male bonding in college fraternities. This research will be published in *Fraternity Gang Rape* (New York: New York University Press, in press). Currently she is engaged in a study of Minangkabau animism and culture history.

Alice Schlegel is Professor of Anthropology at the University of Arizona. She is the editor of *Sexual Stratification* (New York: Columbia University Press, 1977), among other books she has written or edited, and is the author of numerous articles on gender, social organization, and the Hopi. Her current research focuses on adolescent socialization across cultures. Her field areas are the Hopi Indians of Arizona and, more recently, contemporary Europe.

Name Index

Abdullah, Taufik, 143, 154, 155–56, 163, 165, 215
Abidjan, 262, 263
Abu-Lughod, Lila, 4, 7, 14, 15, 311–37
Accra, 260, 263
Adams, Moni, 131
Adorno, T. W., 250
Africa, 17, 75–98, 113–37, 215, 253–80, 281–310
Andaya, Leonard, 159
Appell, Laura, 130
Aquino, Corazon, 77, 96
Ardener, Edwin, 187
Armstrong, W. E., 175, 190, 216
Aryee, A. F., 285
Atkinson, Jane, 173, 201
Awe, Bolanle, 277
Awlad 'Ali, 311–37

Bacdayan, Albert, 177, 181
Bandaranaike, Sirimavo, 77
Barnes, J., 55
Barnes, Sandra, 4, 7, 14, 15, 16, 108, 163, 253–80, 289, 303
Barthes, Roland, 160
Basso, Ellen, 127
Battaglia, Debbora, 198
Beauvoir, Simone de, 1, 2, 3, 12, 130, 171, 173, 201
Bedouin, 15, 311–37
Beidelman, T. O., 115, 122, 126
Benda-Beckmann, F. von, 141, 146, 149, 150, 161, 165
Benda-Beckmann, K. von, 141, 150, 165
Benedict, Ruth, 2
Beng, 10, 113–38

Bennett, Lynn, 128
Berde, Stuart, 175
Berndt, R. M., 198
Bernheimer, Richard, 25
Berry, Sara, 290
Bhutto, Benazir, 75, 77
Bledsoe, Caroline, 4, 7, 14, 15, 16, 87, 117, 261, 264, 269, 277, 278, 281–309
Bleek, Wolf, 297, 301
Bloch, Maurice, 5, 11, 12, 159, 162
Bourdieu, Pierre, 65, 69, 284, 314, 333, 334
Brandon, Anastasia, 285
Brightman, Robert, 182
Brown, Judith, 180, 195, 209
Brown, Paula, 46, 171
Buchbinder, Georgeda, 171
Buckley, Thomas, 127
Bujra, J., 262, 263, 264, 277

Caldwell, John, 290
Calvados Chain Islands, 201, 206
Chafetz, J., 250
Chambers-Schiller, Lee Virginia, 92
Chodorow, N., 250
Chowning, Ann, 175
Clignet, Remi, 303
Cohen, Ronald, 285
Colemen, Linda, 111
Collier, Jane, 4, 108, 115, 202–3, 210, 211, 215, 283, 284
Comaroff, Jean, 133, 333, 334
Comaroff, John, 277, 285, 286, 303, 305
Conklin, Harold, 216
Conteh, James, 288
Corsaro, W., 250

Name Index

Craton, Michael, 333

De Lauretis, Teresa, 6
Divale, William, 172, 180, 204, 209, 210
Dobu Island, 180
Douglas, Mary, 126, 127, 128
Drewal, Henry John, and Margaret Thompson Drewal, 131
Drucker, Philip, 215
Dundes, Alan, 200
Durkheim, Emile, 94, 128

Ebin, V., 133
Egypt, Western Desert, 311–37
El-Guindi, Fadwa, 335
Ember, Melvin, and Carol Ember, 180
Enga, 50, 69, 215
Engels, F., 275
Estioko-Griffin, Agnes, 182
Etienne, Mona, 130, 174, 177, 208, 262, 278
Evans-Pritchard, E. E., 216, 334

Fadipe, N. A., 277
Faithorn, Elizabeth, 116
Fapohunda, O. J., 278
Feil, D., 49, 51, 52, 55, 56, 64, 215
Fernandez, James, 133
Fischer, Michael, 333
Fortune, Reo, 180
Foucault, Michel, 311, 314–15, 323, 333, 334
Frankel, S., 62
Franklin, K., 68
Freetown, 263, 293, 301, 302
Friedan, Betty, 91
Friedl, Ernestine, 172, 180

Gandhi, Indira, 75–77, 96
Gandhi, Rajiv, 96
Gaspar, David B., 333
Genovese, Eugene, 333
Gewertz, Deborah, 15, 208, 209, 215
Ghana, 133, 297, 301
Giddens, Anthony, 305
Gilbert, Michelle, 133
Glasse, R., 55, 62, 68, 198
Glaze, Anita, 131
Gluckman, Max, 286
Godelier, Maurice, 51, 70
Goldman, L., 48
Goodale, Jane, 182

Goodenough, Ruth Gallagher, 4, 7, 13, 17, 163, 225–51
Goodenough, Ward, 7, 79, 88, 250
Goodenough Island (Mwalatau), 199
Gordon, R., 45
Gottlieb, Alma, 4, 8, 9, 10, 113–38
Gough, Kathleen, 179
Gramsci, Antonio, 284, 314, 334
Grandmaison, C., 278
Gray, Robert, 134
Guha, Ranajit, 333
Guyer, Jane, 284

Haddon, A. C., 175
Hafkin, Nancy, 284
Hakimy, H. I., 142, 144, 148, 151, 154, 163
Halpenny, P., 278
Hammond, Dorothy, 177, 180
Hamy, E. T., 175
Handwerker, W. Penn, 288
Hansen, K. T., 262, 277
Haraway, Donna, 333
Harrell-Bond, Barbara, 285, 302
Harris, Marvin, 172, 180, 204, 209, 210
Harris, Olivia, 130
Harrison, S., 56
Heizer, Robert, 215
Herdt, Gilbert, 48, 110, 196
Herskovits, Melville, 87
Heusch, Luc de, 133
Hoffer, Carol, 215, 262
Hoffman-Ladd, Valerie, 335
Hopi, 9, 12, 16, 21, 24, 27–39, 174, 189, 210, 227
Howell, Martha, 91
Hua, 6, 9, 13, 99–112, 117, 173, 211, 248
Huxley, Julian, 207

Ilahita Arapesh, 26–27
India, 77, 152, 333
Indonesia, 11, 139–68
Isiugo-Abanihe, U. C., 261, 277
Islam, 139, 146–47, 153, 154, 156, 160, 331–32
Ivory Coast, 10, 113–38

Jablow, Alta, 177, 180
Jameson, Frederic, 333
Jansen, Joan, 91
Jordanova, L. J., 149
Josephides, L., 51, 53, 56, 63

Name Index

Kaberry, Phyllis, 182
Kagura, 122, 126, 133
Kampala, 263, 264
Kartiwa, Suwati, 165
Kato, Tsuyoshi, 152
Kay, Paul, 111
Kelly, Raymond, 48, 51, 55, 196
Kerkvliet, Tria, 333
Kessler, Suzanne J., 116
Kilson, M., 278
Kinshasa, 261, 263
Knight, Chris, 17
Kono District, 288
Kopytoff, Igor, 4, 5, 7, 16, 21, 75–98, 108, 150, 292
Korn, V. E., 164
Kristeva, Julia, 333
Kuo, Shirley, 77
Kuper, Adam, 116

LaFontaine, J. S., 117, 130, 261, 277, 278
Lagos, 14, 15, 253–80
Laguerre, Michel, 133
Lamphere, Louise, 174
Lancy, D., 69
Landes, Ruth, 182
Langness, L., 54
Leacock, Eleanor, 3, 130, 172, 173, 174, 177, 179, 182, 208
Lederman, Rena, 1, 4, 5, 6, 7, 8, 9, 10, 11, 16, 43–73, 211
Lepowsky, Maria, 4, 12, 16, 169–223, 225, 227
Levine, Lawrence, 333
Lévi-Strauss, Claude, 2, 3, 12, 30, 173, 200, 205
Lewis, B. C., 278
Liberia, 263, 289
Linton, Ralph, 7, 78, 88, 94, 188, 196
Little, K., 257–58
Lloyd, P. C., 277
Louisiade Archipelago, 174, 182, 185–86

MacCormack, Carol, 11, 200, 287, 307
Maccoby, E. E., 250
Macgillivray, John, 207
Macintyre, Martha, 175, 209, 217
Madagascar, 11, 159
Mae Enga, 46, 49, 64
Malinowski, Bronislaw, 175–76, 181, 185, 198, 200, 215, 216

Manggis, M. Rasjid, 142, 146
Mann, Kristin, 263, 278, 285
Marcus, George, 333
Margold, Jane, 215
Martin, Biddy, 335
Martin, Emily, 333
Marxism, 333, 334
Massim, 171–223
Matthews, Glenna, 92
Mauss, Marcel, 128, 273
McKenna, Wendy, 116
Mead, Margaret, 1, 2, 3, 23, 171, 188, 209
Meggitt, M., 45, 46, 53, 55, 64, 171, 198
Meigs, Anna, 4, 6, 8, 9, 10, 13, 21, 33, 99–112, 117, 171, 173, 195, 196, 198, 213, 248, 250
Melanesia, 4, 49, 178
Melpa, 46, 49, 69
Melville Island, 182
Mende, 14, 15, 215, 281–309
Mendi, 8, 10, 43–73, 211
Merina, 11, 159
Mervis, Carolyn, 130
Messick, Brinkley, 334
Miers, Suzanne, 292
Minangkabau, 6, 11, 12, 13, 16, 139–68, 209, 210, 211, 225, 227
Mintz, Sidney, 215
Misima Island, 201, 208
Mitchell, Timothy, 334
Modjeska, C. N., 51
Moi, Toril, 333
Moran, Mary, 289
Morauta, Louise, 178
Morgen, Sandra, 333
Mount Hagen, 66, 116, 128, 205
Munn, Nancy, 68, 69, 216
Murphy, Robert, 211
Murphy, William, 288
Murphy, Yolanda, 211
Mushin, 260–61, 266, 269–73
Muslim, 299, 302

Nash, Jill, 210
Nash, June, 333
Nasroen, M., 142
Needham, Rodney, 115
Nehru, Pandit, 92
Ngubane, Harriet, 128
Nigeria, 131, 256–80
Nile Valley, 315

Name Index

Nimowa Island, 208
Normanby Islands, 200
North Africa, 334
Nyoro, 25, 126

Obbo, Christine, 262, 263, 264, 277, 278, 285, 290
O'Brien, Denise, 25
Ogbu, John, 193
O'Hanlon, Rosaline, 334
Okely, Judith, 129
Olson, Ronald, 215
Ong, Aihwa, 333
Oppong, Christine, 285
Ortner, Sherry, 3, 31, 48, 115, 171, 172, 173, 177, 197, 201, 211, 284, 306
Ottenberg, Simon, 131

Pacific Northwest, 200, 215
Paige, Jeffrey, 313
Paley, V., 250
Panaeati, 175, 201
Papua New Guinea, 25, 116, 117, 128, 169–223
Papua New Guinea (Central Highlands), 55, 68
Papua New Guinea (Eastern Highlands), 65, 99–112
Papua New Guinea (Northern Highlands), 46–47
Papua New Guinea (Southern Highlands), 43–73, 69, 70
Papua New Guinea (Western Highlands), 50, 69
Parkes, Peter, 115
Parkin, David, 286
Parmentier, Richard, 215
Peil, M., 270
Pellow, Deborah, 291
Philippines, 77, 182
Pitcher, E. G., 250
Pittin, R., 262, 264, 278
Poole, Fitz John Porter, 17, 23, 171, 195, 196, 198
Poro, 117
Price, R., 65
Prindiville, Joanne, 141, 164

Quran, 154, 331

Radcliffe-Brown, A. R., 284
Rahman, Khalida Zia, 77

Rapp, Rayna, 307
Reichard, Gladys, 215
Richards, Audrey, 179, 180
Roberts, Simon, 285, 303, 305
Robertson, C. C., 227, 260, 278
Rogers, Susan, 127, 211
Róheim, Geza, 200, 216
Rosaldo, Michelle, 171, 173, 177, 201, 202–3, 210, 211, 215
Rosaldo, Renato, 334
Rosch, Eleanor, 111, 130
Rosman, Abraham, 215
Rossel Island, 187, 190, 199–200, 202, 208, 216
Rubel, Paula, 215
Ryan, D'A., 52, 68

Sacks, Karen, 3, 31, 130, 172, 177, 275
Sahlins, Marshall, 69
Sanday, Peggy Reeves, 1–19, 139–68, 172, 173–74, 177, 179, 180, 181, 194, 197, 201, 209, 210, 211, 225, 229, 247, 250, 255
Sande, 117, 287, 295
Sanjek, R., 259
Sanskrit, 146
Schieffelin, E., 55, 68
Schlegel, Alice, 3, 4, 5, 6, 8, 9, 16, 21–41, 127, 172, 174, 179, 180, 189, 194, 201, 210, 211, 227, 255
Schneider, David, 179
Scholnick, Ellin Kofsky, 130
Schultz, L. H., 250
Schuster, I. M., 262
Schwede, Laurie, 166
Schwimmer, E., 55
Scott, James, 313, 333, 334
Seligman, C. G., 175
Semin, Gun R., 130
Sexton, L., 66, 70
Shore, Bradd, 131
Sierra Leone, 261, 281–309
Sillitoe, P., 55, 62
Simmons, Leo, 195
Smith, Jonathan, 117, 130
Smith, Raymond, 303
Smock, A. C., 278
South Africa, 333
South America, 229
Southeast Asia, 333
Southern Africa, 116, 133
Southern Bantu, 116, 133

Sri Lanka, 77
Stanley, Captain Owen, 207
Steady, F. C., 263, 277
Stoler, Ann, 333
Stoller, R. J., 250
Strathern, Andrew, 48, 51, 54, 55, 61, 63, 66, 68, 69, 70
Strathern, Marilyn, 4, 11, 25, 26, 48, 49, 52, 63, 69, 102, 115, 116, 128, 131, 173, 200, 205, 213, 255, 307
Strobel, Margaret, 87, 90, 278
Sub-Saharan Africa, 133, 262
Sudarkasa, N., 275, 277
Suku, 7, 16, 75–98
Sumner, William, 83
Swaziland, 126
Sweetman, David, 90

Tanner, Nancy, 141, 163, 164
Tanzania, 122, 126, 133, 134
Taussig, Michael, 333
Thatcher, Margaret, 75–77, 96
Thomas, Lynn L., 141, 164
Thompson, Robert Farris, 133
Thune, Carl, 216
Tiffany, Sharon, 130
Titiev, Mischa, 34
Trobriand Islands, 175, 181, 205
Tubetube, 209, 217
Turner, Victor, 133
Turton, Andrew, 333
Tuzin, Donald, 26

Uganda, 25, 126
United States, 13, 17, 21, 33, 36, 75–98, 215, 225–51, 333

Vanatinai, 12, 13, 16, 169–223, 225, 227
Vellenga, Dorothy, 82, 87

Wagner, R., 48, 55, 69
Ware, H., 277
Wazed, Sheikh Hasina, 77
Weiner, Annette B., 127, 130, 175–76, 201, 205, 215
West Africa, 113–38, 253–80, 281–310
West Indies, 303
West Sumatra, 139–68
White, David, 197
Whitehead, Harriet, 3, 48, 171, 172, 177
Wiessmer, Polly, 215
Wikan, Unni, 109
Williams, Raymond, 334
Willis, Paul, 305, 333
Wiru, 46, 49, 64, 66
Wola, 46, 62, 64
Wolf, Eric, 313

Yanagisako, Sylvia, 4, 115, 283
Yoruba, 14, 131, 253–80
Young, Michael W., 175, 198, 216

Zaire, 75–98, 126
Zambia, 133

Subject Index

abortion, 294, 301
accommodation in gender relations, 4, 11–13, 16, 139, 244–46, 248
African: "free woman," 86–88, 90; secret societies, 117, 274, 287–88, 292; woman marriage, 87, 281; women warriors, 85
agency, 4, 14, 46–48, 56, 58, 64, 284
American: career women, 77; conception of womanhood, 91–95; dominant ethos, 93–95; kindergartners, 13, 17, 225–51; marriage, 89–90, 93
anthropological models, 1–4, 8, 15, 43, 48, 54, 57, 60, 64–68, 115, 128–30, 283, 305

big-men, 62–64, 173
big-women, 173
binary opposition, 2–3, 10, 12, 115–18, 120–21, 128–30, 133. *See also* dualism
biological: determinism, 1, 3, 108, 112, 171, 307; differences, 2–3, 9, 229
bridewealth transactions, 52, 82, 87, 193, 215, 267, 284–85, 299, 303

career woman, Sierra Leone, 14, 290–91, 305
child fosterage, 87, 258, 261–62, 270, 287, 294, 299, 301
children and security, 260
circumcision, 81, 83, 85
clan relationships, 43, 47, 49, 51–64, 69, 127
comparative analysis, 1, 7, 16, 65, 171–72, 194, 201
contested social order, 8, 43, 45–73
context, 1, 6, 9–10, 13, 16, 21, 99, 112, 117–18, 130, 162, 211, 247–49, 284
contradiction. *See* social contradiction

cross-sex dyads, 23, 28, 30–31, 230. *See also* husband/wife; mother/father; mother/son; sister/brother
cross-sex interaction, 13, 177, 225, 228–29, 231–42; attraction, 231, 235, 242–49; dependency, 231, 235–36, 242, 247–49; disparagement (*see also* denigration of women), 231, 236–39, 247
cultural construction, 3, 66, 80, 108, 110, 112; of gender categories (*see also* gender, constructions), 1–3, 10, 23–24, 101, 112, 117, 284; and social practice, 48, 284

denigration of men, 27, 34
denigration of women, 9, 11–12, 17, 26–27, 34, 115, 225. *See also* negation of the feminine
division of labor, 50–51, 78–79, 83–84, 173–74, 177, 180–84, 189, 195, 211–14, 261, 267–68
divorce, 53, 125, 193, 259–60, 267, 270
domestic hierarchy, 14, 265–66, 268, 276
domestic relations, 62. *See also* public/domestic
dualism, 115–16, 121–22, 129–30, 132–33, 196. *See also* binary opposition

economic independence and women's security, 257–64, 284–85
egalitarian societies, 12, 169, 171–223, 227
exchange, system of, 8, 12, 46, 49–53, 56–64, 69–70, 169, 175, 195, 212, 215; and clan relations, 8, 43, 56–64, 69; *kula* exchange, 185–86, 217; women's exchange, 52, 175–77, 184–88. *See also* reciprocity

Subject Index   349

female: autonomy, 17, 52–53, 58, 66, 174, 187–88, 194, 253, 255, 266–67, 284; initiation, 117, 178, 287; subordination, 10, 26, 47, 130, 169, 172, 214, 227, 253, 255, 276, 283
female power, 6, 8, 16, 28–29, 75, 96, 106–8, 141, 144–45, 155–56, 161–64, 173, 187–88, 211, 255, 257, 274, 276; and economic independence, 257–64
female status, 9, 15, 86, 101, 106–8, 110, 143, 171, 173, 175, 177, 179; contradictory statuses, 9, 14; multiple statuses, 101–12
feminism. *See* Western feminism
fertility cults, 70
fosterage. *See* child fosterage

gender: classification, 3, 9–10, 12, 23, 39, 108–12, 116–18; constructions, 2, 10–11, 23, 43, 48, 54, 56, 63–65, 108–11, 113, 172, 283; definition of, 5; hierarchy (*see also* social hierarchy), 8, 11, 66, 177, 225, 246, 250, 265; statuses, 101–12; technologies, 6, 10, 17
gender identity, 13; formation of, 230, 247, 249, 283–84. *See also* social identity
gender ideology, 1, 6, 8–12, 23, 101, 110, 172–73, 213; androcentric, 130, 150–53, 211, 256; Bedouin, 320–22, 324, 327–28; Beng, 113; chauvinist, 9, 99, 102–5, 173; contradictory ideologies, 16, 23, 99, 102–3; definition of, 5; egalitarian, 99, 103, 105, 225, 227, 246; general/specific, 6, 8, 10–11, 24, 31, 33–39, 172, 197; Hopi, 24, 37–38; matriarchal, 99, 102, 105, 139, 141; multiple ideologies, 99, 101–12, 130, 211, 246; Polynesia, 31; Vanatinai, 196. *See also* ideology
gender meanings, 1, 9, 127; contradictions in, 21, 24, 172, 202; definition of, 24; general/specific, 5–6, 16, 21, 23–41, 172
gender relations, 4, 43, 45, 66; dualist models of, 115–16, 129; Hopi, 27–31. *See also* pollution
gender representations, 1, 6–8, 17, 38–39, 213, 225, 246; androcentric, 141–68; contradictions in, 5–6, 8–9, 11, 39, 139, 141–43, 159; definition of, 5, 164; matrifocal, 141–68

history, 11, 65, 139, 143, 152–53, 155–56, 212, 324–25, 332
homosexuality, 192

human sexuality. *See* homosexuality; prostitution; sexuality
husband/wife, 52–54, 59, 67, 82–83, 89, 125, 166, 175, 180, 259, 265, 327

ideology, 6, 39, 48, 54, 75, 77, 113, 162, 188, 287; definition of, 5, 164; ethnic, 6, 11, 139, 142, 160; matrilineal, 9, 146–50; Minangkabau, 139, 141–42, 160, 164; production of, 12, 143, 159, 162, 284; Yoruba, 253. *See also* gender ideology
incest, 10, 34–38

killing, dual meaning of, 33, 201–2
kinship relations, 28–29, 37–38, 49, 54, 82, 179, 257–58

life cycle, 11–12, 80–81, 99, 103–5, 109–11, 259–60; Vanatinai, 169, 188–96
literacy, 85, 288–89

male: autonomy, 58; bonding, 14, 104, 225, 234, 248; dominance, 2–4, 6, 9, 14–17, 43, 54, 99, 101, 106, 163–64, 169, 171–73, 194, 197–98, 211, 213, 225, 227, 231, 245–46, 249, 255–56, 276, 311; initiation, 6, 81–82, 99, 102, 117, 169, 178; pregnancy, 33, 102; status, 85, 107
marriage, 49, 69, 119; Bedouin, 326–27, 329; process, 14, 83, 192–95, 283–309, 324; women's resistance to, 317–20, 327; and women's security, 256–64; weddings, 329–30
matrifocality, 11, 139, 141–68. *See also* gender representations
matriliny: Hopi, 27–31; Minangkabau, 11, 139, 142–43, 146; Suku, 78, 81; Vanatinai, 13, 173, 179, 194, 210, 216
matrilocal residence, 28, 194
men's houses, 178
menstrual blood, 9, 81, 116
menstruation, 81, 89, 123, 190, 216
modernization, 15, 85, 139, 166, 281, 289, 311, 315, 324, 331
mortuary rituals, 12, 169, 171, 175–77, 185–87, 204, 212
mother/father, 28–33, 36–38, 141, 144–45, 149–50, 166, 203
mother/son, 13, 156–59

nature/culture, 2–3, 12, 15, 23, 25, 79, 94, 108, 112, 148–49, 173, 197, 200–201, 203, 205, 289, 306
negation of the feminine, 3–4, 10–13, 15–16, 99, 102, 104, 162. *See also* denigration of women; pollution
negotiation. *See* social negotiation

opportunity structure, 7, 15–16, 108, 212, 253, 256–57, 264–68

patriliny, 113, 128, 164, 210, 287; Ilahita Arapesh, 26
patron/client relationships, 269, 273, 286
pollution, 6, 10, 104, 113, 169, 171, 190, 192, 198, 203; Beng models of, 115–38; and gender relations, 118, 198, 246
polygyny, 125, 259, 287, 290
power relations, 60, 68, 213, 227, 255, 284, 311, 330. *See also* resistance
pregnancy, 119–20, 132, 285–87, 293–96, 301, 304, 306
prestige structures, 177, 213–14
property holding, 14, 16, 253, 289; structure of, in urban Lagos, 256, 264–75; and women's economic independence, 263–64, 275–77; women house owners, 268–75; and women's political power, 273–77
prostitution, 86, 88, 262–64, 297, 301
public/domestic, 3, 54, 145, 177, 179, 276, 306

rape, 70, 106, 163, 173, 194
rape-free society, 163
reciprocity, 63, 258, 273. *See also* exchange, system of
reproduction: asexual, 35–37; dual meaning of, 32–33, 35, 201–2
resistance, 16, 313–37; and power, 313–24, 330–32; women's, 15, 311, 315–32
respect for individual, ethic of, 12–13, 169, 178–79, 181, 184, 188, 213–14
role and status, 75–98

school girl as gender category, 283–309
secret societies. *See* African, secret societies
sedentarization, 327
segmentary lineage models, 55–56
self-representation, 7, 13, 17, 306
sex roles, 3, 5, 75–98, 108, 171, 213–15; immanent/existential, 2, 75, 81–82, 87; circumstantial, 84

sex-gender system, 2–3, 108
sexism, 13, 17, 77, 227, 231, 246
sexual: asymmetry, 2–3, 59, 172, 211–12; complementarity, 9–12, 35, 99, 103, 118, 174, 213; equality, 12–13, 16, 172–74, 194, 214, 225, 227; inequality, 1, 4, 15, 45, 77, 253; morality, code of, 119, 320–27; separation or segregation, 6, 30, 169, 213, 315–17, 326. *See also* gender
sexual division of labor. *See* division of labor
sexuality, 10, 35–37, 118–30, 134, 190–92, 194, 293–96, 329. *See also* homosexuality; prostitution
sister/brother, 9, 12–13, 29–30, 33–37, 53, 57, 59, 149–50
social change, 16, 51, 60, 65, 205, 213, 281
social contradiction, 1, 4, 6, 8, 11, 16, 43, 45, 48, 57, 60, 139, 153–59, 253, 255, 281
social hierarchy, 47, 69, 70, 174, 177–78, 181, 213, 265
social identity, 7, 48, 57, 75–98, 284; definition of, 79; existential/role-based, 7, 16, 21, 77, 79, 87–88, 93; identity-personality, 8, 88; immanent features of, 75, 80–84; negotiable features of, 84–85, 306. *See also* gender identity
social negotiation, 6–8, 14–16, 75, 80, 84–85, 108, 281, 283–84, 300–306
stress, 13, 164, 227–30, 245, 249; and population density, 177–79, 215
"sugar daddies," 302–3
symbolic representation, 24

Third World women, 77, 96

uncle, 28–30, 36–38, 145, 151

veiling, 15, 323

warfare, 59–60, 69, 82, 173, 182, 184, 202, 205–7
Western feminism, 17, 311
witchcraft, 31, 67, 194, 201–2, 207, 209, 216
woman marriage. *See* African, woman marriage
women: as hunters, 173, 202; as "second sex," 1–3, 116, 130; as warriors (*see* African, women warriors); exclusion of, 47, 51, 53–54, 56, 59, 67, 70, 173, 225. *See also* female; gender